Blockchain and Web 3.0

Blockchain is no longer just about bitcoin or cryptocurrencies in general. Instead, it can be seen as a disruptive, revolutionary technology which will have major impacts on multiple aspects of our lives. The revolutionary power of such technology compares with the revolution sparked by the World Wide Web and the Internet in general. Just as the Internet is a means of sharing information, so blockchain technologies can be seen as a way to introduce the next level: sharing value.

Blockchain and Web 3.0 fills the gap in our understanding of blockchain technologies by hosting a discussion of the new technologies in a variety of disciplinary settings. Indeed, this volume explains how such technologies are disruptive and comparatively examines the social, economic, technological and legal consequences of these disruptions. Such a comparative perspective has previously been underemphasized in the debate about blockchain, which has subsequently led to weaknesses in our understanding of decentralized technologies.

Underlining the risks and opportunities offered by the advent of blockchain technologies and the rise of Web 3.0, *Blockchain and Web 3.0* will appeal to researchers and academics interested in fields such as sociology and social policy, cyberculture, new media and privacy and data protection.

Massimo Ragnedda is a senior lecturer in mass communication at Northumbria University, Newcastle, UK.

Giuseppe Destefanis is a lecturer in the Department of Computer Science at Brunel University, UK.

Routledge Studies in Science, Technology and Society

34 Imagined Futures in Science, Technology and Society
Edited by Gert Verschraegen, Frédéric Vandermoere, Luc Braeckmans and Barbara Segaert

35 Adolescents and Their Social Media Narratives
A Digital Coming of Age
Jill Walsh

36 Scientific Imperialism
Another Facet of Interdisciplinarity
Edited by Uskali Mäki, Adrian Walsh and Manuela Fernández Pinto

37 Future Courses of Human Societies
Critical Reflections from the Natural and Social Sciences
Edited by Kléber Ghimire

38 Science, Africa and Europe
Processing Information and Creating Knowledge
Edited by Patrick Harries, Martin Lengwiler and Nigel Penn

39 The Sociology of "Structural Disaster"
Beyond Fukushima
Miwao Matsumoto

40 The Cultural Authority of Science
Comparing across Europe, Asia, Africa and the Americas
Edited by Bauer, MW, Pansegrau, P and Shukla, R

41 Blockchain and Web 3.0
Social, Economic, and Technological Challenges
Edited by Massimo Ragnedda and Giuseppe Destefanis

For the full list of books in the series: www.routledge.com/Routledge-Studies-in-Science-Technology-and-Society/book-series/SE0054

Blockchain and Web 3.0

Social, Economic, and Technological Challenges

Edited by Massimo Ragnedda and Giuseppe Destefanis

Routledge
Taylor & Francis Group
LONDON AND NEW YORK

First published 2020
by Routledge
2 Park Square, Milton Park, Abingdon, Oxon OX14 4RN

and by Routledge
52 Vanderbilt Avenue, New York, NY 10017

Routledge is an imprint of the Taylor & Francis Group, an informa business

British Library Cataloguing-in-Publication Data
A catalogue record for this book is available from the British Library

Library of Congress Cataloging-in-Publication Data
A catalog record for this book has been requested

ISBN: 978-0-367-13984-1 (hbk)
ISBN: 978-0-429-02953-0 (ebk)

Typeset in Bembo
by Apex CoVantage, LLC

Contents

Contributors

Betty B. Ackah is a PhD candidate in the School of Communication at Simon Fraser University. Her current research is on the social construction of blockchain technologies. She is particularly interested in the symbiotic relationship between blockchain and the social dynamics of the gender digital divide in Ghana. She has diverse research experience as a member of the School of Communication's GeNA lab, and on projects funded by the IDRC, Ohio University's Tropical Disease Institute and UNICEF. She has an MA in international development studies, and another in Spanish language and culture, both from Ohio University.

Philippa R. Adams is a SSHRC Doctoral Scholar pursuing a PhD in the School of Communication at Simon Fraser University. Her research interests are in technology and society, including gender in social media, blockchain and popular culture. She holds a BA in political science from the University of Victoria and an MA in communication from Simon Fraser University. Philippa works as the Research Manager at the GeNA Lab where she manages a range of quantitative and qualitative research projects.

Walid Al-Saqaf (PhD) is Senior Lecturer at Södertörn University, Sweden.

Jannis Angelis is an Associate Professor of Operations Strategy at Indek, Royal Institute of Technology (KTH), Sweden.

Isabel Azevedo holds a PhD in informatics engineering from the Faculty of Engineering – University of Porto, Porto. She is an associate professor in the Department of Informatics Engineering of ISEP. Isabel Azevedo previously worked in the Documentation Service of Aveiro University and in the Faculty of Engineering of the University of Porto as a software and system programmer in the area of technological infrastructures.

Ivana Beveridge is currently finishing her PhD at the Sorbonne University. Over the past few years she taught a number of marketing courses at the Sorbonne as well as a number of business schools. Ivana is a partner with Sunrise International Education in Beijing. She has worked in international marketing practice in Asia, the Middle East, the US and Europe, with Naspers – MIH Group, Edelman PR, Hill & Knowlton Strategies, Pennebaker and Labbrand.

Balazs Bodo (Institute for Information Law, University of Amsterdam), is the principal investigator at the Blockchain & Society Policy Research Lab. He is a research scientist at the Institute for Information Law, University of Amsterdam. He is a two-time Fulbright Scholar (2006-7, Stanford University; 2012 Harvard University) and a former Marie Skłodowska-Curie fellow (2013-15). Balazs Bodo has a strong interdisciplinary background, having a degree in economics (MSc, Corvinus University, 1999) and a PhD in media studies (ELTE, 2011). In recent years he has worked on copyright piracy and algorithmic information personalization.

Santiago Bragagnolo I am currently working as a transfert technologique engineer and giving first steps into research at INRIA, on many different technologies, mostly on blockchain technologies. My main topics of interests are language and runtime analysis and modeling, parallel/concurrent computation and virtual machines. For that, I work on reflective applications and programming languages. I participate in the open source community of the Pharo programming language and environment. I am a coding enthusiast and software engineering researcher wanna be.

Dr. Peter Chow-White is Professor and Director of the School of Communication and the GeNA Lab at Simon Fraser University (www.genalab.org). The GeNA Lab investigates the development, adoption, and social impact of communication, blockchain and big data.

Marcus Denker is a permanent researcher (CR1, with tenure) at INRIA Lille – Nord Europe. Before, he was a postdoc at the PLEIAD lab/DCC University of Chile and the Software Composition Group, University of Bern. His research focuses on reflection and meta-programming for dynamic languages. He is an active participant in the Squeak and Pharo open source communities for many years. Marcus Denker received a PhD in Computer Science from the University of Bern/Switzerland in 2008 and a Dipl.-Inform. (MSc) from the University of Karlsruhe/Germany in 2004. He co-founded 2Denker GmbH in 2009. He is a member of ACM, GI and a board-member of ESUG.

Stéphane Ducasse is the Inria Research Director. He leads RMoD team http://rmod.lille.inria.fr. He is the expert in language design and reengineering. He worked on traits. Traits have been introduced in Pharo, Perl, PHP and under a variant into Scala, Groovy and Fortress. He is expert on software quality, program understanding, program visualisations, reengineering and metamodeling. He is one of the developer of Moose, an open-source software analysis platform http://www.moosetechnology.org/.

He created Synectique a company building dedicated tools for advanced software analyses. He is one of the leader of Pharo http://www.pharo.org/ a dynamic reflective object-oriented language supporting live programming. He built the industrial Pharo consortium http://consortium.pharo.org.

He works regularly with companies (Thales, Wordline, Siemens, Berger-Levrault, Arolla,...) on software evolution problems. He wrote couple hundred articles and several books. According to google his h-index is 54 for more than 12800 citations.

Malin Picha Edwardsson (PhD) is Senior Lecturer at Södertörn University, Sweden.

Robbie Fordyce (BA Hons.) is a research fellow and Doctoral Academy Convener at the Network Society Institute, The University of Melbourne, Australia.

Scott Freeman is the CEO of crypto exchange C2CX.com, ranked in the top 50 exchanges worldwide in volume by coinmarkcap.com. He co-founded a technology start-up in China and built it into IT Resources, one of China's leading IT service providers. His previous experience includes Deutsche Bank, UBS, HP and Mercedes-Benz. He holds an MBA from St. Gallen University, Switzerland.

Julie Frizzo-Barker is a PhD candidate in the School of Communication at Simon Fraser University. Her current research focuses on the social shaping of emerging technologies, through a study of women in the blockchain space. As a research assistant in School of Communication's GeNA Lab, she has collaborated on a range of projects and publications to do with blockchain, big data, privacy and genomics. She holds an MA in media and communications from Goldsmiths College, University of London.

Alexandra Giannopoulou is a postdoctoral researcher at the Blockchain and Society Policy Research Lab at the Institute for Information Law (IViR), University of Amsterdam. She holds a PhD in law from the University of Paris II Panthéon-Assas. Her PhD thesis entitled "The Creative Commons licenses" assesses the effects that Creative Commons – as a transnational copyright management system – had on copyright reforms. Alexandra was a visiting researcher at Stanford Law School (2012) and a junior lecturer (ATER) at the University of Paris Ouest Nanterre la Défense (2014–2016). Before joining IVIR, she worked as a research fellow at the Humboldt Institute for Internet and Society (HIIG) in Berlin.

Felix Hartmann is a researcher and entrepreneur. After leaving Europe for several years, he returned to Italy and founded his first consultancy company in 2012. Always passionate about innovation of all kinds, he got in touch with Bitcoin back in 2013. He is an active investor in some blockchain projects and started to work full time on blockchain and connected technologies in early 2017. In that year, he founded extus.co, an R&D network that aims to connect highly skilled researchers and developers and support companies with respect to pioneering blockchain innovation.

Luke Heemsbergen (PhD) is a Research Fellow at the Networked Society Institute, The University of Melbourne, Australia, and a lecturer in communication at Deakin University, Australia.

Ralph Holz is a lecturer in networks and security in the School of Computer Science at the University of Sydney, Australia, and a visiting academic at the Technical University of Munich, Germany.

A.T. Kingsmith is a doctoral candidate in political science at York University. His book, *A Schizo-Stroll: Anxious Reflections on Late Capitalism*, examines the advent of generalized anxiety in relation to the affective conditions of neoliberal capitalism since the 2008 global financial crisis. He recently co-edited an essay collection and a special double issue of *Global Discourse*, both of which analyze the dynamics of left-wing organizing on an increasingly hostile, cynical and polarizing political terrain.

Guido Noto La Diega is a lawyer specialising in cyber law, data protection and intellectual property. With a PhD in private law (Unipa) and a postdoc in cloud computing law (QMUL), Dr Noto La Diega is the author of books and papers published in international peer-reviewed journals. Co-convenor of NINSO, the Northumbria Internet & Society Research Group, and Fellow of the Nexa Centre for Internet & Society, Dr Noto La Diega teaches intellectual property and cyber law at the Northumbria Law School, where he is European Research Partnerships Coordinator.

Dr Matthew Lovett is Subject Lead for Music and Media at the University of Gloucestershire; his work explores the common ground between creative practice, continental philosophy and political economy. His research focuses on music economics, technology and creative processes in relation to speculative and new materialist philosophies, whilst his musical practice, which is frequently collaborative, engages with improvisation, environmental performance and audiovisual composition.

Maria Ilaria Lunesu is a research fellow on the computer science faculty at Cagliari University, Italy. After earning a degree in electronic engineering, she got her PhD in electronic and computer engineering at the same university. Since 2010, her main research topic has been lean-agile methodologies applied on modeling and simulation of development and maintenance processes with journal and international conference publications. She recently started studying blockchain applications, with particular interest in smart contracts and ICOs.

Alexia Maddox is Research Officer for Deakin University Library and Sessional Lecturer in Research Methods in the Faculty of Arts and Education at Deakin University, Australia. She also conducts research into the social impacts of cryptomarkets in her role as Research Officer at the National Drug Research Institute, in the Faculty of Health Sciences at Curtin University, where she is supported by funding from the Australian Government under the Substance Misuse Prevention and Service Improvement Grants Fund.

Michele Marchesi is full Professor at the University of Cagliari. He has been one of the first scholars in Italy to study object-oriented programming, since 1986, and agile methodologies for software production, since 1998. He has a vast experience with consulting and company training in application production with object-oriented technologies, software development procedures and quantitative economic analysis.

Bronwin Patrickson got his PhD (2014) at the Department of Media, Music & Cultural Studies, Macquarie University, Sydney, Australia.

Henrique Rocha I have a Computer Science PhD in the Federal University of Minas Gerais (UFMG – Brazil, 2016), working in the research group of Applied Software Engineering. I was a pos-doctoral researcher at Inria (France, 2017–2018) working with blockchain oriented software engineering. I have experience in Computer Science and Electrical Engineering, focusing on Software Engineering, Blockchain, Recommendation Systems, Bugs, and Software Testing.

Sune Sandbeck is currently completing his doctoral degree in political xcience at York University. His PhD dissertation examines the history of offshore finance in relation to monetary policy. He recently co-edited a special issue examining the concept of "authoritarian neoliberalism" for the upcoming 2019 volume of *Competition and Change*. He has also written on the political and monetary dynamics of the European debt crisis for *Competition and Change* and *New Political Economy*.

James Stacey is RA in Blockchain Law.

Duarte Teles holds a bachelor of informatics engineering degree from Instituto Superior de Engenharia do Porto, Portugal. Currently in his final year in a master's degree in informatics engineering with a specialization in computer systems, he has a deep interest in everything related to blockchain, software design and development in particular.

Roberto Tonelli is a researcher in software engineering. He has been working on applications of complex systems network theory to software engineering since 2007. He is the author of more than 80 papers, many of them on open source software, software process simulation and modeling, and simulation of statistical processes to software development and maintenance. He has been chair and organizer for RefTest2013 and RefTest2014 conferences,

WETSoM2015 and 2016; track chair and PC member at XP2014; and PC member for Wetsom since 2011 and will be PC member for XP2015.

Julian von Bargen is a doctoral candidate in political science at York University. His PhD dissertation examines the breakdown of the Barlow model of the Internet and the return to territorialized authority in Internet governance. He recently co-edited a special double issue of *Global Discourse* that analyzed the challenges and transformations of left-wing organizing, mobilizing and imagining in the face of the rise of the far right.

Xiaofeng Wang is a senior lecturer and researcher on the computer science faculty of the Free University of Bozen-Bolzano, Italy. Her main research areas include software startups, agile and lean software development and innovation, and human factors in software engineering. Before moving to Italy, she worked in Lero, the Irish Software Engineering Research Centre, as a postdoc. She is actively publishing in both information systems and software engineering venues, including *Information Systems Research, Information Systems Journal, IEEE Software, Empirical Software Engineering, Journal of Systems and Software*, etc.

Janet Hui Xue is a research associate at the University of Sydney, Australia, where she is affiliated with the Department of Government and International Relations, School of Social and Political Science. She is also a research associate at the One Belt One Road Programme at the Faculty of Law and visiting scholar at Wolfson College, both at the University of Oxford, UK.

Guillermina Yansen holds a PhD in social sciences from the University of Buenos Aires, Argentina (UBA). She has been a CLACSO grant-holder and is currently a postdoctoral fellow with CONICET. She also teaches Informatics Social Relations and Sociological Theory in the Faculty of Social Sciences at UBA and is a member of the e-TCS team, as well as various research projects at the University of Buenos Aires, Centro Ciencia, Tecnología y Sociedad (CCTS), Universidad.

Chapter 1

Blockchain

A disruptive technology

Massimo Ragnedda and Giuseppe Destefanis

Introducing blockchain

Blockchain is no longer just about bitcoin or cryptocurrencies in general, but it can be seen as a disruptive and revolutionary technology which will have a major impact on multiple aspects of our lives. The revolutionary power of such technology can be compared with the revolution sparked by the World Wide Web and the Internet in general. As the Internet can be seen as a means for sharing information, so blockchain technologies can be seen as a way to introduce the next level: blockchain allows the possibility of sharing value.

The problem solved by a blockchain is "consensus". It revolutionizes the concept of trust, introducing elements for generating disruption in the financial sector. Currencies are therefore the first concept which can be implemented upon such technology, but this is only the premise. Satoshi Nakamoto conceived the Bitcoin electronic cash system in 2008 with the aim of producing digital coins whose control is distributed across the Internet rather than owned by a central issuing authority such as a government or a bank. It became fully operational in January 2009, when the first mining operation was completed, and since then it has continuously seen an increase in the number of users and miners. In the beginning, the interest in the bitcoin digital currency was purely academic, and the exchanges in bitcoins were limited to a restricted elite of people more interested in the cryptography properties than in the real bitcoin value. Nowadays bitcoins are exchanged to buy and sell real goods and services, as happens with traditional currencies.

Distributed infrastructure

The main distinctive feature introduced by the Bitcoin system is the distributed infrastructure where all the transfers are recorded. To send and receive bitcoins, a user needs an alphanumeric code called an address. An address can be seen as a bank account number and can be the recipient of funds. An address is public information derived from a public key. No personal information is recorded in a blockchain, and for this reason, the Bitcoin protocol offers pseudo-anonymity. The consensus mechanism allows agents to transfer "value" without having a third party involved in the process, which guarantees that the source actually owns that value which it wants to transfer and which guarantees that the recipient receives (or not) the value being transferred. The elimination of this third trusted party is a major breakthrough. If we think about how banks work at the moment and what they actually do, it is immediately clear that banks match the definition of trusted third parties. The bitcoin blockchain allows the transfer of value without a third party. The disruptive potential of the bitcoin consensus algorithm is enormous. The fact that all the transactions are public and it is not possible to delete them is the key which lets the consensus algorithm work. The whole transaction history (from the first that occurred) is accessible by anyone (any agent which wants check what happened from the genesis), and it cannot be changed.

Consensus is linked with another two elements necessary to let this technology work: peer-to-peer networks and cryptography. The blockchain is built upon a peer-to-peer network, and anyone willing to join the network can do it without asking permission from anyone. Each node of the network exposes a constantly updated version of the blockchain, and this fact gives the possibility (to each node) to verify old and new transactions and to decide if they are valid or not. There is no possibility of "double spending", and by eliminating this possibility, distributed ledgers introduce the concept of digital scarcity.

Introducing scarcity in a digital world has been extremely complex. Scarcity and digital are almost opposite concepts, if we think, for instance, how easy is to duplicate a file (a music file, a document, a film). Speaking about money, it is easy to understand the concept of scarcity: if we have a banknote, we are sure that that banknote is unique, no one else can have the same one, and if someone tries to "make a copy" we are aware of the fact that the action is classified as illegal. Governments, banks, laws and agreements protect a fiat currency from the double-spending problem.

From Web 1.0 to Web 3.0

The advent of blockchain technology brings a new era in the web, what here we define as the Web 3.0. The first era of the Internet was mainly characterized by information carried by static websites without any possibility of interaction. It was primarily made by information portals with flat data where users could "only" read and were not allowed to add any comments, reviews or feedback. A paradigmatic example of this first era of the Internet is the British Encyclopedia (or any other traditional encyclopedia) that "simply" digitalized the content, moving the information from offline to online but without giving the possibilities to users to interact and generate new content. The Web 2.0, or second stage of the World Wide Web's evolution, is characterized by the possibilities to interact, share information, add content and exchange data. This era, also known as participative, gives the possibility to all users to participate, generate content online (user-generated content) and easily interact with other users (usability).

One of the paradigms of this new era is Wikipedia, which, in contrast with the British Encyclopedia, can be written (and not only read) by users. The shift is from the "readable" phase to the "writable" phase, from passive users (simply consuming contents) to active users (becoming active creators of content), from the static to the dynamic web. In this vein, another paradigmatic example of this new phase is given by the advent of social media, which encourages participation (Jenkins, 2006), information sharing and collaboration.

The advent of blockchain technologies brings the third era of the web, the so-called Web 3.0. This new era allows the transfer of value.

The Web 3.0 is based on decentralization, without points of control and unique profit centres. The blockchain enables the transfer of value without a centre of profit or monopolistic service providers. While the advent of social media allowed the exchange of information among users but kept the control among a few private actors (generating digital oligarchy with social media companies, peer-to-peer ridesharing, peer-to-peer hospitality networks), blockchain technologies allow the possibility of creating decentralized networks without centralized points of control. From this stems one of the disruptive aspects of this technology that will enable to operate on a decentralized system without any central centre of profit in charge of coordinating (and taking advantage of) the network. Blockchain technology allows the secure transfer of information, assets and money without a third-party intermediary, such as banks or other financial institutions (Swan, 2015: 15). These third-party intermediaries are not limited to banks, but it also includes the economic platforms of the shared economy and Web 2.0, which make a profit from each transaction, and popular social media platforms, which make profits using users' data.

A blockchain can be used also as a backbone infrastructure for running smart contracts, particular decentralized applications which can be seen as computer programs executed by participants in a blockchain. Smart contracts are an additional disruptive factor and have gained tremendous popularity in the past few years, to the point that billions of US dollars are currently exchanged every day through such technology. However, since the release of the Frontier network of Ethereum in 2015, there have been many cases in which the execution of smart contracts managing Ether coins lead to problems or conflicts. Smart contracts rely on a non-standard software life cycle, according to which, for instance, delivered applications can only be updated or bugs resolved by releasing a new version of the software. Furthermore, their code must satisfy constraints typical of the domain, like the following: they must be light; the deployment on the blockchain must take into account the cost in terms of some cryptovalue; their operational cost must be limited; and they are immutable, since the bytecode is inserted into a blockchain block once and forever.

The idea of a smart contract was originally described by cryptographer Nick Szabo in 1997 as a kind of digital vending machine. In his paper (Szabo, 1997), he imagined how users could input data or value and receive a finite item from a machine.

More in general, smart contracts are self-enforcing agreements, i.e., contracts, implemented through a computer program whose execution enforces the terms of the contract. The idea is to get rid of a central control authority, entity or organization which both parties must trust and delegate such a role to the correct execution of a computer program. Such a scheme can thus rely on a decentralized system automatically managed by machines. The blockchain technology is the instrument for delivering the trust model envisaged by smart contracts.

Since smart contracts are stored on a blockchain, they are public and transparent, immutable and decentralized, and since blockchain resources are costly, their code size cannot exceed domain-specific constraints. Immutability means that when a smart contract is created, it cannot be changed again.

Smart contracts can be applied to many different scenarios: banks could use them to issue loans or to offer automatic payments; insurance companies could use them to automatically process claims according to agreed terms, postal companies for payments on delivery.

No border

The power of such a structure is also given by the fact that there are no borders, and it is possible to transfer value everywhere with low transaction fees. Or at least everywhere we have access to the network. Blockchain technologies will be used for financial products and have opportunities in all those fields, which requires transparency, immutability, certainty and certification. However, one of the main challenges that blockchain technologies are facing is related to the so-called digital divide, often intended as the gap in accessing and using new technologies. According to recent research, it seems that the digital divide in terms of access is narrowing quickly, "driven by the expansion of broadband access in developing countries" (Nye, 2015). However, this assumption is only partly true. Indeed, it depends on what we intend when we say "digital divide". If we consider the digital divide only a matter of accessibility, then this assumption might appear true. Indeed, thanks to the rapid growth of the new mobile and networking technologies and the expansion of broadband availability the digital divide in terms of the availability of the technology is narrowing at both at the national and international level. This definition is reductive and does not explain in detail the different levels of digital inequalities and how these could affect, in different ways, the diffusion, the uses and the benefits users can get from using new technologies. Indeed, there are major divisions in the type, quality, reliability and affordability of access both within and between nations across the globe. Furthermore, available and accessible information and communications technology (ICT) is not the only gap among users and citizens, and it is not the only divide that creates inequalities. For those with access we have moved from simple issues of an access divide (to have the material or physical access) to the capability divide (the ability to use, quality of provision and use of) and then to the outcome divide (to the effects of utilizing digital media). These three elements – access, uses, and benefits – are what we define as the three levels of the digital divide (Ragnedda, 2017) and provide a more sophisticated and complete picture of the multidimensionality of digital inequalities. The digital divide is therefore the actual social and personal consequences of the divide or discrepancy in the levels of connectivity, in the level of capabilities, in the outcomes, in the digital and social skills, in the motivation and in a diversity of combinations of these measures.

These features influence the way in which we access, use and gain benefits from blockchain technologies. In other words, not everybody will benefit from the advent of these new technologies, since inequalities in accessing (the first level of the digital divide), in using (the second level of the digital divide) and in getting tangible outcomes (the third level of the digital divide) are persistent. For this reason and to extend to all users the benefits of blockchain, it would not be enough to implement access to the technologies to offer the possibility of gaining advantage from their uses. Without the necessary (digital) skills, the confidence to use blockchain technologies and the digital capital (Ragnedda, 2018) to "convert" the uses of technologies into concrete and tangible outcomes, the diffusion of blockchain will reinforce previous social inequalities, giving to the most advantageous groups more possibilities compared to their disadvantaged counterparts. In other terms, the full potential of this revolutionary technology is not fully displayed and exploited if the digital divide is not opposed and tackled.

Blockchain technologies: risks and opportunities

This book underlines the risks and opportunities offered by the advent of blockchain technologies and the rise of the Web 3.0. This book, adopting an interdisciplinary perspective, outlines the conceptual development of these technologies in different disciplines, inter alia legal, sociological, media and engineering studies. The core analysis in the book explains how such technologies are disruptive and further discusses the concrete consequences of these disruptions in terms of social, economic, technological and legal consequences.

Such a comparative perspective has also been underemphasized in the debate about blockchain, and this underemphasis leads to weaknesses in our understanding of decentralized technologies. We anticipate that the comparative examination of these features will be helpful in clarifying the dynamics and consequences of the blockchain technologies in a variety of settings. This book aims at filling this gap by hosting an interdisciplinary and comparative discussion of blockchain technologies in a variety of disciplines.

From this unified perspective, the book proceeds with three discipline-focused sections, each one including five chapters. The first includes case studies examining the socio-economic consequences of the advent of blockchain technologies, while the last section focuses on the technological innovations and how this emerging technology has gone beyond cryptocurrencies to include health care, voting systems, energy, transport and so forth.

More specifically, the first section opens with a chapter (Chapter 2) written by Sune Sandbeck, A. Kingsmith and Julian von Bargen that considers the disruptive potential of highly reliable, versatile forms of collective action in open networks that are now possible with blockchains. Sandbeck, Kingsmith and von Bargen argue that blockchain technology is compatible with what they refer to as a commons-based framework for socio-economic interchange, which, in turn, holds the potential to disrupt neoliberal logics of governmentality, production and value that are only reinforced by standard blockchain architectures. Their analysis comprises an evaluation of the development and deployment of blockchains along each of these three parameters. Next, in Chapter 3, Guido Noto La Diega and James Stacey, after a brief introduction on general regulatory issues in the blockchain, explore the impact of the blockchain on copyright. They argue that the more the blockchain becomes widespread, the more lawmakers develop an interest in regulating it. Most existing regulations, policies and case law take a top-down approach and focus on Bitcoin and, therefore, on fraud and anti-money laundering. A more participatory and holistic approach would be more suitable. Indeed, it is important to involve all the stakeholders and keep in mind all the potential socio-legal issues if one wants to ensure that the blockchain unleashes its full potential and benefits all the players involved.

In Chapter 4, Philippa R. Adams, Julie Frizzo-Barker, Betty B. Ackah and Peter A. Chow-White explore the discourses and activities around women in blockchain meetups through a technofeminist lens. This reflexive "social shaping of technology" perspective highlights how gender and technology co-evolve in a seamless web of technical artifacts, social relations and cultural meanings (Wajcman, 2004). This position challenges the prevailing notion of technology as neutral and value free. In the 1990s, feminist scholars celebrated the emancipatory potential of the Internet to close the gap of gender inequalities (Haraway, 1991; Plant, 1997; Turkle, 1995). Yet these claims in many ways fell short, leaving the corporeal realm behind. Technofeminism builds on Haraway's vision, conceiving of technology as both a source and a consequence of gender relations (Wajcman, 2004). Within this framework, both gender and blockchain are viewed as part of the texture that constitutes contemporary life rather than as separate from society. In Chapter 5, Scott Freeman, Ivana Beveridge and Jannis Angelis investigate the enablers and limitations of digital trust, which is enabling the mass mobilization of people across geographical and social boundaries at and to a historically unparalleled speed and extent, bringing them into a circle of trust. Blockchain technology is able to fundamentally transform the boundaries of organizations, thus challenging traditional assumptions about organizations being an ideal entity to manage market transactions. Moreover, it threatens to disrupt existing power structures by questioning their future role and reason for existence. Consequently, traditional notions of trust have to be updated. Drawing on market data, industry cases, anecdotes and academic frameworks, the authors analyze the drivers of digital trust in the crypto industry from historic, institutional, market and sociological perspectives. The author suggests that the ability to endorse distrust as a crucial aspect of digital trust may be essential for the long-term success of the industry. They support the conclusions drawn with empirical findings from first-hand managerial experience with a leading crypto exchange in Asia. Finally, in the last chapter of this section (Chapter 6), Bronwin Patrickson explores the potential implications posed by blockchain technologies for Scotland's digital design industries, particularly in terms of creative IP formation, development and expansion. Patrickson worked with three case study partners of variable sizes (small, medium and large) across Dundee, Edinburgh and Glasgow, conducting a participatory action research study involving three active tests of the networked blockchain beta application Colony. During the beta test, Patrickson conducted tests with each industry partner, recording their experience with and evaluation of these applications. Combined with business profiles/histories and before and after participatory interviews, the test is a vehicle to actively explore the influence of blockchain technologies.

The second section of this book focuses on the implications of blockchain on the media development. More specifically, in Chapter 7, Walid Al-Saqaf and Malin Picha Edwardsson focus on how the peer-to-peer, decentralized and highly disruptive blockchain technology may impact or be used by news media and journalists. In this study, we explore blockchain's potential to make journalism a more sustainable business. By reflecting on the *relative advantage* attribute of the diffusion of innovations theory by Rogers, this study assesses whether a blockchain-based newsroom model can compete against the traditional centralized model. As a case study, the authors explore Civil, a blockchain-based protocol that aims to use cryptoeconomics to incentivize the production of quality journalistic content. They conclude that the main relative advantage of a Civil newsroom model is the ability to enhance news credibility. The protocol achieves this by allowing a greater degree of decentralization, equality, transparency and accountability, which collectively reduce the influence of intermediaries such as advertisers, gatekeepers and media owners. Since Civil and blockchain technology in general are in early stages of development and face many challenges, they argue that it is too early to predict the success of this model and find it useful to track the progress of Civil and similar platforms over time. In the following chapter (Chapter 8), Balazs Bodo and Alexandra Giannopoulou critically examine whether the communities that develop and maintain blockchain technology infrastructures (such as bitcoin or Ethereum) are able to solve the governance issues of their respective, planetary scale technologies; how the governance logics they develop for themselves get reflected in the technology itself; and how the success or failure of the governance of the blockchain technology infrastructure affects blockchain technologies' promise to address the currently unresolved governance challenges of other, planetary scale resources. In this chapter, Bodo and Giannopoulou argue that the genesis of blockchain should not be seen merely as a response to the global financial crisis of 2008 (Nakamoto, 2008) but that the crisis of Web 2.0 modes of governance also played a role in the mainstreaming of blockchain technologies.

Lowett analyses the way in which two blockchain-based platforms – Mycelia's Creative Passport and Steemit – are emerging as examples of a particular paradigm of blockchain-based digital media commerce. Each demonstrates how such networks can generate revenue directly, through enhanced production and distribution systems, and indirectly, via an exponential series of connections. Much has been said about how blockchain systems will increasingly do away with intermediaries – in other words banks, royalty collection agencies, even lawyers and other third parties, etc. – thereby rewarding content creators with higher earnings for their endeavours through frictionless payment systems and smart contracting. However, what is clearly emerging is another form of the "Internet of Value" (Tapscott, 2016), one that does not simply create more revenue by merely simplifying exchange protocols. Steemit co-founder Ned Scott suggests that "It's as though all the [Steemit] users are playing a social media game, and they're earning points based on how well they participate". As network effects are increasingly leveraged as a means to create income, blockchain-based innovations such as Creative Passport and Steemit are emerging as an opportunity to rethink wealth distribution beyond the narrow frameworks that have hitherto dominated the Internet.

Luke Heemsbergen, Alexia Maddox and Robbie Fordyce, in Chapter 10, argue against the ideological tide washing in on peer-to-peer, distributed ledgers based upon cryptography, or phrasing that adds "blockchain enabled" to various forms of digital communication practice. Through a media studies lens we theorize blockchain as "Web 3.0" technology, signalling the emergence of "human programming", where people become the conscious linkages between disparate machineries while serving their underlying vulnerabilities. The authors also draw upon historical analysis of community access television (CATV) and the Internet and World Wide Web to argue that radical ideologies have intertwined with "new media" and specifically networked media since the 1960s and follow an innovation and adoption trajectory of expansion and contraction. Through the case study of Bitcoin, a cryptocurrency based upon the blockchain protocol, they examine its initial innovative frames of expansion through decentralization and disruption of the centralized banking system. They conclude this critique by considering how smart contracts are ledgers of built personal data that are inescapable for their subjects. Guillermina Yensen, in the last chapter of this section (Chapter 11), characterizes an extended way of using blockchain technology in the field of circulation and commercialization of user-generated data through the case of Wibson. Launched in 2017, Wibson is a blockchain-based app that aims to decentralize the data market by "empowering individuals to profit from their data" (Wibson, 2017). This case is relevant for two reasons. First, it represents a clear example of one of the current and most extended modes of blockchain usage in the context of informational capitalism (Castells, 1997; Zukerfeld, 2010). Second, it operates within one of the most profitable branches of the information sector, potentially challenging giant companies like Facebook and Google. This branch has been subject to all kinds of debates about privacy boundaries and abuses and lack of transparency by corporations. Yensen advances the study of Wibson by pointing out some criticisms, underlining how this is a witness case to observe the way in which the potentials of blockchain technology are being subsumed to the logic of the commercialization of the Internet and, thus, leaving aside the discussions about the meaning of the public.

Finally, the last section opens with Chapter 12 by Janet Hui Xue and Ralph Holz, in which the feasibility of using smart contract technology to handle online dispute resolution on a large scale is analyzed. Online dispute resolution is "referred to as the use of technology to carry out the dispute resolution process". Online dispute resolution combines alternative dispute resolution and information and communications technology; it can be used for disputes arising from both online e-commerce transactions and offline transactions such as purchases. The chapter identifies the feasible regulatory space to help understand how smart contracts for ODR platforms can possibly be regulated and embedded within current law systems.

In Chapter 13, Stéphane Ducasse, Henrique Rocha, Santiago Bragagnolo, Marcus Denker and Clement Francomme present SmartAnvil, an open platform to build software analysis tools around smart contracts. The authors illustrate the general components and focus on three important aspects: support for static analysis of Solidity smart contracts, deployed smart contract binary analysis through inspection, and blockchain navigation and querying. SmartAnvil is open source and supports a bridge to the Moose data and software analysis platform.

In the third chapter of this section (Chapter 14), Dario Puligheddu, Roberto Tonelli and Michele Marchesi describe a blockchain technology application able to solve many of the drawbacks and inconveniences presently occurring in standard customer relationship management (CRM) using a completely new approach which exploits the blockchain features offered by Hyperledger. The authors implement this scheme with a permissioned blockchain, which requires a precautionary verification of network participants and use "Fabric" by Hyperledger, a project finalized to the creation of Blockchain for Enterprise. The permission structure of Hyperledger reduces the risk of security problems allowing transactions only between authorized parts.

Chapter 15, written by Duarte Teles and Isabel Azevedo, presents the core aspects of the General Data Protection Regulation (GDPR), and then three scenarios are discussed regarding the right to erasure, complemented with a generic GDPR compliance guideline for Ethereum DApps. The authors present also a case study: DFiles, a decentralized application (DApp) built mainly with decentralized technologies, which additionally adheres to blockchain software engineering (BOSE) principles.

In the last chapter (Chapter 16), Felix Hartmann, Xiaofeng Wang and Maria Ilaria Lunesu investigate what the success factors are for blockchain-based crowdfunding campaigns and how they are related to each other. They applied a mixed-method approach, including an analysis of three key evaluation websites of blockchain-based crowdfunding campaigns and construction of an interpretive structural model based on experts' knowledge. As the results of the study, a list of success factors from both literature and practice is presented, along with a hierarchical model of the relationships among these factors. The chapter provides a more extensive and structured understanding of what can lead to the success of (blockchain-based) crowdfunding campaigns.

In conclusion, by looking at these three main areas, this book sheds light on the potential impact of blockchain technology on the economic, media, social and technological fields. Thus, the volume integrates a number of chapters examining disparate areas, all unified around their focus on the phenomenon of blockchain in a comparative and interdisciplinary perspective. The book presents new theoretical approaches and empirical evidence to help guide the reader through some of the most critical debates of the digital era. Ultimately, this volume fills a gap in the emerging literature about blockchain technologies by proposing an interdisciplinary approach to understand the social, technological and economic consequences of decentralized technologies.

Bibliography

Castells, M. (1997). *Power of Identity: The Information Age: Economy, Society, and Culture.* Cambridge, MA: Blackwell Publishers, Inc. Haraway, D. (1991). A cyborg manifesto: science, technology and socialist-feminism in the late twentieth century. In *Simians, Cyborgs and Women: The Reinvention of Nature* (pp. 149–181). New York: Routledge.

Jenkins, H. (2006). *Confronting the Challenges of Participatory Culture: Media Education for the 21st Century.* Chicago: The MacArthur Foundation.

Nakamoto, S. (2008) *Bitcoin: A Peer-to-Peer Electronic Cash System.* https://bitcoin.org/bitcoin.pdf (Last access January 2019).

Nye, B. (2015), Intelligent tutoring systems by and for the developing world: a review of trends and approaches for educational technology in a global context. *International Journal of Artificial Intelligence in Education.* 25(2): 177–203.

Plant, S. (1997). *Zeros + Ones: Digital Women + The New Technoculture.* London: Fourth Estate.

Ragnedda, M. (2017). *The Third Digital Divide. A Weberian Analysis of Digital Inequalities.* London: Routledge.

Ragnedda, M. (2018). Conceptualizing digital capital. *Telematics and Informatics* 35(8): 2366–2375.

Swan, M. (2015). *Blockchain: Blueprint for a New Economy.* Sebastopol, CA: O'Reilly Media.

Szabo, N. (1997). Formalizing and securing relationships on public networks. *First Monday* 2(9).

Tapscott, D. (2016). *How the Blockchain Is Changing Money and Business.* Available at www.youtube.com/watch?v=Pl8OlkkwRpc&t=49s (Last access January 2019).

Turkle, S. (1995). *Life on the Screen*. New York: Touchstone.

Wajcman, J. (2004). *TechnoFeminism*. Cambridge: Polity.

Wibson. (2017). Official website. Available at https://wibson.org/

Zukerfeld, M. (2010). *Capitalismo y conocimiento. Materialismo cognitivo, propiedad intelectual y capitalismo informacional (Tesis de Doctorado, FLACSO Argentina)*. Available at https://capitalismoyconocimiento.wordpress.com (Last access January 2019).

Part I

Socio-economic aspects and consequences of decentralized technologies

Chapter 2

The block is hot

A commons-based approach to the development and deployment of blockchains

Sune Sandbeck, A.T. Kingsmith, and Julian von Bargen

Introduction

Blockchains are hot right now. To better understand why, we must examine the political conditions that underpin them. David Golumbia (2016) has illustrated in vivid detail the affinities between Bitcoin's technical infrastructures – which replace a 'trusted' third party such as the state or platform with cryptographic proofs – and right-wing economic thought during the twentieth century, embodied in the likes of the John Birch Society and the Chicago School of Economics. Whether viewed as a database, a network, or a distributed ledger, it is clear that blockchain is much more than code or a computational tool for time-stamping data records and transaction. Not only does Bitcoin not exhaust the potential of cryptocurrencies, but cryptocurrencies do not exhaust the potential of blockchains. In fact, to mistake the tokens that accompany blockchains as always being cryptocurrencies is a misleading assumption that precludes alternative applications of blockchains beyond neoliberal incentivizing schemes.

A blockchain is a distributed ledger or database shared across a digital network. What makes it different from most information that runs across the Internet is that blockchains are – like the early Internet – distributed, peer-to-peer systems. What makes a blockchain a blockchain is that every node in the network updates and maintains the distributed ledger independently, rather than leaving a master list in the possession of a single authority or host computer. This innovation caused exhilaration among defenders of the original model of the Internet because it reinvigorated old hopes for a decentralized information system beyond the control of any one authority, while also innovating on the classic model of the Internet by adding cryptography and a protocol to govern incentivization. By solving the problems of authenticity and authorization without a centralized authority, blockchains are said to amplify the capacity of bottom-up and non-hierarchical organizational structures, echoing a longing for the now lost (or more accurately never achieved) classical model of the Internet.

In other words, as Rachel O'Dwyer (2016) observes, what blockchain offers is the possibility of cooperation without trust. Bitcoin and other cryptocurrencies are often propagated as a 'trustless architecture' – a *stand-in* for trust in the absence of traditional intermediaries such as local communities and regional regulators. O'Dwyer (2016) stresses that this configuration is actually something quite different from fostering or building trust. The claim being made by cyberlibertarians and other supporters is not that we can engineer greater levels of cooperation or trust in friends, institutions, or governments but that we can dispense with social and institutional relations altogether in favour of a purely technical solution. Through seemingly innocuous choices to limit algorithmically the supply of bitcoins or by requiring computational 'proof of work' to create new coins, such political commitments, as Golumbia (2016) emphasizes, are integrated into the technical design of the system.

The history of blockchain, so far, has shown limited applications of the technology outside of financial speculation and risky investments in pursuit of spectacular returns. A central part of this dynamic is driven by core assumptions about the relationship between the technical architectures of blockchain and neoliberal modes of social and political governance. As the last decade has shown, there is no linear-causal relationship between decentralization in technical systems and egalitarian or equitable practices socially, politically, or economically (O'Dwyer 2016). Importantly, as Maurizio Lazzarato (2013) points out, features of neoliberalism such as decentralization, horizontality, and structurelessness are not so much threats to institutionalized regulatory mechanisms but an ideal solution to many of the impasses of classical liberal economics that generates the illusion of 'governance with governing'.

By conflating technical architectures with social or political modes of organization, blockchain supplants trust with the technical efficiency of the protocol (Galloway 2004). This chapter is focused primarily on what is – and what will be – at stake in blockchain's continuing embeddedness in the logics of neoliberalism. Through that lens, we begin by examining the transformation of classical liberal relations of exchange into neoliberal relations of competition. What is most important for us is the ways in which this shift in economic relations from exchange to competition constitutes a new mode of 'governmentality', or expansion in the scope of economic subjectivity that has been internalized in the protocols generating value on the blockchain.

In drawing out these internalizations, we examine the monetary arguments advanced by cyberlibertarians to support Bitcoin as an ideal form of currency against fiat money, the latter considered to be defective at its core since it relies on a state-sanctioned authority for trust and legitimacy. To do so, we survey the problems with assumptions underlying the protocols of Bitcoin before turning to three broader social and political factors that affect blockchains: *production*, *value*, and *governance*. The goal of this first section is to strip the blockchain of the neoliberal baggage generated by the incentivization scheme of Bitcoin. Finally, we conclude by investigating what other options might exist for developing and deploying the highly reliable, versatile forms of collective action in open networks made possible with blockchains on behalf of projects opposed to both neoliberal capitalism and libertarian politics. In this regard, we argue that the problem with most existing blockchain applications is not that they attempt to incentivize governmentality but rather that they attempt to incentivize the wrong kind of governmentality. In the final section, we focus primarily on attempts to incentivize a conception of trust as produced for sharing, recorded through an open and participatory consensus process and actualized as a sharing commons.

Homo economicus

Neoliberalism is the restoration not only of class power – of capitalism as the only possible economic system – but of capitalism as fully synonymous with reality. What is imposed (or what is 'restored') is a shift from 'homo economicus' or 'economic (hu)man' as an exchanging creature to a competitive one whose tendency to compete must be fostered. Jason Read (2009, p. 28) summarizes the profound effects of this shift: "while exchange was considered to be natural, competition is understood by the neoliberals of the twentieth century to be an artificial relation that must be protected against the tendency for markets to form monopolies and interventions by the state". This fundamental increase in the scope of economic rationality in neoliberal economics – the assertion that economics is coextensive with all of society, all of rationality – is not a natural state, but, as Michel Foucault (2008) catalogues, a form of naturalized 'governmentality' that requires constant intervention and management.

Competition necessitates this constant intervention on the part of the state, not on the market, but on the conditions of the market. By making desirable activities accessible and undesirable activities socially and political costly, governmentality can influence the parameters of choice so as to render certain outcomes more likely when subjects calculate their 'rational' interests (Lazzarato 2015).[1] In this way, neoliberalism subordinates state power to the conditions of the marketplace, the implication being that 'political problems' can be recast in technical terms. The operative terms of this recasting are no longer rights but interest, investment, and competition. Whereas classical liberalism presumes rights that can be exchanged – as Read (2009) observes, the legal subject of the liberal state (*homo juridicus*) is constituted through the exchange of the social contract – neoliberalism offers the inalienable reality of the market.

In order to produce the illusion of 'governance without governing', actors must have a great deal of freedom to act – to 'choose' between competing strategies. This choice is not a reality but a transformation of ideology in terms of its conditions and effects. As Lazzarato (2015) observes, the main objective is to deproletarianize the population by making everyone an owner without requiring too much direct state regulation. Importantly, this freedom of ownership is not outside of politics but rather, as Read (2009) emphasizes, an integral element of a strategy that operates through interests, desires, and aspirations rather than rights and laws. The regulatory mechanisms of neoliberalism do not directly curtail actions as a sovereign power. They govern by managing the conditions though which those actions can be produced.

As a result, the trajectory of neoliberal governmentality generates a fundamental paradox; as power becomes less restrictive, less grounded in institutional mechanisms of regulation, it also becomes more intense, saturating the field of all possible actions so as to most effectively manage the conditions of competition. On one hand, the state is expected to set the stage for competition. On the other, the state is expected to avoid becoming a player in the market. As Thomas Lemke (2002) suggests, neoliberalism manages this basic contradiction by attempting to create a social reality that it suggests already exists, stating that competition is the basis of social relations while fostering those same relations. The contemporary trend away from long-term, secure work and towards temporary and precarious labour is not only an effective economic strategy – freeing corporations from contracts and the expensive commitments of health care and other benefits – it is an effective political strategy as well.[2]

By encouraging workers to see themselves not as 'workers' in a social and communal sense, who have something to gain through solidarity and collective organization, but as 'entrepreneurs of the self', an economic perspective, that of the market, becomes coextensive with all of society. When it comes to monetary sovereignty, this expansion in the scope of economic relations has been internalized in the protocols that generate value on the blockchain. Bitcoin caused excitement when it proposed a technical solution to a problem that previously required a trusted intermediary – money, or, more specifically, the problem of guaranteeing and controlling money supplies and monitoring the repartition of funds on a global scale.

In the same way that neoliberal governmentality does not actually eliminate governance – but rather curtails the amount of regulation required from any single actor in the system – blockchains do not actually eliminate trust. What they do is minimize the amount of trust. They do this by distributing trust among different actors in the system by incentivizing them to compete as rational agents (read: homo economicus) on the terms defined by the protocol. Blockchains thus herald the arrival of a digital order that effectively merges libertarian philosophies of governance and neoliberal precepts about value creation and distribution, by elevating *laissez-faire* to an autonomous, self-governing algorithm.

Where libertarian and neoliberal visions intersect

Perhaps a more accurate way to describe blockchains is not as 'trustless' but as built on the basis of *distributed trust*: trusting everyone in the aggregate as economic agents participating in a network on the basis of rational self-interest and competition. As the pseudonymous architect of Bitcoin, Satoshi Nakamoto, argued, "the root problem with conventional currency is all the trust that's required to make it work. The central bank must be trusted not to debase the currency, but the history of fiat currencies is full of breaches of that trust" (Nakamoto 2008). Proponents of Bitcoin and other cryptocurrencies commonly aver that the modern monetary system is inherently prone to structural inflation and repeated crises due to its *centralization*. Bitcoin and its distributed blockchain ledger were therefore hailed by cyberlibertarians as a revolution in monetary decentralization – one that takes the supply, distribution, and exchange of money out of the hands of any single individual or institution. Cryptocurrencies like Bitcoin thus represent the culmination of *laissez-faire* so feted by neoliberal ideologues and libertarians alike, but that was a practical impossibility until now.

How is Bitcoin argued to accomplish this feat in monetary decentralization and *laissez-faire* (anti-)governance? First, the supply of Bitcoin is permanently limited to 21 million tokens, which mimics a commodity money minted in non-renewable precious metals such as gold. Bitcoin thus embodies in its very architecture the idealization of the gold standard often found among far-right monetarists opposing fiat currency. This likeness to precious metal coinage is underscored by Bitcoin's irreplaceability: if bitcoins are lost (for example, by forgetting one's wallet password or destroying a hard-drive that contains the only copy of a bitcoin wallet's secret keys), they can never be retrieved.

Second, Bitcoin's proof-of-work algorithm – in which miners compete for new bitcoins by solving a cryptographic problem required to append the next block of transactions to the blockchain – adjusts itself according to the overall computing power or 'hashrate' of the Bitcoin network so that additional bitcoins are released at a steady and predictable rate. Bitcoin is a deflationary currency by design, and the rate of this deflation is intended to proceed in a stable manner over time. Insofar as Bitcoin's supply schedule is indifferent to miners' inherent incentives to compete for bitcoins by increasing their processing power, Bitcoin surpasses even the rarest of precious metals in its rigid deflationary tendencies. In short, the supply of Bitcoin can neither be accelerated nor debased.

Third, since Bitcoin and most other cryptocurrencies are supplied and distributed by a decentralized network of users, no individual or organization can, in theory, monopolize the currency and take on the role that the state or central bank occupies under typical fiat currency regimes. For Bitcoin in particular, the highly competitive proof-of-work algorithm creates an incentive structure that ideally guards against the possibility of malicious forks in the blockchain, since an attacker would have to amass over 50 percent of the computing power of the entire Bitcoin network before they could alter the transaction blocks to their advantage. This is highly unlikely for any single Bitcoin miner to achieve, given the astronomical costs.

However, have cyberlibertarian claims about Bitcoin's revolution in monetary decentralization and *laissez-faire* governance borne out over the past decade of its existence? A cursory overview of Bitcoin's production, value, and 'governance without governing' algorithm suggests that its success as a viable currency has been stymied by the very attributes so emphatically touted by its advocates.

Production (and circulation)

The first and most obvious failure of Bitcoin has been in relation to the claims made about Bitcoin's decentralized production and distribution. As Böhme et al. (2015) point out, there are several levels in the Bitcoin network where there exists significant potential for centralization: currency exchanges, digital wallet services, and mining pools.[3] The first two of these are, strictly speaking, exogenous to the core protocols of Bitcoin and other cryptocurrencies since there is no practicable method of ensuring that users avoid the use of currency exchanges to swap between crypto- and fiat currencies or to forgo the convenience of relying on online wallet services that offer a host of security functions above and beyond the base cryptocurrency client. And to the chagrin of cryptocurrency's neoliberal advocates, such currency exchanges and online wallets offer a lucid example of how even in the most free-market of online environments, monopolistic tendencies quickly establish themselves because early entrants gain a significant advantage and create immense barriers to entry for latecomers.

Mining cartelization, however, has been an endogenous and intractable problem for Bitcoin's champions. Although anyone in theory can become a miner, the chances of solving a block and being rewarded with bitcoins is negligible for the individual miner given the overwhelming competition in processing power they face. Moreover, the hashrate required to profitably mine Bitcoin has long since rendered personal PCs obsolete, and the vast majority of mining pools now rely on application-specific integrated circuits (ASICs), most of which are now located in China and other emerging market economies (EMEs), given the relative affordability of both hardware and electrical costs there. The costs associated with such set-ups has placed the necessary hardware for Bitcoin mining beyond the reach of most individuals, and the only recourse for most new entrants into the market is to rent a portion of an ASIC-based mining center's processing power. Even then, it can take years before such individuals see any return on their investment, if ever.

The cartelization of mining underscores the fact that trust is ever present in blockchain systems and vital for cryptocurrencies to function. Mining cartelization presents an inherent problem to proof-of-work blockchains, since any pool that acquires over 50 percent of the hashrate of the entire cryptocurrency network could, in theory, 'fork' the blockchain to its advantage and begin to double-spend cryptocurrency tokens, rendering the blockchain illegitimate and destroying trust in the currency. But as Dowd and Hutchinson (2015) suggest, the monopolistic tendencies of cryptocurrency mining are theoretically absolute, since each individual miner would be best off contributing to a *single* mining pool, where the probability of success for all mining pool members would be 1. And in practice, such tendencies have become intractable for some of the more established cryptocurrencies like Bitcoin and Litecoin, whose oligopolistic mining networks are dominated by a small number of large pools; over 90 percent of Bitcoin's hashrate is distributed amongst just eight mining pools, with the four largest pools accounting for approximately 70 percent of the network's processing power.[4]

In the face of this competitive breakdown, Bitcoin and other proof-of-work cryptocurrencies effectively depend upon the good will of mining pools to never exceed the 50 percent hashrate mark, and there is no intrinsic failsafe to ensure that such a scenario could never transpire. In other words, the spectre of governance reinserts itself into Bitcoin's blockchain in the form of the decisions that a small, unelected cabal of mining pools make, who could collectively amass the kind of power to debase Bitcoin, given enough hashing power. The similarity here with the kind of arbitrary central bank power that Nakamoto decried is glaring.

Value

The second problem for the monetary validity of cryptocurrencies has been the erratic and unpredictable changes in value that most cryptocurrencies suffer from, with the price of a single Bitcoin having seen a spectacular rise in 2017 only to subsequently collapse at the beginning of 2018 (see Figure 2.1).

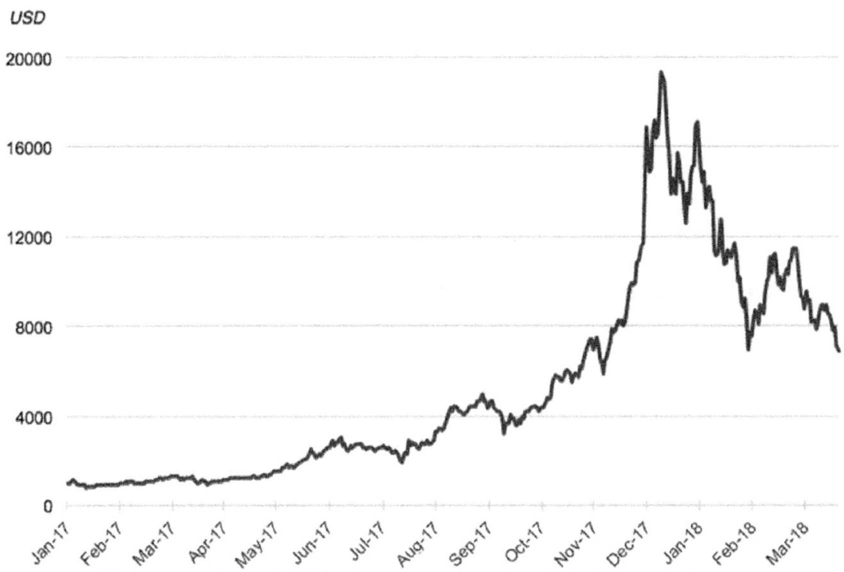

Figure 2.1 Price of Bitcoin in USD

Source: Quandl

This purchasing power volatility has rendered it fundamentally useless as a store of value, and most long-term holders of Bitcoin have invested in it speculatively, as an asset that should theoretically increase in value given its deflationary architecture (Weber 2016). For those who intend to use bitcoins as a medium of exchange, however, there is an inherent incentive to minimize the amount of time that bitcoins are held, since its value oscillates unpredictably. Similarly, sellers who accept Bitcoin as a means of payment typically quote prices that float according to Bitcoin's exchange rate with an established currency such as the US dollar. In this sense, Bitcoin not only fails as a store of value but also as a *unit of account*, since its instability leads to prices being implicitly denominated in established fiat currencies.

What the instability of many cryptocurrencies reveals is that a fixed nominal supply and a predictable trajectory of monetary creation cannot ensure deflationary tendencies proceed in any orderly manner (Harwick 2016). Absent of any centralized mechanism for controlling the currency's value and supply, the price of Bitcoin and other cryptocurrencies are at the mercy of market speculation, which inevitably manifests itself in extreme volatility.

As Figure 2.2 shows, the daily volatility of Bitcoin far exceeds stock indices such as the S&P 500. And these bouts of sudden appreciation and decline have been so severe and regular in occurrence that they rendered it nigh impossible for retailers and other online service providers to commit to acceptance of Bitcoin for payment. Microsoft, Valve (the largest online game distributor), and

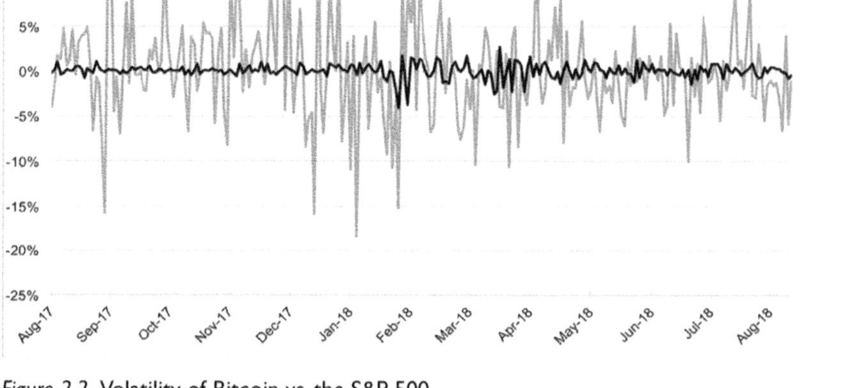

Figure 2.2 Volatility of Bitcoin vs. the S&P 500
Source: Quandl

Reddit are only the most recent companies to have quietly dropped support for Bitcoin.

Governance (without governing)

The third problem – the monetary viability of Bitcoin in the absence of any central authority responsible for monetary governance – is perhaps the most daunting challenge to Bitcoin's survival and underscores the misplaced faith in the principle of *laissez-faire*. For if the value of a currency is unresponsive to economic conditions or, obversely, responds to prevailing market sentiments in an uncontrollable manner, then that currency's ability to effectively facilitate market exchanges becomes undermined by declining trust in the currency and a growing propensity to treat it as a speculative asset instead. As a result, governance may appear less restrictive and less grounded in institutional mechanisms of regulation yet simultaneously becomes more crucial for facilitating the field of economic conditions and market sentiments so as to most effectively manage the conditions of competition. In this regard, the ostensibly trustless architecture of Bitcoin does not eliminate trust or even minimize it so much as relocate trust to the protocol.

By enabling investors on the blockchain to see themselves as 'entrepreneurs of the self', Bitcoin caused excitement when it proposed a technical solution to a problem that previously required a trusted intermediary. However, while neoliberalism is highly governed through the regulatory power of the competitive self-entrepreneur, there are no mechanisms in place to address the problem of guaranteeing and controlling monetary supply and monitoring the repartition of value on a global scale. Without some sort of centralized, distributed, or alternative form of participatory engagement that can break from the cartelization of cryptocurrency mining, the sanctity of the blockchain as an accurate, trustworthy, and socially transformative ledger for managing, distributing, and assuring the stability of a token's value in times of crisis is perpetually endangered.

The core critique of institutions by cyberlibertarian advocates of Bitcoin and other cryptocurrencies – i.e., that currencies can be effectively managed by non-market forces – condemns the very regulatory features of money that allow it to function in the first place. In a sense, cyberlibertarians are unable to confront the endemic limits of digital currencies because they stubbornly cling to the prevailing myth about money's origins, a narrative that paints a picture of some anarchic ur-community in which the state and money were once separated and money was free to function efficiently as a utility-maximizing technology to avoid the encumbrances of barter (Gammon 2012). But even more importantly, such advocates have ignored the basic nature of modern money in that the only difference between money and paper lies with the kind of intervention brought to bear by variously constituted regulatory bodies that function as an ultimate guarantor of money's *status quo* money.

As with any privately mined commodity, the irrevocable *laissez-faire* features that are embedded within the Bitcoin protocol and other proof-of-work cryptocurrencies are defenseless against the kind of monopoly tendencies and speculative spikes in value that are difficult to avoid. Bitcoin and other so-called 'trustless' cryptocurrency architectures have merely served to promote neoliberal governmentality by relying on financial subjectivity and speculative futurity as the primary impetus for governance on the blockchain.[5] However, as we discuss in the following section, if we approach the problem of governance differently, sidestepping the Bitcoin paradox of 'trust-in-technicalities', blockchain can offer possibilities for developing and deploying the highly reliable, versatile forms of collective action, engagement, and exchange in open networks on behalf of projects opposed to both neoliberal capitalism and libertarian politics.

Can blockchains shed their neoliberal governmentality?

Despite the failure of Bitcoin and other blockchain algorithms to usher in a form of governance that truly disrupts the dominant logics of the present era, the question remains: can the neoliberal logic of financial and individual incentivization be extirpated from the architecture of the blockchain? If, as we have demonstrated, neoliberal governmentality is coded into the protocol of Bitcoin and similar cryptocurrencies, then what do blockchains look like without this logic? Does the influence of neoliberal governmentality taint the idea of blockchains, decentralization, or trust, or merely their neoliberal variants? What we suggest here is that blockchains, in fact, have something significant to offer commons-based projects and might be successfully leveraged to inculcate alternative conceptions of trust, exchange, shared governance, and the deployment of collective resources. The key, however, lies in a recognition of the fact that blockchain architectures are not merely technical designs but a series of political choices that always-already entail governance, as we have argued.

Though neoliberal governmentality has been a staple of the most popular applications of blockchain, the problem is not located in blockchains or in the ideas of decentralization, 'trustless' architecture, cryptography, or a distributed ledger. What taints blockchains is our contemporary socio-historical moment. Blockchain applications such as Bitcoin were admittedly designed to subvert this contemporary moment, even if, as we argue, they ultimately reinscribed neoliberal governmentality. In fact, this is precisely what buttresses the allure of Bitcoin and blockchains: the financial system is not neutral and serves some interests and not others. Therefore, even if one disagrees with the politics of Bitcoin or insists correctly that Bitcoin was an unsuccessful design that has ultimately been appropriated by the very financial interests it set out to disrupt, it is nevertheless possible to imagine a commons-based approach to blockchain that does not simply reinscribe the logic of neoliberalism.

While commons-based applications of blockchain do not share the same concerns as Bitcoin, they likely share a preoccupation with the spectre of the state intervening to incentivize competition. This is because the state is more than just a state; as we have argued, it is a neoliberal capitalist state. And one of the primary functions of this state is to incentivize competition, privatization, and deregulation in place of a shared, commons-based mode of governance over collective resources. The neoliberal state can therefore always be relied upon to allocate shared resources to the private sector as the basis for stimulating competition. This pattern is deeply embedded within the logic of the state itself, as demonstrated by countless failed attempts by left governments to install a different economic order through state power. Thus, until the character of the state itself is fundamentally altered, there is little hope of instituting an alternative order through the deployment of statism. For some, blockchain is a bulwark against this problem and perhaps even a solution to the breakdown of social provisioning provided by the Keynesian state.

A blockchain might therefore provide key advantages to commons-based projects, to build coherence and trust among a community of people with shared values, to build alternative sources of value, and to protect commons and allow sharing of resources among underserved communities. As such, blockchains have the potential to facilitate and amplify a growing desire for alternatives to a privatized commons, neoliberal governmentality, austerity politics, and a global financial system dominated by state and corporate power.

Trust

In a small organization in which everyone knows one another and relations are already structured, a blockchain is unnecessary. The blockchain only emerges as a useful tool for a defined community in which members share values but do not necessarily know one another, where no formal governance structures exist, and where state institutions and financial interests are dominant. Under these conditions, if a community seeks to pool or manage resources in a framework that emphasizes participation and shared governance, blockchains offer a potentially revolutionary technology for maintaining trust and managing a shared resource. By using a blockchain for transparently managing, distributing, and assuring the stability of the shared resource, trust can be fostered within a community even as, externally, market relations are foisted upon every facet and domain of social life and the politics of austerity force further cuts to the services provisioned by the state (Gammon 2012). In this way, blockchains are seen by some as a way to evade this reduction of existence to a profit margin and the exhaustion of a Fordist model that, at the very least, linked profits and productivity growth to wages.

But a key element here is that the design of the blockchain application would have to be limited in scope: instead of offering to disrupt the dominant economic and political system, such a blockchain would aim to *evade* it and offer alternative tools for small-scale organization. The first step in this evasion would be to build local blockchains that are not structured in the manner of start-ups, which ultimately aim to scale globally (Pazaitis et al. 2017), because in scaling globally, consensus must be derived from a wide variety of global actors with diverging and conflicting interests. This requirement restricts the ability of actors to pursue local goals as part of a shared community. By scaling communally instead, the shared values and goals of a defined community can maintain their guiding role in the social reproduction of the blockchain.

At this reduced scale, blockchains have been deployed with real success, as part of commons-based projects that are attuned to the needs and desires of local communities (Gloerich, Lovink, de Vries eds, 2018). The project that has taken this vision the furthest is the Social Wallet, a series of pilot projects across Europe. One implementation of the Social Wallet is Macao in Milan, a community of artists who have organized themselves using the Social Wallet's blockchain, which records the distribution of resources amongst the community. This ledger is visible to all members of the community, ensuring that the distribution of resources is fully transparent, which provides a vital incentive to maintaining fairness and equity. The primary resource distributed is a basic income, but community members are also endowed with the power to create, assign, and track the distribution of resources and exchange coins based on hours contributed to the community. These contributions are in service of organizing events, taking care of public space, or contributing to an urban commons, and they are based on labor time (www.macaomilano.org, 2018).[6]

Value

The implementation of the Social Wallet is suggestive of a very different conception of value. Unlike value in Bitcoin, which is linked to the idea of the speculated worth of a financial asset's exchange value, for the Social Wallet, the value is derived from fairly rewarding all facets of labor related to social reproduction without reducing that value to an exchange value. According to the developers of Freecoin, whose blockchain architecture provides the basis for the Social Wallet, the specific architecture was designed to "let people run reward schemes that are transparent and auditable to other organisations. It is made for participatory and democratic organisations who want to incentivise participation, unlike centralized banking databases" (https://freecoin.dyne.org/, 2018). Blockchains are essential to this system because they create a trust management system that allows communities to uphold the sanctity of their contributions without the reduction of these contributions to an exchange or monetary value. This means trust is not located in a central authority, nor is it located in a 'trustless architecture', but rather it is located in the community, which is vested with the capacity to assert the value of particular contributions. These hours are tracked, logged, and reciprocated. Members put in time by contributing to community goals and in return receive coins which they might spend on other services provided by other contributors to the community.

Incentivization

By scaling at the community level and using share values and goals as the foundation of blockchain architecture, incentives do not have to mimic the speculative and financialized logic of established cryptocurrencies, which, as we have seen, merely replicate a mode of neoliberal governmentality. Moreover, there is no need to view cryptocurrencies and established forms of money as mutually exclusive. For example, some common-based blockchains have been designed as 'complementary currencies'. These currencies are designed to supplement instead of replace national currencies and aim to incentivize spending within local communities. The SantaCoin, for instance, is used at the Santarchangelo Festival. It allows festival goers to trade Euros into the SantaCoin and to spend their coins at participating local vendors. The idea is to keep money internal to the local community, building trust, networks, and solidarity in the process. According to the designers, the idea is to build "welfare from the ground up" (www.santarcangelofestival.com/en/santacoin/, 2018). This reminds us that money is not merely a means of exchange but an embodiment of social relations, which is never neutral in its design. By carefully choosing how we design monetary architecture – which is now possible at the local level through blockchain technology – new incentives can be established that foster collective values and relationships which run counter to the dominant logics of neoliberalism. This revolutionary potential in commons-based organization is what has commons-activists, left movements, and participatory democracy advocates so excited about blockchains, and with good reason.

Conclusion

Social investment in blockchain technology is critical at this precise moment in time because it remains outside of the purview of established institutional interests and state control, and its potential is still boundless. Hype surrounding blockchains has reached fever pitch over the past few years based largely on the notion that the technology is inherently counter-hegemonic and disruptive of the state and established fiat currencies (Herian 2018). However, as we have shown here, there are substantial limitations to the revolutionary potential of blockchain technology given the dominance of libertarian blockchain architectures and their implicit adherence to neoliberal logics and incentives of financialized competition. What underlies these limitations is the fundamental belief that blockchains are inherently trustless and therefore free of governance. But as the history of Bitcoin and other cryptocurrencies has shown, by turning the spectre of homo economicus into an organizing principle, such blockchains have merely reproduced the worst traits of neoliberal governmentality and have done little to undermine the tendencies towards cartelization and monopoly control. In short, cryptocurrencies with global ambitions of revolutionizing the established order have served as speculative and highly volatile digital assets, turning blockchain technology into a grotesque platform for financial profiteering.

What we have illustrated, however, is that blockchain technology need not serve such ends. By recognizing the inherently political dimension of blockchain architecture and, consequently, *blockchain governance*, it becomes possible to reengineer the technology to the benefit and empowerment of local communities and organizations. In this sense, we have argued that commons-based approaches to the application of blockchain are possible, ongoing, and full of potential. However, such commons-based approaches to blockchain must temper the scope of their scaling to ensure that the technology is deployed locally and serves the ends of the community rather than aiming to spark counter-hegemonic transformations through the mere deployment of blockchain alone. To paraphrase Polanyi (1944/2001), commons-based projects must aim to embed blockchain within the community rather than seeking to embed social relations within the blockchain itself (as its libertarian proponents might advocate). In so doing, however, blockchain technology has the real potential to promote the kind of social relations and collective organizations needed to achieve blockchain's original aim of systemic change.

Notes

1 For instance, the example of education demonstrates the idea behind the proposal for university business plans. The social sciences are often seen to be a drain on a public university's budget, so the choice for more profitable diplomas is promoted. According to Foucault (2008), governmental power does not trump the freedom of the governed in this scenario. Students are still 'free' to choose the social sciences if they estimate the benefits outweigh the costs of unemployment, high student loans, etc.

2 Importantly, as Earl Gammon (2012) points out, this idea of long-term, secure work under Fordism never really existed. Despite relative increases in economic equality (as a ratio of purchasing power), Fordism was built on the acceptance of certain entrenched inequalities that elicited challenges to the post-war Keynesian compromise. Internationally, it was premised on a division of labour in which colonies and former colonies continued in their role as producers of raw materials for Western nations, while domestically it was grounded in the gendering of industrial work – by presenting manufacturing as the embodiment of masculinity – and the creation of a new normal Fordist self, based on notions of frugality, hygiene, punctuality, and temperance largely dependent on racial and ethnic stereotyping.

3 A fourth level that the authors discuss, Bitcoin 'mixers', are intended to enhance the anonymity of transfers, since, strictly speaking, the Bitcoin addresses of the sender and recipient are publicly viewable on the blockchain itself. The mixers split the payment into chunks that are then rerouted through various addresses at random times in order to obscure the underlying addresses of transfer. However, more recent cryptocurrencies such as DASH and Monero have embedded this feature within the core client protocol.

4 See https://blockchain.info/pools.

5 The intentional misspelling of 'hold', which has become a popular meme among Bitcoin's proponents, originated in a 2013 online post on the Bitcointalk forums that was written by an apparently inebriated user. It has since become a popular rallying cry for Bitcoin and other cryptocurrency enthusiasts, signaling their intention to buy and hold cryptocurrencies, whatever the volatility or decline in value.

6 From the website: "The future we imagine is made of decentralized technological infrastructures, distributed and based upon algorithms. They are governed by democratic

discussions and decisional processes, put into place by communities that share values and ideas. In other words: in a plausible future in which algorithms control our economic, relational and spatial behaviours, the real challenge is to find a way to question them without creating a democratic deficit as a collateral effect".

References

Böhme, Rainer, Nicolas Christin, Benjamin Edelman, and Tyler Moore. 2015. "Bitcoin: Economics, Technology, and Governance." *Journal of Economic Perspectives*, 29(2): 213–238.

Dowd, Kevin and Martin Hutchinson. 2015. "Bitcoin Will Bite the Dust." *Cato Journal*, 35(2): 357–382.

Foucault, Michel. 2008. *The Birth of Biopolitics: Lectures at the Collège de France, 1978–1979*. New York: Palgrave Macmillan.

Galloway, Alexander. 2004. *Protocol: How Control Exists After Decentralization*. Cambridge, MA: The MIT Press.

Gammon, Earl. 2012. "The Psycho- and Sociogenesis of Neoliberalism." *Critical Sociology*, 39(4): 511–528.

Golumbia, David. 2016. *The Politics of Bitcoin: Software as Right-Wing Extremism*. Minneapolis, MN: University of Minnesota Press.

Harwick, Cameron. 2016. "Cryptocurrency and the Problem of Intermediation." *Independent Review*, 20(4): 569–588.

Herian, Robert. 2018. "Taking Blockchain Seriously." *Law and Critique*, 29(2): 163–171.

Inte Gloerich, Geert Lovink and Patricia de Vries (eds) (2018), *MoneyLab Reader 2: Overcoming the Hype*. Institute of Network Cultures, Amsterdam.

Lazzarato, Maurizio. 2013. "Governmentality in the Current Crisis." *Generation Online*, This text is a translation of a lecture delivered in Berlin. Available at www.generation-online.org/p/fp_lazzarato7.htm

Lazzarato, Maurizio. 2015. *Governing by Debt*. Los Angeles: Semiotext(e)/Intervention Series.

Lemke, Thomas. 2002. "Foucault, Governmentality, and Critique." *Rethinking Marxism*, 14(3): 49–64.

Nakamoto, S. (2008) *Bitcoin: A Peer-to-Peer Electronic Cash System*. https://bitcoin.org/bitcoin.pdf (Last access January 2019).

O'Dwyer, Rachel. 2016. "Blockchains and Their Pitfalls." In Trebor Scholz and Nathan Schneider (eds) *Ours to Hack and to Own: The Rise of Platform Cooperativism, A New Vision for the Future of Work and a Fairer Internet*. New York: OR Books.

Pazaitis, Alex, Primavera De Filippi, and Vasilis Kostakis. 2017. "Blockchain and Value Systems in the Sharing Economy. The Illustrative Case of Backfeed." *Technological Forecasting and Social Change*, 125: 105–115.

Polanyi, Karl. 1944/2001. *The Great Transformation*. Boston: Beacon Press.

Read, Jason. 2009. "A Genealogy of Homo-Economicus: Neoliberalism and the Production of Subjectivity." *Foucault Studies*, 6(1): 25–36.

Weber, Beat. 2016. "Bitcoin and the Legitimacy Crisis of Money." *Cambridge Journal of Economics*, 40: 17–41.

Chapter 3

Can permissionless blockchains be regulated and resolve some of the problems of copyright law?

Guido Noto La Diega and James Stacey[1]

Introduction

In October 2018, the European Parliament passed a resolution (European Parliament resolution of 3 October 2018 on distributed ledger technologies and blockchains: building trust with disintermediation (2017/2772(RSP))) on distributed ledger technologies that recognised blockchains' potential to disrupt copyright. The aim of this chapter is to examine blockchain technologies and provide an assessment of their disruptive potential upon the legal sphere of intellectual property, and in particular copyright in the music industry. In order to do so, this chapter will start off by clarifying that *the* blockchain does not exist, because there are several different types of blockchains and, accordingly, different legal and regulatory issues. After identifying the type of permissionless blockchain that is analysed in this chapter, we move on to identify the definitional and non-definitional features of blockchain technologies. For the blockchain to unleash its disruptive potential, it must be clarified whether it complies with existing laws and whether new regulations are needed. Should existing regulations be found insufficient, only then could a serious discussion around new regulations be started, and it should take into account the necessity not to stifle innovation, the level of development of the relevant technologies, the importance of involving all the stakeholders, and the placement of the discussion at a supranational level. The focus of the chapter is to critically assess whether public permissionless blockchains can be used to disrupt intellectual property law by resolving some of the problems in copyright law, with particular regard to the issues of copyright registration and infringement. It will be shown how blockchains can resolve the registration issues by allowing forms of tamper-resistant, censorship-resistant, user-friendly, and privacy-friendly copyright registration. As to infringement, blockchains can prevent it by making it easier for copyright owners to track the use of their works and for music consumers to identify the owners, seek a license, and pay the royalties. It is perhaps too soon to conclude that a 10-year-old technology will ultimately disrupt copyright, but there already seem to have emerged some indications that the blockchains' features of being permissionless, distributed, transparent, without a single point of failure, tamper resistant, and peer to peer will radically change copyright by fixing some of its more urgent problems.

Does *the* blockchain exist?

Arguably, *the* blockchain does not exist; there are several different types of blockchains, each with different legal issues.

This said, a good starting point is the technological overview presented by the US National Institute of Standards and Technology (NIST) in October 2018 (Yaga et al., 2018). Blockchains are defined as 'distributed digital ledgers of cryptographically signed transactions that are grouped into blocks'. After an agreement is reached on the validation of a new block, the latter is added to the chain and cryptographically linked to the previous one. The participants will notice if someone tries to tamper with a transaction inscribed in a block (tamper evidence), and the older a block is the more difficult it is to tamper with it (tamper resistance). The distributed character of the blockchains derives from the fact that every participant has a full copy of the chain, and 'new blocks' are replicated across copies of the ledger. However, not all blockchains are fully distributed. Indeed, a major distinction in this field is between permissionless blockchains and permissioned ones. The main example of the former is Bitcoin, where every user can view all the transactions, has a full copy of the chain, and in principle has the same power as the other participants (peer to peer). Permissioned blockchains, in turn, are not peer to peer, disintermediated, and fully transparent because there are administrators or consortia granting user permissions.

This chapter focuses on a permissionless blockchain that is open, distributed, peer to peer, transparent, tamper resistant and censorship resistant. The resistance to censorship derives from the lack of a central point of failure: being distributed, it is virtually impossible to take down content, because even if a node goes down, the rest of the network still stands (Sermpinis, 2018). The blockchain whose legal issues we are exploring is not, however, a Bitcoin-type blockchain. Indeed, even though we are referring to a permissionless technology, since we want to apply it to be multipurpose, we have in mind an Ethereum-type blockchain (Popper, 2017). The latter is Turing complete and therefore more versatile than the Bitcoin, which can be used only for simple transactions and does not allow users to build smart contracts – protocols to automatically execute actual contracts (Mik, 2017) – on top of it (Brent, 2018).

Core and non-definitional components of blockchain technologies

It is important to note that there are differing opinions as to which features of blockchain technology are strictly definitional and not subject to change (Fairfield, 2015). However, this chapter is of the opinion that 'blockchain technology' is actually an umbrella term for three distinct technologies combined, not all of which will remain apparent in every deployment of blockchain-based applications (Maas, 2018).

The first of those three technologies is the blockchain itself, as a way to structure data. What makes a blockchain unique is its use of cryptography. By utilising certain cryptographic functions, a blockchain is able to create a persistent, tamper-evident record of any item of data and authenticate the identity of the parties involved in each transaction (UK Government Chief Scientific Adviser, 2017). Unsurprisingly, a blockchain is a definitional feature of blockchain technology that will be apparent in each and every blockchain application (Maas, 2017).

The second element is the network. Early applications of blockchain technology such as Bitcoin and Ethereum operate on a publicly visible, permissionless blockchain that is distributed across a peer-to-peer network (Bacon, 2018). In that, anything that happens on a blockchain is a function of the network as a whole. A network of computers known as 'nodes'[2] manage the network jointly, meaning that there is no central authority (Rosic, 2018). In this type of blockchain, anyone can become a node, and the entire contents of the blockchain are publicly visible. However, this is not to say that every application of blockchain technology will be this way. Distributed peer-to-peer networks or those that are public or permissionless may not be necessary or even permissible in certain circumstances. Alternative applications include networks that are 'private' or 'permissioned', where participation is limited to a certain group of users and can only be viewed by specified parties. It is often predicated that the blockchain is a trustless system[3] in that participants can transact without necessarily trusting each other and without intermediaries (e.g., banks). However, this can be said only with regards to permissionless blockchains. In permissioned blockchains, conversely, there is likely to be an aspect of trust among the users required as there will be some element of 'centralisation' (Bacon, 2018). Venture capital-backed Ripple is one example of a blockchain application that has amended the underlying technology to operate in an environment where a degree of trust is required for transactions to be validated (UK Government Chief Scientific Adviser, 2017). Governments are also exploring the idea of blockchains using a centralised trusted third party. Estonia, for example, has utilised blockchain technology since 2012 to help maintain the integrity of data across health, judicial, and legislative areas ('E-Estonia, 2018). For these reasons, this chapter considers public, permissionless distributed peer-to-peer networks to be a fundamental characteristic of early blockchain-based applications rather than a definitional feature that is apparent in all versions of blockchain technology. Nonetheless, when we do not specify otherwise, a reference to the blockchain must be understood as a reference to a permissionless distributed peer-to-peer network, since these characteristics have the potential to disrupt, or at least profoundly affect, the law, and copyright in particular.

The final component is the consensus mechanism, i.e., a 'process to achieve agreement within a distributed system on the valid state (the main consensus mechanisms are proof of work, round robin, and proof of stake". The latter is used in Ethereum and can be either Byzantine fault-tolerant proof or chain-based).

Consensus is what enables the nodes in a distributed peer-to-peer network to work together without having to know or trust each other. The consensus mechanism is a set of rules that are agreed upon by the network of nodes running the software in which the rules regulate the addition of new blocks (Maas, 2018). These rules ensure consistency across the network and that participant/system behaviour is valid and appropriate (Bacon, 2018). Given that consensus mechanisms solve problems of trust in distributed peer-to-peer networks,[4] it follows that if the deployment of a blockchain application is anything other than distributed, such a consensus mechanism may not be required. Therefore, this chapter considers consensus mechanisms to be a fundamental characteristic of early applications that may change dependent on the purposes for which the technology is adopted, rather than a definitional feature apparent in all blockchain-based applications. Nonetheless, since the distributed character of the blockchain is likely to have a disruptive impact on the law and on copyright in particular, we will refer to blockchains using a consensus mechanism, unless stated otherwise.

To regulate or not to regulate: that is the question?

For the blockchains to unleash their potential in the music industry and beyond, the regulatory conundrum must be untangled. Overly restrictive regulation may stifle innovation, but the lack of any regulation may lead to legal uncertainty, which in turn would slow down the adoption of the blockchains (Telpner, 2018). The regulatory treatment of blockchain or of some of its aspects and applications will be a major factor in determining the level of success the technology will have regarding all its use cases. Given the importance of blockchains' regulation and music copyright being highly regulated, it is necessary to dig deeper and explore the regulatory treatment of blockchain in general.

The more blockchain becomes widespread, the more lawmakers develop an interest in regulating it. Most existing regulations, policies, and case law take a top-down approach and focus on Bitcoin and, accordingly, on evidence and tax issues.

For example, the EU Court of Justice exempted Bitcoin transactions from VAT because they regard only 'currency, bank notes and coins used as legal tender' (*Skatteverket v David Hedqvist Skatteverket v David Hedqvist*, Case C-264/14). For the focus on evidence, see Arizona Revised Statutes, 44–7061.

The most common approach, however, is to assess whether and how existing laws apply to the blockchains[5] and avoid the introduction of new regulations 'given that the technology is still evolving and practical applications are limited both in number and scope' (European Securities and Markets Authority, *Report The Distributed Ledger Technology Applied to Securities Markets* (ESMA, 2017) 4).

In the US, a similar 'wait-and-see' approach has been taken by the Federal Reserve Board, as well as the Federal Reserve Banks of New York and Chicago (see Mills, David, Kathy Wang, Brendan Malone, Anjana Ravi, Jeff Marquardt, Clinton Chen, Anton Badev, Timothy Brezinski, Linda Fahy, Kimberley Liao, Vanessa Kargenian, Max Ellithorpe, Wendy Ng, and Maria Baird (2016). 'Distributed ledger technology in payments, clearing, and settlement,' Finance and Economics Discussion Series 2016–095. Washington: Board of Governors of the Federal Reserve System, https://doi.org/10.17016/FEDS.2016.095. Cf., similarly, Financial Industry Regulatory Authority, *Distributed Ledger Technology: Implications of Blockchain for the Securities Industry* (FINRA, 2017)). Contrary to popular belief, blockchains are not a lawless technology; recent research underlined that we should abandon the naivety whereby blockchain transactions would be 'free from the travails of conventional law, thus offering the promise of grassroots democratic governance without the need for third-party intermediaries' (Yeung, 2019). Most of existing laws apply to the blockchains, but should new regulations be introduced, a participatory and holistic approach would be preferable. Indeed, it is important to involve all the stakeholders and keep in mind all the potential socio-legal issues if one wants to ensure that the blockchain unleashes its full potential and benefits all the players involved.

Bitcoin, the first and most widely used blockchain, set out to remove state institutions' influence on currency. Permissioned blockchains inherited the features of being intrinsically transnational and (potentially) state free, which begs the fundamental questions on whether it is at all possible to regulate them and, if so, how. These problems, however, are not new, since the Internet is transnational and yet is highly regulated. Recent research has showed that most of the physical world rules can be applied in cyberspace, though there is a clear problem concerning which authority can legitimately regulate it (Chris Reed and Andrew Murray, *Rethinking the Jurisprudence of Cyberspace* (Elgar 2018)). Bitcoin and blockchain have moved on from the cypherpunk days (Lopp, 2016), where the community using Bitcoin and the like were mostly made up of individuals with libertarian and anti-establishment political stances (Stankovic, 2018). Nowadays, Bitcoin has entered the mainstream, even becoming a legal payment method in Japan (Garber, 2017). Blockchain, in turn, has stepped out of Bitcoin's shadow and now offers a wide variety of potential use cases, some of which promise to be revolutionary (Swan, 2015). However, for blockchain to realise its full disruptive potential, it will need to appease the legal and regulatory environments in which it will operate ('Blockchain – Key Legal and Regulatory Issues' *Lexis PSL TMT*). Indeed, beyond cryptocurrency, blockchain has potential application across a number of heavily regulated industries, which have been designed without blockchain in mind. This may ultimately mean that the use of blockchain could be found to be incompatible with the current regulatory framework (Finck, 2017). If so, the uncertainty that this incompatibility inevitably creates will no doubt restrict innovation and ultimately prevent large-scale adoption of blockchain into these areas. In order to successfully navigate these heavily regulated industries, it would seem necessary that regulation is seen as a tool to provide certainty for those involved in blockchain's development and encourage innovation rather than one used by the regulators to stifle it (where not otherwise specified, the term 'regulators' is used generically to refer to any lawmakers and regulators across jurisdictions, whether they operate a transnational, supranational, national or subnational level; 'Blockchain – Key Legal and Regulatory Issues' (n 35)). The problem does not apply, however, only to regulated industries but to all sectors where personal data is processed. Indeed, the EU General Data Protection Regulation (GDPR), which came into force in May 2018, introduces principles, obligations, and rights whose implementation can be difficult if at all possible in a blockchain context (Berberich, 2016; Herian, 2018). For example, data subjects have the right to rectify their personal data, but once the data is in the blockchain, it is virtually impossible to change it (Ibáñez, 2018; CNIL, *Blockchain, 2018*).

Part of the literature is of the opinion that regulation of blockchain is inevitable, and in the end the community of developers will in fact welcome such regulation. According to this view, regulators will win the developers around by accepting creative solutions to achieve the right balance between protecting the relevant public interest objectives and stimulating innovation (Kevin, 2017). The rationale behind said opinion is based on the fact that the same scenario happened twenty years ago at the early stages of the Internet. The more recent phenomenon of the platform economy (Kenney, 2017) has also reinforced how this scenario plays out (Noto La Diega, 2016). Uber, for example, who were once notoriously reluctant to cooperate with regulators (Arvelo, 2018), have now actively sought regulatory intervention regarding insurance legislation that applies unanimously across the United States (Uber, 'Insurance Aligned', 2018), and as of March 2018, they have instructed insurance companies in order to comply with those requirements (Uber, 'An Update on Insurance', 2018).

If regulation is inevitable, the next question is how to regulate. Going forward, it would seem that successful regulation is dependent on a number of factors. First of all, the regulators need to learn from their past mistakes regarding other emerging technologies and be sure not to repeat them. Although blockchains remain an immature technology with evolving use cases, it is arguable that early regulatory acknowledgment and interest should be seen as positive, as it is important to be mindful of the negative impact that delayed interest in an emerging technology can have (as noted by Finck, (Finck, 2017), the early stages of the Internet's development suffered the negative impact of a delayed interest).

Second, successful regulation is not only dependent on the regulators themselves. Rather, the industry and those involved with the development of blockchain should also actively collaborate with each other and the regulators to tackle the complex challenges at hand (Finck, 2017). If those involved in the development of blockchain do decide to resist regulatory attempts, it is suggested that '[i]f anything, the innovators stand to lose the most by delaying government involvement in adopting reasonable solutions' (Werbach, 2017).

The third factor concerns the level at which blockchain is regulated. Generally, regulators regulate the use of a technology as opposed to regulating the technology itself. However, blockchain's ever-growing use cases mean that regulators are finding it difficult to regulate ('Blockchain – Key Legal and Regulatory Issues' (n 35)). Yet some scholars suggest that this remains the best approach and claim that a use-case-focused approach is supported by the experience with other emerging technologies such as the Internet (Maupin, 2017). If such an approach is to be successfully adopted, the aforementioned collaborative effort of all the parties involved in that specific use case will be key. Not only that, the unpredictability of blockchain will require a flexible, open approach to each use case that will allow the law to develop as and when the technology does (Finck, 2017).

That being said, even if flexible, agile, use-specific regulation is developed, if that regulatory model is only applicable in one country, its positive impact may be limited. The distributed potential of blockchain, coupled with its intangibility, means that its application could operate simultaneously over multiple jurisdictions. This may mean that it is unclear who is performing the regulated activity. If this proves to be the case, regulators may struggle to determine whether or not a particular blockchain's activities need to be regulated, and if so, under which jurisdiction. Further, if something goes wrong, it may prove difficult to determine the precise location and identity of the culprit who is responsible for said breach or failure ('Blockchain – Key Legal and Regulatory Issues' (n 35)). Therefore, successful regulation will also require regulators to engage in transnational conversation and cooperation in an attempt to formulate some sort of consistent collaborative governance.[6] Although international conventions would appear the most suitable level of regulation, practically it is unlikely that an agreement will be reached and that, if reached, the rules will be fit for the blockchains or for the particular use that will be taken into consideration.[7]

In conclusion, no regulation is better than bad regulation. More evidence is needed to clarify whether existing regulations suffice when it comes to the blockchains. Should existing regulations be found insufficient, only then could a serious discussion around new regulations be started, and it should take into account the necessity of not stifling innovation, the level of development of the relevant technologies, the importance of involving all the stakeholders, and of placing the discussion at a supranational level. Only in this way can legal certainty be achieved and the blockchains unleash their disruptive potential.

The disruptive potential of blockchain on copyright law

Having defined blockchain technology and set out the technical and regulatory essentials, the rest of this chapter will concern the disruptive potential that blockchain may have upon the legal sphere of intellectual property, using music copyright as a use case.

This section is focused on intellectual property and, in particular, copyright, i.e., the body of law that protects aesthetic and artistic creations such as literary, musical, dramatic, and artistic works.[8] Blockchain technologies can affect copyright in manifold ways, as recognised by the European Parliament's resolution of 3 October 2018 on distributed ledger technologies and blockchains: building trust with disintermediation. The EU resolution underscores that distributed ledger technologies can be used to track and manage intellectual property, thus facilitating copyright and patent protection.[9] It further acknowledges the technology's potential to develop artists' ownership through an 'open public ledger that can also clearly identify ownership and copyright". It is then recognised that in collaborative and open innovation contexts (e.g., 3D printing), blockchain's capability to link creators to their works is of the utmost importance. Finally, authors can benefit from transparency and traceability in the use of their works as well as the smoothening of royalty distribution and increase in revenues that can be expected by cutting down on intermediaries. On the last point, it is important to critically note that blockchain's promise to eliminate traditional intermediaries is unlikely to be fulfilled (O'Dair, 2016). Evidence of the trend towards re-centralisation is the investment of traditional intermediaries in the blockchain (PRS for Music, 2018) and the rise of permissioned blockchains, where the disintermediation is only partial (Bacon, 2018).

Although it is still unclear whether blockchains will revolutionise copyright, it can be argued that they can resolve some of the issues that affect this body of law and the relevant industries, with particular regards to copyright registration, infringement, management,[10] and transactions.[11] For the sake of brevity, this section will focus on how, if at all, the type of blockchain described earlier can resolve some of the problems of copyright registration and infringement (popularly known as 'piracy').

Blockchains for a privacy-friendly, agile, tamper- and censorship-resistant registration

One of the main innovations brought by the Berne Convention[12] has been that copyright arises with the creation of the work (e.g., once a book has been written) without the need for any formalities, i.e., systems of public registration (Berne Convention, art 5(2)). Such formalities enabled governments to control ex ante the contents of the books, thus enabling them to censor those works that went against the governmental policies or the dominant ethical values (Mann, 2016). The abolition of registration formalities is positive because it favours the authors by making copyright easily obtainable and by reducing the opportunities for governments to censor them. However, without registration there are evidentiary problems in copyright infringement proceedings, because it is hard to prove who created what and in which moment in time.[13] For example, if John shares without Jerry's permission a picture the latter had posted on Instagram, how does Jerry prove that he created said work (the picture), that he did it before John, and that he is the sole legitimate author and owner? To resolve these kinds of problems, some countries such as the US effectively sidestepped the Berne Convention and *de facto* reintroduced the copyright registration. Indeed, even if copyright arises with the creation of a work, in infringement proceedings, statutory damages and attorney's fees will not be awarded in the absence of registration.[14] In the UK, there is no such limitation, but without registration said evidentiary issues remain. Therefore, new registration mechanisms have been introduce to ensure evidence; however, they often are a burden for the author (e.g., they are expensive and not user friendly), and they can be forged; particularly with paper ledgers there is a 'high level of forgery' (UK Government Chief Scientific Adviser (n 11) 7). Alongside the problems of censorship, forgery, and lack of user friendliness, existing registration systems are open to criticism from a privacy perspective. This is the case in the US, where rules of procedure of the Copyright Office and attitudes of the US District Courts make it very hard for pseudonymous and anonymous authors to be successful in infringement lawsuits (Bell, 2016).

All these problems can be resolved through a blockchain-enabled copyright registration. Indeed, a blockchain platform could issue a token, which would serve as proof of authenticity, in which a timestamped copyright registration is contained. Arguably, such a disruptive system would enable a cheaper, more transparent, and more user-friendly registration (Buntinx, 2018) – as noted by Savelyev (2018), 'blockchain can introduce long-awaited transparency in matters of copyright ownership chain'. Thus, the problem of forgery also would be addressed, considering that the blockchain is tamper resistant.[15] Moreover, one of the key features of permissionless blockchains is that they have no single point of failure. Therefore, if an author deposited a work to register it and a government wanted to take it down for censorship purposes, this would be practically impossible[16] because '(e)ven if several nodes failed, the network would still continue to function' (Bacon, 2018), and the work would still be available, since all data is maintained by all nodes.[17] Finally, moving on to anonymous and pseudonymous authors' privacy, a public, permissionless blockchain distributed across a peer-to-peer network may resolve their problems by providing robust digital pseudonyms, 'a mask that, while hiding (the author's) real identity, would nonetheless be unique to him or her' (Bell, 2016).

A blockchain registration would be optional, thus complying with the Berne Convention, and it would ensure the benefits of traditional registration in terms of evidence in infringement proceedings whilst preventing its drawbacks in terms of costs, forgery, censorship, and privacy.

Blockchains and copyright infringement: an ambiguous relationship

Copyright infringement, popularly known as 'piracy', is a widespread issue, as exemplified by the fact that 53 percent of young users access music illegally[18] and by the fact that new intermediaries such as Spotify often make available music without its owners' consent, allegedly because they do not know who the owners are.[19] Copyright infringement thrives for a number of reasons, two of which can be addressed by blockchain. The first one is that it is difficult for copyright owners to track the use of their works. Once a song is published, the owners currently have limited or no means to know who is accessing it and how. The problem is exacerbated by the sharing practices that are becoming commonplace in the time of social media. Indeed, it can be said that we live in the sharing society,[20] where sharing copyright material is easy, particularly on social networking sites, e.g., by retweeting someone's tweet which, in turn, had retweeted someone else's tweet.[21] This means not only that many people infringe copyright, possibly without being aware of it, but also that after repeated sharing and linking it is difficult to track back who was the original owner. Ultimately, the difficulty for copyright owners to track the use of their contents decreases the incentives to access contents legally, since end users have the reasonable expectation that the owners cannot track the consumption of their content, and therefore, they cannot enforce their rights.

The second reason why copyright infringement is so common, particularly in the music industry, is that it is often impossible to know who the author and owner is.[22] This is because there is not a requirement to register copyright, and, more importantly, because of the lack of a single updated database of music metadata. Music metadata are data about who did what in music. Music metadata are fragmented in databases that do not sync and that are owned by corporations with conflicting views about what should be public and what should, in turn, be kept private (DA Wallach, 2014). Music ownership is extremely complex for legal and business reasons. On the one hand, under the Copyright, Designs and Patents Act 1988[23] – the main UK statute on copyright – a single song has at least three owners, i.e., the author of the lyrics, the author of the music, and the producer of the sound recording. From a business point of view, music is a collaborative enterprise; indeed, most 'recorded music is a collaboration between songwriters, singers, musicians, producers, recording engineers, mastering specialists' (DA Wallach, 2014). All these subjects and other new intermediaries such as Spotify and iTunes have a stake in the industry and some expectations in the distribution of music's revenues. For these reasons, the artists receive only a limited share of the revenues and only after a long time (Heap, 2016). If artists are finally paid a slice of the 'royalties cake', this reaches them between six and eighteen months after the publication (Heap, 2016). The problem of music's attribution and royalty distribution are not new, but they are made worse by new technologies and new ways of consuming musing. While at the time of vinyl records and CDs it was easy to understand who contributed and how, iTunes, Spotify, etc., create a credits conundrum where the listener knows only who the singer is and nothing else. A final reason why identifying copyright owners (and rewarding them) is difficult is that even though there is a presumption the author (of the music, of the lyrics, etc.) is the owner of the relevant work,[24] this is often not the case, either because the work had been made in the course of employment and therefore is owned by the employer or because ownership has been transferred to third parties by means of a contract of copyright assignment. These contracts are often accompanied by the so-called paternity waiver, whereby the author gives up their right to be acknowledged as the author.[25] If copyright paternity can be waived, it is likely that it will be, because the relevant relationships in many creative industries are often characterised by an imbalance of bargaining power (one needs to keep in mind that the industry tends to 'oblige authors and artist to enter standard-form contracts that require them to waive their integrity rights' (Lionel Bently and Brad Sherman, *Intellectual Property Law* (4th ed, OUP 2014) 290)). For all these reasons, music is often consumed without the owners' permission, and the system does not reward artists sufficiently and in a timely manner, if at all.

Permissionless blockchains could tackle both issues. A blockchain-based music platform such as Mycelia can allow artists to issue a token that can be transferred only when the owner signs off on the transaction with their private key. This disincentivises end users from accessing music illegally. As to the music metadata's conundrum, a public, permissionless blockchain distributed across a peer-to-peer network may resolve the problems of copyright infringement by enabling the creation of a global updated database of music metadata. The blockchain could be the backbone of a decentralised, open-source global platform, *controlled* by no single entity, and with the potential to contain accurate, real-time, global data encompassing credits and rights ownership (Wallach (n 85)). As noted by some scholars, most copyright registry are territorial, but the creation of a global registry would not require governments to trust other government or third parties, '(r)ather, trust can be placed in the mathematical certain provided by blockchain technology' (Wright, 2015). Moreover, blockchain could be a technological means to practically nullify the practice of imposing paternity waivers, thus contributing to fixing the structural imbalance of power of the creative industries, music included. Once recorded in a blockchain platform, no one could contest the authorship and ownership.

In making it easier to access copyright content legally, the blockchain can prevent copyright infringement. At the same time, however, it can constitute a problem because, in light of the distributed nature of the blockchain and its lack of single point of failure, infringing content cannot be taken down: once it is on the blockchain, it is stored in every node, potentially forever.[26] In recent years, the prevailing way that copyright owners react to copyright infringement is not bringing lawsuits against the end users or the actual infringer but targeting the intermediaries that enable said infringement (e.g., the Internet service providers, such as BT or Sky).[27] However, in permissionless blockchains, in principle, there are no intermediaries or, better, the latter have a different, more elusive identity. The virtual impossibility of removing a file once on the blockchain and the inherent disintermediation is likely to make it difficult to enforce copyright. However, the disruptive potential of the blockchain may manifest itself in preventing infringement altogether by allowing copyright owners to track the use of their works and by powering a global updated database of music metadata, which will make royalty distribution smoother and fairer.

Conclusions

The blockchain, at least in its permissionless form, has the potential to disrupt copyright law by resolving two of its problems, namely registration and infringement.

Currently, there are no reliable registers of copyright ownership, which creates problems of evidence, because it is difficult for claimants to prove the link between them and the infringed work, as well as to prove the time of creation. Current registration systems are prone to forgery, can be used as a means of censorship, are cumbersome, and are unfavourable to anonymous authors. A blockchain-based registration mechanism would resolve this problem by providing the means for a tamper-resistant, censorship-resistant, user-friendly, and privacy-friendly platform.

As to copyright infringement or piracy, this is on the rise because owners cannot track the use of their works and because it is often difficult to know who the owners are, which in turn makes it virtually impossible to seek a license and pay the royalties. However, using the blockchain, artists could decide to transfer music by transferring a token signing off on the transaction with their private key. No unauthorised use would be possible. The blockchain, moreover, would allow the creation of global, constantly updated music metadata that would make it easier to find and reward the copyright owners.

It is too early to assess whether blockchains will disrupt the music industry and fix all the problems of copyright, a body of law whose inadequacy for the digital age is striking (on the compatibility of the blockchain with some copyright principles see Bodó, B., Gervais, D., and Quintais, J. P. (2018). Blockchain and smart contracts: the missing link in copyright licensing? *International Journal of Law and Information Technology*, *26*(4), 311–336). From this analysis, however, it would seem that blockchains could contribute to the resolution to some problems encountered by copyright owners and authors. In order to succeed, these potential solutions must be accompanied by a twofold caveat. First, the immature blockchain technology must overcome its technical issues to prove, beyond doubt, that it is a better proposition than the technology it is replacing. Second, it will have to appease the current regulatory framework to allow these technological advancements to achieve large-scale adoption. Whilst new regulations are not necessarily the best way forward, regulators should work closely with law academics and industry stakeholders to clarify how existing laws apply to this new technology. Indeed, without legal certainty, the blockchains are unlikely to unleash their disruptive potential.

Notes

1 The authors are grateful to the anonymous reviewers for their helpful comments. Nonetheless, the responsibility for any errors and opinions rests with the authors. This chapter has been a collaborative enterprise, but Guido Noto La Diega is responsible for the legal sections and James Stacey for the technical ones.

2 These are the computers that are connected to the blockchain network. All blockchain-based applications are made up of nodes. However, who can become a node and the level of involvement that is permissible by each node will differ depending on the type of blockchain application deployed. Nodes store a local copy of the blockchain. 'Full' nodes store a copy of the blockchain in its entirety, while 'light' nodes only hold a portion of the blockchain needed to verify transactions (Bacon (n 14) 11).

3 Yaga (n 2) 38 underlines, however, that trust is needed even in supposedly trustless systems, e.g., trust in the cryptographic technologies and that users are not colluding in secret. For other critical remarks, see Carl, Uggla, and Hallström Carl-Johan, 'Is It as Trustless as They Say?: A Functional Analysis of the Blockchain and Trust' (2018).

4 Consensus mechanisms, however, do not always lead to correct execution results, because participants may be affected by economic interests in the smart contracts, as pointed out by Chen, L., Xu, L., Gao, Z., Lu, Y., & Shi, W. (2018). 'Tyranny of the Majority: On the (Im)possibility of Correctness of Smart Contracts'. *IEEE Security & Privacy*, 16(4), 30–37.

5 In the UK, for example, the Financial Conduct Authority believe that most initial coin offerings (ICOs) are unregulated, but they take a case-by-case approach to decide whether ICOs fall within their remit – Financial Conduct, Consumer warning about the risks of Initial Coin Offerings ('ICOs') (FCA, 2017).

6 Peter Yeoh, 'Regulatory Issues in Blockchain Technology' (2017) 25 *JFRC* 196, 200.

7 On the problem of 'legal hysteresis', i.e., the delay with which innovation is necessarily regulated, see Roberto Pardolesi, '"Software", "property rights" e diritto d'autore: il ritorno dal paese delle meraviglie'. (1987) 3, II *Foro it.*, 300. The idea was applied to copyright regulation by Guido Noto La Diega, 'In Light of the Ends. Copyright Hysteresis and Private Copy Exception after the British Academy of Songwriters, Composers and Authors (BASCA) and others v Secretary of State for Business, Innovation and Skills Case'. (2015) no. II *Diritto Mercato Tecnologia* 1–16.

8 Charlotte Waelde, Abbe Brown, Smita Kheria, and Jane Cornwell, *Contemporary Intellectual Property* (OUP 2016), 3.

9 2017/2772(RSP), para 22.

10 The blockchain can smoothen royalty distribution by decreasing the role of traditional intermediaries, though one can doubt that the middleman will actually be eliminated. There are a number of reasons that suggest that the blockchain will not get rid of intermediaries. These include the fact that traditional intermediaries are substantially investing in the blockchain and the fact that the enforcement of copyright online tends to target the intermediaries rather than the end users; therefore, lawmakers and courts have a strong interest in keeping the middlemen in the loop.

11 Copyright transactions can be secured thanks to blockchain-based smart contracts. However, it can be argued that these self-executing protocols are neither 'smart' nor 'contracts', and this has practical legal consequences. The fact that contracting parties using smart contracts (and smart licenses) do not have the flexibility to breach the contract risks limiting the practical impact of this application of the blockchain to very simple and routinary transactions. The efficient breach doctrine is evidence that, in most jurisdictions, the legal systems protect the fundamental right of contracting parties to change their mind and reallocate the resources in a more efficient way by breaching the contract. Society and law are built upon the assumption that individuals can change their mind, and this does not seem to be reflected in the lack of flexibility of this new technology.

12 Berne Convention for the Protection of Literary and Artistic Works of September 9, 1886, completed at Paris on May 4, 1896, revised at Berlin on November 13, 1908, completed at Berne on March 20, 1914, revised at Rome on June 2, 1928, at Brussels on June 26, 1948, at Stockholm on July 14, 1967, and at Paris on July 24, 1971, and amended on September 28, 1979.

13 It should be kept in mind that copyright is not a monopoly; therefore, the independent creation of identical works does not constitute infringement. For infringement to occur, the claimant needs to prove that the defendant carried out a restricted act (e.g., made a copy of the book, picture, etc.) with regards to the whole or a substantial part of the work, and there is a causal connection between the claimant's work and the defendant's one. The latter requirement means that either there is direct evidence of copying or this can be inferred from the similarities between the works and the opportunity to copy. See the UK Copyright, Designs Patents Act 1988, s 16.

14 US Copyright Office, Circular 1, *Copyright Basics*, section 'Copyright Registration'.

15 Nonetheless, the blockchain is not absolutely immutable, as proved by the DAO breaking the rules of their blockchain in order to react to some hackers exploiting a bug in the code. On this matter and its implications see O'Hara, K. (2017). 'Smart contracts-dumb idea'. *IEEE Internet Computing*, 21(2), 97–101.

16 This circumstance, coupled with the disintermediation that may come with the adoption of the blockchain, would make copyright enforcement very complicated, since the trend in recent years has been to target intermediaries rather than end users. The most obvious example of this is constituted by the injunctions against ISPs, for instance, in the event of illegal download of music or videos.

17 This depends on the type of blockchain; for instance, it does not apply to permissioned blockchains.

18 'Share of Global Internet Users Who Access Music Through Copyright Infringement as of 2017, by Age Group'. *Statista* (2018) <www.statista.com/statistics/609114/music-copyright-infringement-by-age/> accessed 5 December 2018. A more general empirical analysis of intellectual property infringement can be found in European Intellectual Property Office, *Synthesis Report on IPR infringement 2018* (EUIPO 2018). This is not to say that copyright infringement is always and necessarily a negative thing, as proved by ECORYS, *Estimating displacement rates of copyrighted content in the EU* (European Commission 2017).

19 Therefore, Spotify had to pay $112 million USD to songwriters in the settlement of *Ferrick, et al. v. Spotify USA Inc., et al.*, No. 16-cv-8412 (AJN) United States District Court, S.D. New York.

20 'All Eyes on the Sharing Society'. *World Intellectual Property Review* (March/April 2015) <www.rightsdirect.com/wp-content/uploads/sites/6/2015/04/WIPR-Kim-Zwollo-04-2015.pdf> accessed 30 May 2018.

21 On the matter of copyright on 'tweets' and infringement by retweeting see R. Haas, 'Twitter: New Challenges to Copyright Law in the Internet Age'. (2010) *J Marshall Rev Intell Prop L, 10* i.

22 In principle, the author is the first copyright owner of the relevant work, but there are some exceptions, the main one being works created by employees in the course of employment. See the UK Copyright, Designs and Patents Act 1988, s 11.

23 Copyright, Designs and Patents Act 1988, ss 3(1), 5A, and 10A.

24 Copyright, Designs and Patents Act 1998, s 9.

25 Copyright, Designs, and Patents Act 1988, s 87(2). In many civil law jurisdictions such waivers are not enforceable; see French *Code de la propriété intellectuelle*, art L. 121–1 and *Huston v TV5, Cour de Cassation, Chambre civile* 1, 28 May 1991, 89–19.522 89–19.725 [1991] RIDA 149, 197, where the French Supreme Court stated that moral rights are a matter of public policy, and therefore, waivers that were lawful under US copyright law were not enforceable in France.

26 The difficulty of taking down content is likely to have significant consequences even beyond copyright. One need only think of the research that found child porn links on a blockchain which begs the question whether all participants can be held liable for illegal content on the blockchain (Matzutt, R., Hiller, J., Henze, M., Ziegeldorf, J. H., Müllmann, D., Hohlfeld, O., and Wehrle, K. (2018). A Quantitative Analysis of the Impact of Arbitrary Blockchain Content on Bitcoin. In *Proceedings of the 22nd International Conference on Financial Cryptography and Data Security* (FC) (Springer).

27 In the UK, the trend of addressing copyright infringement by targeting Internet service providers and other intermediaries, as opposed to the end user or the primary infringer, can be seen in Dramatico v BSkyB (2012) EWHC 268 (Ch); Paramount & Others v British Sky Broadcasting (2013) EWHC 3479; 1967 Ltd v BSkyB, BT and others (2014) EWHC 3444. In the EU, see e.g. UPC Telekabel Wein v Constantin Film Verleih (C-314/12) (2014) EC.D.R. 12; Svensson & others v Retriever Sverige AB (C-466/12) (2014) All ER 609 (EC); GS Media BV v Sanoma Media Netherlands (C-160/15) (8 September 2016).

Bibliography

Case law

1967 Ltd v BSkyB, BT and others [2014] EWHC 3444.

Dramatico v BSkyB [2012] EWHC 268 (Ch).

Ferrick, et al. v Spotify USA Inc., et al., No. 16-cv-8412 (AJN) United States District Court, S.D. New York.

GS Media BV v Sanoma Media Netherlands (C-160/15) ECLI:EU:C:2016:644.

Huston v TV5, Cour de Cassation, Chambre civile 1, 28 May 1991, 89–19.522 89–19.725 [1991] RIDA 149.

Paramount & Others v British Sky Broadcasting [2013] EWHC 3479.

Skatteverket v David Hedqvist Skatteverket v David Hedqvist (Case C-264/14) ECLI:EU:C:2015:718.

Svensson & others v Retriever Sverige AB (C-466/12) [2014] All ER 609 (EC).

UPC Telekabel Wein v Constantin Film Verleih (C-314/12) [2014] EC.D.R. 12.

Books

Pilkington, M., 'Blockchain Technology: Principles and Applications.' In Olleros, F. and Zhegu, M. (eds.), *Research Handbook on Digital Transformations* (Edward Elgar 2016).

Reed, C. and Murray, A., *Rethinking the Jurisprudence of Cyberspace* (Elgar 2018).

Swan, M., *Blockchain: Blueprint for a New Economy* (1st edn, O'Reilly & Associates 2015).

Waelde, C., Brown, A., Kheria, S., and Cornwell, J., *Contemporary Intellectual Property* (OUP 2016).

Reports and white papers

Commission nationale de l'informatique et des liberté, *Blockchain. Premiers éléments d'analyse de la CNIL* (CNIL 2018).

ECORYS, *Estimating Displacement Rates of Copyrighted Content in the EU* (European Commission 2017).

European Intellectual Property Office, *Synthesis Report on IPR Infringement 2018* (EUIPO 2018).

European Securities and Markets Authority, *Report the Distributed Ledger Technology Applied to Securities Markets* (ESMA 2017).

Financial Conduct Authority, *Consumer Warning About the Risks of Initial Coin Offerings ('ICOs')* (FCA 2017).

Financial Industry Regulatory Authority, *Distributed Ledger Technology: Implications of Blockchain for the Securities Industry* (FINRA 2017).

Mills, D., Wang, K., Malone, B., Ravi, A., Marquardt, J., Chen, C., Badev, A., Brezinski, T., Fahy, L., Liao, K., Kargenian, V., Ellithorpe, M., Ng, W., and Baird, M., 'Distributed Ledger Technology in Payments, Clearing, and Settlement.' *Finance and Economics Discussion Series 2016–095* (Washington: Board of Governors of the Federal Reserve System, 2016) <https://doi.org/10.17016/FEDS.2016.095>.

O'Dair, M. et al., *Music on the Blockchain* (Blockchain For Creative Industries Research Cluster, Middlesex University 2016).

Telpner, J., *The Lion, the Unicorn, and the Crown: Striking a Balance Between Regulation and Blockchain Innovation* (Blockchain Research Institute 2018).

UK Government Chief Scientific Adviser, *Distributed Ledger Technology: Beyond Block Chain* (Government Office for Science 2017).

Yaga, D., Mell, P., Roby, N., and Scarfone, K., *Blockchain Technology Overview* (NIST 2018).

Journal articles

Bacon, J. et al., 'Blockchain Demystified.' Queen Mary University of London, School of Law Legal Studies Research Paper No. 268/2017 (2018) <https://ssrn.com/abstract=3091218> accessed 29 January 2018.

Bell, T.W., 'Copyrights, Privacy, and the Blockchain' (2016) 42 *Ohio Northern U L Rev* 439, 464.

Berberich, M. and Steiner, M., 'Blockchain Technology and the GDPR – How to Reconcile Privacy and Distributed Ledgers.' (2016) 2 *Eur Data Prot L Rev* 422, 426.

Bodó, B., Gervais, D., and Quintais, J.P., 'Blockchain and Smart Contracts: The Missing Link in Copyright Licensing?' (2018) 26 (4) *International Journal of Law and Information Technology* 311–336.

Brent, L., Jurisevic, A., Kong, M., Liu, E., Gauthier, F., Gramoli, V., Holz, R., and Scholz, B., 'Vandal: A Scalable Security Analysis Framework for Smart Contracts.' arXiv preprint arXiv:1809.03981 (2018).

Carl, U. and Carl-Johan, H., 'Is It as Trustless as They Say?: A Functional Analysis of the Blockchain and Trust.' Thesis (2018).

Chen, L., Xu, L., Gao, Z., Lu, Y., & Shi, W., 'Tyranny of the Majority: On the (Im) Possibility of Correctness of Smart Contracts.' (2018)16 (4) *IEEE Security & Privacy* 30–37.

DA Wallach, 'Bitcoin for Rockstars' (Wired, 12 October 2014) <http://www.wired.com/2014/12/bitcoin-for-rockstars> accessed 1 June 2018.

Fairfield, J., 'Bitproperty.' (2015) 88 (4) *SCL Rev* 805.

Finck, M., 'Blockchain and Data Protection in the European Union.' Max Planck Institute for Innovation and Competition Research Paper No. 18–01 2 (2017) <https://papers.ssrn.com/sol3/papers.cfm?abstract_id=3080322> accessed 22 March 2018.

Finck, M., 'Blockchain Regulation.' Max Planck Institute for Innovation and Competition Research Paper No. 17–13 (2017) <https://ssrn.com/abstract=3014641> accessed 26 March 2018.

Haas, R., 'Twitter: New Challenges to Copyright Law in the Internet Age.' (2010) 10 *J Marshall Rev Intell Prop L* i.

Herian, R., 'Regulating Disruption: Blockchain, GDPR, and Questions of Data Sovereignty.' (2018) 22 (2) *Journal of Internet Law* 1.

Ibáñez, L.-D., O'Hara, K. and Simperl, E., 'On Blockchains and the General Data Protection Regulation.' (2018).

Imogen Heap and Don Tapscott, 'Blockchain could be Music's next Disruptor' (*Fortune*, 22 September 2016) <http://fortune.com/2016/09/22/blockchain-music-disruption> accessed 1 June 2018.

Kenney, M. and Zysman J., 'The Rise of the Platform Economy.' (2016) 32 (3) *Issues in Science and Technology*.

Kevin, W., 'The Song Remains the Same: What Cyberlaw Might Teach the Next Internet Economy.' (2017) 69 (3) *Florida Law Review* 887.

Li, J., 'Data Transmission Scheme Considering Node Failure for Blockchain.' (2018) *Wireless Personal Communications*.

Mann, A.J., 'The Anatomy of Copyright Law in Scotland Before 1710.' In Alexander, I. and Tomás Gómez-Arostegui, H. (eds.), *Research Handbook on the History of Copyright Law* (Elgar 2016), 99.

Matzutt, R., Hiller, J., Henze, M., Ziegeldorf, J. H., Müllmann, D., Hohlfeld, O., and Wehrle, K., 'A Quantitative Analysis of the Impact of Arbitrary Blockchain Content on Bitcoin.' In *Proceedings of the 22nd International Conference on Financial Cryptography and Data Security (FC)* (Springer 2018).

Maupin, J., 'Mapping the Global Legal Landscape of Blockchain Technologies.' (2017) 149 *CIGI Papers*.

Mik, E., 'Smart Contracts: Terminology, Technical Limitations and Real World Complexity.' (2017) 9 (2) *Law, Innovation and Technology* 269–300.

Noto La Diega, G., 'In Light of the Ends. Copyright Hysteresis and Private Copy Exception After the British Academy of Songwriters, Composers and Authors (BASCA) and others v Secretary of State for Business, Innovation and Skills Case.' (2015), no. II *Diritto Mercato Tecnologia* 1–16.

Noto La Diega, G., 'Uber Law and Awareness by Design. An Empirical Study on Online Platforms and Dehumanised Negotiations.' (2016) no. II *Revue européenne de droit de la consommation/European Journal of Consumer Law* 383–413.

O'Hara, K., 'Smart Contracts-Dumb Idea.' (2017) 21 (2) *IEEE Internet Computing* 97–101.

Pardolesi, R., '"Software", "property rights" e diritto d'autore: il ritorno dal paese delle meraviglie.' (1987) 3, II *Foro it.* 300.

Savelyev, A. 'Copyright in the Blockchain Era: Promises and Challenges.' (2018) 34 (3) *Computer Law & Security Review* 550–561.

Sermpinis, T. and Sermpinis, C., 'Traceability Decentralization in Supply Chain Management Using Blockchain Technologies.' arXiv preprint arXiv:1810.09203 (2018).

Werbach, K. and Cornell, N., 'Contracts Ex Machina.' (2017) 67 (2) *Duke Law Journal* 313.

Yeoh, P., 'Regulatory Issues in Blockchain Technology.' (2017) 25 JFRC 196.

Yeung, K., 'Regulation by Blockchain: The Emerging Battle for Supremacy Between the Code *of* Law and Code *as* Law.' (2019) 82 (2) *Modern Law Review* 207 (33).

Newspapers, websites and blogs

Arvelo, F., 'RESIST – Uber and Subverting Regulations.' *The Bespoke Lawyer* (10 March 2017) <www.bespokelawyer.com/resist-uber-and-subverting-regulations/> accessed 28 March 2018.

Buntinx, J.-P., 'Future Use Cases for Blockchain Technology: Copyright Registration.' *Bitcoin News* (4 August 2015) <news.bitcoin.com/future-use-cases-for-blockchain-technology-copyright-registration> accessed 30 May 2018.

'E-Estonia – We Have Built a Digital Society and So Can You.' *e-Estonia* <https://e-estonia.com/> accessed 7 February 2018.

Garber, J., 'Bitcoin Spikes After Japan Says It's a Legal Payment Method.' *Business Insider* (3 April 2017) <http://uk.businessinsider.com/bitcoin-price-spikes-as-japan-recognizes-it-as-a-legal-payment-method-2017–4?r=US&IR=T> accessed 22 March 2018.

Lopp, J., 'Bitcoin and the Rise of the Cypherpunks.' *CoinDesk* (9 April 2016) <www.coindesk.com/the-rise-of-the-cypherpunks/> accessed 22 March 2018.

Maas, T., 'Blockchain: The 3 Core Components.' *LinkedIn* (24 October 2017) <www.linkedin.com/pulse/blockchain-3-core-components-thijs-maas> accessed 29 January 2018.

Maas, T., 'What Is Blockchain Technology?' *Lawandblockhain.eu* (21 June 2017) <www.lawandblockchain.eu/post-template/> accessed 29 January 2018.

Popper, N., 'Understanding Ethereum, Bitcoin's Virtual Cousin.' *The New York Times* (2 October 2017).

Rosic, A., 'What Is Blockchain Technology? A Step-By-Step Guide for Beginners.' *Blockgeeks* (2016) <https://blockgeeks.com/guides/what-is-blockchain-technology/> accessed 3 February 2018.

'Share of Global Internet Users Who Access Music Through Copyright Infringement as of 2017, by Age Group.' *Statista* (2018) <www.statista.com/statistics/609114/music-copyright-infringement-by-age/> accessed 5 December 2018.

Stankovic, S., 'An Introductory Guide to Cryptocurrency Regulation.' *Unblock* (15 January 2018) <https://unblock.net/cryptocurrency-regulation/> accessed 22 March 2018.

Wright, A. and De Filippi, P., 'Decentralized Blockchain Technology and the Rise of Lex Cryptographia.' *SSRN* (10 March 2015) <ssrn.com/abstract=2580664> accessed 1 June 2018.

Press releases

'An Update on Insurance.' *Uber Newsroom* (1 March 2018) <www.uber.com/newsroom/an-update-on-insurance/> accessed 26 March 2018.

'Insurance Aligned.' *Uber Newsroom* (24 March 2015) <www.uber.com/newsroom/introducing-the-tnc-insurance-compromise-model-bill/> accessed 26 March 2018.

'PRS for Music, ASCAP and SACEM Initiate Joint Blockchain Project.' (*PRS for Music*, 7 April 2017) <www.prsformusic.com/press/2017/prs-for-music-ascap-and-sacem-initiate-joint-blockchain-project> accessed 4 December 2018.

Legal encyclopaedias

'Blockchain – Key Legal and Regulatory Issues.' *Lexis PSL TMT* <LexisPSL> accessed 23 March 2018.

Chapter 4

Meetups

Making space for women on the blockchain

Philippa R. Adams, Julie Frizzo-Barker, Betty B. Ackah, and Peter A. Chow-White

Introduction

Blockchain has a gender problem. Gender disparity in the tech sector remains a persistent, well-documented challenge for women (Byrne, 2017). Blockchain represents an even worse case of this familiar trend, with only 5–7 percent female cryptocurrency investors (Tans, 2018). In its short history since the emergence of Bitcoin (Nakamoto, 2009) blockchain has been a male-dominated space. It is rooted in the financial and technological industries it purports to disrupt and characterized by stereotypes such as the 'Bitcoin Bros' (Bowles, 2018). In an extreme example, at a recent North American Bitcoin Conference in Miami, 3 of the 88 speakers were women, and the event concluded with a party at a strip club (Primack, 2018). Yet women are increasingly influencing blockchain development and becoming more visible at the helm of some of its most successful start-up organizations (Bowles, 2018). More broadly, local meetups for women interested in blockchain present accessible opportunities for women at various levels of expertise to learn and network around blockchain (Griffith, 2018). As an emerging technology, the definition, development, and diffusion of blockchain is still solidifying. This offers scholars an opportunity to assess the early stages of the technology and potentially influence its development in order to benefit as many users as possible (Callon, Law, & Rip, 1986). It is therefore important to consider the technical, economic, and gendered aspects of blockchain when investigating this new techno-social assemblage (Kitchin, 2014). In doing so, we can identify relevant actors and social groups and explore the process of who has power to shape this emerging technology as it unfolds. We are interested in how blockchain can be a potentially "disruptive innovation" (Christensen, 1997) as it diffuses unevenly across gendered divides.

Blockchain will turn ten in 2019. It has undergone several developmental phases already. Blockchain 1.0 demonstrated the feasibility of a digital currency that could be created and managed by people instead of governments. Blockchain 2.0 expanded the scope of the technology from currency to other applications. The smart contract enables developers to use blockchain for other applications and self-managed exchange propositions. The Ethereum community is the key example of blockchain expansion into other domains.

Blockchain 3.0 technologies move beyond cryptocurrency and smart contracts to revolutionize a broader range of social applications including government, health, arts, and culture (Swan, 2015). This represents promise for women in particular, with access to financial services for the 42 percent of global women who do not have bank accounts, secure identification records and land title registries on the blockchain for women in the developing world, and potential financial gain for those who invest in cryptocurrency (Allen, 2018; Thomason, 2017; Lielacher, 2018). Improving gender inequality is not only a pressing moral and social issue but an economic one as well. A 2015 report found that $12 trillion USD could be added to global GDP by 2025 by advancing women's equality in work and society (Woezel et. al.). Sandra Ro, chief executive of the Global Blockchain Business Council, commented, "(T)here is as much a human, culture shift element to what is going on as well as the technical evolution" (Bond, 2018). While blockchain is a decade old, it is still in the very early stages of adoption and diffusion. Blockchain has a long way to go to scale up to mainstream use as a digital currency or decentralized web. However, developers and early adopters argue it has potential to reorganize and democratize the way value is distributed in order to bring about a fairer world. Of course, we have heard this type of promising discourse before with other 1.0s and 2.0s, such as the Internet and social media. The future of blockchain remains unclear. This space of uncertainty is a key moment to understand how people are negotiating their hopes and fears about its future.

In this chapter, we investigate blockchain as a vital site to explore gendered instantiations of a new, emerging technology. We analyze women's discourses and practices around blockchain meetups through a technofeminist lens. Technofeminism's reflexive "social shaping of technology" perspective highlights how gender and technology coevolve in a seamless web of technical artifacts, social relations, and cultural meanings (Wajcman, 2004). This position challenges the prevailing notion of technology as neutral and value-free. Within this framework, both gender and blockchain are viewed as part of the texture that constitutes contemporary life rather than as separate from society. Our observations explore some of the socioeconomic aspects and consequences of decentralized technologies included in this volume.

Theoretical framework

The social shaping of technology approach (Pinch & Bijker, 1987; Mackenzie & Wajcman, 1999) highlights that human bias, whether intentional or unintentional, influences the design, trajectory, and social worth of an innovation. These scholars argue technologies are linked directly to culture, values, and socially accepted practices. Technology historian Ruth Schwartz Cowan (1976) painted a compelling picture of this, contrasting the extensive documentation of the steam engine with the comparably dismissed innovation of the baby bottle, both socially significant technologies. New technologies often help certain social groups consolidate power while diminishing the power of others. For example, Winner's (1980) study of suburban development in New Jersey revealed the geopolitical context of race relations in the US. Architects designed bridges that prevented buses from working class and predominantly black neighborhoods from accessing beaches located in predominantly white middle-class areas. Physicist Ursula Franklin conceptualized technology as a mindset and a practice, and therefore: "when certain technologies and tools are predominantly used by men, then maleness becomes part of the definition of those technologies" (1999, p. 8).

In the 1990s, feminist scholars celebrated the emancipatory potential of the Internet to close the gap of gender inequalities (Haraway, 1991; Plant, 1997; Turkle, 1995). Cyberfeminism emphasized women's agency and subjectivities. Technology itself was viewed as liberating for women. However, this techno-evangelist approach overemphasized the role of technologies. Enthusiasm over cyborgs, flexible identities, and social change often overlooked persistent gendered challenges. By the early 2000s, scholars began a fruitful exchange between gender theory and science and technology studies in order to study technologies as sociomaterial or sociotechnical practice. In particular, Judy Wajcman's technofeminism blended insights from cyberfeminism and the social shaping theory of technology, conceptualizing "a mutually shaping relationship between gender and technology, in which technology is both a source and a consequence of gender relations" (2004, p. 7).

Technofeminism strikes a balance between technophilia and technophobia, "to explore the complex ways in which women's everyday lives and technological change interrelate in the age of digitization" (Wajcman, 2004, p. 6). Women's use of technology often simultaneously enables and constrains their identities and experiences. For instance, social media has allowed for new forms of misogyny and harassment toward women while also facilitating women's collective resistance against such mistreatment, as seen in the #metoo movement (Mendes, Ringrose, & Keller, 2018). Similarly, women in blockchain are enthusiastically networking for global movement toward economic empowerment despite its male-dominated culture (UN Women, 2018). Technofeminism offers a nuanced perspective from which to analyze the complexities and contradictions inherent in both gender and technology.

A complementary theoretical lens we use to analyze how and why certain technologies are adopted in particular ways is Rogers' (2003) diffusion of innovation. Diffusion refers to the process by which an innovation is communicated through various channels among members of a social system. It is a specific type of communication concerned with the spread of new ideas. At the present, blockchain is in the earliest stages of diffusion. The very definition of blockchain remains in flux, both literally and figuratively. On the semiotic level, we observe that many news stories, scholarly papers, and local meetups open with the question, "What is blockchain?" Once a technology has successfully diffused into everyday usage and public discourse, the definition solidifies, and there is less of a need to define it. On the socioeconomic level, blockchain also remains in its earliest stages of diffusion. Which groups and causes will it best serve?

STS research on infrastructure investigates how innovations diffuse, solidify, and fade into the background of everyday use. This process carries socioeconomic implications. Star (1999) characterizes infrastructures as embedded, transparent, learned as part of membership, linked to conventions of practice, and built on an installed base. In this case, blockchain is built on an installed base of existing structures from the male-dominated tech and finance industries. Viewed as an infrastructure, blockchain requires a type of sociotechnical expertise that has traditionally excluded women. As one technology historian put it, "a gendered history of top-down structural discrimination defines the shape of the modern computing industry in the Anglo-American world" (Hicks, 2017). This project seeks to disentangle the complex relationships between male-dominated spaces and cultural practices (Wajcman, 2004; Gill, 2007; Gill, 2011; Byrne, 2017 cite; Neely, 2018). We explored how women create their own spaces and inroads into the male-dominated world by examining the role of meetups in blockchain. We focus our investigation by asking several research questions: How are local meetups shaping the definition, development, and diffusion of blockchain technologies? How are women shaping and being shaped by blockchain meetups? How do actors use discourses of gender in blockchain meetups? What is the role of gender in blockchain development?

Methodology

In our fieldwork, we observed local meetups through a technofeminist lens to analyze how gender and blockchain influence one another. We conducted participant observation at various blockchain meetups in Vancouver, British Columbia, Canada, a technology industry hub known for vibrancy, diversity, and innovation (Simon Fraser University Ethics Approval #2018s0237). The city is home to a burgeoning blockchain community including companies like Etherparty, which specializes in smart contracts, Vanbex, a blockchain consulting firm, and Axiom Zen, the studio that created the first blockchain-based game, Cryptokitties. Local interest in blockchain is also evident through the many blockchain-related events happening in the city and surrounding area on a weekly basis.

Scholars have researched meetups as valuable sites to study social networking and information sharing in ways that differ from other spaces like workplaces or online communities (Sessions, 2010; Shen & Cage, 2015). A 'meetup' is a face-to-face gathering of people with similar interests. It can be a periodic, informal meeting in a local coffee shop or a short-term learning event in a formal setting. A semiprofessional peer group can emerge and meet periodically. Participants combine real-world meetings and digital platforms to support one another and transmit information, job opportunities, and practice-based social relations (Benkler, 2006; Hindman, 2009). The events we attended ranged in size from 15–90 attendees (see the Appendix). The majority of the events took place on weekday evenings, while two were daylong events. We identified some as presentation focused and more corporate in tone, while others were discussion based and informal. The corporate-run events often involved a brief sales pitch for their service, product, or work space, related to blockchain. Some events were free, and others were $50 or $100 per ticket.

We found meetups to be an ideal site of observation to analyze both the development and the gendering of blockchain. A simple web-based search for local blockchain meetups yields a list of gendered gatherings, including "Bitcoin Gentlemen's Club" and "Crypto Witch Futurist Brunch." We attended and analyzed various local blockchain meetups and events in order to gather detailed observations and rich insights from naturalistic settings (Babbie & Benaquisto, 2010). The meetups we attended targeted a variety of audiences, including blockchain beginners, students, women in male-dominated industries, professionals, programmers, and potential cryptocurrency investors. These spaces where people commune around common interests and themes are local examples of a global trend (Griffith, 2018). Blockchain meetups attract people with different levels of technological experience, backgrounds, and motivations. Attendees gather together in a way that connects abstract technological tools and innovations into the embodied, social world. As attendees at these events we observed the form and content of the meetups, paying particular attention to the role of discourse and gender among participants. The open, enthusiastic nature of meetups and other blockchain events in Vancouver made them excellent sites to examine the ways participants shape the conversations and focus. We analyzed where, why, and how women interact with emerging technologies like blockchain, as their interactions shape the very definition and development of the technology itself.

Since blockchain technology is in its early stages, entrepreneurs, technology workers, and curious citizens of the general public all play a role in determining its course. The social shaping of technology happens in part through conversation, debate, and discussion in the public sphere, as exemplified by meetups. We made observations about the framing and focus of the meetups, the attendees, and the questions raised. We attended a range of different meetups, some aimed at women or minority interest groups and others with no particular gender focus, in order to compare and contrast them, although we remained observant of the gendered dynamics at each meetup. Of the many events we identified online through social media, Meetup.com, and Eventbrite.com, our research team attended eight meetups in person over a period of five months, from March to June 2018.

Findings

From the many observations we made over the course of the study, two major themes emerged. First, blockchain meetups reflect the opportunities and challenges typically observed at the beginning of the adoption curve for a new technology. Second, women-focused blockchain meetups serve as both spaces of resistance and spaces of support.

Blockchain 101: from "What is blockchain?" to "Beyond Bitcoin"

Each of the meetups we attended began with an introduction of blockchain, designed for a nontechnical, nonexpert audience. Most presenters opened with a slide outlining "What is blockchain?" The question is so persistent because of the newness of the technology, but also because it is a difficult question to answer for a broad audience. The apparent technical density of blockchain contributes to the perception that blockchain is more technologically complicated than it is. Presenters and meetup hosts dealt with this complexity with varying degrees of success. Some facilitators and panelists used metaphors, diagrams, or jokes to convey the technology as relatable and useful. At one event, after a lengthy discussion of how blockchain works, the presenter seemed to switch gears by suggesting, "You don't really know how your computer or your car works, you just know how to use them and what they can do for you. It will be similar with blockchain." However, to follow the car metaphor, blockchain is still in such early stages, most average users would not yet know how to turn the key and start it up. All these discussions point to the newness of the technology and curiosity about how it will unfold.

Each meetup was unique in tone, spatial orientation, and motivation for both presenters and participants. For instance, some had a more corporate inclination in terms of jargon, seating arrangements, and networking. In contrast, there were more informal events, several of which were aimed at women and minority groups. The informal events tended to be more collegial and conversational, while others had a more corporate inclination in terms of jargon, seating arrangements, and networking. For example, one of the meetups for women played up the gendered focus by beginning with wine and appetizers in a lounge setting before attendees took their seats at tables with fresh cut flowers. The women in attendance ranged in age from younger to more seasoned professionals. All attendees introduced themselves and their motivation for attending to the entire group before the presentation began. Some had come to learn about blockchain for the first time, some were blockchain programmers, and some were successful cryptocurrency investors. This group-wide introduction style was a marked contrast to the more typical exercises we observed at other meetups, introducing yourself to the people sitting next to you as a brief, informal icebreaker.

Overall, we found the informal meetups to be more productive in terms of allowing for participants to connect and for organizers to tailor the content to attendees' interests. In contrast, the more polished, corporate events positioned attendees more as audiences, with less agency in the course of the event, which set the tone for the conversational segments before and after the presentation as well. One unifying factor we observed across the meetups was a sense of community and support. This tone was very different than the competitive and individualistic culture associated with tech companies. Using Franklin's definition of technology as practice, we can view meetups as open access technologies in and of themselves. Even at the meetups sponsored by Microsoft or local tech companies, there was a sense of shared learning and collaboration about something new and exciting. Several meetups concluded with an invitation to join a social media group or a mailing list for follow-up conversation among participants.

A majority of presentations focused on cryptocurrency as the best-known blockchain example, and indeed many attendees voiced interest in how to begin investing in this new market. One presenter spent over an hour of the presentation describing the details of a Bitcoin transaction, complete with a simulation exercise that involved the attendees signing and swapping pieces of paper. Often there was a conflation of the definitions of blockchain and Bitcoin, contrasted by a growing awareness of blockchain's potential benefits across other areas of public life. For example, after lengthy cryptocurrency discussions at two events, audience members asked if the presenter could discuss blockchain applications beyond cryptocurrency. At another meetup, a physician asked about where she could find more information about health-focused blockchain applications. To contrast different types of expertise, the student-led event we attended comprised mainly computer science undergraduate students who had complex questions about how to mine various cryptocurrencies. Most of the presenters gave enthusiastic presentations about the potential benefits and opportunities of blockchain. In various cases, it was the skeptical or confused audience members who raised important discussion about blockchain's potential risks or challenges. For instance, one attendee questioned the value of blockchain's claims to food provenance. If it involves physically or digitally tagging products, couldn't this information be compromised? This raised a useful discussion on the quality and verification processes of data entering the blockchain. Some meetups capitalized on attendees' skepticism, such as one titled "To Blockchain or Not to Blockchain: Does your company need a blockchain solution?"

The rapid proliferation of blockchain meetups and events in Vancouver are indicative of the current formative stage of the development of blockchain. Even a year ago, there were far fewer events or public discourse about blockchain. We noticed that some of the events were polished and professional in terms of logistics and presentation. Others seemed to be thrown together haphazardly or hastily. Early adopters, or those eager to position themselves as such, are clamoring to enter the blockchain arena. Two examples from our observations illustrate this. We attended one "Intro to Blockchain" event organized by a local "women in blockchain" group, as advertised on meetup.com. When we arrived, we realized that in fact various groups, all associated with the same start-up incubator organization, had advertised this same meetup. We were expecting to attend a meetup targeted at women, led by the woman pictured on the event listing. Instead, she was unable to make it that day, and one of her male business partners, who advertised the same event through a different local blockchain group, gave the presentation, which was attended by a mixed group of men and women, with women slightly less represented and far less vocal in the discussion. We noticed a shift in tone when the host announced he would be the only presenter. A number of female participants expressed disappointment that the event was not what they were expecting. For the participants, the communicative context mattered. In another instance, when we arrived at a "Women in Blockchain" meetup as per the Eventbrite ticket listing, we realized it had been cancelled and rescheduled for a later date with no notice given, so we showed up to an empty room. There is a sense of urgency and immediacy associated with these types of meetups, which in these cases came along with disorganization. These observations support our assessment of blockchain's current position at the earliest stage of the diffusion of innovation curve.

Gendered spaces of resistance and support

Blockchain's gender problem was apparent in all the meetups we attended. All of the women-focused meetup presenters and one of the male presenters at a start-up organization's "Intro to Blockchain" meetup highlighted the gender discrepancy in the technology sector, adding that this disparity is even more stark within blockchain. The male presenter suggested that organizing meetups with the aim of introducing more people to blockchain was a way of balancing the gender scales. Gender was at work in the meetups aimed at general audiences as well as the meetups specifically aimed at women. The existence of meetups such as "Meet the Women in Vancouver's Top Blockchain Start-ups" goes to show that there is a need to create a space for meetups hosted by women, primarily targeted to women. These meetups function both to resist the hyper-masculine blockchain space and to foster supportive connections for women in blockchain by highlighting their leadership in the space.

At the start of one of the women's meetup presentations, the host asked the audience, "Why do you feel there aren't more women in blockchain?" After a pause, it was one of the few men in attendance who spoke up first, commenting that women have historically been left behind in technology and finance. This cultural in-group dynamic continues with blockchain. Weeks later, we spoke to a woman at a meetup for Women in Male Dominated Industries, who explained how she enjoys women-focused events in the tech and video gaming sectors. But she noticed more men had been attending them, and those men tend to be more outspoken than the women in a way that intruded on one of the few arenas women in tech could lay claim to.

We asked the organizer of the Women in Male Dominated Industries about her motivation for starting this monthly event held at a coffee shop downtown. Her response echoed several of the conversations we had with other attendees.

"If there isn't a space in the field for you, you need to make your own space to succeed and improve at what you do," she said. She had worked in the mining industry and wanted to make connections with other women who were similarly minorities in their fields, for support, networking, and professional development. Organizing these meetups was therefore her way of highlighting women's successes and struggles across various male-dominated industries. One attendee of the Women in Male Dominated Industries meetup spoke about how she attends all sorts of events but really enjoys the women-created events because the energy and conversation "is just different" at them. Women are more comfortable speaking up about their hopes and fears without being dismissed or harassed.

We found that women-created and women-focused events were spaces of resistance to the male-dominated sectors of both technology and finance, as well as spaces of support for one another in a broader context of an inhospitable tech sector. In various conversations, women saw blockchain as a platform to make their presence known in the technology and finance worlds. Some women organizers spoke of the necessity of getting into the general blockchain space through the various educational and networking opportunities that the meetups afforded. One presenter opened her talk on blockchain with a rallying cry about how women are missing out on great opportunity if they don't understand and participate in the blockchain space, recounting how men have disproportionately benefited from financial and technological innovations in the past. In one of her introductory slides, she used side-by-side screenshots of Reddit and Pinterest to highlight online communities dominated by men and women, respectively. This example illustrated the gendered, sociocultural aspects of these tech platforms.

We noted that at the meetups designed by women for women, the organizers asserted their positions as leaders rather than followers or beginners in the blockchain field. In contrast, the majority of the general-audience events had predominantly male panelists and presenters. This highlights the bias toward men as the de facto experts in the field, especially where digital and financial technologies are concerned. At "The Future of Blockchain" summit, men constituted over 70 percent of the speakers. Male presenters covered such topics as the financial and technical aspects of blockchain. In contrast, female presenters focused on how blockchain may impact other fields, such as health care, art, and marketing. This illustrates the fact that, since women have achieved better gender parity in those industries in recent years, they were perceived as credible enough to speak to blockchain in relation to those areas to a wider audience. In contrast, the male presenters at the same event were more likely to focus on cryptocurrency or business-related aspects of blockchain, which seemed like a 'natural fit' based on men's overrepresentation in those areas.

Panels on cryptocurrencies like Bitcoin and Ethereum were popular attractions for attendees seeking new investment opportunities. Both cryptocurrencies had received extensive media attention following their skyrocketing value in late 2017 and early 2018. Many attendees viewed meetups as opportunities to gain relevant information and contacts towards making educated investment decisions. Other participants who have already invested in cryptocurrencies and other blockchain-based products attended meetups to acquire and share more advanced knowledge. For instance, during the introductions at a Blockchain from Women's Perspectives meetup, one participant, who runs a successful online business, commented that she had encouraged her husband to invest in cryptocurrency one year prior. When he disagreed, they did not invest because he managed their investments. Bitcoin's value increased dramatically since then. She did not want to miss out on future investment opportunities, so now she was being proactive and investigating how to invest on her own. Her participation at this event was therefore her way to educate herself and subsequently initiate investment proceedings.

Women-focused events subvert the norm to showcase women's diverse expertise. Meetups specifically for women allow women to have conversations that do not center around gender. To illustrate, the first "Women on the Block Diversity Blockchain Conference" took place in New York City, with over 50 female blockchain experts who spoke on raising capital, creating startups, and legal issues, with proceeds going toward a charitable fund to support women and girls in technology (Women on the Block, 2018). At a gathering like this, there was no need for a panel on 'women in blockchain.' In our own observations, we noticed women at such meetups exchanging personal stories, business cards, and professional insights. Many of these events also allowed space for hearing about the attendees' interests in terms of which topics should be covered, with presenters then tailoring the conversation towards those topics. The Women in Male Dominated Industries meetup was entirely participant-driven, in that the attendees determined the topics, parameters, and pace of the conversations. The facilitator's only direction was to periodically remind participants to change seats regularly to interact with different people. The women-focused events were inherently agentic and encouraged women's participation.

Conclusion

Through our fieldwork, it is clear that women are cognizant of the gendered disparities in technology and finance. Both organizers and participants viewed blockchain meetups as sites for learning more about the technology and achieving personal and career goals. We found that women are indeed influencing blockchain development, just as blockchain is shaping women's experiences of technology and finance despite lower representation. We also found that women have enthusiastically created many of these meetups in response to the need for accessible, supportive, educational social networks for women to participate in the blockchain milieu. Blockchain is at the very early stages of diffusion and innovation. Those involved in all the various techno-social practices surrounding blockchain at the present will shape where it goes, how it develops, and how it is used. It is therefore vital to interrogate the role of women in this phase of blockchain development.

Our research of local blockchain meetups has shown the importance of the role of discourse in the development of new technologies. Much of the existing research on women in technology focuses on workplaces or industries and the trends or specific policies that affect gender disparity. Blockchain is an emerging, decentralized technology that is diffusing in a decentralized, organic way. This technology poses new challenges for scholars but has great potential for future research, development, and innovation. Technofeminism highlights the fact that each of these social dynamics are both influencing and being modified by our relationship to technologies. Technologies enable or constrain individuals differently based on aspects of identity. These meetups show the social side of blockchain technologies and help illustrate some of the ways in which women are making their voices heard in a space that historically excludes them. Through our research on the local Vancouver blockchain community, it is clear to us that blockchain's gender problem persists. However, it is also clear that women, whether from a technological or financial background or with no blockchain experience at all, are interested in gaining access to the potential benefits blockchain offers.

Blockchain proponents claim a positive vision of decentralization and democratization, with the potential to improve the lives of women. In these early days it is hard to tell whether the technology will in fact evolve this way. The active players in the blockchain community now are those whose ideas will shape blockchain as it develops. At several of the meetups we observed, attendees and presenters noted the gender discrepancy in blockchain, an element that detracts from proponents' claims of decentralization. Meetups reflect that blockchain holds great promise of opportunity, even amidst the challenges and volatility of an emerging technology. Through conversations at events like the ones we attended, women are actively shaping the blockchain space. Through meetups, these women are working to educate themselves and others about the technology and innovate solutions to myriad problems using the technology and their own social connections. What blockchain developers build on the platform is more important than the technology itself. Similarly, without a diversity of voices proactively shaping the technology, blockchain is in danger of re-inscribing the existing power structures it purports to dismantle. Meetups for women in blockchain are one example of how a small yet proliferating movement can shape the course of a new technology in the making.

References

Allen, B. (2018). *Commentary: 3 ways blockchain can empower women worldwide.* Retrieved March 1, 2018 from http://fortune.com/2018/02/13/blockchain-bitcoin-cryptocurrency-womens-rights/

Babbie, E., & Benaquisto, L. (2010). *Fundamentals of social research* (2nd ed.). Toronto: Nelson Education.

Benkler, Y. (2006). *The wealth of networks: How social production transforms markets and freedom.* New Haven, CT and London: Yale University Press.

Bond, F. (2018, June 21). *Women at the top are driving cryptocurrency evolution.* Retrieved July 19, 2018 from www.raconteur.net/finance/women-at-the-top-are-driving-crypto-evolution

Bowles, N. (2018, February 25). Women in cryptocurrencies push back against "blockchain bros". *New York Times.* Retrieved from www.nytimes.com/2018/02/25/business/cryptocurrency-women-blockchain-bros.html

Byrne, C. (2017). *4 charts that show tech is still a man's world.* Retrieved April 6, 2018 from www.weforum.org/agenda/2017/08/women-in-tech-gender-parity/

Callon, M., Law, J., & Rip, A. (1986). How to study the force of science. In *Mapping the dynamics of science and technology* (pp. 3–15). London: Palgrave Macmillan. https://doi.org/10.1007/978-1-349-07408-2_1

Christensen, C. (1997). *The innovator's dilemma: The revolutionary book that will change the way you do business (Collins Business Essentials).* New York: Harper Paperbacks.

Cowan, R. S. (1976). The "Industrial Revolution" in the home: Household technology and social change in the 20th century. *Technology and Culture, 17*(1), 1–23.

Franklin, U. (1999). *The real world of technology.* Toronto: House of Anansi.

Gill, R. (2007). *Gender and the media.* Cambridge: Polity Press.

Gill, R. (2011). Sexism reloaded, or, it's time to get angry again! *Feminist Media Studies, 11*(1), 61–71. doi:10.1080/14680777.2011.537029

Griffith, E. (2018). *For women in cryptocurrency, a new effort to grow their ranks.* Retrieved April 6, 2018 from www.wired.com/story/for-women-in-cryptocurrency-a-new-effort-to-grow-their-ranks/

Haraway, D. (1991). A cyborg manifesto: Science, technology and socialist-feminism in the late twentieth century. In *Simians, cyborgs and women: The reinvention of nature* (pp. 149–181). New York, NY: Routledge.

Hicks, M. (2017). *Programmed inequality: How Britain discarded women technologists and lost its edge in computing* (W. Aspray & T. J. Misa, Eds., 1st ed.). Cambridge, MA: The MIT Press.

Hindman, M. (2009). *The myth of digital democracy.* Princeton, NJ: Princeton University Press.

Kitchin, R. (2014). *The data revolution: Big data, open data, data infrastructures and their consequences.* Thousand Oaks, CA: Sage.

Lielacher, A. (2018, March 3). *Femtech in Africa: Meet the women who are pioneering Bitcoin in Africa.* Retrieved April 6, 2018 from http://bitcoinafrica.io/2018/03/03/femtech-in-africa-women-in-tech-pioneering-blockchain-africa/

MacKenzie, D., & Wajcman, J. (Eds.). (1999). *The social shaping of technology* (2nd ed.). Buckingham and Philadelphia: McGraw Hill Education/Open University.

Mendes, K., Ringrose, J., & Keller, J. (2018). #MeToo and the promise and pitfalls of challenging rape culture through digital feminist activism. *European Journal of Women's Studies, 25*(2), 236–246.

Nakamoto, S. (2009, May 24). *Bitcoin: A peer-to-peer electronic cash system.* Retrieved March 5, 2018 from https://web.archive.org/web/20140320135003/https://bitcoin.org/bitcoin.pdf

Neely, M. T. (2018). Fit to be king: How patrimonialism on Wall Street leads to inequality. *Socio-Economic Review, 16*(2), 365–385.

Pinch, T., & Bijker, W. E. (1987). The social construction of facts and artifacts: Or how the sociology of science and the sociology of technology might benefit from each other. In W. E. Bijker, T. P. Hughes, T. Pinch, & D. G. Douglas (Eds.), *The social construction of technological systems: New directions in the sociology and history of technology* (pp. 17–51). Cambridge, MA: MIT Press.

Plant, S. (1997). *Zeros + ones: Digital women + the new technoculture.* London: Fourth Estate.

Primack, D. (2018, January 26). *Bitcoin conference ends at a strip club*. Retrieved April 6, 2018 from www.axios.com/bitcoin-conference-stripclub-1516983254-35e78aad-ee30-4872-bfe6-13190dd46061.html

Rogers, E. M. (2003). *Diffusion of innovations* (5th ed.). New York, NY: Free Press.

Sessions, L. (2010). How offline gatherings affect online communities. *Information, Communication, and Society*, *13*(3).

Shen, C., & Cage, C. (2015). Exodus to the real world? Assessing the impact of offline meetups on community participation and social capital. *New Media and Society*, *17*(3), 394–414.

Star, S. L. (1999). The ethnography of infrastructure. *American Behavioral Scientist*, *43*(3), 377–391.

Swan, M. (2015). *Blockchain: Blueprint for a new economy* (1st ed.). Beijing and Sebastopol, CA: O'Reilly Media.

Tans, G. (2018). Why it's vital we close the tech gender gap. Retrieved April 6, 2018, from World Economic Forum website: https://www.weforum.org/agenda/2018/01/close-the-tech-gender-gap-gillian-tans/

Thomason, J. (2017). Blockchain: An accelerator for women and children's health? *Global Health Journal*, *1*(1), 3–10.

Turkle, S. (1995). *Life on the screen*. New York, NY: Touchstone.

UN Women. (2018). UN Women's innovation and technology projects. Retrieved February 28, 2018, from UN Women website: http://www.unwomen.org/en/digital-library/publications/2019/03/innovation-for-gender-equality

Wajcman, J. (2004). *TechnoFeminism*. Cambridge: Polity.

Winner, L. (1980). Do Artifacts Have Politics? *Daedalus*, *109*(1), 121–136.

Women on the Block Blockchain Conference - May 13, 2018. (2018). Retrieved August 15, 2018, from website: https://www.womenontheblock.io/

Appendix

Table 4.1 Vancouver blockchain events

Date	*Event*	*Location type*	*Organizer*
March 6, 2018	Beyond Bitcoin: Blockchain and the Future of Work	University Lecture Hall	University Group
March 29, 2018	Blockchain From Women's #Perspectives	Co-working Space	Event Series
May 8, 2018	The Future of Blockchain by Glance Technologies	Event Hall	Technology Company
May 17, 2018	Vancouver Women in Male Dominated Industries	Coffee Shop	Individual
May 28, 2018	Intro to Blockchain | Why It's Important, How It Works and Its Key Applications	Start-up Incubator	Technology Company
May 29, 2018	Blockchain 101: Learn the Basics of Blockchain Technology and Why It Matters	University Classroom	University Student Group
June 11, 2018	#Perspectives 2	Co-working Space	Event Series
June 12, 2018	Indigenous Blockchain Roundtable	Corporate Meeting Room	Tech Company

Chapter 5

Drivers of digital trust in the crypto industry

Scott Freeman, Ivana Beveridge, and Jannis Angelis

Introduction

In this chapter we focus on the role of trust as a digital enabler, with a particular focus on blockchain technologies. A high degree of cooperation among the users is the core element of shared ledger technologies. This in part creates a stronger bond among them and also puts pressure on the users to act in an agreed-upon manner. Such coordination and agreement of permissible behavior plays center stage when it comes to successfully employing blockchain technology, which in practice highlights the importance of trust among the users. In covering the issue, we discuss the characteristics of trust in a digital and cryptocurrency context and consider concerns relating to technology design, conditions of decentralization and transparency, and ways in which trust can be managed in a crypto-environment.

Trust and cooperation as key human success factors

There is much dispute over the key factors that helped humans to dominate the planet. Was it the invention of controlled fire? Or of tools such as spears and traps? Language, cooking, or agriculture? No doubt all of the above played an important role. Yet it can hardly be denied that at least one somewhat more abstract innovation must certainly have had a crucial impact: humans' ability to cooperate together in order to achieve common goals and ultimately share in the fruits of those endeavors. To do this, humans evolved the ability to create comprehensive trust relationships with others. Such trust is central to the functioning of the modern society (Watson, 2009).

Anthropologists Richerson and Boyd (1998) suggest that to override their more basic selfish instinct to maximize personal gain, humans have evolved a kind of tribal instinct. This permitted our ancestors to share both resources and rewards and was thus key to enabling humans to begin the process of creating increasingly complex social and economic structures. The ability to cooperate for mutual benefit seems to initially have been limited to – as the term implies – known persons, i.e., other members of one's tribe. This seems to have remained the state of affairs until recently in evolutionary terms. Even a mere 2,500 years ago in Europe, those not belonging to one's own group were for the most part considered to be without rights, essentially nonpersons, or "barbarians," as the Greeks termed them. The idea that humankind in general was worthy of cooperation was a new concept and a decisive step that led to the almost infinitely complex interlocking patterns of cooperation and exchange that characterize our modern world.

Trust remains a fairly complex and a multidimensional concept to define, since it draws on both rational and idiosyncratic perceptions and even lacks a common definition (Möllering, 2001). Trust has been researched by many disciplines, and it is influenced by many tangible and intangible factors. Traditionally, economists viewed trust as calculative (e.g., Williamson, 1993) or institutional (North, 1990) and psychologists assessed it in terms of attributes of trustors and trustees (Tyler, 1990), while sociologists interpret trust in terms of relationships between people or institutions (Granovetter, 1985). Rousseau, Sitkin, Burt, and Camerer (1998) suggested that these different interpretations of trust are also related to different usage of language in its denotative vs. connotative terms. Mayer, Davis, and Schoorman (1995, p. 712) proposed what became one of the most cited definitions of trust as a "willingness of a party to be vulnerable to the actions of another party" in a situation of risk. What unifies many definitions of trust is that rather than being defined as an individual mental predisposition, trust is mostly seen in relational terms (Castelfranchi & Falcone, 2001).

Trust has evolved through history from being confined to immediate and restricted individual networks to being extended to third parties deemed to have the needed authority. Undoubtedly, trust could only be understood in context, as it is always constructed in unique contexts (Bohnet & Meier, 2005). In this respect, blockchain presents a unique, relatively new context that calls for revisiting of the aforementioned traditional notions of trust. In particular, decentralized models have the potential to reorganize all manner of human activity (Foroglou & Tsilidou, 2015), showing a new kind of creative potential and a capacity to deliver a new kind of trust (Walport, 2016).

Complex cooperation models in the modern economy

That humans have developed the tribal instinct or "ultra-sociability" (Richerson & Boyd, 1998) does not change the fact that they also retain an instinct to seek to maximize personal gain while at the same time minimizing the personal effort. This means that successful cooperation is dependent on a mechanism to limit the free rider problem by punishing cheaters and rewarding fair players in proportion to their contribution. If such a framework can be devised, trust relationships can be created and deepened between participants. In a business context, voluntarily organized joint-stock companies were a means to essentially pool resources together for specific and limited purposes without the need to change tribes or affiliations.

Using written rules enforced by contracts, both contributions and rewards were regulated, which in turn increased the level of trust between the participants. The existence of such a systematic and formalized approach to trust meant that humans could effectively participate in multiple tribes. Initially, people who knew each other personally came together, but stocks and bonds were increasingly abstracted from their founding companies and allowed people who had never met physically to combine resources. These increasingly complex models of cooperation were closely correlated with productivity gains. Trust plays a significant role in corporate collaborations because successful and sustainable business relationships typically require an established and mutual level of trust (Kwon & Suh, 2004). This is especially true for large networks where complex transactions and information sharing must be managed in a timely and reliable manner (Eurich, Oertel, & Boutellier, 2010).

In the twenty-first century, facilitated by an increase in the use of information technology to both enable and survey investments and trades, those initial joint-stock companies evolved into complex corporate structures mostly owned and controlled via financial markets. Those financial market and corporate structures became more complex and convoluted but also created new opportunities for added value for participants. Yet, at the same time, something in their basic nature changed. Governments and specialized lawyers increasingly took over the structuring of these relationships, to the extent that in most countries today, these relationships can hardly be said to be the result of voluntary cooperative agreement between the participants.

These entities not only took over control but also demanded an increasingly large cut of the fruits of those cooperative structures. While governments typically claim that this is done for investor protection, ultimately these structures can be seen as classic protection rackets. As their voluntary nature ebbed, trust in the honesty of these structures understandably fell. Offering an alternative model to this traditional one, blockchain has challenged the assumption about traditional organizations being best suited to manage market transactions, disrupting the existing power structures and calling for the updates on the traditional notions of trust (Seidel, 2017; Yermack, 2017).

Erosion of trust is not only apparent as it pertains to the traditional financial institutions, but it also extends to online centralized systems. For example, Facebook collected more personal customer's data in the first ten years than the Library of Congress in 200 years (Zyskind, Nathan, & Pentland, 2015). Massive mining of user data, notably on Facebook, has significantly contributed to the erosion of the public trust in the centralized online entities (The Harvard Gazette, 2018).

Blockchain systems and digital currencies present a shift from the traditional financial and centralized infrastructures, allowing for more transparent, decentralized organization in contrast to the traditional centrally coordinated and less transparent monetary system structures. Considering that many online services in the future could run as decentralized applications on blockchain systems, it will be important to understand the new notions of trust both in terms of social as well as technological components of these systems.

Trust and digital technology

Although much of human cooperation has historically been achieved through violence and coercion, voluntary cooperation has proven to be more efficient, and it has grown steadily over time. Today, technology is intertwined with and changes how trust is manifested among people and in society at large. The development of the digital arena in general and the use of decentralized systems such as blockchain in particular have both a significant and substantial impact on how trust is manifested. We see the unique culmination of voluntary trust in the largely unregulated cryptocurrency industry. Thanks to the Internet – and more recently the distributed technology platforms such as blockchain – people all around the world can now choose from a vast number of technology platforms and even investment opportunities. The webs of trust that thereby are created reach connection numbers and speeds unprecedented in history.

Despite the creation of an interconnected, worldwide electronic web enabling instant communication and trading in ways unimaginable to investors living a mere half a century earlier, they would likely find the structures we observe today in traditional financial markets to be quite recognizable. This is because the regulatory bodies have essentially cemented those structures into place. Given the highly bureaucratic nature of financial markets in most countries, the decentralized and transparent nature of cryptocurrencies and their associated distributed ledgers offer a real alternative to existing financial structures. Exchanges, brokers, and derivative merchants can flog their services worldwide. Value propositions can be promoted and funds raised to support projects from investors in all corners of the world. A team with a promising project in Kazakhstan can get investment from an enthusiastic investor in Japan or Tanzania, and it is fairly difficult for governments and third parties to extract a share. A key underlying enabler to all this is digital trust. The unprecedented transparency of the feedback mechanism offered by the Internet and transparent distributed ledgers offer market participants new avenues to judge the reliability of potential contract partners.

Research on trust and technology has mostly been conducted on the premise that a third party exists, and thus trust has been defined in relation to another party that is trusted (Bracamonte & Okada, 2017). Not having to rely on a trusted third party to validate transactions by users or to maintain the security of the system is considered as one of the most important characteristics of blockchain technologies (Nakamoto, 2008). This tendency toward decentralization resides in the essence of blockchain technology (Manski, 2017). Nonetheless, decentralized applications based on smart contracts rely on a combination of technical components to achieve a system where it is not necessary to trust an individual node (Bonneau et al., 2015). Furthermore, the system also relies on traditional architecture, with websites acting as the user interface being susceptible to downtime. Thus, the concept of trust in blockchain should be measured as social as well as technology trust (Bracamonte & Okada, 2017).

Blockchain characteristics and trust

The use of blockchain technology in the crypto industry – or the broader distributed ledger technologies it falls under – provides potentially four different but connected advantages: *safety, efficiency, scalability*, and *improved access* (Heires, 2016). But to be realized, the relationship between various parties must move from purely transactional to a more integrated relationship. For instance, the network-based consensus approach to decision making and information processing helps prevent fraudulent transactions, but it also places a significant degree of responsibility on all participants. In its core, this is an issue of trust in the network.

Distributed ledger technologies have the ability to lower transaction costs and make intellectual property ownership and payments more transparent, seamless, and even automated. They give any authorized party access to the entirety of or parts of the ledger of recorded transactions by distributing digital copies of the ledger instantly and simultaneously, and with the transaction record indelibly recorded through advanced computational algorithms and various cryptographic locks. This has the potential to facilitate significant levels of trust among the participants, which in turn supports value creation and exchange. Blockchain technologies have even been named the *Fourth Industrial Revolution* (Schwab, 2016), categorized as a disruptive and transforming technology in a similar way that email removed the need for a trusted third party such as the post office (Lee, 2016; Iansiti & Lakhani, 2017). A growing interest in the industry has resulted in the high degree of venture capital investments in blockchain startups, estimated at around $1.3 billion in 2018 and growing (The Crunch, 2018). In this light, it's hard to deny that the blockchain industry has been disrupting the key traditional economic sectors, and it has attracted substantial attention from the financial, tech, and academic sectors.

At the core of technological innovation behind it is the so-called "Nakamoto consensus" protocol for maintaining a decentralized ledger known as the blockchain. Under the pseudonym Satoshi Nakamoto, an individual or a group published in 2008 the paper "Bitcoin: A Peer-To-Peer Electronic Cash System". It describes the ideal of direct peer-to-peer transactions without a third party or intermediary (Nakamoto, 2008). Previously, if not held in its physical form, money was tracked on the ledger of a centralized intermediary. Blockchain is the first digital currency system that does not require such centralized intermediary. This allows users to conduct economic exchanges without an intermediary (Werbach, 2018). When the Bitcoin blockchain later emerged in 2009, it was little known outside of the crypto community and was for the most part considered obscure until more widely recognized around 2012.

In blockchains, trust is built on the decentralized nature of the ledger and the immutability of the shared data. The former means that parties can interact with each other and have confidence that records of any interactions and transactions are permanently archived. The latter means that any changes to the shared information on such interactions cannot be altered or modified without all participants being aware of the changes. Both of these conditions foster an environment of increased trust among the blockchain participants, even in blockchains where participating parties are anonymous. Moreover, each transaction in a shared (or public) ledger is verified by consensus of a majority of the participants in the system, allowing for traceability and, in turn, security without the need of a central authority. Since every block is connected to the previous one, as the number of participants and blocks grow, it is very difficult to modify information without having a network consensus (Corea, 2019; Crosby, Nachiappan, Pattanayak, Verma, & Kalyanaraman, 2015). Such a consensus-seeking system both requires and builds trust among its participants.

The nature of digital trust

The concept of trust appears ambiguous in the blockchain space, and it is often referred to as "trustless trust" (Cohney et al., 2018). This is not to say that blockchains do not require trust or exist without trust; rather, trust is distributed among different actors (otherwise not knowing each other enough to trust one another) who place trust in the system, providing them with the economic incentives to cooperate. Decentralization in this case leads to more transparency due to near-real-time transactions monitored via the public peer-to-peer network, whereby each transaction is verified by consensus of a majority of participants, contrary to the traditional centralized financial mechanisms. Furthermore, each past and present transaction remains stored and can be verified at any point in the future. The extent to which trust is encompassing naturally leads to an embarkation between those trusted and those not trusted. In blockchains, this is the boundary between public and private chains. In the former, access to participate in the consensus process of operating the blockchain is not regulated. In contrast, in the latter, permissions are kept centralized. Read permissions may be public or restricted to an arbitrary extent. Hybrid blockchain versions such as so-called consortia have the consensus process controlled by a preselected set of parties (or nodes).

The decentralized nature of blockchain technology eliminates the need for a third party controlling the ledger. This is beneficial in terms of shared decision making and ensuring information is not forged or modified in secret, since copies remain synchronized with the other network participants. But the shared access or ownership to contracts, transactions, and records also places a substantial responsibility on these participants. They need to conform to agreed-upon rules and procedures so as not to cause problems for the network as whole. They also have to make decisions on such things as changes to procedures and offered services that follow a shared vision. The participants are expected to make decisions that are beneficial to the network as a whole. Since the dynamic and often rapidly changing business environment may require fast decision making on unexpected issues, it is typically difficult to preplan for all eventualities.

Network participants must be trusted to make the right decisions. For instance, the blockchain immutability of data, where the shared ledger means information cannot be modified without leaving a trace, does provide a notable degree of operational security. But the shared decision making means that participants in some circumstances can overrule others through "majority attacks", where the common decision making is controlled through a majority (e.g., the "51% attack"). Retaining the shared benefits means that participants have to be trusted to refrain from such behavior, possibly through a hybrid permissioned-permissionless approach that limits the decision-making ability to those participants that share a common vision.

What may be one of the main drivers behind the growing research interest in blockchain is in fact the ambiguity found in the fundamentals of blockchain, and in particular behind the notion of trust underpinning the industry. Bonneau et al. (2015) note two opposing research views on blockchain technologies, symbolized in attitudes to Bitcoin. Bitcoin is a decentralized digital currency in which encryption techniques are used to allow peer-to-peer transactions in a system that works without a central bank or single administrator. The first research view suggests that "Bitcoin works in practice but not in theory", dismissing it due to its lack of a solid theoretical foundation. The second view is that its stability relies on an unknown combination of socioeconomic factors "hopelessly intractable to model with sufficient precision, failing to yield a convincing argument for the system's soundness" (ibid, p. 104).

Undoubtedly, the same factors serving as trust enablers in the crypto world present a challenge – conceptually at least – for traditional institutions and in particular for the institutional investors. One important reason for this is the ecosystem nature blockchain technologies typically operate within. An ecosystem refers to a network comprising a focal organization, its suppliers, and customers (Adner & Kapoor, 2010). As such, the ecosystem is the wider network of parties that influence how value is created and captured. Organizations operating within the ecosystem have to consider their function in the ecosystem and design and employ the blockchain accordingly. Without a doubt, the notion of digital trust in the blockchain industry has disrupted the traditional notions of organizing in the market economy as we know it.

Incorporating trust

The complexity of the trust concept has increased in the digital space due to a combination of technological and sociological components. In the crypto space, the concept of trust can be largely explained with the way blockchain is designed. Previous research analyzing the notion of trust in the blockchain systems has been limited, focusing on issues such as social components of Bitcoin use (Zarifis, Cheng, Efthymiou, & Dimitriou, 2014) or wallet providers (Eskandari, Clark, Barrera, & Stobert, 2015). In particular the notion of "technology trust" in blockchain systems remains under-researched. Bracamonte and Okada (2017) suggest that the focus of research on user behavior in blockchains should also be on the technology as a trustee. Because governance mechanisms rely on the architecture of the system and its developers (Kroll, Davey, & Felten, 2013), it is misleading to suggest that blockchains are characterized with "trustless trust". Within the distributed ledger technologies (DLTs), code substitutes for trust, and this allows for a new type of market interactions (Kewell, Adams, & Parry, 2017). A shared consensual ledger replaces the traditional need for trusted third-party intermediaries with a consensus of rightness, whereby DLTs replace the old concept with "trust in the algorithm".

Iansiti and Karim (2017) suggest five basic principles behind blockchain technology: a distributed database: – each party on a blockchain has access to the entire database and its history, and no single party controls the data of information; peer-to-peer direct communication; transparency with pseudonymity – every transaction is visible while the users can choose to remain anonymous or provide proof of identity to others; irreversibility of records; and computational logic (users can set up algorithms).

Bonneau et al. (2015) suggest that blockchain operates without any specific trusted third parties as well as without pre-assumed identities of the participants. One of the key drivers of trust is certainly the way that blockchain technologies are designed: rather than being centralized, the ledger is replicated and distributed across a wider network. This enables the anonymous parties to enforce complex agreements via cryptographic proof protecting each transaction through a digital signature, rather than trusting a third-party mechanism.

Blockchain thus presents a self-regulating mechanism that incentivizes correct behavior, enticing "miners" to work on valid blocks (that is, those accepted by the majority) and reject invalid ones and remain motivated to solve a computational puzzle in order to gain financial incentives. This was originally described by "Nakamoto" as "incentive compatibility" – that there is an assumption that Bitcoin will remain stable as long as miners follow their economic incentives. Furthermore, the underlying blockchain technology eliminates the ability for any single entity to change the ledger without other parties (or nodes) being able to detect the changes made (Hackett, 2016).

Managing decentralization

Blockchain technology enables the type of new structures reflecting the manner in which way we communicate and share information today – that is, the decentralized way we conduct communication and business exchanges. This trend for decentralization, fueled by distributed communication systems of the Internet now culminating in the blockchain systems, is ultimately what underpins social media, crowdfunding, and what is commonly referred to as the "Internet of Things" (IoT). To a degree, this quest for decentralization has been accelerated with the erosion of trust in centralized systems and concerns over privacy.

Decentralization is a key blockchain feature. Its decentralized approach addresses "the centuries-old problem of *trust*, a social resource that is all too often in short supply, especially amid the current era's rampant concerns over the security of valuable data" (The World Bank, 2016). Blockchain relies on the group consensus mechanism regulating transactions in the competing environments without third authoritative parties (Tapscott & Tapscott, 2016). Transactions in the blockchain are validated through the process known as "mining" by the network members, whereby it is the network that performs the centralized function of the trusted third party. Network members validate transactions, and this is achieved by the consensus of majority (Welch, 2015). Because blockchain has the potential to create an infrastructure that no single person has the power to change, it might as well hold the potential to avoid the "tragedy of the commons" in the sense we know it.

Traditionally, we place trust in the third parties perceived to have the authority, and they are the ones who verify identities of all parties involved in market transactions. Conversely, consensus on the blockchain is achieved through a decentralized, pseudonymous protocol, which as an innovation plays a central role in its success. Simply put, it takes financial intermediaries out of the equation, allowing parties without a preestablished trust to conduct transactions safely: the security mechanisms are provided by the peers rather than by the third authoritative party.

Decentralization is a key disruptor of the existing structures. The need for a trusted third-party intermediary is replaced with a shared consensual ledger. This fundamentally challenges the traditional management thinking and organizational theory, where the starting assumption is that legitimate organizations or third parties are best suited to take up on the role of trust coordinators, assuming a source of power in their centralized positions (Seidel & Greve, 2017). Conversely, blockchain technologies enable trusted market transactions without a central authority, challenging the fundamental organizing principles of capital markets.

Managing transparency

If a bank claims to have deposits of $1 billion, it is nearly impossible for anyone on the outside to assess if that is true or if the bank hasn't already lost those $1 billion by handing out bad loans. For the average saver, the answer is that he or she basically cannot know. He can only hope that some regulating authority is watching over their shoulder.

The situation in the crypto world is completely different. If an exchange X claims that it has 100,000 bitcoins, or $1 billion in USD tether deposits, this is very swiftly verifiable on the associated blockchain. For example, if both Bitfinex and Binance have holdings of approximately 168,000 bitcoins in their principal Bitcoin wallet addresses, then this is visible on websites such as bitcoinforcharts.com that track such figures.

What about smaller players, new entrants, or simply entities located in other countries? Investors looking to buy into a promising new project need to open an account at an exchange located in another country. How can they decide whether it is trustworthy? For starters, just as with a local bank, they can take a look at the building it occupies – in this case the digital building. Is it well built? Is it riddled with spelling mistakes? Do deposits and withdrawals in multiple currencies work smoothly? After sending a minor amount, does the deposit credit to the account quickly, and is withdrawal possible equally promptly? Is it listed on the major exchange listing sites? Does it offer responsive customer service?

Building and promoting websites with all these functions is not cheap – it takes money, valuable time, and know-how. If everything more or less works – keeping in mind that the entire industry is in a constant state of flux – then it is a fair bet that the business is far more valuable as a running concern than as a one-time tool to rob depositors. Who would go to all that trouble just to steal a bit of money from depositors while at the same time risking arrest? Most users intuitively use this logic to assess potential service providers, and thus far losses from fraud have been minimal.

The same difference in transparency holds true even if something goes wrong. In the traditional financial world, as soon as something goes wrong, typically, a government entity becomes involved. The processes may take years, and in the meanwhile, investors are largely out of luck. For instance, in the 2011 MF Global bankruptcy, it took five years to complete handling of all claims, and for several years it appeared probable that small investors would essentially end up penniless. This long and indeterminate delay was disastrous for many of those investors. By contrast, in the digital world, far more efficient options are available to resolve such dilemmas. For example, investors can be offered a tradable token in lieu of immediate repayment. This was precisely the approach taken by Bitfinex after its servers were hacked in August 2016, leading to the loss of 119,756 bitcoins.

Although this hack left Bitfinex technically insolvent, they were back online within two weeks, issuing their users "BFX tokens" representing 36 percent of the total value of their previous holdings calculated in US dollars. This meant that not only were their users able to immediately regain access to 64 percent of their assets, they were also able to opt to trade away their BFX tokens at whatever price the market had on offer. Obviously, for most users this result was far more attractive than waiting five years for an uncertain payout. For those with confidence in Bitfinex, results were even better. They were able to pick up additional BFX tokens for as little as 15 percent of their par value of $1 USD. BFX holders could optionally convert these into Bitfinex equity, or simply wait for Bitfinex to pay them at par. Bitfinex redeemed all BFX tokens at par within 10 months of their issuance. Those who converted their BFX tokens into equity ended up with a return of over 1,000 percent on those investments.

Managing mistrust

Digital trust in the crypto world is certainly a numbers game. To a degree, the platforms are trustworthy because thousands use them, and if they are abused, the consequences are potentially high for a large number of users. Moreover, deposit amounts held by many platforms are somewhat transparent and thus speak for themselves in terms of capital backing. Nonetheless, digital trust in the crypto world is enabled by a dynamic interaction between other complex factors. It also results from the fact that there is a healthy equilibrium between "honest" and "dishonest" players.

The hacks particularly highlight the power of these newly created trust networks. Perhaps one of the most known breaches of security was the Mt. Gox hack revealed in 2014, whereby approximately 540,000 bitcoins were lost in total. This ultimately resulted in Mt. Gox declaring bankruptcy; as of November 2018, creditors are still waiting to be compensated. Mt. Gox was a Japan-based Bitcoin exchange, and at the time the largest in the world. High-value hack cases are, however, abundant, such as the DAO hack, which led to the controversial Ethereum transaction rollback, the Parity Wallet hack, and the Bitfinex hack mentioned earlier. And while security measures have clearly improved since Mt. Gox days, rapid expansion of the industry was probably been a major reason why major hacks continued to occur, at least until early 2018. One of the last publicized major cases was the January 2018 XEM hack of the Japanese Coincheck cryptocurrency exchange, resulting in the loss of $534 million USD equivalent.

Although these hacks do send ripples of fear across the trading community, at the same time, they have not managed to cripple the enthusiasm. Arguably, they lead to the overall increase of the industry standards, inspiring the evolutionary development through a "survival of the fittest", making the cryptocurrency industry more secure long term (Zycrypto, 2018). A study by Suberg (2018) shows that blockchain-related majority attacks, so called 51% attacks where a group of miners control the network mining hash rate, are both a credible and significant threat and something that directly impacts partner trust.

Another risk is that a user with a compromised private key cannot recover it, unlike in a centralized system, where reissue typically is possible. Personal identity preservation is nowhere near a guarantee and points to a need for a degree of trust among the participants for the blockchain to operate well. Christoffer De Geer, vice president of the first Swedish Bitcoin company, BTCX, stated to Crypto News (2018), hacks are "good for the industry as a whole. The more hacks we can have, while the industry is young, the better for the industry when it is established. If companies today learn how not to store digital value, and customers learn how not to give over everything they own to centralized third parties, while we can still change, and while the hits are not too devastating, that's all the better for the industry".

A short story from early 2018 entitled "*How I ended up with $55,000 in Crypto for free because of a hack*" illustrates this issue well. After originally appearing on Reddit (2018), the post went viral. The developers of the hacked blockchain decided to give people double what they had before the hack, but what the developers gained was increased value, making up for the loss after the company proved to be trustworthy following the hack. As suggested by the Redditor "Juicy Spark", that decision "was intentional. It was a lot easier for them to give everyone double what they had . . . then to sit through all this mess. It wasn't bad. We were only talking maybe a million extra coins in circulation compared to over a billion coins".

Millions of dollars in coins and tokens have repeatedly been stolen from cryptocurrency exchanges or wallets due to hacks. Consequently, the mainstream financial press has repeatedly labelled cryptocurrencies as a "moral hazard" with "too many hacks, too little security" (e.g. Bloomberg, 2018; CNN Money, 2018). Nonetheless, the interest in the industry continues to grow exponentially, and this is to a large degree related to the redefined notion of trust in this space.

A trust-mistrust equilibrium as a basis for investment

There is a balance between trust and mistrust in all human endeavor, and the digital world is no exception. The investment proposition offered by BiblePay, a "charity-focused Christian cryptocurrency", is a good example to illustrate this idea. This organization's mission – or value proposition – is described as giving to charity in abundance, helping to find cures for diseases, sharing the Gospel of Jesus, and decentralizing money. Considering that they have managed to stay afloat in the industry for a while, their proposition apparently proved appealing to at least some clients or investors. They allegedly funnel funds to BiblePay researchers who use "distributed Computing to assist in fighting diseases like cancer and HIV/AIDS", all while appealing to the environmentally conscious demographics.

Rather than "wasting energy that essentially just generates heat", they suggest that BiblePay takes a completely different approach: most of their computing resources "are used in research projects focused on finding cures for diseases", thus pioneering the energy-efficient method that is also respectful to the environment and "helps provide hope to people all around the world: when you participate as a BiblePay researcher you get BiblePay coins (BBP) based on the amount of research you do. This BBP is created in a block, but instead of being in the standard 7-minute block it is included in a daily 'superblock' that is distributed to researchers" (BiblePay.org).

For investors who view the BiblePay coin to be an investment worth considering, the question remains: do the gains from trust relationships offset the losses from relationships with other, seemingly less trustworthy parties? If an investor invests one bitcoin in nine projects that collapse, plus one bitcoin in a project which succeeds, how successful must that project be for the overall investment to generate a positive return? The answer is that one successful project must have the quite substantial returns of 1,000 percent. In the blockchain industry, such returns have for some time been achieved.

Concluding thoughts

The digital revolution is undoubtedly disrupting traditional structures. Early adopters have set about applying blockchains to everything from supply chain management to hospital records, the workings of government through transparent voting, and the digital signatures of e-ID (Roehrs, da Costa, & da Rosa Righi, 2017; Sullivan & Burger, 2017; Sun, Yan, & Zhang, 2016). Thus, the impact of blockchain use on society is significant, and the implications this may have on the creation of trust quite substantial. Similarly, cryptocurrencies are based on the fundamental idea of disintermediation, decentralization, and peer-to-peer networks enabling complete strangers to reach consensus without a third-party authority. This is in contrast to the centralized power model of the traditional financial sector. Such disruptions challenge how many people think of market transactions. However, they also provide opportunities to create new value propositions, allowing organizations to move beyond their traditional business models and to redefine their notions of trust in the contemporary organizing context.

It is apparent in the crypto world that trust and distrust serve as enablers of digital trust: prioritizing one dimension over the other (i.e., seeing trust only as beneficial and distrust only as harmful) implies that the interrelationship between the two is not fully understood. Mistrust reinforces trust. The problem of focusing only on a seemingly positive pole implies that the interrelationship between the two is not fully understood, and this leads to a negative reinforcing cycle (Lewis, 2000). Trust alone can lead to poor results. Thus, rather than eliminating the inherent paradox embodied in the notion of trust, embracing it helps to "construct a more workable certainty" (Lüscher & Lewis, 2008, p. 234). The ability to endorse distrust as a crucial aspect of digital trust may be essential for the long-term success of the industry. Understanding the balance between trust and suspicion, which exist in each society, helps to understand how societies actually work.

Whether blockchain is destined to replace traditional structures and usher in new business models and decentralized governance structures is yet to be seen, as well as how it will interact with traditional financial institutions. What is apparent, though, is that it is disrupting our thinking about the fundamental rules of a market economy and the traditional approach to organizations and interactions between them. Seidel (2017) suggests that we currently do not have adequate organizational theory to explain the phenomenon of distributed trust in the crypto world; it fundamentally transforms boundaries of organizations, thus challenging traditional assumptions about organizations being an ideal entity to manage market transactions. It has fundamentally disrupted existing power structures, questioning their future role and reason for existence (Yermack, 2017). Consequently, traditional notions of trust may need to be updated (Seidel, 2017).

References

Adner, R., & Kapoor, R. (2010). Value creation in innovation ecosystems. *Strategic Management Journal, 31*(3), 306–333.

Bitcoinforcharts.com. (2018). *Top 100 richest bitcoin addresses.* Retrieved September 19, 2018 from https://bitinfocharts.com/top-100-richest-bitcoin-addresses.html

Bloomberg. (2018). *$2.3 Billion in Losses Highlights Crypto's Moral Hazard. Too many hacks. Too little security.* Retrieved July 10, 2018 from www.bloomberg.com/view/articles/2018-06-11/-2-3-billion-in-losses-highlights-crypto-s-moral-hazard

Bohnet, I., & Meier, S. (2005). Deciding to distrust. *KSG Working Paper No. RWP05.* Retrieved September 19, 2018 from https://ssrn.com/abstract=839225

Bonneau, J., Miller, A., Clark, J., Narayanan, A., Kroll, J., & Felten, E. (2015). Research perspectives on Bitcoin and second-generation cryptocurrencies. *Symposium on Security and Privacy.* San Jose, CA, Retrieved October 18, 2018 from www.ieee-security.org/TC/SP2015/papers-archived/6949a104.pdf

Bracamonte, V., & Okada, H. (2017). *The issue of user trust in decentralized applications running on blockchain platforms, 2017 IEEE International Symposium on Technology and Society (ISTAS).* Sidney, Australia. Retrieved October 29, 2018 from https://ieeexplore.ieee.org/document/8318975

Castelfranchi, C., & Falcone, R. (2001). *Trust and deception in virtual societies.* Norwell, MA: Kluwer Academic Publishers.

CNN Money. (2018). *Crypto hacks: Is your bitcoin investment safe?* Retrieved July 10, 2018 from https://money.cnn.com/2018/06/13/investing/bitcoin-cryptocurrency-hacks-security/index.html

Cohney, S., Hoffman, D. A., Sklaroff, J., & Wishnick, D. A. (2018, July 17). *Coin-Operated Capitalism.* Retrieved September 1, 2018 from https://ssrn.com/abstract=3215345

Corea, F. (2019). The convergence of AI and blockchain. In *Applied artificial intelligence: Where AI can be used in business* (1st ed., pp. 19–26). Cham, Switzerland: Springer.

Crosby, M., Nachiappan, Pattanayak, P., Verma, S., & Kalyanaraman, V. (2015). *Blockchain technology: Beyond bitcoin. Sutardja center for entrepreneurship & technology.* California: Berkeley University of California.

The Crunch. (2018). *With at least $1.3 billion invested globally in 2018, VC funding for blockchain blows past 2017 totals.* Retrieved August 1, 2018 from https://techcrunch.com/2018/05/20/with-at-least-1-3-billion-invested-globally-in-2018-vc-funding-for-blockchain-blows-past-2017-totals/

Crypto News. (2018). *An interview: Hacks are good for the crypto industry.* Retrieved August 28, 2018 from https://cryptonews.com/exclusives/vp-of-the-first-swedish-btc-company-hacks-are-good-for-the-i-1222.htm

Eskandari, S., Clark, J., Barrera, D., & Stobert, E. (2015). *A first look at the usability of bitcoin key management.* Workshop on Usable Security, San Diego, US. Retrieved August 28,

2018 from www.ndss-symposium.org/ndss2015/ndss-2015-usec-programme/first-look-usability-bitcoin-key-management/

Eurich, M., Oertel, N., & Boutellier, R. (2010). The impact of perceived privacy risks on organizations' willingness to share item-level event data across the supply chain. *Electronic Commerce Research, 10*(3), 423–440.

Foroglou, G., & Tsilidou, A. L. (2015). *Further applications of the blockchain.* 12th Student Conference n Managerial Science and Technology, Athens, Greece. Retrieved October 28, 2018 from www.researchgate.net/publication/276304843_Further_applications_of_the_blockchain

Granovetter, M. (1985). Economic action and social structure: The problem of embeddedness. *American Journal of Sociology, 91*, 481–510.

Hackett, R. (2016). *Wait, what is blockchain*? Retrieved July 18, 2018 from http://fortune.com/2016/05/23/blockchain-definition/

The Harvard Gazette. (2018). *On the web, privacy in peril.* Retrieved August 18, 2018 from https://news.harvard.edu/gazette/story/2018/03/facebooks-privacy-problem-may-erode-web-trust-harvard-analyst-says/

Heires, K. (2016). The risks and rewards of blockchain technology. *Risk Management, 63*(2), 4.

Iansiti, M., & Lakhani, K. (2017, January–February). The truth about blockchain. *Harvard Business Review, 95*, 118–127.

Kewell, B., Adams, R., & Parry, G. (2017). Blockchain for good? *Strategic Change: Briefings in Entrepreneurial Finance, 6*(5), 429–437.

Kroll, J. A., Davey, I. C., & Felten, E. W. (2013). *The economics of bitcoin mining, or bitcoin in the presence of adversaries.* The Twelfth Workshop on the Economics of Information Security (WEIS 2013), Washington, US. Retrieved August 28, 2018 from www.econinfosec.org/archive/weis2013/papers/KrollDaveyFeltenWEIS2013.pdf

Kwon, I., & Suh, T. (2004). Factors affecting the level of trust and commitment in supply chain relationships. *Journal of Supply Chain Management, 40*(1), 4–14.

Lee, L. (2016). New kids on the blockchain: How Bitcoin's technology could reinvent the stock market. *Hastings Business Law Journal, 12*(2). Retrieved August 23, 2018 from papers.ssrn.com/sol3/papers.cfm?abstract_id=2656501

Lewis, M. (2000). Exploring paradox: Toward a more comprehensive guide. *Academy of Management Review, 25*(4), 760–776.

Lüscher, L., & Lewis, M. (2008). Organizational change and managerial sensemaking: Working through paradox. *Academy of Management Journal, 51*(2), 221–240.

Manski, S. (2017). Building the blockchain world: Technological commonwealth or just more of the same? *Strategic Change, 26*(5), 511–522.

Mayer, R. C., Davis, J. H., & Schoorman, F. D. (1995). An integrative model of organizational trust. *The Academy of Management Review, 20*(3), 709–734.

Möllering, G. (2001). The nature of trust: From Georg Simmel to a theory of expectation, interpretation and suspension. *Sociology, 35*(2), 403–420.

Nakamoto, S. (2008). *Bitcoin: A peer-to-peer electronic cash system.* Retrieved May 28, 2018 from www.bitcoin.org/bitcoin.pdf

North, D. C. (1990). *Institutions, institutional change, and economic performance.* New York: Cambridge University Press.

Reddit. (2018). *How I ended up with $55,000 in Crypto for free because of a hack.* Retrieved April 8, 2018 from www.reddit.com/r/CryptoCurrency/comments/88wx8z/how_i_ended_up_with_55000_in_crypto_for_free/

Richerson, P., & Boyd, R. (1998). The evolution of human ultrasociality. In I. Eibl-Eibesfeldt & F. K. Salter (Eds.), *Ethnic conflict and indoctrination* (pp. 71–95). Oxford: Berghahn.

Roehrs, A., da Costa, C. A., & da Rosa Righi, R. (2017). OmniPHR: A distributed architecture model to integrate personal health records. *Journal of Biomedical Informatics, 71*, 70–81.

Rousseau, D. N., Sitkin, S. B., Burt, R. S., & Camerer, C. (1998). Not so different after all: A cross discipline view of trust. *Academy of Management Review, 23*(3), 393–404.

Schwab, K. (2016, January 14). *The fourth industrial revolution: What it means, how to respond.* World Economic Forum. Retrieved April 21, 2018 from www.weforum.org/agenda/2016/01/thefourthindustrialrevolutionwhatitmeansandhowtorespond/

Seidel, M. (2017). Questioning centralized organizations in a time of distributed trust. *Journal of Management Inquiry*, 1–5.

Seidel, M., & Greve, H. (2017). Emergence: How novelty, growth, and formation shape organizations and their ecosystems. In M. Seidel & H. Greve (Eds.), *Emergence* (Research in the Sociology of Organizations, Vol. 50, pp. 1–27). Bingley, UK: Emerald Publishing Limited.

Suberg, W. (2018). *Ethereum classic 51% attack would cost just $55 Mln, Result in $1 Bln profit: Research.* Retrieved September 23, 2018 from https://cointelegraph.com/news/ethereum-classic-51-attack-would-cost-just-55-mln-result-in-1-bln-profit-research

Sullivan, C., & Burger, E. (2017). E-residency and blockchain. *Computer Law & Security Review, 33*(4), 470–481.

Sun, J., Yan, J., & Zhang, K. (2016). Blockchain-based sharing services: What blockchain technology can contribute to smart cities. *Financial Innovation, 2*(26), 1–9.

Tapscott, D., & Tapscott, A. (2016). *Blockchain revolution: How the technology behind bitcoin and other cryptocurrencies is changing the world.* New York, NY: Portfolio/Penguin.

Tyler, T. R. (1990). *Why people obey the law.* New Haven, CT: Yale University Press.

Walport, M. (2016). *Distributed ledger technology: Beyond block chain.* Technical Report, UK Government Office for Science. Retrieved November 18, 2018 from www.gov.uk/government/uploads/system/uploads/attachment_data/file/492972/gs-16-1-distributed-ledger-technology.pdf

Watson, R. (2009). Constitutive practices and Garfinkel's notion of trust: Revisited. *Journal of Classical Sociology, 9*(4), 475–499.

Welch, A. (2015). The Bitcoin blockchain as financial market infrastructure: A consideration of operational risk. *Legislation and Public Policy, 8*, 837–893.

Werbach, K. (2018). *The blockchain and the new architecture of trust.* Cambridge, MA: MIT Press.

Williamson, O. (1993). Calculativeness, trust, and economic organization. *The Journal of Law & Economics, 36*(1), 453–486.

The World Bank. (2016). *Blockchain technology: Redefining trust for a global, digital economy.* Retrieved September 17, 2018 from http://blogs.worldbank.org/ic4d/blockchain-technology-redefining-trust-global-digital-economy

Yermack, D. (2017). Corporate governance and blockchains. *Review of Finance, 21*(1), 7–31.

Zarifis, A., Cheng, X., Efthymiou, L., & Dimitriou, S. (2014). Consumer trust in digital currency enabled transactions. *Business Information Systems, 183*, 241–254.

Zycrypto. (2018). *Survival of the fittest: Can hacks strengthen the crypto industry?* Retrieved August 28, 2018 from https://zycrypto.com/survival-of-the-fittest-can-hacks-strengthen-the-crypto-industry/

Zyskind, G., Nathan, O., & Pentland, A. (2015). *Decentralizing privacy: Using blockchain to protect personal data.* Conference: 2015 IEEE Security and Privacy Workshops (SPW). Retrieved November 23, 2018 from https://ieeexplore.ieee.org/document/7163223

Chapter 6

Lightbulb concrete

Bronwin Patrickson

Introduction

The term trustless transactions (Swan 2015; Kiviat 2015) refers to the notion that blockchain technologies enable trust where it wouldn't normally exist so that even strangers can transact with confidence online without the need for costly and cumbersome third-party authentication. But what happens when technologies designed to automate 'trust' amongst strangers are applied to creative collaborations between colleagues? By enabling data sharing between distributed, but linked, ledgers accessed by a team of cooperative and yet separate entities, blockchain technologies are increasingly framed as tools for collaborative business models (Deloitte 2018).

This study explores that potential in the context of the games industry. Games development involves cross-disciplinary teams of artists, animators, designers and programmers. Working collaboratively, this sort of creative teamwork can build high levels of trust. At the same time, since computer game development is a highly mediated craft, much of that work is tracked by the digital software programs that simultaneously enable it. Team members work on computers, share screens and also often communicate with each other through audiovisual gaming channels. Data about time spent, platforms used and tools employed, for example, can potentially be shared in order to build a collective intelligence resource for the games industry. For start-up teams in particular, this rich knowledge base could provide a valuable guide to best practice (Chen, Chiang, and Storey 2012).

Mediation of games development processes also introduces the potential to map and automate complex micro payments. Automated payments of multiple, distinct contributors have already been successfully trialled on the *Musicoin* platform, for example, and this level of automation is likely to increase. Could the capacity to automatically track code changes seen in collaborative open-source coding repositories like Github be helpful in this regard? As society becomes increasingly systematised (Zimmerman 2015) and subsequently increasingly tracked (Van Dijck 2014), the question whether automated contribution records might potentially be linked to future licensing agreements is increasingly pertinent.

Despite these alluring possibilities, it is still not clear what digital collaborations authorised by trustless technologies might mean for the people involved, however. For example, a review of the literature related to blockchain technologies and trust in the sharing economy[1] shows that "the conceptualization of trust differs substantially between the (two) contexts" (Hawlitschek, Notheisen, and Teubner 2018: 50). "Trust machines", or blockchain systems that "industrialise trust"(Berg, Davidson, and Potts 2017: 2) by managing self-interest towards a cooperative goal, create positive expectations due to their systematic capacities to withstand human intervention, whereas the more multifaceted conceptions of trust in sharing economy contexts are more likely to collaborate with human intervention and therefore tend to be based upon judgements of interpersonal ability, benevolence and integrity (Gefen and Straub 2004; Lu, Zhao, and Wang 2010), in partnership with system design (Keymolen 2013). In this case, trustworthiness is signalled by a range of means including verification, ratings and reviews, insurances and support, web design and user representation (Teubner and Hawlitschek 2018). These multilayered judgements can be cognitive or affect based (Yang, Lee, Lee, Chung, and Koo 2016) and also involve power relations (Castelfranchi and Falcone 2010).

The divergence between these two concepts of trust reflects the limits, as much as the specific capacities of automated trust, or the '(a)lgorithmic authority' (Lustig and Nardi 2015) of the underlying smart contracts, derived from such characteristics as the perceived clarity of the contract and its integrity over time, as well as its ability to resist subsequent manipulation (Fröwis and Böhme 2017). It also indicates the confusion that can arise when a term like trust that is commonly used to describe "the intention to accept vulnerability based upon positive expectations" (Rousseau, Sitkin, Burt, and Camerer 1998: 395) is applied interchangeably in different contexts.

Bearing this difference in mind, the primary case study for this exploration involves young start-up games development teams chosen to be part of the UK Games Fund's Tranzfuser program, designed to help new UK games production graduates make the transition from university studies to a professional production career. The £5000 Tranzfuser grants sponsor the production of game demos which emerging developer teams can take to market. As part of their support, the UK Games Fund has been experimenting with a blockchain-based IP management tool dubbed The Global Tal Registry. This experimental IP management tool aims to help teams develop flexible revenue shares as project proofs until they are ready to tackle the more formal and potentially costly legal process of company formation (Durrant and Hogarth 2016). In the early phases of creative development, teams are often fluid and changeable. The Tal Registry is designed to respond to that creative flux yet at the same time provide enough structural support to give developing teams the confidence to work outside of their immediate circles of trust.

The following sections of this chapter explain the ways in which the various creative collaborations unfolding during that development process were interrogated, as well as the results that emerged. What these results imply for future automated licensing and knowledge-exchange strategies are discussed in the final section of this chapter, with reference to the potential opportunities posed by emerging Web 3.0 technologies, linked to Tim-Berners Lee's vision of a semantic data network

> [in which computers] become capable of analysing all the data on the Web – the content, links, and transactions between people and computers. A 'Semantic Web', which makes (it) possible, (for) the day-to-day mechanisms of trade, bureaucracy and our daily lives (to) be handled by machines talking to machines.
>
> (Berners-Lee and Fischetti 2001: chapter 12)

In Steve Whittaker's 2002 meta-review of "Theories and Methods in Mediated Communication", he argues that in order to effectively map the affordances of any mediation technology, there first needs to be a rich and nuanced consideration of definitions of interaction, context and expressivity. With that in mind, I will now review these three considerations in turn, before turning to the empirical study.

Interaction

Interaction is a loose term that can incorporate collaboration as much as consensus. Game-writer Chris Crawford defines interaction as "a cyclic process between two or more active agents in which each agent alternately listens, thinks and speaks (terms taken metaphorically)" (Crawford 2012: 159). This conversational image implies a feedback loop or enacted dialogue that emphasises a shared process of meaning making and includes metaphoric dialogues, such as dancing.

Blockchain technologies also create a type of dialogue: an algorithmic, collective encounter that generates a proven record. Reijers and Coeckelbergh (2018) argue that these sorts of organising technologies configure transactions in a way that makes them increasingly rigid, like plots. Indeed, by capturing the fluid mutability of digital identity and freezing it in a moment of authenticated time, blockchain technologies have formalised a type of digital rarity that never existed before. Reijers and Coeckelbergh (2018) also argue that when automated code mediates collective identities it configures a narrative (about money or security, for example) that refigures social interaction in the form of a transaction. The potential implications of reducing that which is priceless (art, friendship, love) to a transaction are concerning. At the same time, quantification, or counting, can provide value recognition for those whose work traditionally goes under-rewarded, like domestic workers and care givers (Waring and Steinem 1988). In other words, formal acknowledgment where none previously existed is potentially transformational, but not always reductive. Perhaps quantification itself is less the issue than is the potential it introduces for one aspect of the networked self (fluidity, fractionalism, for example) to exclude the other (form), along with the value judgements being challenged as a result of this process. As rules for encoded, procedural engagement, blockchain technologies also create new procedural possibilities, such as financial and social value reconfiguration in collaboration with other variable conditions like the decision to tokenise or certify particular behaviours within the supply chain. By privileging a more collaborative, sector approach, public blockchain technologies may therefore require substantial business model transformations. Despite the challenges that such disruptions pose, the efficiencies gained as a result of the ability to break down data silos and support consortium actions via data-sharing technologies are driving these efforts (Ølnes, Ubacht, and Janssen 2017).

Context

Ironically, blockchain technologies create consensus on the back of self-interest and competition. For example, Bitcoin is still the most secure of all the cryptocurrencies due to a costly and energy-consuming proof-of-work authentication process driven by the promise of financial reward (O'Dwyer and Malone 2014). Miners compete to be the first to solve a complex, cryptographic puzzle in order to win the allotted Bitcoin cash reward (the transaction fee). Their problem-solving efforts act like a de facto timestamp that proves these transactions were recorded on this block, in this time period. The new block is given a cryptographic hash number ID that includes the hash of the previous block, and in this way each block in the chain is authorised and linked to the previous block in turn. Over time these cryptographic puzzles have become harder and demand more computing power to solve. In other words, blockchain technologies can successfully coordinate self-interest for shared benefits, but they are not by their nature public services, and they need to be designed accordingly.

Automation is a valuable tool. It can save time and offer additional computation enhancements, such as GPS navigation, as much as proof of work. The challenge is how to best integrate automation and humanism within digitally mediated creative contexts. The gaming industry, which is commercialised and highly mediated but also motivated by collaboration and creativity goals, thus provides a helpful case study of the ways that formality, informality, independence, interdependence, machines and people might coexist.

Whilst the blockchain is ingenious precisely because it coordinates self-interested profit motives, nevertheless, as the team from UK Games Fund points out in their "Tal Stories" white paper (Durrant and Hogarth 2016), ingenious is not the same as astute. As yet, no level of automation can substitute for a basic team agreement at the outset. Teams still need to discuss and decide responsibility for prior work, as well as the alignment and/or differentiations between personal and collective visions, "so a real 'smart contract' would need to read minds if it could automate this initial step"(Durrant and Hogarth 2016: 3).

Expressivity

In this context, expressivity is both an individual and group concern. Just as digital environments mediate the participatory level of "influence [upon] the form or content" (Nakevska, van der Sanden, Funk, Hu, and Rauterberg 2017: 97), so too the task at hand, the team collaborating on that task and the tools employed to undertake that collaboration will all inform and influence that process.

Automated working environments act like assembly spaces. For example, the sort of game-play that can be produced using a game development software tool suite like Unity, a self-described 'game engine', is limited by the design of the Unity software (UnrealForum 2018). Working within these limits, game developers can still build and personalise seemingly endless varieties of two-dimensional and three-dimensional games. Thus, the limits of the system can either be experienced as creative aids or as frustrations, depending on the aims and experience of the maker.

In terms of expressive interactions, the more meaningful those mediated actions or choices are within that context, the more "agency" (Murray 2001: 394) that users are said to enjoy. But what sorts of meaningful agency exists in automated collaborations, "characterized by the fact that their core capability is algorithmic coordination" (Roio and Jelincic 2017), such as data sharing and proof of work? For some, agency is only possible when there is also some sense of personal control over that data. For example, the quantified self-movement embraces personal data-monitoring practices such as behaviour monitoring, location tracking, medical self-diagnostics and personal genome sequencing as a form of self-knowledge (Wolf 2010; Swan 2013). For others, agency equates to the chance or challenge to game the system and make the numbers work to personal advantage. For instance, the appeal of big data for corporate advantage could be classified as the appeal of uncovering the hidden laws or patterns in play and responding accordingly. Both of these aspects need to be considered in the design of any data-sharing application.

The study

For this study, the Global Tal Registry tool was tested during the EGX Games Expo. Billed as "the UK's biggest game event"(EGX 2018), EGX is a video game trade fair that gives consumers the chance to play over 200 games ahead of their official release and has attracted over 80,000 attendees (Batchelor 2017). During the 2018 EGX event, 18 hopeful Tranzfuser teams, each consisting of four or more budding games makers, gathered to show a demo game to prospective publishers and gaming enthusiasts, whilst also competing for further development funds.

The UK Games Fund coined the term Tal with reference to the dual meaning of the word talent, first in terms of who does the work and also with reference to the ancient currency of Talents. Much like shares in a company, Tals are a much simpler distribution of shares in creative IP. The Tal system is divided between those stakes that offer voting rights (silver Tals), or only revenue shares (copper Tals), or both. There is also a facility for external dispute resolution with no revenue entitlement (The gold Tal, a facility which the UK Games Fund holds at this point).

In order to explore the broader implications and logistics of such an application, an interview-based, qualitative approach was chosen. This allows for in depth analysis of participant responses and gives participants more freedom to express their unique perspectives. Combined with observation of a Tal allocation meeting and hands-on social network analysis conducted by a selection of four teams, this study provides insight into the participatory experience of mediated collaboration, linked to the prospect of automated authentication.

During the four-day 2018 EGX event held at Birmingham's NEC Stadium from September 20–23, a series of interviews were conducted with a sample of 36 young games makers (those on location at the Tranzfuser stand, available to speak with the researcher and familiar with the Global Tal Registry system) regarding their IP management approach and data-sharing practices. These opinion-based samples were then supplemented by an in-depth social network analysis study conducted with four members of four select Tranzfuser teams. Those four teams were chosen according to location (two were based in Scotland, where this study originated) and context: two of the teams had already formed a limited company prior to the competition. Also, at least two of these teams had experienced challenging line-up changes prior to the competition.

Four members of each sample team were interviewed individually, apart from the other members of their team, and asked to represent the demo development process both in terms of contribution and communication flows using a hands-on method of social network analysis known as net-mapping developed by Schiffer and Hauck (Schiffer and Hauck 2010). Net-mapping generally involves visualising and making explicit those networks, people and things that can help a team or individual to achieve their goals. The process also measures the perceived reach of that influence. During interviews, participants first identify relevant actors of influence, then how and whom they influence (e.g., through funds, commissions, feedback, inspiration, social acceptance, etc.) and then the value or strength of their influence (articulated in the height of representative influence towers). In this study, the net-mapping technique was adjusted to demonstrate the contribution of team members to the development of a particular demo rather than focusing upon the influence of external networks. To complete the process, goals and conflicts were strategically compared and discussed, and communication flows mapped.

For the purposes of this study, the net-mapping method provided an ideal way to help articulate team work contributions. One of the key aspects of emerging technology applications that this research focuses upon are the potential tensions between formal versus informal working methods. Thus, this method was deliberately chosen to help articulate those potential nuances in an easy-to-use and yet also tangible visual and kinaesthetic format.

For this task, each team member was asked to place a stack of coloured blocks like dominos on a piece of butcher's paper, so that each individual stack would represent a different team member. Each member was also asked to represent their fellow team member's comparative level of contribution by changing the height of the stack. Beyond these two directions, each interviewee was invited to freely choose the colour and placement of each block on the page. Whilst they did so, each participant was encouraged to explain their choices. Participants were also asked to complete the representation by drawing lines between the stacks in order to show the lines of communication between the various team members.

Although photos of these team work development maps are shared in this paper, for the sake of privacy, the interview transcripts are kept private, and the researcher did not share them with the rest of the team without the relevant permission of those individuals concerned. This sort of subjective documentation can't be taken as a "mirror" of an event, but the comparison of these individual "selective interpretations" (McCarthy and Wright 2004: 119), where some details can be withheld depending on what participants deem relevant or how they frame their perspective of their individual role within a group dynamic, can also help to build a more multidimensional view of the team experience.

Bias in participant demographics was difficult to avoid due to the male-dominated nature of the gaming industry (Gray, Buyukozturk, and Hill 2017), and in the case of Tranzfuser competition, a focus upon recent graduates. Participants were generally between the ages of 20 and 30 years old, and most had experience of undergraduate education, although some team members were also working on these projects as contractors. Only one of the 16 core team members interviewed was female, whilst two of the participants interviewed on location in the Tranzfuser stand were also female.

In addition to the in-depth, individual net-mapping interviews, 36 members of the general Tranzfuser cohort were asked a shorter series of three questions:

1 What can you tell me about your experience using the Global Tal Registry?
2 Are you aware it is intended to be a blockchain registration system? Would blockchain registration change your decision to use it again?
3 What are your thoughts about also potentially sharing (anonymised) information on workflows, platforms, working processes and times with the broader gaming community using these sorts of secured, automated technologies?

Findings: the Tal redistribution meeting

Team 1 revised their Tal distribution during the development phase, largely because the project lead reduced his share of the silver Tals, preferring to acknowledge the importance of the emerging team identity. Adjustments were made to even out those distributions (previously 190,000 lead/170,000 rest of team, now 175,000 lead/165,000 rest of team), whilst ensuring that the founder retained a final decider vote. Extra copper Tals were also awarded to a contract artist who was working remotely and busy on other projects but whose advice had proven influential to the development of the team's visual design approach.

The short survey

1 **What can you tell me about your experience using the Global Tal Registry?**

For those who were unfamiliar with business practice, this simplified rights management system was a universally positive experience. Perceived benefits included the simplicity of the process combined with the ability to use it as a test bed team management structure. Teams that had already incorporated as a limited company found the Tal Registry's more informal system less useful for their purposes.

2 **Are you aware it is intended to be a blockchain registration system? Would blockchain registration change your decision to use it again?**

Only two people were familiar enough with blockchain technologies to attempt to answer this question. One said they liked the idea of it being secure and anonymised. Another thought blockchain was used for criminal transactions, and they couldn't see why it would be relevant for creative IP registration.

3 **What are your thoughts about also potentially sharing (anonymised) information on workflows, platforms, working processes and times with the broader gaming community using these sorts of secured, automated technologies?**

Perhaps reflective of the open-source tradition in the games industry, all bar 3 out of 36 respondents thought this was a good idea in principle. Perceived benefits included the ability to gain an overview perspective regarding best practice, as well as the potential to hold the industry more accountable in terms of realistic working hours and crunch time demands. Reservations focused upon the risk to competitive advantage or fears regarding the loss of personal control and the risk of comparative critique, which underlines the potential importance of cooperative ownership of the data but may also reflect a lack of familiarity with this approach.

The net-mapping exercise

Due to the intensity of the Tranzfuser game development challenge, at EGX, team trust levels were rated highly amongst all present. However, at least two of the teams had experienced work management issues, so that trust was also conditional upon the demonstrated investment of other team members.

Team 1: team work takes priority

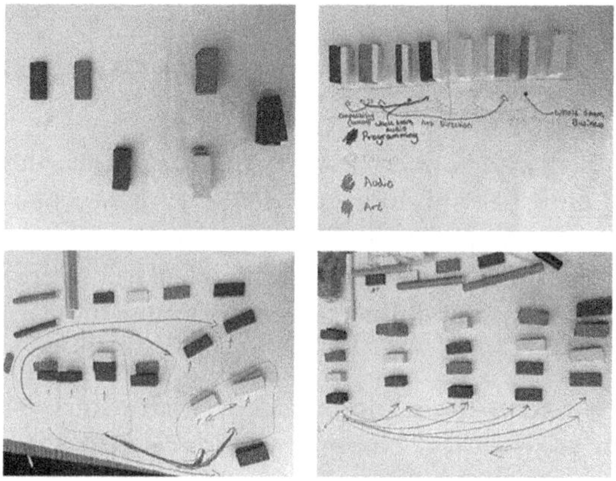

The core members of this team met at university but planned to continue as a company, taking on freelance work to help fund their efforts. Whilst one member suggested the original idea, the game demo concept was substantially developed by the group overall. The team thus claimed relatively equal IP distribution and also enjoyed generally positive relations. Collaboration strategies refined in process included rules like anybody could attend a special interest meeting and had a right to be heard.

Team 2: value compositions

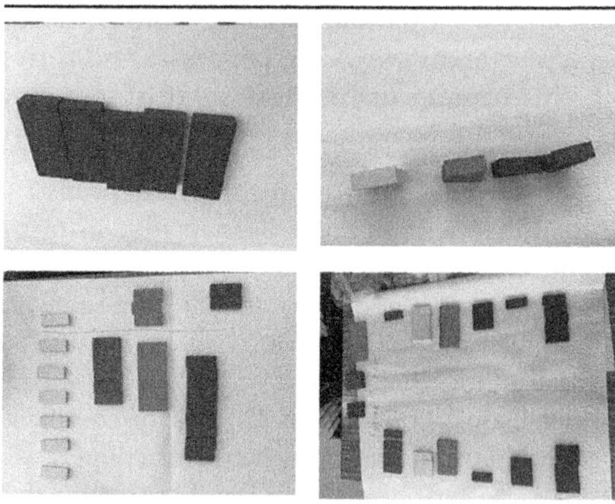

This team has ambitions to become Scotland's top VR games producer. Members met through business incubation programs, which, according to the founder, informed their professional approach. This team was already incorporated, and with a complex share structure already in place, Tal allocation was less relevant. Work-tracking records had helped adjudicate a past dispute. Nevertheless, it was pointed out that time on task is still only one measure of contribution.

Team 3: contribution vs influence

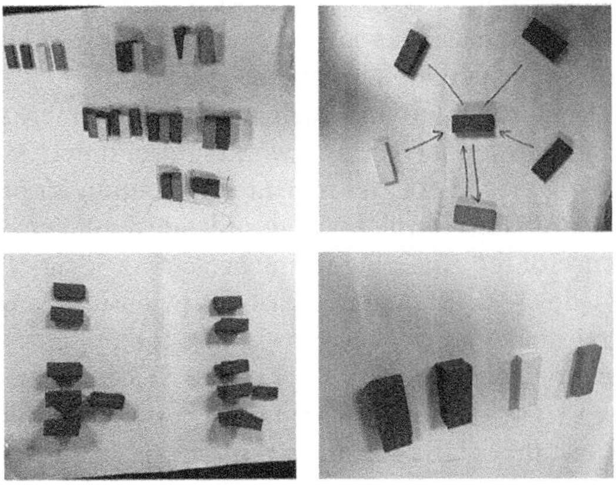

This team worked across two businesses, so that the main conduit for team communication across both was a creative manager rather than a coder, which led to a discussion about the distinction between contribution and influence (see the two differing blue spreads). Team goals centered upon gaining a publisher for their demo game and establishing flat team structures long term.

Team 4: the Importance of dev logs

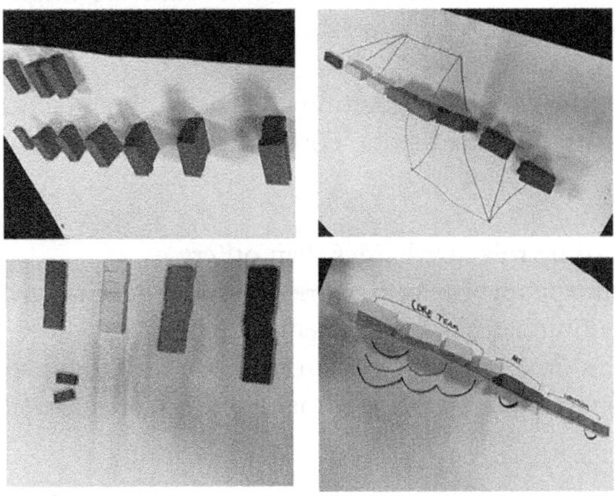

This university team kept daily developer (dev) logs using the basecamp software. Tied to dev log results, this team decided revenue shares according to time- and result-based contributions. The dev logs also helped to adjudicate a difficult team dispute when one member wasn't seen to be pulling their weight. The team's ambitions centered upon winning Tranzfuser.

Discussion

One of the reasons for using social network analysis in this study was to check whether these communication flows influenced the distribution of Tals. From these results, it appears that they have a significant influence. For instance, contractors who work remotely are generally less embedded in the team structure, reflected in a tendency to allocate contractors copper Tals (monetary rewards) rather than silver Tals (monetary rewards combined with voting rights). Also, whilst the project leads tended to commit more time than the rest of the team, all four of the founders interviewed were mindful to recognise the value of the emerging team identity. The observed Tal redistribution meeting is indicative of this shift over the course of the project. The motivational value of flat management structures and shared value recognition was also commonly deemed to be an important consideration. These cultural values are likely to reflect the close interdependencies of collaborative game development work.

Further research is required in order to ascertain which aspects of the emerging group identity might also be reflected in social networking data flows. As Team 3's experience made clear, for example, development contribution is not always the same as creative influence. This is true for both individual influence and the more ephemeral influence of the emerging team character or identity. Even if social networking data flows can document changes in group team communication activity, it is still unlikely that they can capture the full character of an emerging group identity and its influence upon creative decisions.

Thus, although automated work tracking systems are highly convenient and useful ways to track contribution, they don't capture everything. Measuring contribution purely according to time, for example, can miss important social considerations and also invites system gaming. Time-based measurements can encourage long working days but also potentially less productive working hours. Equally, as one interviewee also pointed out, a short meeting might be key to a team's success – and yet that value might only become apparent months later.

Another participant made the astute suggestion that any attempt to reward participants based on output needed to be contextualised by four key considerations:

- Difficulty of task, because some roles are harder than others.
- Time available, because some people can only work part time, or remotely.
- Quality of output, because time does not always equal ability.
- Prior knowledge, because in situations where team members are taking on a number of roles, they are just as often novice as master of those combined tasks.

Whilst differentiating the value of individual contributions may be a useful consideration, it also risks team work relationships that place a strong emphasis upon hierarchical contribution measures. Another consideration is whether output is always the best measure of time efficiency. Even time spent daydreaming can become essential as long as it is linked to a work program and broad-based development trajectory. This indicates the value of a broader, sectoral analysis of workflows over time and also across a number of teams in order to better understand the nature and/or importance of these productivity peaks and troughs to the overall development trajectory.

Supplemented by an open and supportive management style, automated work-tracking systems were most useful in terms of work contribution management. Whilst they didn't necessarily motivate hard work (since creative teams are generally motivated by creative goals, rather than productivity outcomes

(Malik and Butt 2017)) and indeed can potentially demotivate workers if those being watched feel unsafe and lack a sense of ownership, or respect within that process (D'Urso 2006), nevertheless they provide useful evidence of a problem when issues do arise, as they can in remote teams. Each team interviewed preferred the transparency and camaraderie of face-to-face teamwork (which can also mitigate the risk of system gaming) but also valued the availability and skill of remote workers.

Any ability to ease the administrative load through automation systems was generally welcomed. The teams that used manual dev logs regarded them as an invaluable work management resource and an essential aspect of their practice but also time consuming and easy to forget, so they require constant reminders and value reiteration. When doing so, care needs to be taken to ensure that they don't overly formalise the creative development process and introduce the sort of prescriptive rigidity that Reijers and Coeckelbergh (2018) refer to, however.

Thus, there is a lot to be gained by sharing those records beyond the immediate team in order to build up a collective knowledge that enables the entire sector to price and schedule itself and potentially also share the costs of machine learning analytics that support efforts to work smarter rather than harder. Ideally, such records would either be anonymous, or to some extent private, so that individual workers aren't publicly compared without their consent and penalised as a result of these comparisons (a fear expressed by at least one young developer). It is also likely to be important that individual contributors have the right to share ownership of that data so that they have the option to co-opt their own work record, for example, and make it simultaneously available for potential recruiters in an automatically updated profile feed (another possibility which a few developers discussed, with interest).

What blockchain registration of creative IP offers is at this point unclear. Although creative commons licenses have been recognised in European courts of law (CreativeCommons 2018), the legal status of blockchain registration is still quite abstract. Blockchain registration systems like *Ascribe*, for example, are more likely to grant a sense of ownership rather than guaranteed legal recourse (Christies 2018). It is also worth bearing in mind that company registration regulations may well be complex for a reason, such as to ensure that companies adhere to fair trade principles. Without some mechanism to also promote ethical business practice, blockchain business registration risks becoming a strategy for compliance avoidance. Nevertheless, for start-ups, the process of forming a limited company can seem overwhelmingly complex and prohibitively costly (one participant wondered whether that was the point in order to prompt lucrative fines), so there is value in exploring simpler, more streamlined test bed structures. It may be that future solutions to the challenge of keeping legislative pace with the fast-changing nature of digital disruption is to partner something like the Global Tal Registry with a more flexible and responsive ethics review board system. One participant suggested that these semi-formal alternatives might also be particularly useful for fan creation networks, which can often continue for many years with numerous contributors over time.

The value of emplotment (Reijers and Coeckelbergh 2018) or formalisation is precisely so that agreed interactions proceed without subsequent human intervention, and "code is law" (Lessig 1999). As computing science theorist Kieran O'Hara argues, to assume that code is therefore interchangeable with law is a "dangerous fallacy" (O'hara 2017: 100), however. Laws are developed democratically, can be challenged (for example, when fraud, or duress, or compromised capacity are proven) and can also be broken, whereas software development is a much more opaque process (O'hara 2017). Nevertheless, parties to coded smart contracts still have agency; they may negotiate the initial terms and can choose to participate, or not. When problems do arise, those agreements are also potentially negotiable when mechanisms are in place to enable this. Similarly, whilst smart contracts may lack social context (O'hara 2017), that can also be their strength. For example, smart contracts can relatively easily enforce clear-cut agreements across jurisdictions and potentially support that transaction as well via the provision of transparent, shared data (Eenmaa-Dimitrieva and Schmidt-Kessen 2017). They also enable distributed governance on a scale never previously possible, which in some cases is more efficient and can reduce the risk of conflicts of interest, or fraud (De Filippi 2018).

Conclusion

This research explored what automated trust and blockchain technologies offered for efforts to streamline games production licensing, knowledge exchange and business registration. In order to better understand these questions, participants of the UK Games Fund's Tranzfuser initiative were interviewed regarding their collaboration experience and their use of the UK Games Fund's Global Tal Registry IP management tool.

This empirical study of the collaborative experience of young game developer teams indicates that potential future Web 3.0 creative enterprise tools like blockchain business registration and data-sharing frameworks can expedite creative collaboration practice in a way that is potentially enhancing, if not entirely suitable for all contexts. Automated work records are a valuable tool to help streamline the licensing and creative development process, but they work best in collaboration with human insight. The overall value of these enhancements is likely to depend upon the agency of those involved.

Whilst the emerging semantic web (Hendler 2009) can already provide disarming insights into the nature of human behaviour, there is still a lot that it does not capture, such as the amorphous and potentially transformational insights that only emerge through the psychological, emotional and even energetic interplay of human subjectivities in collaboration with systematic data flows. In terms of creative production processes artificial data intelligence still needs to be combined with social intelligence.

Further research needs to be undertaken to interrogate the tensions between company secrets (which may be closely guarded due to a tradition of competitive business relationships) and the value of collective intelligence, but in principle the prospect that data-sharing technologies can be used to pool algorithmic knowledge networks offers great potential value for start-up game companies. In future, by taking advantage of enhanced, collective insights, these sorts of collaborative intelligence pools may increasingly disrupt their more competitive, secretive forebears.

Acknowledgement

Thank you to Coffee Box Games, Deep Fried Games, Darkroom Interactive, Out Of The Box Games and the UK Games Fund.

Note

1 The sharing economy has been defined by Lessig (2008) as "collaborative consumption made by the activities of sharing, exchanging, and rental of resources without owning the goods" (Lessig 2008: 143).

References

Batchelor, James. 2017. "Record Attendance for Tenth Anniversary EGX, 2018 Dates Revealed." *gamesindustry.biz*. Accessed 3.9.18. www.gamesindustry.biz/articles/2017-09-25-record-attendance-for-tenth-anniversary-egx-2018-dates-revealed.

Berg, Chris, Sinclair Davidson, and Jason Potts. 2017. "Blockchains Industrialise Trust." Accessed 18.6.18. SSRN: https://ssrn.com/abstract=3074070 or http://dx.doi.org/10.2139/ssrn.3074070.

Berners-Lee, Tim, and Mark Fischetti. 2001. *Weaving the Web: The Original Design and Ultimate Destiny of the World Wide Web by Its Inventor*. Collingdale, PA, United States DIANE Publishing Company.

Castelfranchi, Christiano, and Rino Falcone. 2010. *Trust Theory: A Socio-Cognitive and Computational Model*. Vol. 18. Hoboken, New Jersey, United States John Wiley & Sons.

Chen, Hsinchun, Roger H. L. Chiang, and Veda C. Storey. 2012. "Business Intelligence and Analytics: From Big Data to Big Impact." *MIS Quarterly*: 1165–1188.

Christies. 2018. "Art + Tech Summit: Exploring Blockchain – Is the Art World Ready for Consensus?" *YouTube*. Accessed 15.8.18. www.youtube.com/watch?v=KT-gPtK5uHY&t=25689s.

Crawford, Chris. 2012. *Chris Crawford on Interactive Storytelling*. Stanford, California, USA: New Riders.

CreativeCommons. 2018. "Case Law." Accessed 24.9.18. https://wiki.creativecommons.org/wiki/Case_Law.

De Filippi, Primavera De Filippi. 2018. *Blockchain and the Law: The Rule of Code*. Cambridge, MA: Harvard University Press.

Deloitte. 2018. "Breaking Blockchain Open: Deloitte's 2018 Global Blockchain Survey." *Deloitte*. Accessed 28.8.18. www2.deloitte.com/content/dam/Deloitte/cz/Documents/financial-services/cz-2018-deloitte-global-blockchain-survey.pdf.

Durrant, Paul, and Mark Hogarth. 2016. "TalTM Stories: A New Concept for Creative Teams to Share Project Ownership and Revenues." Accessed 4.4.18. www.talregistry.com/about.html.

D'Urso, Scott C. 2006. "Who's Watching Us at Work? Toward a Structural – Perceptual Model of Electronic Monitoring and Surveillance in Organizations." *Communication Theory* 16(3): 281–303.

Eenmaa-Dimitrieva, Helen, and Maria José Schmidt-Kessen. 2017. "Regulation Through Code as a Safeguard for Implementing Smart Contracts in No-Trust Environments." Accessed 30.9.2018 http://cadmus.eui.eu/bitstream/handle/1814/47545/LAW_2017_13.pdf?sequence=1&isAllowed=y

EGX. 2018. "EGX Home." *EGX*. Accessed 3.9.18. www.egx.net/egx.

Fröwis, Michael, and Rainer Böhme. 2017. "In Code We Trust?" In *Data Privacy Management, Cryptocurrencies and Blockchain Technology*, 357–372. Berlin: Springer.

Gefen, David, and Detmar W. Straub. 2004. "Consumer Trust in B2C e-Commerce and the Importance of Social Presence: Experiments in e-Products and e-Services." *Omega* 32(6): 407–424.

Gray, Kishonna L., Bertan Buyukozturk, and Zachary G. Hill. 2017. "Blurring the Boundaries: Using Gamergate to Examine 'Real' and Symbolic Violence Against Women in Contemporary Gaming Culture." *Sociology Compass* 11(3): e12458.

Hawlitschek, Florian, Benedikt Notheisen, and Timm Teubner. 2018. "The Limits of Trust-free Systems: A Literature Review on Blockchain Technology and Trust in the Sharing Economy." *Electronic Commerce Research and Applications* 29: 50–63.

Hendler, Jim. 2009. "Web 3.0 Emerging." *Computer* 42(1).

Keymolen, Esther. 2013. "Trust and Technology in Collaborative Consumption. Why It Is Not Just About You and Me." *Bridging Distances in Technology and Regulation*: 135–150.

Kiviat, Trevor I. 2015. "Beyond Bitcoin: Issues in Regulating Blockchain Transactions." *Duke LJ* 65: 569.

Lessig, Lawrence. 1999. "Code Is Law." *The Industry Standard* 18.

Lessig, Lawrence. 2008. *Remix: Making Art and Commerce Thrive in the Hybrid Economy*. London: Penguin.

Lu, Yaobin, Ling Zhao, and Bin Wang. 2010. "From Virtual Community Members to C2C e-Commerce Buyers: Trust in Virtual Communities and Its Effect on Consumers' Purchase Intention." *Electronic Commerce Research and Applications* 9(4): 346–360.

Lustig, Caitlin, and Bonnie Nardi. 2015. "Algorithmic Authority: The Case of Bitcoin." 2015 48th Hawaii International Conference on System Sciences (HICSS).

Malik, Muhammad Abdur Rahman, and Arif N. Butt. 2017. "Rewards and Creativity: Past, Present, and Future." *Applied Psychology* 66(2): 290–325.

McCarthy, John, and Peter Wright. 2004. "Technology as Experience." *Interactions* 11(5): 42–43.

Murray, Janet. 2001. "Agency, Hamlet on the Holodeck." In *Multimedia: From Wagner to Virtual Reality*, 1st ed., pp. 380–397, 394 p. New York: Norton.

Nakevska, Marija, Anika van der Sanden, Mathias Funk, Jun Hu, and Matthias Rauterberg. 2017. "Interactive Storytelling in a Mixed Reality Environment: The Effects of Interactivity on User Experiences." *Entertainment computing* 21: 97–104.

O'Dwyer, Karl J., and David Malone. 2014. "Bitcoin Mining and Its Energy Footprint." Hamilton Institute National University of Ireland Maynooth, http://karlodwyer.com/publications/pdf/bitcoin_KJOD_2014.pdf

O'hara, Kieron. 2017. "Smart Contracts-dumb Idea." *IEEE Internet Computing* 21(2): 97–101.

Ølnes, Svein, Jolien Ubacht, and Marijn Janssen. 2017. *Blockchain in Government: Benefits and Implications of Distributed Ledger Technology for Information Sharing. Government Information Quarterly*, Volume 34, Issue 3, Pages 355–364.

Reijers, Wessel, and Mark Coeckelbergh. 2018. "The Blockchain as a Narrative Technology: Investigating the Social Ontology and Normative Configurations of Cryptocurrencies." *Philosophy & Technology* 31(1): 103–130.

Roio, Denis, and Ivan Jelincic. 2017. "DECODE: Multidisciplinary Framework on Commons Collaborative Economy." Accessed 3.3.18. https://files.dyne.org/decode/D3.3_Data_Privacy_and_Smart_Language_requirements.pdf.

Rousseau, Denise M., Sim B. Sitkin, Ronald S. Burt, and Colin Camerer. 1998. "Not So Different After All: A Cross-discipline View of Trust." *Academy of Management Review* 23(3): 393–404.

Schiffer, Eva, and Jennifer Hauck. 2010. "Net-Map: Collecting Social Network Data and Facilitating Network Learning Through Participatory Influence Network Mapping." *Field Methods* 22(3): 231–249.

Swan, Melanie. 2013. "The Quantified Self: Fundamental Disruption in Big Data Science and Biological Discovery." *Big data* 1(2): 85–99.

Swan, Melanie. 2015. *Blockchain: Blueprint for a New Economy*. Newton, Massachusetts, United States: O'Reilly Media, Inc.

Teubner, Timm, and Florian Hawlitschek. 2018. "The Economics of Peer-to-Peer Online Sharing." In *The Rise of the Sharing Economy: Exploring the Challenges and Opportunities of Collaborative Consumption*, pp. 129–156. Santa Barbara, California, United States. ABC-CLIO.

UnrealForum. 2018. "Can You Give Me Detailed Reasons for Why Unreal 4 Is Better Than Unity?" *Unreal*. Accessed 18.11.18. https://forums.unrealengine.com/community/general-discussion/1434198-can-you-give-me-detailed-reasons-for-why-unreal-4-is-better-than-unity.

Van Dijck, José. 2014. "Datafication, Dataism and Dataveillance: Big Data Between Scientific Paradigm and Ideology." *Surveillance & Society* 12(2): 197–208.

Waring, Marilyn, and Gloria Steinem. 1988. *If Women Counted: A New Feminist Economics*. San Francisco: Harper & Row.

Wolf, Gary. 2010. "The Data-driven Life." *The New York Times*, 28 April 2010.

Yang, Sung-Byung, Kyungmin Lee, Hanna Lee, Namho Chung, and Chulmo Koo. 2016. "Trust Breakthrough in the Sharing Economy: An Empirical Study of Airbnb1." PACIS. https://aisel.aisnet.org/pacis2016/131/

Zimmerman, Eric. 2015. "Manifesto for a Ludic Century." *The Gameful World: Approaches, Issues, Applications*: 19–22.

Part II

Blockchain and digital media

Chapter 7

Could blockchain save journalism? An explorative study of blockchain's potential to make journalism a more sustainable business

Walid Al-Saqaf and Malin Picha Edwardsson

Introduction

Dozens of initiatives have emerged in recent years to explore the use of distributed/decentralised ledger technologies (DLTs) in general and public blockchains in particular for various purposes and by different industries and governments (Hileman and Rauchs, 2017). Use cases vary widely and go well beyond the traditional financial technology (fintech) sector (Underwood, 2016) and into health care (Mettler, 2016), insurance (Mainelli and von Gunten, 2014), education (Sharples and Domingue, 2016), identity verification (Shrier, Wu and Pentland, 2016) and many other domains (Al-Saqaf and Seidler, 2017; Tapscott and Tapscott, 2016).

It is established that blockchain's distributed ledger functionality can eliminate the need to trust an intermediary, making it attractive for solving some of the problems facing financial as well as non-financial industries where eliminating middlemen is desired (Crosby et al., 2016, p. 17). In journalism, intermediaries can be viewed as those who are positioned between journalists and readers in such a way that give those intermediaries direct or indirect influence on editorial decisions. Examples of such intermediaries include media owners, gatekeepers, politicians and businesses.

However, a reality check at this stage is due, since blockchain technology is at an early development phase; much of the discussion is hypothetical and highlights the potential benefits while not sufficiently reflecting on the hindrances and challenges that would prevent mass adoption. This leads to a widening gap between expectations and results and subsequently feeds blockchain-sceptical narratives (Pisa, 2018).

This is further complicated by the fact that most blockchain and cryptocurrency start-ups end up failing relatively quickly (Biggs, 2018; Froelings, 2017). Much of the hype around blockchain is often driven by a perceived gold rush to generate wealth, either through speculation in the volatile cryptocurrency market or investing in initial coin offerings (ICOs) with the expectation of yielding very high returns in a short period of time (Zetzsche et al., 2017).

However, the use of blockchain in the field of journalism is relatively new and lacks substantial research into how this technology can impact the news media industry, which is currently going through many challenges, such as low public trust and profitability (Newman et al., 2017, p. 9).

Journalism's role in society, among other things, is to inform the public by presenting the news. If the public does not perceive the news as credible, journalism fails in achieving its core objective. Such a scenario leads to a lack of the means to remain sustainable and relevant.

Traditionally, credibility of news has been assessed based on the credibility of the following layers: (1) the medium (newspaper, website, TV channel, etc.), (2) the source (journalist, writer) and (3) the message itself (text, images, video, etc.) (Kiousis, 2001; Sundar, 1999).

Research has found that lower news credibility leads to less trust in the media where the news is published. This in turn leads to media scepticism and lower media exposure (Tsfati and Cappella, 2003). It can therefore be concluded that stronger news credibility can enhance sustainability, since higher media exposure naturally translates to higher revenues from advertisements, subscription fees, sponsorships, etc.

Building on the connection between news credibility and media exposure, the aim of this study is to explore blockchain's potential to enhance news credibility and thereby make journalism a more sustainable business. It is important to note here that being a sustainable business is but one of the consequences of news credibility, which also contributes to enhancing the audience's trust and loyalty and creating a more informed public.

By reflecting on the *relative advantage* attribute of the diffusion of innovations theory by Rogers (2003), this study assesses whether a blockchain-based, decentralised newsroom model can compete against the traditional centralised model. We would like to emphasise, however, that this attribute alone is not necessarily sufficient to prove that the innovation will be diffused to the masses.

As a case study, we explore Civil, a blockchain-based protocol that aims at using cryptoeconomics to incentivise the production of journalistic quality content (Civil White Paper, 2018).

Our research question is: How can blockchain enhance sustainability of journalism as a business? We address this by looking into the potential of blockchain to enhance news credibility in each of the aforementioned layers: (1) the medium, (2) the source and (3) the message.

To answer this question, we use several methods. We first highlight blockchain's main operating principles that set it apart from traditional database systems, namely (1) *decentralisation*, (2) *transparency*, (3) *equality* and (4) *accountability* (Al-Saqaf and Seidler, 2017). The greatest potential for using blockchains is mainly in areas that could benefit from one or more of these principles.

Decentralisation eliminates the need for intermediaries or central points, as all operations are peer to peer. *Transparency* keeps all activities done on the blockchain timestamped and openly visible to all peers. *Equality* guarantees that all peers on the network that are represented by corresponding wallet addresses are treated equally with the exact same rules. *Accountability* necessitates that data on the blockchain is secure and immutable, making it immune from being hacked or manipulated or changed. Absolute accountability is vital for smart contracts on the blockchain to operate as expected without possibility for manipulation or exceptions.

Second, we draw connections between the aforementioned operating principles and how they affect each of the three layers influencing news credibility. Our method involves studying the Civil white paper and other texts available on the project's official website (https://civil.co) and carrying out a test on the trial version of the Civil platform in order to experience how it functions in real time. To obtain information not available on the website, we conduct interviews by email with key members of the Civil Media Company leadership team, namely co-founder and CEO Matthew Iles, co-founder and head of marketing Matt Coolidge and co-founder and engineering lead Dan Kinsley. We also interview Maria Bustillos, who is the editor of Popula (https://popula.com), one of the newsrooms created on the Civil platform.

Third, we analyse our results in view of the *relative advantage* attribute of the diffusion of innovations theory by Rogers (2003).

The diffusion of innovations theory

In this study, we attempt to explore the potential use of blockchain in making journalism a more sustainable business. When doing so, we use the *relative advantage* attribute of the diffusion of innovations theory by Rogers (2003).

Everett M. Rogers first presented his theory about diffusion of innovations in 1962, and ever since then the theory has been widely applied by communications scholars. Rogers defines *diffusion* as "the process by which an innovation is communicated through certain channels over time among the members of a social system. Diffusion is a special type of communication concerned with the spread of messages that are perceived as new ideas" (Rogers, 2003, p. 35). Furthermore, he argues that "diffusion is a kind of *social change*, defined as the process by which alternation occurs in the structure and function of a social system" (ibid, p. 6).

Rogers describes five innovation attributes – useful for understanding why some ideas diffuse more easily than others. These attributes are

1 *Relative advantage*, which is "the degree to which an innovation is perceived as being better than the idea it supersedes" (ibid, p. 229).
2 *Compatibility*, which is "the degree to which [the] innovation is perceived as consistent with the existing values, past experiences, and needs of potential adopter" (ibid, p. 240). Compatibility can help the individual give meaning to the new ideas so they are regarded as more familiar. "An innovation can be compatible or incompatible with 1) sociocultural values and beliefs, 2)

previously introduced ideas, and/or 3) client needs for the innovation" (ibid, p. 240).

3 The *complexity* of an innovation is the degree to which an innovation is perceived as relatively difficult to understand and use. According to Rogers, the complexity "is negatively related to its rate of adoption" (ibid, p. 257).
4 *Trialability* is the degree to which an innovation may be experimented with on a limited basis. New ideas that can be tried easily are generally adopted more rapidly than others (ibid, p. 258).
5 *Observability* is the degree to which the results of an innovation are visible to others. Some ideas are easily observed and communicated to other people, whereas other innovations are not (ibid, p. 258).

It is still important to note, however, that several critics, including Rogers himself, indicate that diffusion of innovations theory is not without limitations. One such limitation is that the theory has a "pro-innovation bias", implying that innovations are desirable and should be adopted quickly and without modification (Rogers, 2003; Ekdale et al., 2015).

Due to time and space limitations, this paper will be confined to the theory's first attribute of *relative advantage* by examining whether a blockchain-based journalism newsroom, with Civil as a case study, can be superior to a traditional newsroom in enhancing sustainability and news credibility. The aim is to take this as the first step that would then allow future research into this domain to cover the other attributes.

Use cases in journalism

When mapping the field of blockchain and journalism, we briefly present six main areas that can either directly or indirectly utilise blockchain for journalism.

1 **Combating fake news and disinformation:** Creating an ecosystem or mechanism that encourages the publishing of accurate information and preventing the spread of fake news and disinformation. This requires marking and rating news items based on whether they contain any inaccuracies and filtering them over time so that readers are exposed to factual stories and informed about any fake news that may have been produced earlier. Projects that aim at limiting the distribution of fake news by using the blockchain include Trive (https://trive.news), DNN (https://dnn.media), Snip (https://media.snip.today), Civil (https://civil.co), PressCoin (https://presscoin.com), Userfeeds (https://userfeeds.io), Bitpress (https://bitpress.network), Truepic (https://truepic.com/). For example, Truepic allows content creators of audiovisual content to embed geolocation, camera and software information and other metadata to the photo/video file and store a hashcode representation of the file on the Bitcoin blockchain (Berkhead, 2017). It has been argued that blockchain technology has the

potential in theory to facilitate the detection and tracking of fake news on social media content with blockchain (Jing and Murugesan, 2018).

2 **Preserving intellectual property:** Blockchain's ability to keep immutable records allows the creation of *proof of publication* of original media content to be one way through which intellectual property (IP) can be protected by providing means to authenticate and certify original content creation. As long as this original record is recognised by all beneficiaries, there will be consensus on who owns the intellectual property for any article or creative work that is timestamped and stored on the blockchain. While Civil and Reporter (http://reportercommunity.tech) offer a method to resolve IP disputes between authors, Snip detects the reuse of original content and informs the original writer automatically. The other two projects, Stock Block (https://stockblock.io) and Binded (https://binded.com), aim to provide this function only for visual content. Truepic, on the other hand, allows the verification and certification of photo and video authenticity by storing on the Bitcoin blockchain a hash of the content and metadata such as date, time and location of any image or videos captured. Blockchain and smart contract uses for protecting IP has also been argued to be useful in supporting online open innovation by allowing creators of original work to timestamp an IP disclosure or creation on the blockchain (de la Rosa et al., 2016).

3 **Limiting bias and external influence:** One of the problems that several blockchain-driven journalism projects emphasise is the bias and lack of objectivity that mainstream media often suffer from. The main reason for this is often the reliance on advertising revenues from corporations and other powerful entities. To combat this, Civil, PressCoin, DNN and Publicism (https://publicism.nl) offer incentives in cryptocurrency payments to discourage bias and encourage objectivity and writing openly on subjects that may be sensitive, such as reporting cases of corruption or abuse of power. Since writers do not rely on advertising, they are compensated with cryptocurrency rewards – often in units called tokens – based on how factual and objective their reporting is. Civil in particular has highlighted this as a major aim behind the project (Iles, 2016).

4 **Resisting censorship:** The high degree of decentralisation offered by open permissionless blockchains allows them to be inherently censorship resistant, since they necessitate storing transaction data on multiple devices. Civil, DNN, PressCoin, OngSocial (https://ongcoin.io), Steemit (https://steem.io), SocialX (https://socialx.network), Publicism, Bitpress and PUBLIQ (https://publiq.network) are examples of blockchain-enabled projects that aim at using open and public blockchains to ensure that data is accessible to readers despite attempts by gatekeepers to prevent access through domain filtering and other technical censorship methods (Mattila, 2016, p. 9).

5 **Protecting whistleblowers:** Allowing individuals to hide their identity when providing sensitive data is a domain that appears to be supported by

the pseudonymous nature of public blockchains such as Bitcoin and Ethereum. The two start-ups Trutheum (https://trutheum.com) and Publicism have explicitly mentioned protecting whistleblowers as one of their main objectives and do so by not requiring any personal information when connected with the source via cryptocurrency addresses. While Bitcoin and Ethereum can provide partial anonymity, other permissionless blockchains such as Zcash and Monero can be used to give a high degree of privacy and anonymity (Henry, Herzberg and Kate, 2018).

6 **Encouraging content creation by users:** While some of the blockchain journalism projects, such as Civil, are meant to be used to create complete newsrooms, other projects such as DNN, PressCoin, OngSocial, Steemit and Hashtiv (https://hashtiv.io) aim at using the blockchain instead of centralised services to store user content. Unlike centralised services such as Facebook or Twitter, Steemit, for example, allows users to use different web applications to produce and view text content that is stored on the Steemit blockchain in a decentralised manner without relying on a central server. Using third-party applications such as *d.tube*, Steemit also allows users to store videos in a distributed manner using the InterPlanetary File System (IPFS) protocol (Chohan, 2018). This in turn encourages citizens to produce original content including journalistic articles without the fear of censorship or control. Blockchain-based social media projects can develop a reputation system that allows users to evaluate and rate published content in an incentive-driven manner (Kolonin et al., 2018).

The six areas presented here are not mutually exclusive, which explains why we found several projects covering more than one. Furthermore, the list is not exhaustive and does not consider scalability or limitations. What is noticeable in most of the aforementioned projects is that they mostly focus on integrating the blockchain technology into the media content production process, and several focus exclusively on journalistic content. Yet since the technology is rather new and untested, there will certainly be challenges and, in some cases, hindrances that may prevent their realisation.

Due to limitations on time and resources, we have only looked into Civil as a single-case study representing a start-up promising to make journalism more sustainable. Civil was the case study of choice due to its prominence in the media, high profile partners, comparatively advanced stage of development and increased willingness to share its information and platform details compared to similar projects. It also is the only platform of its kind that already has a functional backend where testing the various functions was possible.

Civil: betting on cryptoeconomics

Established in 2016, the Civil Media Company created Civil as a decentralised communications protocol that aims at using blockchain-enabled cryptoeconomics to facilitate the creation and governance of and financially sustain distributed, independent and decentralised newsrooms. The aim is to produce high-quality and local, international, investigative and policy journalism (Civil White Paper, 2018).

As the birthplace of blockchain and cryptoeconomics, Bitcoin has proven that it is possible to create a reward system by using incentives and cryptography (Stark, 2017). Blockchain entrepreneur Josh Stark defines cryptoeconomics as "the practical science of using economic mechanisms to build distributed systems, where important properties of that system are guaranteed by financial incentives and where the economic mechanisms are guaranteed by cryptography" (ibid).

With capital totalling $5 million, Civil launched 14 projects representing the first fleet of newsrooms doing local, policy, investigative and foreign reporting. Popula editor Maria Bustillos said her newsroom decided to be a subscription-based publication. Her first question to the Civil team upon joining the first newsroom fleet was about the platform's capacity to keep a permanent archive on the blockchain. "Those archives are indelible and can be shut down only by shutting down the 17,000-plus computers worldwide that currently comprise the Ethereum network," she said (Bustillos, 2018). Apart from being used to creating newsrooms, an investment from ConsenSys was also used to create Civil Studios to fund and pilot some projects that use the Civil platform as well as media projects on the blockchain at large (Roberts, 2018).

The company's co-Founder and CEO, Matthew Iles, states in a 2016 blog post on Medium that Civil's goal is to use cryptoeconomics to *save* the journalism industry from an ongoing crisis caused by a broken revenue model, disinformation and unfair compensation to curators and content providers (Iles, 2016).

To do this, the Civil team created a new Ethereum ERC20-based token named CVL instead of establishing an independent blockchain. The CVL token serves as a *utility* that is necessary for the functioning of the Civil protocol, which utilises Ethereum's smart contract capabilities. The token is used to create newsrooms, reward writers and newsroom editors, and vote on various matters ranging from assessing challenges to newsrooms to dealing with potential complaints of violations of journalistic standards. Additionally, CVL holders can be sponsors by pooling tokens together to cover the deposit staked for somebody else's newsroom. While this dependency on Ethereum takes advantage of its robust and massive network and resources and reduces the risk of 51% attacks, which have become a strategy to attack young blockchains in recent years (Hertig, 2018), it also exposes Civil to Ethereum's vulnerabilities and risks, such as slow transaction speed, especially during peak periods. One example of this scalability problem happened when the whole Ethereum network came to a temporary grinding halt in 2017 due to the spike in use of the CryptoKitties' decentralised application (Khalif, 2017). Furthermore, it was found that the ERC20 standard lacks an event-(transaction)-handling mechanism and has other weaknesses, which led to the introduction of alternative standards (Mulders, 2018).

On 18 September 2018, Civil kicked off its official ICO to sell up to 34 million CVL tokens out of a total of 100 million. Applicants wishing to buy CVL through the ICO had to meet stringent requirements, including taking a quiz that even some journalists failed (Wang, 2018). A month after its launch, however, the ICO did not achieve its intended initial $8 million soft target, as only $1.4 million of sales took place. About $1.1 million of the raised amount came from ConsenSys, which is the main initial backer of the project. Since the sale was unsuccessful, Civil refunded all investors and announced that it will launch a second ICO with less stringent requirements (De Silva, 2018).

The scrutiny that buyers of CVL tokens had to go through was meant to prevent the amassing of tokens by possible malicious attackers or speculators (Wang, 2018). However, this very scrutiny may have been one of several contributing factors behind the failed ICO, which explains why Civil is pledging to make the second ICO simpler. Nonetheless, the scrutiny is meant to apply only to the ICO stage, after which Civil's initial plan is to only make CVL available on AirSwap's secondary market for at least a year, which would continue to require those interested in purchasing CVL to provide evidence that they have used CVL within the Civil platform before they can liquidate them (Coolidge, 2018c). If demand increases, it is likely that CVL would become publicly tradable via third-party exchanges. Using such external intermediaries involves the risk of losing deposits due to cyberattacks or mismanagement (Moore and Christin, 2013). The implications of relying on third-party exchanges for blockchain projects exposes them to higher risk of having their funds hacked, since millions of US dollars have been stolen from centralised exchanges in the past (Khatwani, 2018). Additionally, such exchanges defeat the main purpose of blockchain in enhancing decentralisation and can arguably be seen as a bottleneck for many who wish to purchase CIVIL. While there are several emerging decentralised exchanges, they remain far less popular, with fewer traders, and have fewer tradeable cryptocurrencies.

Defined as the "the heart of Civil," the Civil Constitution describes the mission, purpose and values that newsrooms need to abide by to remain part of the platform (Civil Constitution, 2018). The initial version of the constitution was drafted in consultation with journalists and cryptoeconomics and legal advisors. The constitution is similar to the traditional terms of service (ToS) but with a focus on a commitment to high standards of ethical journalism (Coolidge, 2018b). It is worth noting that the Civil team plans to make it possible in the future to have the constitution amended through a process, allowing any CVL token holder to propose an amendment, stake CVL tokens and go through a voting process. If a newsroom disagrees fundamentally with a new Constitution amendment, it has the right to withdraw its CVL application deposit stake and be removed from the registry.

To create a newsroom on Civil, applicants need to deposit $1,000 worth of CVL tokens, which is then held by one of the protocol's smart contracts as insurance in case the owner or writers in the newsroom violate the constitution. Once accepted, the newsroom joins the token-curated registry (TCR) and has its entry added to the Ethereum blockchain.

Since the CVL token had not yet been publicly tradable at the time this chapter was submitted for publication, the Civil team provided us with 3,000 units of free tokens (TESTCVL) on the Ethereum Rinkeby Test Network. These tokens were meant purely for testing purposes. We created a test newsroom after staking 100 TESTCVL and had it approved after it went unchallenged. We also challenged another newsroom for demonstration purposes and won that challenge, earning our account 100 TESTCVL as a reward (Etherscan.io, 2018). The process went rather smoothly and promptly. However, one would naturally expect a longer processing time when the service is officially launched on Ethereum's Main Network, since it can only handle a maximum of 20 transactions per second, which is extremely slow compared to the 10,000 transactions per second average of Visa (Peck, 2017).

The process of applying to create a newsroom and joining the Civil Registry is composed of several steps, as illustrated in Figure 7.1. The first requires writing the name of the newsroom and the wallet addresses of any additional members who are part of the newsroom (if any). Thereafter, required details on the mission and other information about the newsroom in addition to a charter

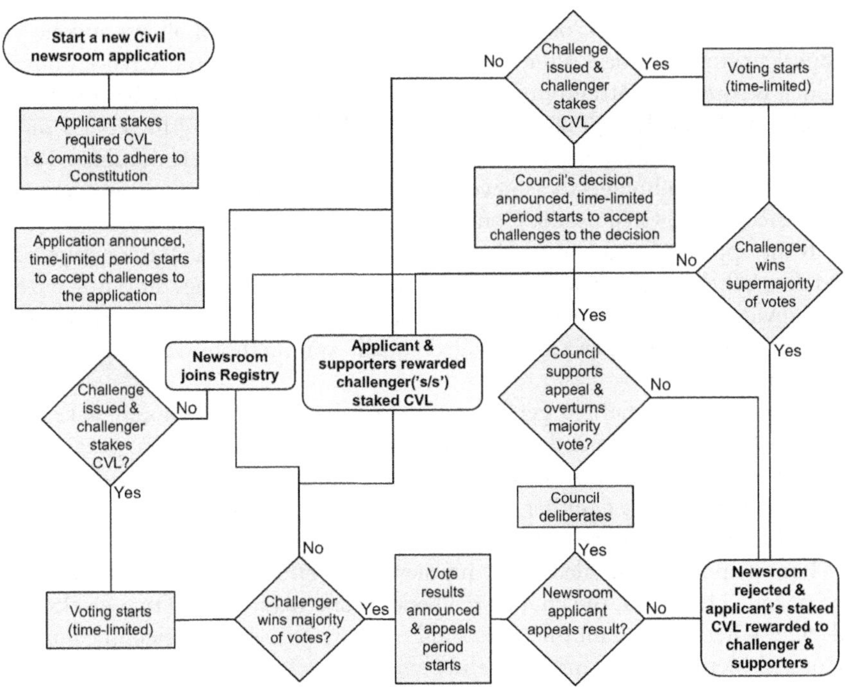

Figure 7.1 A flow chart illustrating the cryptoeconomics model of Civil

are supplied. The third step involves depositing an amount of CVL tokens equivalent to $1,000 to have the application officially filed.

At this stage, the filed application remains pending for 14 days, during which any CVL token holder has the opportunity to review the application and challenge the newsroom by staking $1,000 worth of CVL tokens. Challenges should be derived from an interpretation that the newsroom's mission or other attributes may be in violation of the constitution. Challenges to a newsroom can also take place after a newsroom is accepted into the registry, for example, when an article published by the newsroom is viewed as being in violation of the constitution. The only condition is that there can be only one challenge per newsroom at any given time.

The process of voting for or against the challenge is allowed within ten days after the challenge. An additional seven days are reserved for vote commitment, i.e., making votes count. This system is meant to incentivise members to examine the challenge carefully and vote in a way that would increase their chances of voting with the majority. For a challenge against a newsroom to succeed, it has to garner at least 50 percent of the votes cast.

This scenario would work in a situation where the majority behave in accordance with expected norms. However, there is still risk of malicious intent to take over the network by launching a 51% attack against any newsroom. Additionally, it is still theoretically possible to form alliances and win a majority vote needed to take down a newsroom.

To minimise the risk of such attacks, the Civil protocol allows anyone to appeal up to three days after the votes are committed to the Civil Council, which is composed of a group of experts. This group will initially be composed of nine individuals appointed by the Civil Media Company to serve a one-year term. In the future, Civil plans to have council members nominated and elected by token holders to achieve community self-governance away from any influence by the Civil Media Company (Civil Constitution, 2018).

If the appeal period ends without any appeal to the council, the newsroom is taken off the registry and the full amount staked by the newsroom is seized and divided so that 50 percent of the total sum is awarded to the challenger and the remaining 50percent is divided equally among those who voted for the challenge.

If the challenge fails to get 50 percent of the vote, the amount staked by the challenger is seized and divided so that 50 percent of the total goes to the newsroom and 50 percent is divided equally among those who voted against the challenge. Voters in either case do not need to stake any CVL, limiting any risk of losing CVL tokens and encouraging voters to participate.

For an appeal to be filed, the equivalent in CVL tokens of $1,000 needs to be staked. Thereafter, the council deliberates for a maximum of two weeks and decides whether to grant the appeal and overturn the vote or reject the appeal. Council members vote independently, with a simple majority being necessary to make a decision. Council members who end up winning the vote need to produce a public document to justify their decision based on the constitution. Unlike the voting process regarding challenges, votes of council members regarding appeals are neither on-chain nor transparent, as the final decision is delivered via a single Gnosis Multisig wallet representing a binary decision to either grant or reject the appeal. This prevents the community from knowing which of the council members voted for or against an appeal and which (if any) did not vote or abstained. Civil's lead engineer, Dan Kinsley, acknowledges this issue and notes that the Civil team is looking into developing more sophisticated ways to automate the process and make it more transparent (Kinsley, 2018).

It is to be noted that the council has the power to overturn the result of the vote if an appeal is granted and the council has strong reason to believe that the vote outcome violated the constitution. If the council grants the appeal, any token holder can stake $1,000 worth of CVL to call for challenging the council's decision within seven days after the appeal was granted. For the veto to succeed, it needs at least a two-thirds supermajority. If the decision was not vetoed within seven days or the veto failed to secure a supermajority, the council's granting of the appeal practically means that the vote results are overturned and flow of tokens is reversed.

In the exceptional situation of a deliberate malicious attack that results in the control of more than two-thirds of the vote, for example, by owning most of the CVL tokens, the Civil platform would then be rendered hijacked, resulting in a possible fork of the whole network or even the close-down of the platform to prevent further damage.

According to Coolidge, the aim of using cryptoeconomics and giving an intervention role to the council when needed is to help inform the voting process, and it reinforces the role of the constitution as the "primary document that should guide voter rationale" (Coolidge, 2018c).

Relative advantage of a civil-based newsroom

Despite limitations such as the "pro-innovation bias" mentioned earlier (Ekdale et al., 2015), it is useful to reflect on Rogers' theory of innovation in relation to a Civil-based newsroom. That being said, we also look into shortcomings and weaknesses that Civil may introduce and address them openly in this paper.

Rogers describes five innovation attributes that are useful for understanding why some ideas diffuse more easily than others. One of these attributes is *relative advantage*, which is "the degree to which an innovation is perceived as being better than the idea it supersedes" (Rogers, 2003, p. 229).

When reflecting on this attribute in relation to a Civil-based newsroom, we argue that the cryptoeconomic dynamics in Civil appear to *partially* take advantage of the four operational principles of blockchains (*decentralisation*, *equality*, *transparency* and *accountability*) in order to make newsrooms more sustainable by enabling them to produce news content that could be perceived as more credible.

Decentralisation on Civil is partial and mainly introduced by giving a decentralised network of CVL holders the ability to create and challenge newsrooms instead of having that done by a specific centralised authority. Although the Civil protocol interface operates via a website hosted on a central server, forcing the Civil community to rely on it for voting and applications to join the registry, newsrooms remain autonomous and are able to generate revenues from other CVL token holders who could purchase licenses and stories, as well as from external sources.

With more newsrooms joining, there will be more demand for CVL tokens, leading to higher profitably for token holders, since the total number of tokens is finite. As newsrooms receive and are rewarded CVL tokens through their services, they, too, would profit and be more sustainable. By being more sustainable, they are less prone to external pressure by business and politics, hence enhancing their news credibility as a medium of news content.

However, to be fully decentralised, Civil newsrooms would need to be self-sustaining without relying on Civil's website. This is necessary to avoid centralising control in the hands of Civil, which would defeat the main purpose of blockchain. Due to current reliance on Civil's website and servers, all Civil newsrooms may suffer if the Civil server is exposed to an attack or malfunction. Once fully operational, the Civil ecosystem may also collapse if the company owning it runs out of business, which is a possibility given that most blockchain startups have failed (Biggs, 2018). In order to avoid such a scenario, Civil would have to create and allow access to an open-source decentralised application (dApp) that would run on the devices of CVL holders and communicate directly with the blockchain without Civil's server as an intermediary.

Equality on Civil is also partial, even though all votes are counted equally with no preferential treatment. Those with more CVL are able to issue more challenges and create more newsrooms, which can theoretically lead to abuse. The possibility of abuse is reduced by the fact that challengers cannot win without the backing of the majority of voters.

In a situation where the majority of participating nodes support the constitution, a clear positive influence can be expected by upholding journalistic values, which in turn enhances news credibility. In cases where the majority of voters seem to act against the constitution, equality may be perceived as a weakness, and the Civil Council can therefore overrule the majority if the decision is appealed. This clearly gives the Civil Council tremendous power and makes it vital to properly interpret the constitution if it is to take fair decisions. It also presents an apparent paradox where having a gatekeeper may be necessary in occasions where voters don't act rationally, leading to asking if blockchain is perhaps *not* the right technology to use in this situation, since its main advantage is to *eliminate* the intermediary.

Transparency within Civil's ecosystem largely depends on the newsrooms, since they can decide whether to publish online content via a smart contract on the blockchain or bypass it and publish directly on the web. In the former case, changes can be tracked, since articles would be timestamped and traceable to the individual author or group of authors, forming a permanent archive.

Since one key factor to consider in news credibility is the source, using the blockchain as a means to publish content can lead to enhancing news credibility by revealing the ultimate source (author) and having that immutably recorded on the blockchain.

On the other hand, the fact that Civil newsrooms maintain a high degree of autonomy in receiving external funding can potentially open the door to outside influence and lead to biased editorial decisions. To prevent this, Civil allows CVL holders to challenge newsrooms when any of their authors seem to violate the constitution. Therefore, we conclude that Civil allows *transparency* as long as the newsrooms opt to use the blockchain for publishing content and maintain a transparent record of their revenues.

Accountability in the technical sense is ensured through smart contracts, because they insulate the voting process from manipulation. This creates a system of checks and balances, since smart contracts are immutable and their behaviour is predictable in advance of code execution, provided that the source code of smart contracts is properly audited, which is a major challenge in this space (Nikolic et al., 2018).

Another serious concern that arises here is the inability to verify the identity of the wallet address holders, whether voters or challengers. By design, public permissionless blockchains such as Bitcoin and Ethereum do not care about identity of the node so long as it can verify the legitimacy of a transaction. Some situations require linking a node to the real identity of the person behind it; otherwise, voting may end up being abused with the same individuals possibly voting multiple times using different wallet addresses. Additionally, lax security on the device may lead to hackers infiltrating the wallet and taking over control from the real owner, effectively voting on his/her behalf. This may open the door for vote fraud and buying. Furthermore, the vote is immutable, making it impossible to invalidate or make corrections after the fact. Hence, there has been some scepticism about whether blockchains are the right technology to use for real voting purposes (Juels, Eyal and Naor, 2018).

For the voting process on Civil to be truly democratic, each vote would have to come from a unique individual. It is possible to imagine a scenario in which CVL tokens have changed hands several times and that a single individual or entity was able to vote multiple times using different wallet addresses. Such a scenario leads to weakening the democratic process by giving more voting power to a particular individual/entity and leads to a less accountable system. The ability of using blockchain to establish and verify digital identities is debated due to the dependency on external central authority (Olshansky and Wilson, 2018). This, again, presents the question of whether blockchain is suitable for a system that requires voting to be done in a one-person-per-vote fashion.

Conclusion

Our study concludes that blockchain-enabled journalism projects such as Civil *have* a relative advantage compared to traditional journalism models. Civil takes partial advantage of blockchain's operating principles as it promotes a journalism ecosystem with a higher degree of transparency, equality, decentralisation and accountability than traditional newsrooms.

Civil's cryptoeconomics model incentivises community members to act in accordance to the Civil Constitution, which in turn would lead to higher quality journalistic content. A newsroom producing high-quality factual news content would naturally enhance news credibility and make journalism more sustainable.

That being said, a lot of conditions and variables need to be considered for a platform like Civil to succeed in attracting professional journalists and cause a network effect where more newsrooms and readers perceive their news content as credible. The elephant in the room, however, is the assumption that CVL holders would be committed to the constitution and act predictably and rationally rather than try to abuse the system. It also heavily depends on the state of the health and effectiveness of Ethereum as the underlying technology. This exposes Civil as well as hundreds of other projects that use ERC-20 tokens to the risk of failure if Ethereum's own cryptocurrency (ether) collapses or if the whole project is shut down for any reason.

The question of voter rationality is key when considering, for example, the way voters would react to the publishing of a fake image or unsubstantiated information. Ideally, CVL holders would be able to spot such content and issue a challenge that would then be supported so that the newsroom is held accountable. Such a scenario would be a strong deterrent that would enhance the credibility of messages and thereby lead to higher overall news credibility of the source and the newsroom in question. The more high-quality newsrooms joining Civil, the higher the value of CVL would be, and the more profitable it becomes for all involved.

In this chapter, we demonstrate that the blockchain can reduce the influence of intermediaries in the journalistic process, which in turn can reduce bias and lead to greater trust in the news media, making the journalism industry more sustainable. On the other hand, blockchain technology is best utilised for cases where intermediaries are *totally* eliminated, which is not the case of Civil. Although Civil relies on its community members – as peers – to properly interpret the constitution, the Civil team understands that it may be necessary to have intervention by the council to handle delicate borderline issues that are difficult to interpret.

The fact that Civil compromises full decentralisation by appointing itself – at least for the initial period – as the intermediary that appoints the council to resolve some disputes is a major gamble that may be its Achilles heel, which could have unforeseen negative consequences down the line. It also poses the question of whether blockchain is after all the solution needed for the creation of truly decentralised newsrooms.

One additional bet that Civil has taken is relying on Ethereum, which exposes it to the risks and vulnerabilities of the blockchain, which remains in its early stages of development and is expected to go through a series of changes if it is to become more scalable.

Despite partial leveraging some of blockchain characteristics, we find that the risks involved in the project remain high. The abuse of the system by CVL holders is a real possibility, particularly as the identities of voters are not possible to verify using Civil. Nor is it clear if blockchain is the right technology to use for a system that relies heavily on democratic voting but where wallet addresses are not strictly connected to particular individuals.

Yet according to Civil co-founder Matt Coolidge, taking *risk* was necessary to save journalism. He remains hopeful that the rewards will outweigh the risks in the long run, and even if Ethereum becomes unusable for whatever reason, Civil's concept and framework can move to another blockchain or entirely different system if necessary (Coolidge, 2018a).

We therefore see great value in continuing to follow Civil and similar projects to assess progress over the years and to evaluate the level and type of adoption by journalists and readers. While acknowledging the risks ahead, Civil CEO Iles argues that journalism is at a stage in which someone needs to take initiative, adding that "it's foolish to say it won't be bumpy or take time. But what is important is that 1) there's a strong market need for something different, and 2) categorically, nothing like our approach has ever existed before" (Iles, 2018).

The journey for Civil and other blockchain-based projects in the field of journalism has begun, and in the words of Maria Bustillos of Popula, "The blockchain world changes at a very rapid pace, so we're kind of surfing this gigantic wave. So far, we're still standing; it's terrifying and exhilarating" (Bustillos, 2018).

Bibliography

Al-Saqaf, W., and Seidler, N. (2017). Blockchain technology for social impact: Opportunities and challenges ahead. *Journal of Cyber Policy*, 2(3), 338–354.

Berkhead, S. (2017, December 22). Truepic app lets journalists instantly verify images, videos. *International Journalists Network*. Retrieved November 22, 2018 from https://ijnet.org/en/story/truepic-app-lets-journalists-instantly-verify-images-videos

Biggs, J. (2018, June 29). Thousands of cryptocurrency projects are already dead. *TechCrunch*. Retrieved September 7, 2018 from https://techcrunch.com/2018/06/29/thousands-of-cryptocurrency-projects-are-already-dead

Bustillos, M. (2018, June 20). *Interview about Popula and Civil* [E-mail to W. Al-Saqaf].

Chohan, U. W. (2018). *The Concept and Criticisms of Steemit*. Discussion Paper Series: Notes on the 21st Century, University of New South Wales (UNSW), UNSW Business School. https://papers.ssrn.com/sol3/papers.cfm?abstract_id=3129410

Civil Constitution (2018, September 7). The Civil constitution. *Civil*. Retrieved from https://civil.co/constitution

Civil White Paper (2018, September 7). The Civil white paper. *Civil*. Retrieved from https://civil.co/white-paper

Coolidge, M. (2018a, March 21). *Skype Interview about Civil* [Interviewer W. Al-Saqaf].
Coolidge, M. (2018b, May 4). *We Published the Civil Constitution, and Launched a Venture Studio*. Received by Civil Newsletter Subscribers [E-mail to W. Al-Saqaf].
Coolidge, M. (2018c, September 10). *One last look at Civil* [Email to W. Al-Saqaf].
Crosby, M., Pattanayak, P., Verma, S., and Kalyanaraman, V. (2016). Blockchain technology: Beyond bitcoin. *Applied Innovation*, 2.
de la Rosa, J. L., Gibovic, D., Torres, V., Maicher, L., Miralles, F., El-Fakdi, A., and Bikfalvi, A. (2016, December). On intellectual property in online open innovation for SME by means of blockchain and smart contracts. In *Proceedings of the 3rd Annual World Open Innovation Conference WOIC*, Barcelona, Spain (pp. 15–16).
Ekdale, B., Singer, J., Tully, M., and Harmsen, S. (2015). Making change: Diffusion of technological, relational, and cultural innovation in the newsroom. *Journalism & Mass Communication Quarterly*, 92(4), 938–958.
Etherscan.io (2018, September 4). *Address 0x1080c71d6cb3e06cdb2ba41e49b7cb6c49920876*. Rinkeby Accounts, Address and Contracts. Retrieved September 8, 2018 from https://rinkeby.etherscan.io/address/0x1080c71d6cb3e06cdb2ba41e49b7cb6c49920876
Froelings, L. (2017, September 7). Deloitte reports more than 26,000 blockchain projects launched in 2016. *CoinTelegraph*. Retrieved September 7, 2018 from https://cointelegraph.com/news/deloitte-reports-more-than-26000-blockchain-projects-launched-in-2016
Henry, R., Herzberg, A., and Kate, A. (2018). Blockchain access privacy: Challenges and directions. *IEEE Security & Privacy*, 16(4), 38–45.
Hertig, A. (2018, June 9). Blockchain's once-feared 51% attack is now becoming regular. *CoinDesk*. Retrieved September 8, 2018 from www.coindesk.com/blockchains-feared-51-attack-now-becoming-regular/
Hileman, G., and Rauchs, M. (2017). *2017 Global Blockchain Benchmarking Study*.
Iles, M. (2016, December 14). *Why Civil* [Blog post]. Retrieved September 8, 2018 from https://medium.com/@matthewiles/why-civil-5e018f3e101d
Iles, M. (2018, July 7). *Interview about Civil* [Email to W. Al-Saqaf].
Jing, T. W., and Murugesan, R. K. (2018, June). A theoretical framework to build trust and prevent fake news in social media using blockchain. In *International Conference of Reliable Information and Communication Technology* (pp. 955–962). Springer, Cham.
Juels, A., Eyal, I., and Naor, O. (2018, October 18). Blockchains won't fix Internet voting security – and could make it worse. *The Conversation*. Retrieved November 27, 2018 from https://theconversation.com/blockchains-wont-fix-internet-voting-security-and-could-make-it-worse-104830
Khalif, O. (2017, December 4). CryptoKitties mania overwhelms Ethereum network's processing. *Bloomberg*. Retrieved September 8, 2018 from www.bloomberg.com/news/articles/2017-12-04/cryptokitties-quickly-becomes-most-widely-used-ethereum-app
Khatwani, S. (2018, October 13). Top 5 biggest Bitcoin hacks ever. *Coinsutra*. Retrieved November 27, 2018 from https://coinsutra.com/biggest-bitcoin-hacks/
Kinsley, D. (2018, September 7). *Technical questions about Civil* [Email to W. Al-Saqaf].
Kiousis, S. (2001). Public trust or mistrust? Perceptions of media credibility in the information age. *Mass Communication & Society*, 4(4), 381–403.
Kolonin, A., Goertzel, B., Duong, D., and Ikle, M. (2018). A reputation system for artificial societies. arXiv preprint arXiv:1806.07342.
Mainelli, M. and von Gunten, C. (2014). *Chain of a Lifetime: How Blockchain Technology Might Transform Personal Insurance*. Long Finance Report prepared by Z/Yen Group.
Mattila, J. (2016). *The Blockchain Phenomenon*. Berkeley Roundtable of the International Economy.

Mettler, M. (2016). Blockchain technology in healthcare: The revolution starts here. In *e-Health Networking, Applications and Services (Healthcom), 2016 IEEE 18th International Conference on* (pp. 1–3). IEEE.

Moore, T., and Christin, N. (2013, April). Beware the middleman: Empirical analysis of Bitcoin-exchange risk. In *International Conference on Financial Cryptography and Data Security* (pp. 25–33). Springer, Berlin, Heidelberg.

Mulders, M. (2018, February 19). Comparison between Ethereum standards: ERC20 – ERC223 – ERC777. *Cointelligence*. Retrieved September 8, 2018 from www.cointelligence.com/content/comparison-erc20-erc223-new-ethereum-erc777-token-standard/

Newman, N., Fletcher, R., Kalogeropoulos, A., Levy, D. A., and Nielsen, R. K. (2017). *Reuters Institute Digital News Report 2017*.

Nikolic, I., Kolluri, A., Sergey, I., Saxena, P., and Hobor, A. (2018). Finding the greedy, prodigal, and suicidal contracts at scale. arXiv preprint arXiv:1802.06038.

Olshansky, S., and Wilson, S. (2018, March 13). Blockchain and digital identity – A good fit? *Internet Society*. Retrieved September 17, 2018 from https://internetsociety.org/blog/2018/03/blockchain-digital-identity-good-fit/

Peck, M. E. (2017). Blockchain world-do you need a blockchain? This chart will tell you if the technology can solve your problem. *IEEE Spectrum*, 54(10), 38–60.

Pisa, M. (2018). Reassessing expectations for blockchain and development. *Innovations: Technology, Governance, Globalization*, 12(1–2), 80–88.

Roberts, J. J. (2018, May 2). Civil, the blockchain media firm, tries a "Netflix Original" strategy. *Fortune*. Retrieved September 8, 2018 from http://fortune.com/2018/05/02/blockchain-venture-media-civil/

Rogers, E. (2003). *Diffusion of Innovations* (5th ed.) New York, NY: Free Press.

Sharples, M., and Domingue, J. (2016). The blockchain and kudos: A distributed system for educational record, reputation and reward. In *European Conference on Technology Enhanced Learning* (pp. 490–496). Springer, Cham.

Shrier, D., Wu, W., and Pentland, A. (2016). Blockchain & infrastructure (identity, data security). *Massachusetts Institute of Technology-Connection Science*, 1(3).

Silva, M. D. (2018, October 17). ConsenSys bought most of the tokens in Civil's disappointing ICO. *Quartz*. Retrieved from https://qz.com/1426382/consensys-bought-most-of-the-cvl-tokens-in-civil-medias-disappointing-ico/amp/

Stark, J. (2017, August 19). Making sense of cryptoeconomics. *Coindesk*. Retrieved September 7, 2018 from www.coindesk.com/making-sense-cryptoeconomics/

Sundar, S. (1999). Exploring receivers' criteria for perception of print and online news. *Journalism & Mass Communication Quarterly*, 76(2), 373–386.

Tapscott, D., and Tapscott, A. (2016). *Blockchain Revolution How the Technology Behind Bitcoin Is Changing Money, Business and the World*. London: Portfolio Penguin.

Tsfati, Y., and Cappella, J. N. (2003). Do people watch what they do not trust? Exploring the association between news media skepticism and exposure. *Communication Research*, 30(5), 504–529.

Underwood, S. (2016). Blockchain beyond Bitcoin. *Communications of the ACM*, 59, 15–17.

Wang, S. (2018, July 25). Want to support journalism with cryptocurrency on civil? First you must pass this really hard quiz. *Nieman Lab*. Retrieved September 8, 2018 from www.niemanlab.org/2018/07/want-to-support-journalism-with-cryptocurrency-on-civil-first-you-must-pass-this-really-hard-quiz/

Zetzsche, D. A., Buckley, R. P., Arner, D. W., and Föhr, L. (2017). *The ICO Gold Rush: It's a Scam, It's a Bubble, It's a Super Challenge for Regulators*. Working Paper No. 11/2017.

Chapter 8

The logics of technology decentralization – the case of distributed ledger technologies

Balazs Bodo and Alexandra Giannopoulou

Distributed ledger technologies and the ideology of decentralization

In the history of the Internet there seems to be a recurring hope that open-source, decentralized, and distributed digital technologies would give rise to novel, revolutionary modes of social, political, and economic organization, which build upon and reflect the intrinsic characteristics of the underlying technology. Roughly twenty years after J.P. Barlow's declaration of the independence of cyberspace (Barlow, 1996), which heralded the birth of Web 1.0, and ten years after Benkler's *The Wealth of Networks* (Benkler, 2006), which marked the mainstreaming of Web 2.0, in 2016, blockchain technologies captured the imagination of a diverse group of social actors from crypto-anarchist software geeks, via investors, to governments. Their hope was, again, that technological decentralization would provide a solution to a wide range of problems that include the governance of the global financial system, the excessive power of online platforms, or the way societies maintain property registries.

The term "blockchain technologies", or distributed ledger technologies (DLTs), describes a wide range of technological innovations which use advanced cryptographic techniques to create decentralized technological network infrastructures to facilitate social coordination among strangers without relying on existing institutions or traditional intermediaries. The coordination takes place via a shared database. The integrity of this database is guaranteed by an algorithmic consensus among the members of the network. The database has no limitations on what it contains: it can record time-stamped documents, transactions of unique tokens, or software code that allows for the automatization of coordination. (Narayanan, Bonneau, Felten, Miller, & Goldfeder, 2016)

Blockchain technologies brought together long existing ideas in a new constellation (Narayanan & Clark, 2017), which created an opportunity to see this new technology as a point of discontinuity, a revolutionary moment, rather than a marginal advance in, for example, the science of cryptography or the design of peer-to-peer systems. Such moments of perceived discontinuity create uncertainties around the unexplored, unknown potentials of the technology, which, in the case of DLTs, led to widespread and enthusiastic speculation about an imminent political, economic, and social disruption. After two failures for the brave new, self-governed, autonomous world to emerge, there was again a widespread hope that on a decentralized and disintermediated technological basis, technologically empowered individuals would create horizontal, just, meritocratic, self-governing communities, emancipated from the oppression of states, corporations, and other traditional economic or political middlemen (Swan, 2015; Tapscott & Tapscott, 2016; Wright & de Filippi, 2015; Wright & de Filippi, 2018).

The term "decentralization" enjoys an almost mythical status in the discourses around DLTs in particular and digital technologies in general. This is partly due to the original design of the Internet architecture, which found an effective safeguard against a nuclear attack on a communication network by eliminating central points of failure or control. This has led to more metaphorical interpretations of the advantages of decentralized architectures in the form of John Gilmore's quote: "The Net interprets censorship as damage and routes around it" (Elmer-DeWitt, 1993). In 2006, Benkler stressed the relevance of decentralization in similar, albeit seemingly less loaded terms: "[The] primary attribute [of centralization] is the separation of the locus of opportunities for action from the authority to choose the action that the agent will undertake. . . . 'Decentralization' describes conditions under which the actions of many agents cohere and are effective despite the fact that they do not rely on reducing the number of people whose will counts to direct effective action" (Benkler, 2006, p. 62). In the context of DLTs, decentralization (and anonymity, not discussed here) provides immunity against laws: "It's only through decentralization and anonymity that the system can remain free from outside influence, such as government regulation" (Van Wirdum, 2015). "Policy neutrality" – as legal impunity is referred to by the same text – is achieved because it's difficult and costly to coordinate enforcement against many, small, geographically dispersed, anonymous network constituents.

The normative discourse on decentralization

Decentralization in the technology discourse is rarely a descriptive category with its own particular costs and benefits but rather a normative ideal. Centralization means the rule of the few over the many, the potential for censorship, for coercion. Decentralization is seen as the architectural guarantee of censorship resistance and a safeguard against the coercive influence of any centralized, top-down force. The external forces of control – institutions, intermediaries, rules, laws, and norms – prevent the ideal, purely technological modes of private ordering, based on the horizontal self-organization of equal peers. The social order that is expected to emerge on decentralized technologies is seen as inherently superior to what the status quo has to offer. The teaser of the Internet Archive's Decentralized Web Summit perfectly encapsulates this approach to the cascading social and political impact of technological decentralization: "The Internet Archive's Decentralized Web Summit is dedicated to creating the web we want (and the web we deserve). We are convening those who want to build a web that . . . remembers. Forgets. That's safe. That cares about people. That's a marketplace. That's a public square. That learns. That's magical. That's fun. A web with many winners. A web that's locked open for good."[1] Decentralization is a technological architecture that replaces existing modes of control and reverses their negative effects. It is a higher technological ideal to be strived for, a superior mode of technological design, a "step forward in the evolution of systems" ((Kelly, 2014) quoted in (Baldwin, 2018)) which could enable its users to effectively neutralize or counter the tyranny of states, the injustices of markets, and the untrustworthiness, corruptibility, or outright corruption of various middlemen.

Looking at technological decentralization as a utopian ideal to strive for leaves little room for a more analytical approach. We agree with Baldwin that the actual extent and mode of decentralization of complex techno-social assemblages are the products of concrete social, political, and economic conditions "based upon a geopolitical decision, being a contingent choice, serving a specific historical function, and with appropriate cost-analysis" (2018, p. 3). In the next section we outline some of these forces which shape the degree of centralization of a techno-social system in different dimensions.

The logics and dimensions of decentralization

What are the relevant dimensions of decentralization?

Decentralization of a complex techno-social assemblage can be discussed in relation both to all the resources which are necessary for the production of the assemblage and for all the domains the assemblage offers its products/services to. In the case of DLTs, they must secure inputs from a wide variety of markets: financial resources such as investment; human resources such as software development or legal expertise; technical resources such as the capacities required to mine or run a full node; or infrastructural resources such as access to specialized hardware, energy, network connectivity, or cloud services. Similarly, the concentration (centralization) of markets which use the services offered by or through a technology can also be considered: the number of users both human and institutional and their concentration in various dimensions, such as legal/illicit uses, volume, and geography; the number and distribution of holders of different rights related to the technology (such as ownership, management, extraction, exclusion, etc.); and the distribution of costs and of any rewards.

Decentralization, in the context of DLTs, is usually discussed in terms of software decentralization, which according to Buterin (2017a) has much fewer dimensions: (1) architectural ("How many physical computers is a system made up of? How many of those computers can it tolerate breaking down at any single time?"); (2) political ("How many individuals or organizations ultimately control the computers that the system is made up of?"); and (3) logical ("If you cut the system in half, including both providers and users, will both halves continue to fully operate as independent units?"). According to this classification, "Blockchains are politically decentralized (no one controls them) and architecturally decentralized (no infrastructural central point of failure) but they are logically centralized (there is one commonly agreed state and the system behaves like a single computer)" (Buterin, 2017a). This classification is only little more than a thought experiment, but we quote it here because it comes from one of the most influential architects of the blockchain technology space. It is admittedly rough and debatable, and indeed, various studies that measured DLTs' decentralization suggest a number of additional dimensions, the (de)centralization of which may have far-reaching impact on the political goals technical decentralization tries to achieve. It has been shown that the (de)centralization at the deep networking level, such as bandwidth, network latency, or fairness (Gencer, Basu, Eyal, van Renesse, & Sirer, 2018), the control over the production of code (Azouvi, Maller, & Meiklejohn, 2018), or various dimensions of users, such as marketplaces or web wallets (Gervais, Karame, Capkun, & Capkun, 2014; Srinivasan, 2017), all affect the degree of decentralization of DLTs. The studies also confirm that the decentralization of the different components of a complex techno-social assemblage are not independent of each other. Their mutual interdependence creates a highly dynamic system subject to often unforeseen external forces.

The forces that produce (de)centralization

The history of the Internet is also the history of the recentralization of networks which were initially designed to be decentralized. DLTs are no exception to this rule. In recent years, we also witnessed the lack of decentralization or substantial recentralization of DLTs in terms of, for example, mining power, at the layer of core code developers or at major cryptocurrency exchanges (de Filippi & Loveluck, 2016). In response, a number of social, and technical innovations are being proposed. On-chain governance is supposed to submit the governance of the technology to the rules encoded in the technology, supposedly making it more transparent, accountable, and less arbitrary. Novel consensus mechanisms such as Ethereum's Casper[2] try to address the concentration of proof-of-work mining (Bonneau et al., 2015) and the cartelization of proof-of-stake approaches.[3] Specialized mining hardware (ASIC) resistant protocols are being proposed to address dynamics of recentralization at the levels of hardware. As these dynamics suggest, at any given time multiple, often interdependent forces shape the degree of centralization in often more than one layer of DLTs. In the following, we'll discuss a number of such forces, which we were able to identify through the analysis of (1) discussions that take place in the generalized online fora and in specialized venues; (2) white papers that spell out the technical, economic, social, and political visions of various blockchain projects. The items on this list roughly map onto Lessig's (1999) pathetic dot theory – markets, architecture, laws, and norms – but they offer a more detailed, context-specific insight into the actual workings into these forces. The list is far from being complete, and further work is needed to fully account for all the logics that produce (de)centralization in a techno-social system. Yet – we believe – the most important of these forces are the following: (1) ideology/systems design; (2) internal control/governability; (3) external recognition; (4) external threats; and (5) endogenous and exogenous economic incentives.

1. Ideology/systems design

While the quest for technological decentralization is often seen as a highly political endeavour, rooted in specific, techno-libertarian, or neoliberal ideologies (Barbrook & Cameron, 1995; Chohan, 2017; Golumbia, 2016; May, 1994; Morozov, 2014), the foundational paper introducing Bitcoin (Nakamoto, 2008) does not directly invest in introducing an ideology of decentralization. However, an indirect reference exists in the Bitcoin genesis block and in subsequent posts published by Nakamoto on the functioning of Bitcoin (Nakamoto, 2009). The message in the genesis block references an article in *The Times* newspaper on the proposed second bailout of commercial banks during the 2008 financial crisis. The Nakamoto paper describes a technology that can be applied without needing established, centralized, and trusted intermediaries. Focused on currencies, which are formed based upon the most centralized models, Nakamoto explains that "while the system works well enough for most transactions, it still suffers from the inherent weaknesses of the trust based model". Nakamoto delivered a detailed road map on how to reverse this model.

The success of Bitcoin as an incorruptible trustless system incited a renewed interest in decentralization as a technological solution to power inequalities and inspired the generalization of the Bitcoin idea. The Ethereum white paper (Buterin, 2013) presented blockchain technology as an underlying infrastructure that could apply the impersonal disintermediarized trustless model proposed by the Nakamoto paper to "more than just money". Ethereum introduced decentralized applications (Dapps) and decentralized autonomous organisations (DAOs), all running on a peer-to-peer network instead of running on a centralized computer.

Yet decentralized technologies are proven to be prone to occasional recentralization due to forces we discuss later. For example, some blockchain technology architects, like Zamfir (2016), are focusing their work on the direct and indirect incentives which may lead to the recentralization of power in decentralized blockchain networks. More specifically, the preferred method of establishing consensus on the blockchain has been a dividing issue among different projects. Miner competition in validating blocks is an essential part of decentralized blockchain projects. The recentralization (Gencer et al., 2018) of mining power proves to be not only a practical issue but also a political one. Building technological resistance to centralization of miners has become an integral part of new cryptocurrencies, demonstrating their belief that decentralization on the consensus level and above is fundamental to the design of the DLTs. For example, the cryptocurrency Monero opted to change its consensus validating algorithm every six months to resist ASIC miner centralization. These technological choices ultimately correspond to the decentralization ideals of the techno-social assemblage, while also determining the internal power balance of the community and the success of the project.

With the introduction of smart contracts, the logic of decentralization reached the level of blockchain governance itself. This was a development to be expected: despite all the ideological commitment to decentralize social processes through technology, DLT development remained heavily centralized in terms of software developers and their governance mechanisms. The communities behind the code were, and many still are, weakly organized; they tend to lack formal institutions and processes; they often operate in the state of anarchy or under the rule of benevolent dictators; and in absence of more sophisticated conflict resolution mechanisms, they often have to resort to splitting (forking) the code and the networks to resolve their ideological or systems design differences. Consequently, the governance of DLTs turned out to be of central importance (de Filippi & Loveluck, 2016). The question that in these contexts emerged was whether the production of DLTs can be governed using DLT technologies themselves: is it possible to govern, in a decentralized manner on a decentralized technology, the production of that decentralized technology? In response, multiple efforts started to work on what is called the problem of "on-chain governance". For example, the Tezos blockchain implements a decentralized modular governance model for smart contracts and decentralized applications that would permit more coordinated "radically decentralized protocol forks" (Goodman, 2014). Similarly, decentralized applications like Aragon[4] offer modular decentralized organization models that can be used by companies developing their blockchain project or by decentralized autonomous organizations. These additional layers address the goal of decentralization by inserting mechanisms that would resist centralization tendencies on the governance and decision-making levels.

The efforts to implement automated, decentralized decision-making mechanisms for the governance of blockchain-based applications and organization have provoked a number of conflicts between ideas of decentralization and system design. As will be shown later on, examples of these controversies can be found on the block-size debate for Bitcoin, the Tezos foundation lawsuits, and the Ethereum DAO hack (DuPont, 2017). The ideology-driven decentralization maximalist approach could only be realized at the expense of other important values, such as technical efficiency, governability, or social recognition and diffusion. Take, for example, the now infamous and still ongoing block-size debate. The issue in that controversy is the implication of increasing the size of the blocks on the Bitcoin blockchain. On the one hand, bigger blocks would increase the throughput of the system, allowing for more transactions per minute to be processed and a potentially higher level of recognition of the cryptocurrency as a payment system. Opponents of the increase, however, pointed out that larger blocks mean that individuals with less computing resources and on slower networks are discouraged from participating in the mining process, while big mining consortia would enjoy a number of self-reinforcing advantages (van Wirdum, 2015). A larger block size may help the network to scale up, but it threatens the recentralization of the network. This dilemma has caused divisions and the ultimate schism in the Bitcoin community (de Filippi & Loveluck, 2016). Many members adhering to the "true spirit" of decentralization according to Nakamoto's vision protected the cap for ideological reasons. Others disagreed and decided to create and sustain a forked alternative version of the Bitcoin blockchain that is still maintained as an independent cryptocurrency. The disagreement has demonstrated that non-architectural choices have important consequences on the decentralized nature and the development path of the technology.

2. *Internal control and governability*

One of the biggest challenges a decentralized system faces is its continuous maintenance and community governance. Every additional measure of decentralization to minimize external control also diminishes the control powers of the creators of the system. The decision-making processes that are required by the maintenance of a control-proof decentralized system cannot be fully automated away. The elimination of single points of control makes the maintenance of the system slow and the social coordination of the participating members cumbersome. It proved to be harder than expected to implement in practice the "governing without a government" vision of Nakamoto. The Nakamoto consensus, as a technical approach to create a self-governing system, is only useful to maintain a distributed nature of the ledger but is unable to operate on other levels where decentralization may be desirable. The technology that allows avoiding reliance on external intermediaries was not sufficient to guarantee the decentralized nature of the technology when it came to core developers, full nodes, or miners and other interests and stakes in the techno-social system.

Take, for example, the current governance of the Bitcoin technology. Lacking a formal governance structure, the Bitcoin community coordinates ideas for improvements through the Bitcoin Improvement Proposal (BIP) system. It consists of a transparent process very similar to the code review process available on open-source and free software projects (de Filippi & Loveluck, 2016). Everyone can review the code and documentation and can make suggestions to modify and improve the system. However, the implementations of the code come from the team of core developers who make the decisions "on behalf of the community" and after the proposed BIP has an ultimate consent from "the consensus of the Bitcoin users".[5] From a technical point of view, this (re)centralization tendency around the core developer team makes sense by virtue of their technical skills and very frequent involvement with the code.

The veto powers of the other members of the community act as a counter-balance to the power of the developer oligarchy. The blockchain core developers' protocol decisions have to be approved of and implemented by miners and other nodes. In case they disagree with the changes, they could also make the decision to fork the whole chain. Compared to miners and full nodes, plain users have less veto power, but they still do possess some level of control, by, for example, not assigning market value to the tokens issued by the network.

One can argue that these built-in control mechanisms and the possibility that actors can freely choose between competing chains and implementations stabilize and potentially counteract recentralization tendencies. Yet only in a decentralized network does such an indirect voting mechanism produce an effective democratic, horizontal self-governance of equals. In case of recentralization, there is a chance that this system of decentralized approval/rejection degenerates into a competition of highly centralized powers and leads to a potential tragedy of the anti-commons (Heller, 1998). This is exactly what is at stake with the current levels of concentration of mining power in the Bitcoin network. A small group of miners control more than 51 percent of mining power in the network, so it is relatively cheap and easy for them to prevent any changes in the protocol that might hurt their interests through coordination and collusion. Under such conditions, the built-in informal governance mechanisms in the Bitcoin network were unable to handle the block size disagreement, which could only be solved by the forking of the codebase and the network.

The ability to maintain different versions (forks) of the blockchain and users' freedom to decide which version to embrace can also be read as the expression of technical decentralization. On the other hand, while nothing prevents already centralized miners to produce the code, it is difficult for a small and dispersed group of coders to produce sufficient amounts of capital-intensive mining power. This means that it is very likely that the current separation of code production and mining will consolidate under the miners, removing another layer of checks and balances which currently add to the decentralized nature of the system.

3. *External recognition*

While, as was stated earlier, the purported examples of Bitcoin and foundational blockchains like Ethereum are motivated by the goal of achieving "policy neutrality", the need to build compatibilities with existing systems creates a tendency to recentralize. If blockchain-based systems and applications have to or want to interface with existing institutions, practices, and networks because there is no other way to achieve their stated goals, the mere existence of this interface creates strong external and internal incentives for legal compliance and a corresponding "drift towards legality". This drift implies that the legal, political, and economic systems and institutions develop the necessary tools to adopt the decentralized system. In a similar vein, DLTs also have to build the capacities to be recognizable by existing formal institutions and legal systems. Since legal compliance rests on parties being clearly identifiable and rights and obligations being well defined, this drift towards legality further creates pathways of recentralization. Control of the blockchain through identifiable actors and processes translates into control of the code, of the network, and/or of the decision-making process.

From a legal perspective, the most prominent challenge for wide adoption stems from the need of identifying legal structures under which the constituents of a blockchain project can be recognized. The consequences of such a choice can be found in the identification of formal liable actors, in the regulation of the product, and, finally, in the wider adoption by society. The case of the Tezos Foundation demonstrates the high stakes around the external recognition of DLTs, the interplay between the external and internal status of a blockchain system, the interdependence of the external governance of a techno-social system, and the self-governance of the system which the project is promising to build (Lewis-Kraus, 2018). The Tezos Foundation was established as a Swiss foundation in Zug, Switzerland. A foundation under Swiss jurisdiction is a popular choice for some emerging blockchain projects because it allows DLT developers to escape the regulations of the Securities and Exchange Commission in the US or similar regulatory bodies in other countries. However, being a Swiss foundation showed its limitations when the collapse of trust among board directors of the Tezos Foundation locked up the funds raised during the ICO. Due to regulatory governance and compliance issues, Tezos has yet to launch its promised network to this date, and it is named in numerous class action lawsuits for investor fraud and securities law violations.

On a technological governance level, the irregular nature of code contributions and technological updates among core developers and community contributors appears to inhibit the wider adoption of DLTs in more formal economic and governance contexts. The assumption that the semi-formal technical governance of the software code of DLTs will suffice to permit its integration with governmental and corporate institutions is incompatible with the reality of how institutions function, especially in the financial sector implement technology. In these settings, trusted intermediaries emerge in order to formalize the technical processes and to create liable actors or procedural guarantees. For example, efforts to formalize code production through standardization and the adoption of ISO certifications to DLTs heavily centralizes/(re) intermediates the technological stack via the validation process by external actors. A priori, de facto and de jure standardization of blockchain technology can facilitate the integration to existing trading and economic systems.

These (partial) recentralization processes do not necessarily mean that DLTs have failed their purported self-governing idealistic goals. Recentralization could create the conditions for wider adoption by formal corporate and government structures. Ultimately, the value of decentralization is measured against the value that will be derived from the wider adoption due to the embrace and approval of institutional actors. In any case, such approval requires that part of the decentralization ideal is sacrificed for a more sophisticated governance that includes more robust regimes built for conflict resolution, technological auditing, or risk management. For example, code vulnerabilities discovered on the Bitcoin blockchain illustrate the need for reinforcing code review processes. Similarly, the validation of the longest chain is still the only available predominant conflict resolution mechanism. It thus becomes evident that, for the moment, the safeguards created are still in an early stage, and since they already have demonstrated their shortcomings, there is ample room for improving the overall decentralized governance structure.

4. External existential threats

If we look at the history of the Internet, of the open-source software domain, of privacy enhancing technologies (PETs), or of file sharing networks, existential threats emerge to be the most effective drivers of technological decentralization. Such threats present a clear and present danger to the practices, freedoms, autonomy, or mere existence of technology-enabled communities and practices. The network topology and the protocols of the Internet were shaped by military concerns over the vulnerabilities of centralized communication networks and the direct threat of a nuclear war. The open-source software movement was galvanized by the enclosure of software due to the copyrightability of software code and led to the decentralization of the loci of software development, the political decentralization of competing software implementations, and the legal decentralization through FLOSS licences. The Tor Onion Network is a decentralized network which provides anonymous communication to its users (Syverson, Dingledine, & Mathewson, 2004). Its development is partly funded by the US intelligence services to obfuscate law enforcement and intelligence communications. File-sharing technologies, from Napster to the BitTorrent protocol, became decentralized step by step, as lawsuits identified points where rights holders could shut down networks (Bodó, 2011; Giblin, 2011).

External threats do not produce absolute technological decentralization. The exact degree of decentralization is set by the marginal costs and benefits of the attack and the defense. The BitTorrent protocol decentralized p2p file sharing to the extent at which the extra costs associated with online copyright enforcement exceed the achievable extra benefits. The Tor network does not provide full anonymity; it only renders monitoring and deanonymization prohibitively costly for anyone except probably state actors. Blockchain networks are not immutable, but a 51% attack is usually more costly than any potential benefits it can provide. Such decentralization is thus very pragmatic. While it responds to legal, political, or economic threats, it is also based on more or less precise cost-benefit estimates and tends to not spend more resources on decentralization than what is absolutely made necessary by the economic, technological, and political conditions of the external threat. In blockchain-based systems, this cost-benefit analysis is also modelled in advance and used to incentivize the production of the network. Such decentralization is also gradual and responsive and develops in sync with the expected changes in the nature and the shifting economics of external threats.

5. Endogenous and exogenous economic incentives

The development of cryptoeconomics is one of the major, possibly long-term contributions of the blockchain domain to science. It refers to the use of game theory to design economic incentive systems to encourage certain desired properties in techno-social systems to hold into the future and discourage others to emerge (Buterin, 2017b), or to a "formal discipline that studies protocols that govern the production, distribution, and consumption of goods and services in a decentralized digital economy. Cryptoeconomics is a practical science that focuses on the design and characterization of these protocols" (Zamfir, 2015).

When Benkler formulated his commons-based peer production (CBPP) paradigm, his central concern was how to organize the production of a common resource pool through nonmarket incentives. The CBPP literature focuses on the intrinsic and social sources of motivation to explain the production of shared resources and warns that extrinsic, monetary incentives actually crowd out other forms of motivations (Benkler, 2006, pp. 92–99). In contrast, blockchain-based cryptoeconomic techno-social systems differ from the logic of peer production in that they have built-in remuneration logics in the form of cryptoassets, or native tokens, which are used to incentivize the production of the resources the networks needs for its operation. Tokens are also used to compensate for the costs that such production activity incur (in forms of energy costs, investment, or expertise) (Narayanan et al., 2016). The token-based economic systems in DLTs are thus vehicles to extract and redistribute value. They are also designed in a way to only allow value extraction in certain, limited ways which preferably prevent the reconcentration in various dimensions, such as value extraction power.

The blockchain technology community has paid a great deal of attention to the cryptoeconomic consequences of architectural choices, i.e., how the incentive structures of stakeholders and the corresponding Nash-equilibria of the games they are locked in may change due to different, on the surface purely technical, decisions. The aforementioned Bitcoin block size debate is the obvious case to demonstrate how the game-theoretical consequences were having an effect on the application of a technological, architectural choice. Yet not all such consequences can be modelled at the time of taking a technical decision, which leads to situations where exogenous economic incentives (those that weren't taken into account in the design) produce recentralization and the endogenous incentives (those that are built in the system) are unable to prevent this – or in the worst case, they (unintendedly) aggravate the problem.

As Braudel (1992) and, in his footsteps, de Landa (1996) warn us, market players have an inherent incentive to eliminate market competition and the rules that control and ensure such competition. Blockchain-based techno-social systems are no exception to this rule. Apparently, different blockchain stakeholders find ways through which they can eliminate competition from the provision of services the network relies on, resulting in the recentralization of decentralized systems. This antimarket, centralizing behavior can take multiple forms. Changing the endogenous incentive structures through majority vote or, if that fails, through a hard fork is one approach. The block size debate played out exactly in this manner, and as the improvement protocols aiming to increase the block size were voted down (Andresen, 2015), a number of hard forks ensued. Alternatives like Bitcoin Cash, Bitcoin XT, Bitcoin Classic and Bitcoin Unlimited allow for a higher degree of potential centralization in exchange for higher capacity. On the other hand, exploiting exogenous economic factors can also lead to recentralization. To illustrate this point, consider the dynamics of recentralization of the Bitcoin network. The specific algorithm used by Bitcoin's Proof of Work (PoW) encouraged the development of highly efficient, specialized mining hardware components (Dev, 2014), a market which turned out to be highly centralized. In a different layer, PoW mining turned out to be energy intensive, as both the running and the cooling of mining hardware requires substantial amounts of energy. Consequently, miners tend to geographically cluster around cheap sources of energy and cooler climates. For any given block, only one miner can claim the mining reward, which produces a very unpredictable revenue flow for each individual miner. In response, miners organized themselves into a very small number of extremely influential mining pools which share mining revenues across members in a more predictable fashion.

Some of these centralizing economic incentives can be foreseen and mitigated on the technology layer. Ethereum technology developers realized quite soon that market concentration through cartel formation is an issue to be dealt with on the level of the consensus protocol: "Cryptocurrency is incredibly concentrated. So is mining power. Oligopolistic competition is the norm in many 'real-life' markets. Coordination between a small number of relatively wealthy validators is much easier than coordination between a large number of relatively poor validators. Cartels formation is completely expected, in our context. . . . Blockchain architecture is mechanism design for oligopolistic markets" (Zamfir, 2016). Yet such solutions are rarely straightforward, and there is no guarantee that the protocol design correctly predicts all potential exogenous incentives to recentralize.

Conclusion

At the moment, there is a wide gap between the forms and extent of decentralization, as prescribed by the ideology, and the practical forms in which it manifests in various blockchain networks. Different blockchain implementations serve as case studies in unexpected recentralization of a technological infrastructure designed to be decentralized out of pure ideological reasons. Focusing on decentralization as an end-goal or as an ideologically supreme design choice "conceals relations and systems of domination, exploitation, and alienation" (Baldwin, 2018, p. 6). In addition, looking at decentralization at the technical layer alone is hardly enough. As countless studies on technological communities clustered around decentralized technological infrastructures suggest, a decentralized technical architecture does not automatically produce decentralized governance structures or more just worlds in general.

As we have seen with blockchain technology evangelists, and the Web 3.0 summit organizers, ideological commitment to decentralization may produce decentralization, but it is hardly the only and, by all accounts, may not even be the most effective driver. Decentralization comes with severe trade-offs in terms of scalability, efficiency, usability, security, etc. The optimal choice in these trade-offs differs context by context, and there is hardly a one-size-fits all degree of decentralization in the many interdependent layers of a techno-social system (Wang, Vergne, & Hsieh, 2017).

Decentralization is a powerful architectural feature of digital technology, because it can raise the costs of enforcing legal rules, rights, and obligations for private parties and the state alike. Unlike others (Wright & de Filippi, 2018), we are not convinced that decentralized blockchain networks would be able to bypass or negate the rule of law (Quintais, Bodó, Giannopoulou, & Ferrari, 2019) and would lead to the replacement of law by code. But different technological designs have a different enforcement calculus attached to them. More decentralized technologies, if done right, can be more difficult to rein in. What we have tried to argue in this chapter was that it is important for lawyers and policymakers, as well as those closely involved in the development, monetization, or use of the technology, to understand how the regulation capacities of technological systems interact with, reinforce, contest, and complement the regulatory capacity of legal instruments. Technology and law tend to develop in tandem: law develops to address new practices enabled by new forms of technology, and technology development reflects legal developments. This interlocking coevolution of law and code has sometimes been referred to as an arms race or a whack-a-mole game, describing, for example, the relationship of copyrights and file sharing technologies. However, such an approach locks technology and law in a binary opposition, a mutually antagonistic struggle for supremacy, sovereignty, revolt, and evasion. While this is a plausible scenario, it is not the only one. The concept, the process, and the practical outcome of technology decentralization is more complex than what the code vs. law approach offers, and it is definitely not only about technological sovereignty and legal impunity. As we have shown, the decentralization efforts, so central in the blockchain discourse, enable a wide variety of technology development trajectories which produce different configurations of how law *and* code could work together to order technology-enabled practices and processes. In that process, some outcomes pose less of a challenge than others. The file sharing technology development ultimately produced a situation in which law enforcement is only possible at the deepest infrastructural levels, at the wires controlled by legally not liable ISPs. The understandable resistance to such a drastic approach created a situation where a decentralized technology enables sustained infringing activity. The emergence of a similar outcome in the blockchain space is both possible and avoidable through the better understanding of the processes that drive technology development.

Notes

1 Retrieved from www.decentralizedweb.net/.
2 Retrieved from https://github.com/ethereum/wiki/wiki/Casper-Proof-of-Stake-compendium.
3 Retrieved fromhttps://github.com/ethereum/wiki/wiki/Proof-of-Stake-FAQs.
4 According to the project's white paper, "the Aragon Network provides a subjective governance layer that improves the overall usability of Ethereum by providing a mechanism for pseudo-anonymous blockchain entities, including decentralized autonomous organizations (DAOs) and individuals, to create flexible human-readable agreements that are enforceable on-chain". Retrieved from https://github.com/aragon/whitepaper.
5 Retrieved from https://github.com/Bitcoin/bips/blob/master/README.mediawiki.

References

Andresen, G. (2015). *Bitcoin improvement proposal 101: Increase maximum block size.* Retrieved from https://github.com/Bitcoin/bips/wiki/Comments:BIP-0101

Azouvi, S., Maller, M., & Meiklejohn, S. (2018). Egalitarian society or benevolent dictatorship: The state of cryptocurrency governance. In *22nd International Conference on Financial Cryptography and Data Security*, University College London.

Baldwin, J. (2018). In digital we trust: Bitcoin discourse, digital currencies, and decentralized network fetishism. *Palgrave Communications*, *4*(1), 14. Retrieved from https://doi.org/10.1057/s41599-018-0065-0

Barbrook, R., & Cameron, A. (1995). The Californian ideology. *Alamut.*

Barlow, J. P. (1996). A declaration of the independence of cyberspace. *Eff.Org*. San Francisco, CA: Electronic Frontier Foundation. Retrieved from https://projects.eff.org/~barlow/Declaration-Final.html

Benkler, Y. (2006). *The wealth of networks: How social production transforms markets and freedom.* New Haven, CT: Yale University Press.

Bodó, B. (2011). *A szerzői jog kalózai.* Budapest: Typotex.

Bonneau, J., Miller, A., Clark, J., Narayanan, A., Kroll, J., & Felten, E. (2015). SoK: Research perspectives and challenges for Bitcoin and cryptocurrencies. *2015 IEEE Symposium on Security and Privacy* (pp. 104–121). Retrieved from https://doi.org/10.1109/SP.2015.14

Braudel, F. (1992). *Civilization and capitalism, 15th-18th century, vol. II: The wheels of commerce* (Vol. 2). Berkeley and Los Angeles, CA: University of California Press.

Buterin, V. (2013). *Ethereum white paper: A next-generation smart contract and decentralized application platform*. Retrieved from https://github.com/ethereum/wiki/wiki/White-Paper

Buterin, V. (2017a). The meaning of decentralization. *Medium.com*. Retrieved from https://medium.com/@VitalikButerin/the-meaning-of-decentralization-a0c92b76a274

Buterin, V. (2017b). *Introduction to cryptoeconomics*. Berlin: Ethereum Foundation. Retrieved from www.youtube.com/watch?v=pKqdjaH1dRo

Chohan, U. W. (2017). *Cryptoanarchism and cryptocurrencies*. Discussion Paper Series: Notes on the 21st Century. Canberra.

de Filippi, P., & Loveluck, B. (2016). The invisible politics of Bitcoin: Governance crisis of a decentralised infrastructure. *Internet Policy Review*, *5*(3). Retrieved from https://doi.org/10.14763/2016.3.427

de Landa, M. (1996). Markets and antimarkets in the world economy. In S. Aronowitz, B. Marhnsons, & M. Merser (Eds.), *Technoscience and cyberculture*. New York, NY: Routledge.

Dev, J. A. (2014). Bitcoin mining acceleration and performance quantification. In *Electrical and Computer Engineering (CCECE), 2014 IEEE 27th Canadian Conference on* (pp. 1–6). IEEE.

DuPont, Q. (2017). Experiments in algorithmic governance: A history and ethnography of "The DAO," a failed decentralized autonomous organization. In M. Campbell-Verduyn (Ed.), *Bitcoin and beyond: Blockchains and global governance*. RIPE/Routledge Series in Global Political Economy. New York, NY: Routledge. Retrieved from https://doi.org/10.4324/9781315211909

Elmer-DeWitt, P. (1993). First nation in cyberspace. *TIME International*. Retrieved from http://kirste.userpage.fu-berlin.de/outerspace/internet-article.html

Gencer, A. E., Basu, S., Eyal, I., van Renesse, R., & Sirer, E. G. (2018). *Decentralization in Bitcoin and Ethereum networks*. Retrieved from http://arxiv.org/abs/1801.03998

Gervais, A., Karame, G. O., Capkun, V., & Capkun, S. (2014). Is Bitcoin a decentralized currency? *IEEE Security & Privacy*, *12*(3), 54–60.

Giblin, R. (2011). *Code Wars: 10 years of P2P software litigation*. Cheltenham: Northampton, MA: Edward Elgar Publishing.

Golumbia, D. (2016). *The politics of Bitcoin: Software as right-wing extremism*. Minneapolis, MA: University of Minnesota Press.

Goodman, L. M. (2014). *Tezos: A self-amending crypto-ledger position paper*. Retrieved from https://tezos.com/static/papers/position_paper.pdf

Heller, M. A. (1998). The tragedy of the anticommons: Property in the transition from Marx to markets. *Harvard Law Review*, *111*(3), 621–688.

Kelly, B. (2014). *The Bitcoin big bang: How alternative currencies are about to change the world*. Hoboken, New Jersey, United States: John Wiley & Sons.

Lessig, L. (1999). *Code and other laws of cyberspace*. New York, NY: Basic Books.

Lewis-Kraus, G. (2018, June 19). The blockchain: A love story/horror story. *Wired*. Retrieved from www.wired.com/story/tezos-blockchain-love-story-horror-story/

May, T. (1994). Crypto anarchy and virtual communities. In *Crypto anarchy cyberstates and pirate utopias* (pp. 65–79). Retrieved from www.textfiles.com/internet/anarchy

Morozov, E. (2014). To save everything, click here: The folly of technological solutionism. *PublicAffairs*.

Nakamoto, S. (2008). Bitcoin: A peer-to-peer electronic cash system. *Bitcoin.org*. Retrieved from https://Bitcoin.org/Bitcoin.pdf

Nakamoto, S. (2009). *Bitcoin open source implementation of P2Pcurrency*. Retrieved from http://p2pfoundation.ning.com/forum/topics/bitcoin-open-source

Narayanan, A., Bonneau, J., Felten, E., Miller, A., & Goldfeder, S. (2016). *Bitcoin and cryptocurrency technologies*. Princeton, NJ: Princeton University Press.

Narayanan, A., & Clark, J. (2017). Bitcoin's academic pedigree. *Communications of the ACM, 60*(12), 36–45.

Quintais, J. P., Bodó, B., Giannopoulou, A., & Ferrari, V. (2019). Blockchain and the law: A critical evaluation (Book Review). *Stanford Journal of Blockchain Law & Policy, 2*(1).

Srinivasan, B. S. (2017). *Quantifying decentralization*. Retrieved from https://news.earn.com/quantifying-decentralization-e39db233c28e

Swan, M. (2015). *Blockchain: Blueprint for a new economy*. Sebastopol, CA: O'Reilly Media. Retrieved from https://doi.org/10.1017/CBO9781107415324.004

Syverson, P., Dingledine, R., & Mathewson, N. (2004). Tor: The second generation onion router. *Usenix Security*.

Tapscott, D., & Tapscott, A. (2016). *Blockchain revolution: How the technology behind Bitcoin is changing money, business, and the world*. New York, NY: Portfolio.

van Wirdum, A. (2015, September). The decentralist perspective, or why Bitcoin might need small blocks. *Bitcoin Magazine*. Retrieved from https://Bitcoinmagazine.com/articles/decentralist-perspective-Bitcoin-might-need-small-blocks-1442090446/

Wang, S., Vergne, J. P., & Hsieh, Y.-Y. (2017). The internal and external governance of blockchain-based organizations: Evidence from cryptocurrencies. In M. Campbell-Verduyn (Ed.), *Bitcoin and beyond: Blockchains and global governance*. RIPE/Routledge Series in Global Political Economy. New York, NY: Routledge.

Wright, A., & de Filippi, P. (2015). Decentralized blockchain technology and the rise of lex cryptographia. *SSRN Electronic Journal*, 4–22. Retrieved from https://doi.org/10.2139/ssrn.2580664

Wright, A., & de Filippi, P. (2018). *Blockchain and the law: The rule of code*. Cambridge, MA: Harvard University Press.

Zamfir, V. (2015). *What is cryptoeconomics*? Mountain View, CA: Cryptoeconomicon. Retrieved from www.youtube.com/watch?v=9lw3s7iGUXQ

Zamfir, V. (2016). The history of Casper – Chapter 4. *Medium.com*. Retrieved from https://medium.com/@Vlad_Zamfir/the-history-of-casper-chapter-4-3855638b5f0e

Chapter 9

Disruptive blockworks

Blockchains and networks/ acceleration and collision

Matthew Lovett

Introduction

In the near quarter-century since the Federal Networking Council (NITRD, 1995) first defined the term 'the Internet', our use and our understanding of this most quintessentially disruptive technology has evolved considerably. And now, as a further iteration of the Internet is emerging and beginning to establish itself – a semantic web of integrated data – increasingly, blockchain technology is being pushed to the forefront of debates relating to what a future web might look like and how it could work. With decentralised, peer-to-peer communication as a core operating principle, along with a capacity to facilitate anonymous interaction across global networks, blockchain is enabling an economy, and a culture that is ever more concerned with privacy and authentication, to develop and grow.

What follows is an engagement with Steemit (Steemit, 2018) and Mycelia's Creative Passport project (Mycelia, 2018), two blockchain-based platforms designed and built to harness aspects of blockchain's orientation towards authentication and payment systems. The emergence of blockchain technology has been concurrent with a period of development and change for the Internet, where an early twenty-first-century optimism about the capacity of digital networks to create new forms of non-hierarchical labour and association has been displaced by growing concerns over the widespread commercial domination within a supposedly open network. 'Acceleration and collision' signal two aspects of contemporary discourse surrounding our techonomic environment: 'accelerationism' and 'disruptive technology', the former being a latter-day rewiring of the economist Joseph Schumpeter's theory of 'creative destruction', whilst the latter is a term that draws on the work of the philosopher Gilles Deleuze and the psychoanalyst Félix Guattari and has found purchase in contemporary critical theory and debate.

Initially, the chapter establishes a context in which to discuss the emergence of Steemit and Creative Passport in relation to two notable shifts in our conception and understanding of the Internet during the past twenty years, the first being an initial wave of optimism surrounding digital networks' capacity to create new forms of non-hierarchical labour and association, and the second, a more recent cynicism brought on by widespread commercial domination, defined by Nick Srnicek as 'Platform Capitalism'. We then engage more fully with Steemit and Creative Passport in relation to Schumpeterian and Accelerationist ideas to consider how economic theory is both implicitly and explicitly expressed in blockchain-driven technology, and what kind of disruption these technologies might bring.

Steemit

Steemit is a micro blogging platform reminiscent of both Reddit and Twitter. On creating a Steemit account, users are able to engage with a range of familiar social media activities, including uploading text-based posts, photographs and links to off-site content, tagging other users and creating hashtags. According to the *Steem Whitepaper*, Steem, the blockchain database that drives Steemit, 'is the first cryptocurrency that attempts to accurately and transparently reward an unbounded number of individuals who make *subjective contributions* to its community' (Steem, 2017). Steemit offers to pay users for interacting with the Steem ecosystem, and users are rewarded in Steem tokens for posting, voting and curating on the Steemit platform. These tokens can be converted to Steem Dollars, which in themselves can by traded for Bitcoin, and thus – eventually – exchanged for fiat currency. According to the *Steem Bluepaper*, the Steem blockchain is based on delegated proof of stake rather than a proof of work (PoW), and it mints Steem tokens at a rate of one block every three seconds. Steem sets itself aside from the likes of Bitcoin, stating that 'unlike the traditional PoW means of distribution, where miners are competing over raw computing power, the actors in the Steem network are incentivised to compete in ways that add value to the network' (Steem Bluepaper, 2018). As a result, one of Steem's most important innovations is to have tethered content creation to cryptocurrency production, meaning that the blockchain captures users' every interaction with Steemit and continuously distributes payment from the Steem 'rewards pool' (Steem, 2018) based on the quality of this interaction. Steemit is designed to be an entirely democratic platform that enables its users to decide on – or 'vote' – whether or not, and to what extent, user activity on Steemit (including their own) is worthy of reward. The voting process – known as 'upvoting' – is akin to 'liking' something on other social media platforms, with the addition that Steemit attaches a reward to the upvoting process itself: 'If you discover a post and upvote it before it becomes popular, you can earn a curation reward' (Steem, 2017). Because one of Steemit's fundamental operating principles is to embrace the notion that success within social media environments is as much about interlinking as it is about posting, upvoting also becomes a strategic activity, enabling users to fully engage with the benefits of a connected web, where every point of contact with the web – every digitally recorded act of creative decision making – is a potentially monetisable signpost to every other point. Thus, via the production and validation of new connections, the reward system acknowledges these actions as creative activities in their own right. This is a notable departure from previous iterations of the World Wide Web, which, as we shall see, has often allowed for an atmosphere of creativity for its own sake, and if it has been considered as part of the online environment, then commercial exploitation of content has increasingly been seen as the reserve of multinationals rather than everyday users.

Steemit has been designed to work as an integrated ecosystem, one that encourages users to engage with the platform in a number of ways, reconfiguring the social media environment as a mixed economy of practices and behaviours, akin to 'a game system where users compete for attention and rewards by bringing content and adding value to the platform' (Steemit, 2018). Steemit is thus a wholesale rethinking of creating and sharing, something of a blueprint for an Internet to come, where Steem's twin innovation of paying users for engaging with the platform whilst simultaneously providing an overarching cloak of anonymity enables the network to proliferate and users to prosper whilst maintaining their privacy. In addition, because Steemit's game-like qualities enable it to democratise and, perhaps more importantly, *incentivise* the social media environment, Steem presents a new vision of how to harness a user's desire to inhabit and contribute to a network. By enabling users to track the value of Steem whilst simultaneously monitoring theirs and their peers' financial success, Steemit thereby fuses this desire with a newly tooled appetite to engage with an Internet of commerce and value.

Creative Passport

Creative Passport is one of a number of ventures developed by Mycelia, a project platform founded by the musician Imogen Heap, described on its homepage as 'a research and development hub for music makers' (Mycelia, 2018). On the introduction page, Heap explains that:

> The Creative Passport is the digital container for verified profile information, IDs, acknowledgements, works, business partners and payment mechanisms for each music maker. Its aim is to fill a huge gap for the industry by becoming a digital identity standard for music makers, collectively forming the Creative Passport Database and evolving into the essential connective hub for all music related services.
>
> (Heap, 2018: 3)

As with Steemit, Creative Passport has been designed as a corrective to a perceived flaw in the networked media environment. In the case of Creative Passport, it is a means to ensure that musicians' creative contributions to music-based content are registered and rewarded and that these contributions are safeguarded in perpetuity by being stored on an immutable database. Heap goes on to discuss how earlier attempts to create an all-encompassing 'Global Repertoire Database' had been unsuccessful (Heap, 2018: 5), especially the original project to create a GRD. Launched by the EU and involving Apple, Amazon, Google and a range of publishers and rights collection agencies (Music Business Worldwide, 2016), the project incurred costs of £8 million and was eventually abandoned in 2014. In 2017, the US Congress proposed a bill to create a 'searchable digital database' (Digital Music News, 2017a), but this has also met with little success (Digital Music News, 2017b). In essence, Creative Passport is an attempt to capture and store information at scale, and given the sustained growth of the global music industry – with the IFPI's Global Music Report 2018 reporting that revenues for recorded music had increased by a further 8.1 percent during 2017 (IFPI, 2018) – this is clearly an issue that will continue to be a source of speculation and debate until a multilateral solution is found. Whilst there are clear technological and ideological differences between Steemit and Creative Passport – Steemit being a social media platform designed to provide payment to users for a wide range of creative acts and interactions on the platform, whereas Creative Passport is an information storage facility for those offering commercial services within the music industry – there are also important similarities. Each expresses a vision of harnessing blockchain to create infrastructural improvements in digital music and media commerce, an aspect of blockchain that has all-too-easily been overlooked in the drive to see it as a curative for protracted and inefficient commercial transactions. Instead, what the designers of platforms such as Steemit and Creative Passport understand is that blockchain has the potential to enable us to conceive of a new paradigm for online communication. Worth noting at this point is that, whilst we must be careful to not overestimate the scale of technological change that blockchain might bring about, its presence is undoubtedly contributing to a rapid evolution of both our understanding and our expectations of how we interact with the Internet.

The future was bright

In the early 2000s, a certain utopianism about how the Internet could help establish a more creative and equitable economy was clearly in the ascendant. Yochai Benkler's book *Wealth of Networks: How Social Production Transforms Markets and Freedom* and Charles Leadbeater's *We-Think: Mass Innovation, not Mass Production* are both notable examples of this wave of optimism surrounding a perceived capacity for the Internet to create a step change in both the social and industrial spheres. Indeed, Benkler's conviction was that an increasingly networked world, made possible by cheaper and more powerful computers, would mean that 'nonmarket and radically decentralised [patterns of production would emerge] at the core, rather than at the periphery of most advanced economies' (Benkler, 2006: 3). Whilst Benkler has certainly been proven right about the emergence of decentralised production in all its variances, the extent to which non-market forces are influencing contemporary digital economies is less certain. Nonetheless, Benkler was far from alone in thinking that the Internet would catalyse widespread collaborative and non-commercial activity; indeed, in *Making Is Connecting*, David Gauntlett coined the phrase 'everyday creativity' (Gauntlett, 2011) to highlight the way that digital networks greatly enhanced a general capacity for non-market creative expression. In other words, a digitally enabled culture of *doing-for-the-sake-of-doing* was on the rise. Given its origins in the 1960s as the ARPANET, a packet-switching network designed to facilitate non-commercial resource sharing and collaboration (Internet Society, 1997), it is quite understandable that the Internet was seen to contain the seeds of a new kind of organisation of the creative and communications economy. In this regard, Gauntlett's interest in the wealth of amateurish making and invention, facilitated and disseminated by the reinvigorated Web 2.0, was matched by Leadbeater's extensive analysis of how the Internet was facilitating new forms of digital collaboration, enabling users to come together to think and work in more creative ways in new and flattened organisational structures. Such was the current of thought in the 2000s and early 2010s, where a shared optimism about the Internet's potential to radically alter not only our economic environment but also our attitude towards commercial production was in the ascendant, along with a growing sense of ourselves as members of a distributed community of digitally enabled makers and sharers.

More recently, in the book *Who Owns the Future*, the media theorist, programmer and musician Jaron Lanier coined the term 'Siren Servers' (Lanier, 2014) to convey how, via the exploitation of 'information asymmetry', corporations such as Facebook, Google and Apple make huge financial gains from the very acts of everyday making and connecting that Gauntlett's work identified and described. Lanier's book provided an account for how corporate interest monetises commonplace use activity online, most obviously expressed via the selling of advertising space, but he also sought to develop a response to what he saw as a seemingly inexorable slide towards a 'winner takes all star system' (Lanier, 2014: 35), where an increasingly reduced number of corporations and individuals would see ever-higher profits in return for their growing domination of the Internet. Lanier suggested that a more equitable online economy would be possible, at the expense of redesigning the Internet to include 'two-way links' (Lanier, 2014: 218), which would put revenue and data capture within reach of every user rather than simply in the hands of those who already hold the financial and information advantage.

Such widespread harvesting of users' daily and routine activities is a key component of what Nick Srnicek has described as 'Platform Capitalism'. Srnicek's work analyses the way in which commercial practices based on data gathering and analysis are now producing a new kind of economy:

> Platforms are a new type of firm; they are characterised by providing the infrastructure to intermediate between different user groups, by displaying

> monopoly tendencies driven by network effects, by employing cross-subsidisation to draw in different user groups.
>
> (Srnicek, 2017: 48)

As such, Srnicek presents a comprehensive description of the way in which, in the age of the Siren Server, different companies have developed different methods to exploit the web's gold rush of digital information. Central to the question of how a blockchain-based platform such as Steemit operates is Srnicek's use of the terms 'network effects' and 'monopoly tendencies', since both ideas find expression in the way that Steemit is emerging as a challenge to conventional ways of approaching the design and use of social media. For Srnicek, not only has the platform model established itself as a key component motor of the twenty-first-century global economy, it is also altering the way in which we engage with online networks. In addition, 'by providing a digital space for others to interact in' (Srnicek, 2017: 48) at a more fundamental level, platforms are evolving the way in which we think about the production and distribution of music and music-related media, owing to the fact that so much of the contemporary music economy only exists within, and by virtue of, platform environments.

The extent to which platforms such as Facebook, Google, Uber and Spotify have created processes to enable them to extract and exploit data from a range of sources is now widely recognised, and to an extent accepted, suggesting that our conception of the Internet and the types of practice that it affords is now at some remove from the non-market, participative cultures of the future that Leadbeater, Gauntlett and Benkler described. Latterly, Lanier's and Srnicek's analyses have been designed to show that whilst non-commerciality and sharing may be an experience that occurs at an interpersonal or local level, such transactions and exchanges are simply one aspect of a complex web of commodified information flows. Furthermore, although collaborative and non-commercial creativity once occupied an area of discourse that anticipated a future Internet that was not wholly profit driven, Srnicek's analysis would suggest that the opposite may well be the case and that platformisation is driving towards a hyper-monetisation of the online environment, where even the thought of a non-commercial web has become simply a quirk of history. In a latter-day digital landscape teeming with industrial information harvesters in the guise of commercial platforms, it is therefore little wonder that blockchain is often touted as the panacea that will finally cure the ills of our networked world, cutting out the 'middleman' of corporate exploitation and allowing us to keep hold of the 'digital crumbs' of our online identities (Tapscott, 2016).

Clearly, Steemit and Creative Passport have emerged at a time when perceptions of the Internet are rapidly evolving. On one hand, the potential to integrate blockchain with a networked environment beyond its origins as an engine for cryptocurrency and anonymised exchange is considerable, whilst on the other, in the context of our current fixation with protecting privacy and provenance, blockchain presents as a technological solution to a range of both ethical and financial problems. In this context, Joseph Schumpeter's work is well placed to help us consider how Steemit and Creative Passport, due to their disruptive tendencies, could drive transformation in the digital music and media economies. In addition, because each of them is a manifestation of an accelerating desire to interact with the Internet in more autonomous and equitable ways and because Schumpeter's work is concerned with economic modelling at a macro scale, we can also consider how Steemit and Creative Passport might open up perspectives around the ongoing evolution of the general socio-economic environment.

Destructive transformation

In *Capitalism, Socialism and Democracy*, Schumpeter's wider project was the contention that capitalism is an inherently unstable and self-devouring phenomenon. Whereas Engels and Marx concluded that the transition from capitalism to socialism would come about via a process of violent revolution (Engels and Marx, 1848), Schumpeter looked through a different lens. He held that capitalism was inherently unstable and liable to collapse because of the way in which it systematically undermines the structures that it relies on, and indeed the conditions that brought it into existence in the first place. Although Schumpeter's focus was at the macroeconomic scale, we can nevertheless use his ideas as a backdrop to consider how it is that we might understand Steemit and Creative Passport to be agents of collision and acceleration and keep in mind the fact that, in its original formulation, creative destruction drew a parallel between changes at a market level, with an overall systemic transformation:

> The opening up of new markets, foreign or domestic, and the organisational development from the craft shop and factory to such concerns as U.S. Steel illustrate the same process of industrial mutation that incessantly revolutionises the economic structure from *within*, incessantly destroying the old one, incessantly creating a new one. This process of Creative Destruction is the essential fact about capitalism. It is what capitalism consists in and what every capitalist concern has got to live in.
>
> (Schumpeter, 2010: 73)

Later in the book, Schumpeter qualifies his vision of how creative destruction functions at the level of economic infrastructure, suggesting that:

> The same economic process that undermines the position of the bourgeoisie by decreasing the importance of the functions of entrepreneurs and capitalists, by breaking up protective strata and institutions, by creating an atmosphere of hostility, also decomposes the motor forces of capitalism from within.
>
> (Schumpeter, 2010: 144)

Thus we see the full reach of Schumpeter's conceptual framework, encompassing both market dynamics within the framework of capitalism and the overarching instabilities of capitalism itself. As I have explored elsewhere,[1] we inhabit a world marked by the ubiquitous presence of disruptive technology, where the word 'disruption' – the dominant contemporary reading of the notion of creative destruction – now refers to the way in which new technologies, after some initial discomfort, ultimately alter markets and systems for the better (Lovett, 2019). Indeed, with headlines such as 'The future of all industry is disruption – and that's a good thing', we are told that 'disruption is not something to be feared. Emerging technologies and innovative ideas give businesses the opportunity to grow their core services and products, and expand into new markets' (Accenture, 2018). The original formulation for 'disruption' in its current sense contended that disruption is a process that occurs at a holistic level, where not only products are disrupted but entire infrastructures, including supply chain chains, distribution networks, production processes and so on (Bower and Christensen, 1995). The influence of Bower and Christensen's article, which was more a mapping of technological change and challenge to incumbent companies rather than a consideration of the more underlying precepts of a capitalist exchange system, is clearly visible in the Accenture statement. The commitment to embracing disruption as 'a good thing' is emblematic of an increasingly widespread aspect of the discourse surrounding disruption, where the positive and corrective benefits of technological disruption are a clear step away from Schumpeter's holistic and system-level analysis of capitalism. However, whilst the Accenture statement may well be correct to suggest that disruption at the level of a product or a service may well be of benefit for consumers, the prospect of having our entire economic macrostructure disrupted might not be so welcome.

For Schumpeter, it was a common misconception in 'social criticism' that the 'decline of competition' was the cause of the 'decline of capitalism' (Schumpeter, 2010: 125), and he goes on to suggest that this was – and it may well be the case that it remains – the reason why industrial monopolisation is seen as a 'vice' (Schumpeter, 2010: 125). His approach is a manifestly practical one, and his account for the benefits of monopolies simply states that 'there are superior methods available to the monopolist which either are not available at all to a crowd of competitors or are not available to them so readily' (Schumpeter, 2010: 87). Schumpeter's view was that markets do not function according to a perfect competition between different producers battling with each other over the 'price variable' (Schumpeter, 2010: 85). Instead, competition, properly understood, occurs between an established and incumbent monopoly and the emergent forces and organisations which are seeking to enter the market. Although creative destruction might have evolved into a vision of technological disruption that frames the replacement of incumbents by more advanced and efficient innovators as necessary and corrective, Schumpeter's original intention was clearly to articulate a radical reformulation of market dynamics.

For Schumpeter, the idea of permanent threat and the displacement caused by 'the new commodity, the new technology, the new source of supply, the new type of organisation' (Schumpeter, 2010: 72) was intended to oust traditional notions of competition. In this regard, it is also sobering to briefly reflect on Schumpeter's conviction that the pervasive nature of this type of competition which 'disciplines before it attacks' (Schumpeter, 2010: 72) was not simply a mechanism wherein one monopoly replaces another but in fact should be seen as the very foundations of a market economy.

In the book *Zero to One*, Peter Thiel, like Bower and Christensen, takes certain aspects of Schumpeter's work in order to put forward his own economic treatise for the present day. Thiel's approach is not only to provide a rationale as to why the monopoly model is better than perfect competition but to provide concrete examples of technological disruption. Thiel's basic formulation is almost textbook Schumpeter:

> In the real world outside economic theory, every business is successful exactly to the extent that it does something others cannot. Monopoly is therefore not a pathology or an exception. *Monopoly is the condition of every successful business*; [all happy companies earn] a monopoly by solving a unique problem. All failed companies are the same: they failed to escape competition.
>
> (Thiel, 2014: 34)

Not only does the model fit, but his use of the word 'pathology' is strongly reminiscent of Schumpeter's awareness of the way that monopolies had been linked with 'vice'. What is more, Thiel's suggestion that 'the history of progress is a history of better monopoly businesses replacing incumbents' (Thiel, 2014: 32) is an almost exact description of the way in which technologies such as Steemit and Creative Passport are designed to disrupt their respective environments. As with Thiel's description of Apple's iOS ousting Microsoft, the intention is not to make Steemit and Creative Passport compete with existing models and business, and neither are they supposed to do things in a more efficient or cheaper way. Instead, they are both designed to completely transform their respective sectors, ushering in wholesale transformations both in our understanding of the relationship between creating content and being rewarded on social media platforms and in our expectations around direct and indirect rewards for creating and contributing to commercial content. Schumpeter again:

> [Monopolies] not only arise in the process of creative destruction and function in a way entirely different from the basic schema, but in many cases of decisive importance they provide the necessary form for the achievement. They largely create what they exploit.
>
> (Schumpeter, 2010: 87)

Before concluding, and to provide a further perspective on notions of disruption and creative destruction, I shall briefly turn to the development in European and American critical perspectives known as 'accelerationism'. In what is now often regarded is the 'Urtext' of accelerationist thought, the passage titled 'The Civilised Capitalist Machine' in *Anti-Oedipus*, Deleuze and Guattari lay out the fundamental axiom that has gone on to inform a set of accelerationist trajectories that continue to be played out in both academic and online debate, most notably found within the context of the differentiation of the left, right and 'unconditional' strains of accelerationism.[2] Deleuze and Guattari's aim in *Anti-Oedipus* was to produce a new critique of capitalism, one that was outside of traditional post-Marxist frameworks, and which began to formulate a way of seeing beyond capitalism by establishing a connection with desire. In thinking about what kind of 'revolutionary path' could lead out of the impasses they saw in capitalism, Deleuze and Guattari suggested that we should not 'withdraw from the process [of capitalism] but to go further, to "accelerate the process"' (Deleuze and Guattari, 1972: 162), which, in Schumpeterian terms, would suggest that we should help capitalism to reach its self-driven collapse more rapidly and thus find ourselves in a more acceptable socio-economic environment (which for Schumpeter would be socialism).

The theorist Mark Fisher updated Deleuze and Guattari's ideas in the conference presentation *Terminator vs Avatar*, claiming that 'accelerationism can function as an anti-capitalist strategy':

> [Capitalism], dominated by quasi-monopolies such as Microsoft and Walmart, is an anti-market. Bill Gates promises business at the speed of thought, but what capitalism delivers is thought at the speed of business. A simulation of innovation and newness that cloaks inertia and stasis.
>
> (Fisher, 2012: 345)

There is a clear tension between Fisher's appraisal of advanced capitalism and Schumpeter's – and latterly Thiel's – rationalisation for the way in which monopolies are not only the most financially lucrative commercial model but are also the best way of sustaining innovation and development. Indeed, for Thiel, 'to the economist, every monopoly looks the same', whereas in his view, a monopoly is 'the kind of company that's so good at what it does that no other firm can offer a close substitute' (Thiel, 2014: 24–25). Whilst the likes of Thiel and the accelerationist left clearly inhabit different ends of an economic and ideological spectrum, to a degree, Steemit and Creative Passport capture aspects of both positions. Each is an expression of the idea that systemic innovations are required in order to make online music markets more equitable, and at the same time they are both acknowledgments that non-market networks are now the history rather than the future of the web.

Conclusion

Although it might be tempting to lament the passing of an Internet which was thought to carry within its operating parameters the seeds of a new economy where non-market practices would reconfigure our approach to creativity, trade and sharing, we need only to turn back to Schumpeter to see that the future form of Internet was clear from the outset:

> Unlike the class of feudal lords, the commercial and industrial bourgeoisie rose by business success. Bourgeois society has been cast in a purely economic mould: its foundations, beams and beacons are all made of economic material.
>
> (Schumpeter, 2010: 64)

In the case of Steemit and Creative Passport, their operating models are manifestly different from what precedes them; both have radicalised the way that value can be attached to digital content, and Steem's minting function almost entirely encapsulates Schumpeter's notion of creating that which it exploits. Thus, Steemit's pay-per-post function and Mycelia's ambition to simultaneously make Creative Passport a new kind of global database and promotional platform for creative practitioners 'threaten' (in Schumpeterian terms) a complete displacement of the dominant approach to hosting music and media content online and a set of behaviours and assumptions about how we interact with online media that has existed since the beginnings of the commercial web in the 1990s. The extent to which the Steemit platform embodies this drive towards macro-scale disruption comes through in the way that the *Steem Whitepaper*, not unlike Lanier, critiques our current reliance on revenue from advertising as a means of underwriting payments for content. The white paper informs us that:

> With ads, a creator can make money most easily. Without ads, monetization is difficult but the content is richer. Creators posting to social media outlets that are connected to Steem may monetize merely by having their work recognized (or 'liked') by the Steem community. Blockchain-based payouts are completely digital and have no middle-man. Therefore monetization by blockchain-based content rewards should be faster and much lower barrier to use than monetization by advertisements.
>
> (Steem Whitepaper, 2018)

What is at stake here is that the minting and apportioning of Steem tokens represents an entirely different payment system to one based on leveraging advertising for payments or increasing advertising revenue by exploiting platform users' data. Whilst the white paper is telling us that Steemit, by removing third parties such as advertisers, is a platform that is able to pay users in a more efficient way, the underlying message here is that Steemit is a new way of thinking about how an economy can work. This is to say that, although the white paper talks in a language that foregrounds Schumpeter's 'price variable' – in other words, success in the marketplace based on cost and revenue – at a more fundamental level, it is concerned with mapping out a radical vision for market forces as such. In the age of the Siren Server, we have seen a digital economy based on advertising revenue grow exponentially. The white paper, however, speaks of an economy based on engineered scarcity, wherein a range of Internet-era behaviours such as posting, liking, commenting and reposting have become a new form of labour. As such, Steemit is an experiment in determining whether or not it is possible to circumvent established models for online commerce.

Steemit and Creative Passport also draw on the proposition that as a network increases in activity and size, so does its value. In the case of Creative Passport, not only does the passport as 'container' seek to ensure that payment is made where payment is due, but also, because of the anticipated increase in network connections that would result from the fact that the work of one creative acts as a signpost for another (and vice versa) – in effect turning everyone in the Creative Passport environment into an advertisement for everyone else – the potential for financial reward increases as more users join the network. Herein lies the most obvious difference between Steemit and Creative Passport, in that the latter is designed to use blockchain digital watermarking capabilities to both ensure and propagate payments within a conventional model of commerce (albeit one that has as yet not materialised online), whereas the former is a model that could sustain comparison with quantitative easing or the idea of a Universal Basic Income. In this context, given that Steem minting is happening whether or not users contribute to the Steemit platform, to a degree, interacting with Steemit is simply an opportunity to draw down the benefits of that currency creation process. The *Steem Bluepaper* refers to this specifically as one of Steem's primary innovations, claiming that 'the unique properties of STEEM make it both "smart" and "social" compared to others, such as bitcoin and ether' (Steem, 2017: 1). It attributes this innovation to the way tokens are rewarded via the rewards pool and the voting process, and states that 'when combined [these two unique properties] are referred to as Proof-of-Brain, which is an entendre based on Proof-of-Work, meant to emphasise the human work required to distribute tokens to community participant' (Steem, 2017: 1). Thus, Steem's lasting innovation may be the way in which it articulates and puts forward solutions to much a wider issue over how the nature of markets and benefits might manifest on the Internet.

Steemit and Creative Passport are projects that have been designed to operate in, exploit and make equitable an economic environment that is neither in need of being accelerated out of in stasis, and nor is it in danger of burning itself out. At the macro scale, Schumpeter speculates about whether capitalism is a fully self-contained and unique socio-economic form or if it is 'simply' the last stage of the decomposition of what we have called feudalism (Schumpeter, 2010: 124), and thus his ideas may yet have further prescience. Not only, as Fisher suggested, is advanced capitalism equipped with its own feudal lords – Gates, Bezos, Zuckerberg, et al. – but it is also less complete, less resolved than we may think. Whereas Fisher claimed that capitalism was in crisis because of the stasis and stagnation caused by monopolies, it may be the very fact that because it *is* a monopoly, one that is susceptible to disruption and forever in a state of becoming more than it was but remaining less than what it could be, that Schumpeter will have the last word: 'destruction may not be the right word after all . . . perhaps I should have spoken of transformation' (Schumpeter, 2010: 145). If Steemit and Creative Passport are agents of destructive transformation, then they are agents with no teleological imperative of an anticipated socialism and without the accelerationist's enthusiasm for weaponising the disruptive process in order to achieve the downfall of capitalism. Catching the current wave of blockchain-powered disruption is therefore an acknowledgment that technologies, economies and socio-economic systems will only exist as long as they are the best solutions to the issues they have evolved to address. But even that will not save them, for they cannot help but be transformed by the very forces that brought them into being in the first place, which is to say, themselves.

Notes

1 In the chapter 'Disruption as Contingency: Music, Blockchain, Wtf?', via an account of the history of the term 'disruptive technologies', I examine the way in which 'disruption' connects with contemporary philosophical notions of 'contingency', as expressed in the work of Quentin Meillassoux; concluding that a more accurate term might be 'contingency technologies' (Lovett, 2019).

2 In the blog essay 'Unconditional Acceleration and the Question of Praxis: Some Preliminary Thoughts', the writer and blogger Edmund Berger parses the three variances of accelerationist thought, establishing the lineage of the concept and presenting a set of contemporary viewpoints (Berger, 2017).

Bibliography

Accenture. 2018. *The Future of All Industry Is Disruption – And That's a Good Thing*. Available at www.wired.co.uk/article/the-future-of-all-industry-is-disruption-and-thats-a-good-thing (accessed August 2018).

Benkler, Y. 2006. *Wealth of Networks: How Social Production Transforms Markets and Freedom*. New Haven and London: Yale University Press.

Berger, E. 2017. *Unconditional Acceleration and the Question of Praxis: Some Preliminary Thoughts*. Available at https://deterritorialinvestigations.wordpress.com/2017/03/29/unconditional-acceleration-and-the-question-of-praxis-some-preliminary-thoughts/ (accessed 2018).

Bower, J. and Christensen, C. 1995. *Disruptive Technologies: Catching the Wave*. Available at https://hbr.org/1995/01/disruptive-technologies-catching-the-wave (accessed 2018).

Deleuze, G. and Guattari, F. 1972. 'The Civilised Capitalist Machine', in Mackay, R. and Avanessian, A. (eds.), 2014. *#Accelerate: The Accelerationist Reader*. Falmouth: Urbanomic.

Digital Music News. 2017a. *Imagine a Single, Unified Licensing Database for Every Song in the World*. Available at www.digitalmusicnews.com/2017/07/21/congress-public-music-licensing/ (accessed 2018).

Digital Music News. 2017b. *War Erupts Over Whose Global Music Rights Database Is Better*. Available at www.digitalmusicnews.com/2017/08/04/riaa-ascap-bmi-congress-shared-music-database/ (accessed 2018).

Engels, F. and Marx, K. 1848. *Manifesto of the Communist Party*. Available at www.marxists.org/archive/marx/works/1848/communist-manifesto/index.htm (accessed 2018).

Fisher, M. 2012. 'Terminator vs Avatar', in Mackay, R. and Avanessian, A. (eds.), 2014. *#Accelerate: The Accelerationist Reader*. Urbanomic: Falmouth.

Gauntlett, D. 2011. *Making Is Connecting: The Social Meaning of Creativity, From DIY and Knitting to YouTube and Web 2.0*. Cambridge: Polity Press.

Heap, I. 2018. *Mycelia Creative Passport*. Available at http://myceliaformusic.org/wp-content/uploads/2017/12/CREATIVE PASSPORT-vPDF-INSIDE-V3.pdf (accessed 2018).

IFPI. 2018. *IFPI Global Music Report 2018*. Available at www.ifpi.org/news/IFPI-GLOBAL-MUSIC-REPORT-2018 (accessed 2018).

Internet Society. 1997. *Brief History of the Internet: Introduction*. Available at www.internetsociety.org/internet/history-internet/brief-history-internet/#f5 (accessed 2018).

Lanier, J., 2014. *Who owns the future?*. Simon and Schuster.

Leadbeater, C. 2008. *We-think: Mass Innovation, Not Mass Production*. London: Profile Books.

Lovett, M. 2019. 'Disruption as Contingency: Music, Blockchain, Wtf?', in Hepworth-Sawyer, R., Hodgson, J., Paterson, J. and Toulson, R. (eds.), *Innovation in Music: Performance, Production, Technology and Business*. Routledge.

Music Business Worldwide. 2016. *Who Will Build the Music Industry's Global Rights Database?* Available at www.musicbusinessworldwide.com/who-will-build-the-music-industrys-global-rights-database/ (accessed 2018).

Mycelia. 2018. *Mycelia Creative Passport*. http://myceliaformusic.org/wp-content/uploads/2017/12/CP-vPDF-INSIDE-V3.pdf (accessed 2018).

The Networking and Information Technology Research and Development (NITRD) Program. 1995. *FNC Resolution: Definition of "Internet" 10/24/95*. Available at www.nitrd.gov/fnc/internet_res.pdf (accessed 2018).

Schumpeter, J. 2010. *Capitalism, Socialism and Democracy*. London and New York: Routledge.

Srnicek, N. 2017. *Platform Capitalism*. Cambridge: Polity Press.

Steem. 2017. *Steem Whitepaper*. Available at https://steem.io/SteemWhitePaper.pdf (accessed 2018).

Steem. 2018. *Steem Bluepaper*. Available at https://steem.io/steem-bluepaper.pdf (accessed 2018).

Steemit. 2018. *Steemit FAQ*. Available at https://steemit.com/faq.html (accessed 2018).

Tapscott, D. 2016. *How the Blockchain Is Changing Money and Business*. Available at www.youtube.com/watch?v=Pl8OlkkwRpc&t=49s (accessed 2018).

Thiel, P.A. and Masters, B., 2014. *Zero to one: Notes on startups, or how to build the future*. Broadway Business.

Wu, T. 2003. 'Network Neutrality, Broadband Discrimination', *Journal of Telecommunications and High Technology Law*, Vol. 2, pp. 141–175. Available at www.jthtl.org/content/articles/V2I1/JTHTLv2i1_Wu.PDF (accessed 2018).

Chapter 10

Blockchained to what (end)? A socio-material provocation to check distributed futures

Luke Heemsbergen, Alexia Maddox, and Robbie Fordyce

Introduction

This chapter braces against the ideological tide washing in on distributed ledgers materialised through brands, services, markets, and promises bubbling up through signifiers like Bitcoin, smart contracts, altcoins, ICOs, or phrasing that adds 'blockchain enabled' to various forms of digital communication practice. We consider and deconstruct the ideology of these phenomena with a media studies lens that can chart what 'Web 3.0' is considered to be in relation to distributed ledgers. Our argument proposes to understand blockchain through a sudden political widening of blockchain ideal use(rs) followed by a collapse to centralisations of blockchain as practice. This double movement of expansion and contraction has a long history in media studies, mirrored in understandings of how media apparatus (Agamben 2009; Foucault 1980) function, yet also takes into account the creative potential of disruptive media practice (Heemsbergen 2018), including Bitcoin specifically (Maddox et al. 2016). We understand blockchain through media studies in order to position it not as a revolution of networked computation or politics but as a media practice that enables historical comparators. The comparative lens we draw on offers insight, making visible similar ideological promises of decentralised or distributed media-politics that came to be constricted by structural forces. We note that our argument is not meant to offer a complete totalisation of blockchain as an apparatus of capture in the style of Agamben vis-a-vis the cellular phone. Instead, we hope to provide a critical counterpoint to the unrelenting tide of emancipatory blockchain prognoses. We submit that after the current expansionary tide washes in, its recedence will reveal an adulterated communication-life floor that shows the lasting power and meaning of these technologies' use.

Specifically, we argue that radical ideologies have intertwined with 'new media' and specifically networked media since the 1960s, bending away only to bend back to centralising structures of commerce. Two exemplars of this are community access television (CATV), allowed by the expansion of cable TV, and the Internet and World Wide Web (WWW). Both these disruptive systems of creation that ostensibly broke away from centralised control are now better understood through how they re-formed centralised and centralising modes of control.

That blockchain should be any different is a poorly crafted hypothesis that is falsified by the evidence to date. We provide evidence for this argument in the empirical case of Bitcoin and a conceptual consideration of Ethereum's smart contracts futures in relation to the decentralising media that have come before them. The insight garnered from integrating analysis of the blockchain with historical comparators shows that radical communication technologies and practices come to integrate into structures of political economy over time. That economy may bend away from control in response to these disruptions, but rarely breaks. The bending of expansion and contraction at play in blockchain leaves the underlying media ecosystem indelibly altered.

Our discussion addresses how new technologies have origins in radical/emancipatory decentralisation philosophies yet are absorbed into contemporary systems while changing these systems in complex ways, not least in terms of how labour reorganise and labour markets are reorganised in these contexts. The libertarian, anarchic, or indeed any other radical ideological promise built into the deployment of such technologies (whether blockchain or the Internet protocols they sit upon) are largely subsumed to the structures that they sit in, even as they shift these structures in new ways. We thus link blockchain *media activity* to socio-economic practices and potentials concordant with freedom and control.

The substantive discussion surrounds how patterns of expansion and contraction have already been emulated by the exemplar Bitcoin in its markets, forking, and regulation. First though, this chapter frames and details the theoretical approach that we use to understand blockchain as reflective of Web 3.0 yet situated within larger media logics. This chapter also introduces how the radical new media technologies of community access television and the Internet turned into corporate regimes of control so as to enlighten the discussion that follows. We conclude the chapter with consideration of a similar arc of a second exemplar: Ethereum smart contracts. Our work on smart contracts presents some concluding remarks that critique blockchain as an abstracted media practice in terms of its tracking functions. While currently discussed in terms of provenance and transparency in supply chains, smart contracts also can be employed mercilessly as forms of visibility that become inescapable for their subjects. This, we feel, provides synecdoche for the passive ideology that undergirds blockchain.

Theoretical approach

Blockchain technology stands at of the tail end of 'Web 3.0' while also pushing the definition to its limits. Web 3.0 is often defined in relation to Web 2.0's emphasis on platforms for user communication, decentralised online networks, and focus on human-readable content as value (O'Reilly 2005). Web 3.0 emphasises platforms for user practices (Fuchs et al. 2010), distributed online networks paired against a semantic Internet of Things (Beer 2009), and replacing the focus on content with a focus on machine-readable data for value (Russell 2014). Blockchain fits into this schema insofar as it uses digital code and networks to distribute value alongside information; facilitates 'human programming' through smart contracts; represents real-world organisation and governance within distributed algorithmic ledgers; and operationalises models of artificial scarcity. These traits mediate informational exchange in ways that differ from the affordances usually aligned with decentralised digital information as it is experienced by most users. Digital networks and Internet cultures typically rely on an ever-accelerating capacity to store, copy, and transmit data to invoke new ways of organising, prosecuting, and collaborating on informational problems. In some respects, blockchains can upend the assumptions of accelerating abundance with algorithmic scarcity. For instance, the model of material scarcity baked into the additive 'truth' of each blockchain or in implementations such as Bitcoin that designate the limited numbers of coins to be created differ from Internet culture norms and communication forms. This scarcity can create new types of value in sharing information and is supposed to encourage market-oriented behaviour without need for the shadow of hierarchical regulation.

The capacity of algorithmically executed contracts or more complex fully distributed autonomous organisations (DAO) suggests another way that blockchain reconfigures the traditional notions of relationships between user, Internet intermediary, platform, and networks. More than having protocols shape practice (Galloway 2004), blockchain purports to be the rising phoenix of Lessig's (1999) code as law – where cybernetic architecture at a distance controls through devices of chained hashes that, paradoxically, imbue freedom from traditional pressures of market, norms, and law. Yet in the DAO we see also the creation of the ultimate cybernetic bureaucracy that is unswayed by humanity or humanism and instead doles out what we call 'human programing'. Here we imagine that human users are only able to execute the code or forgo remaining in the, otherwise ubiquitous, communication chains. In this context of creating a DAO-facilitated system of governance, we can readily conceive of a future whereby algorithmic processes have an increasingly significant role in governance to the point where people simply become the conscious linkages between disparate machinery (Marx 1857/1973). Interestingly, the first DAO (based on Ethereum) seems to show there actually is an option for human agency – hacking the code. But the hack caused a political crisis for participants' ideals as they undid what the code had brought in a process that nullified the DAO – the observation here being that a system that attempts to iron out human 'frailty' becomes vulnerable through that very artifice. This case example demonstrates the vulnerability of code-based social engineering to the pragmatics of social practice. In doing so, it also highlights the pivotal role of social appropriation as an aftermath to social adoption. Perhaps it is this aftermath that further disrupts the relationships between user, Internet intermediary, platform, and networks.

Finally, blockchain is considered Web 3.0 in that its resources and effects do not have to be merely informational: they do not control or inform supply chains, they are supply chains; they do not offer data that affect currencies, they are currencies. Blockchain disrupts outside of informational constraints that previous disruptive communication technologies have been held within. Blockchain purports to offer a capacity for durable connections *from* material objects and actions in a way that is relatively unique for networked protocols, code, and data. If in the McLuhanesque sense media offers us extensions of self, blockchain flips that logic on its head, instead offering distributed active physical processes extensions back into human-consumed media ecologies.

To take a moment to explore this ontological peculiarity somewhat further, consider how distributed ledgers afford a distributed permanence and action-oriented ontology that differs from previous conceptualisations of networked data. With action-oriented ontology, we play against the object-oriented ontology deployed by media scholars (see Arnold 2003; Parikka 2012) to point out that the makeup, meaning, and importance of the mediated world that blockchain creates is fashioned through considering the importance of ever-evolving action-rules outside of human consciousness – this, rather than considering the importance of external objects. It is the computational facility to action others – or blockchains as their own motive facilitators – that create objects (contracts, coins, ledgers, users). This further degrades a humanist position in the mediated world and reflects the ideal of trustless systems that developers create to obviate not only central institutions but fallible humans. No longer are we merely one of many objects, we are now mere subjects acted upon in action-oriented flows of irrevocable ledgers that provide shape to what is and how it may relate to other action-flows.

More practically, the distributed permanence of blockchain offers regulators, or other humans caught in their grasp, a seemingly Sisyphean task of stopping the signal. Whether prosecuted via policies that try to stop the circulation of the *Anarchists' Cookbook*, or implement a General Data Protection Regulation (GDPR)-type assurance for erasure on request, the removal of data from a blockchain would influence every other piece of data up the chain. This distributed permanence is suggested by blockchain advocates to be a fundamental feature and, quizzically, an action-oriented solution for any such GDPR-esque privacy concerns:

> Legitimate privacy concerns are best addressed not through law, but through decentralizing technology itself. Open blockchain networks, cryptocurrency, and general encryption are the backbone of a new more secure and private Internet on which individuals have more control over their data, and firms are less incentivized to track and spy on their users.
>
> (Brito 2018)

While that is framed to highlight user autonomy, the distributed permanency of blockchain suggests that spying will be unnecessary. In the described instance, any personal information put to 'open blockchain networks' offers radical transparency that cyberlibertarians enact with pseudo-anonymous technologies of distributed record keeping. Rather than have personal data stored away to be cross-tabulated with select third parties at Facebook, or delisted to obscurity by Google, or discretely syphoned by security agencies, personal data on blockchains – by their nature – are available to publics concerned enough to look and connect the bits.

Proponents suggest that this fact, among other unique aspects of blockchain technology, offer a model of oversight that upends risk and opportunity in current social, economic, and legal regimes. This utopic vision, we argue, is mostly unproven, even readily disproven. What is proven, or at least written in the histories of radical and decentralising new media of the past, is the double movement of a tide of excitement rushing in that is later swept away, leaving the ground underfoot radically changed, nonetheless. We suggest a homologous movement is ongoing with blockchain: a similar utopic vision dominates, the radical potential is present, and yet uptake is moving to centralised banking corporations – the antithesis to cryptocurrencies – adopting blockchain. We argue that Bitcoin's tide – its expansive flow – has already peaked and suggest a re-conscription towards structural absorption is underfoot. To provide some context to this expansion–contraction relationship, we briefly turn to disruptive media that foreshadow blockchain's deployment and social integration: CATV and the popularisation of the Internet itself.

Networked for whom?

Community access television (CATV) and the World Wide Web (WWW), as once-new, now-common media, might seem like strange examples from which to profess understanding blockchain. Yet a brief recount of their history provides insight for Bitcoin's current ideological construction and its arc of emerging practices. In separate times and contexts, both cable television and the Internet's popular turn to WWW-based access initially appeared to be radical reconfiguring of networks. As Hu (2015, 25) points out, the US Federal Communications Commission considered CATV as a way for hierarchical power structures and centralised control of content creation to be evened out by a two-way participatory media environment where feedback was content and value was found in decentralising voice.

Under CATV, various community channels sprung up on 'cable' that precipitated a shift in what public broadcast could be. This led to decentralisation of media practices beyond state-run public broadcasting services to local and varied content by actors that were sometimes individuals, using the greatly lowered barriers to entry that video afforded. Access to CATV was envisioned as radically democratic. Indeed Joselit (2002, 153) points out how the emergence of CATV enabled 'openness to unconventional television [that was] seized upon by a raucous community of video artists and activists equipped with a new technology – the Portapak – and underwritten by funding' from meagre civic grants to produce content. The Portapak, a compact video recorder, enabled production teams of one to create mobile content for later broadcast use. While broadcast on CATV represented a decentralised network, the means of production had sufficiently shifted to distributed actors creating unique aesthetic contributions to society through video tape. This is why Joselit (2002, 152) goes on to lament the 'thoroughgoing commercialisation of cable – its rapid devolution from an open form of communication to a highly standardised array of entertainment products'. This presents a different narrative to the fall of public broadcasters themselves (Tracey 1998), which shows the (civic) centre not being able to hold. Instead, here we see, as part of the departure from that centre, the rapid distribution of voice that is simultaneously, if slowly, re-centralised by market forces and subsumed into hyper-commercialised cable TV. Indeed, this is where Hu (2015) picks up the critique of networked communications by offering a cultural critique on what networks themselves are and become.

The parallel of CATV to the WWW is not lost on either Joselite or Hu: in 2002, the electronic frontiers of the Internet had already been largely replaced by corporate dot-coms, while by 2015, new behemoths of the cloud era of Internet communications had arrived. Google, Apple, Facebook, and Amazon now elicit their own acronym, GAFA, which signals the predominance of the specific economic model Internet-enabled communication practice now presents. In this model, content creation is driven through ad consumption, with two of the GAFA firms controlling more than half of that advertising revenue, while the other two have each surpassed market capitalisation of one trillion dollars based on investor sentiment towards growth forecast on services that facilitate the acceleration of commerce. We can envision the web, then, as born from protocols that democratically expanded distributed content creation across linked networks and then contracted through slick interactive apps and services that entrench corporate control over what was once thought to be wild cybernetic frontiers. Web 2.0 grew up to be corporate.

We note that radical politics of the net, whether found in apps that implement encryption like Signal or Tor, do exist and work to disrupt and otherwise disturb prevailing orders. In the context of both Signal and Tor, encryption protocols function to allow a degree of autonomy by users on Internet-linked systems without subordinating the user to any kind of platform content moderation. In this way they present something of a challenge to large corporate social media platforms that tend to be defined by content review (see Gillespie 2018). Yet Hu (2015) reminds us that this was always so of the Internet, subversive ideologies put to networks through groups like Antfarm in the same breath as RAND and Paul Baran (1964) considered the military applications of distributed communication. In this way, attempting to overlay libertarian temporality to Baran's original graph of centralised, decentralised, and distributed networks through a narrative of control to freedom is a misreading. Control exists throughout. Throughout networked media, or in Joselite's action-oriented language, a 'thoroughgoing' that extends completely is the capacity for control. This control reflects structural and narrative constraints on networked communication practice.

In sum, then, the point of both these historical comparators is to show that radical communication technologies and practices come to be integrated into structures of political economy over time. That economy may bend in response to these disruptions but rarely breaks. Even as new media technologies emerge surrounded by praise for perceived radical, liberatory, or hyper-disruptive aspects, these ideological promises seem to disappear when the ideological tide recedes. These same technologies are taken up by incumbent power structures with new groundings to reassert control in the market, politics, or elsewhere.

Nevertheless, optimistic approaches to the future see a normalisation of cryptocurrency in everyday emancipatory life. The more pessimistic suggest antagonistic sociocultural critiques of Bitcoin's user base (Golumbia 2016), criticism of the radicalness and the anonymity of ledger-based cryptocurrencies (de Jong et al. 2015), the problem of heat and energy (Brunton 2015), and the staggering inequalities in currency ownership (Kondor et al. 2014; Ermann et al. 2018). This is set against observations that there are real and substantial needs to diversify how transactions in value operate internationally (Sassen 2015), the capacity for managing provenance in property such as artworks (Davidson et al. 2018), identity management (Augot et al. 2017), and new possibilities in urban sensor systems (Potts et al. 2017). Cryptocurrencies of all sorts are caught in a tension between their actuality, their potentiality, and perception.

Indicative case study: Bitcoin

Here we consider the arc of the exemplar case of media deployed through blockchain technologies: Bitcoin. We critique Bitcoin's centralisation of value and governance and related commercialisation of the underlying technologies. The peer-to-peer payments system of Bitcoin was imagined as indicative of an alternative digital economy built on affordances of a trustless and efficient system. This includes, as Maddox et al. (2016) notes, functions that were 'intended by developers to engender a politically motivated discourse' eventually subverting 'sovereignty and state power'. Yet the extent that these normative considerations have been usurped by third parties offer a related critique: the spectacular inequality within cryptocurrency markets and forthcoming regulation of cryptocurrencies being signalled by the IMF and national governments, centralised energy concerns, and ongoing issues of trust demonstrate how incumbent structures reappropriate the blockchain to their own ends. The centre retook what was not held. Next we detail the expansion and contraction of the Bitcoin tide.

Bitcoin expands – the hope of a chain

From a social lens, cryptocurrencies represent emerging financial technologies that are imbued with overlapping community values of decentralised peer-to-peer exchange and the use of encryption technologies to support user privacy and (pseudo-)anonymity. Cryptocurrencies such as Bitcoin are a recent sociotechnical innovation designed by their developers to disrupt the existing monetary system. The creation of Bitcoin is attributed to an anonymous group of developers (Nakamoto 2008), with its social uptake dated from 2009 (Maddox et al. 2016). The origin community contributing to the development and social uptake of cryptocurrencies is described by Maurer et al. (2013) as based upon libertarian politics, and they argue that Bitcoin combines practical materialism with a politics of community and trust that puts code front and centre. In this way, we can understand cryptocurrencies and the blockchain as materialising the 'rules of engagement', where code becomes law. Originating from the cypherpunk movement, this self-organising network of people has come together through the development and adoption of open-source cryptocurrency software such as that which underpins Bitcoin. The social profile of members, Maurer argues, consists of a diverse network of interests incorporating 'goldbugs, hippies, anarchists, cyberpunks, cryptographers, payment systems experts, currency activists, commodity traders, and the curious' (Maurer et al 201, p. 2).

Similarly, Dahlberg (2010) observes the origins of the values underpinning the cryptocurrency community as espoused by the cyberlibertarians of the 1990s. In an expansionist view of an emergent, peer-to-peer technology of the time, they idealised the Internet as a space for democratic culture autonomous from the state and other forms of centralised control. This version of 'democracy', Dahlberg (2010, 333) argues, saw the subject pursuing personal liberty to satisfy private interests through technologically mediated networking and access to free information flows and individual decision making free of bureaucracy. The resonance between these ideas and the function of the blockchain and cryptocurrencies are clear; these values were articulated in the early adoption cases of Bitcoin, such as its use as a pseudonymous digital currency with which to buy drugs on cryptomarkets (Maddox et al. 2016; Barratt et al. 2016). However, Dahlberg (2010, 333–337) argues that Bitcoin is a technology engendered through the values of cyberlibertarianism 2.0. Dahlberg's definition of cyberlibertarianism 2.0 sees users as 'cybernauts', a term very similar to the psychonaut drug-use cultures engaging with cryptomarkets, which leverages off the metaphor of travellers to outer space who move beyond the reach of state regulation and social control and become responsible only to themselves. This autonomous agent was often articulated within the cryptomarkets through a notion of personal sovereignty. These sovereign astronauts of the Internet and perceived users of cryptocurrencies operated as, in Dahlberg's words, 'DIY prosumers freed from external constraint'. This freedom from constraint, however, is contextualised through the nodal governance practices within which cryptocurrencies and the blockchain are deployed.

By drawing on Dahlberg's (2010) notion of cyberlibertarianism 2.0 as describing the community values giving rise to the development of cryptocurrencies, we can also follow his argument that these values inform the anarcho-capitalism of the sharing economy and the more radical anti-statism of Bitcoin. As has been argued previously (Maddox et al. 2016), this developer and cryptographic community share an overarching agenda of disrupting centralised banking within the fiat economy. From the cyberlibertarian lens at the core of this attitude, the fiat system was perceived to reinforce structural inequalities and create financial exclusion through the decision-making processes within the banking system that resulted in outcomes counter to the interests of the individual user. Whether this movement implies a radical capitalist individualism with a strong and radical right-wing view of government and the masses is outside our scope. However, we can see this community in its broader sense as seeking to provide radical technological solutions to these structural inequalities. The cryptocurrency developer community identified gaps and possibilities for new technical solutions to existing problems in the flows of money. These included lag times in the movement and reporting of movement of money between accounts and, secondly, the high level of 'friction' between banks and mediating institutions on the transnational flows of money through regulations, mediation, and conversion processes. Through this focus upon innovations in financial technologies solving wicked problems, the nature of this community broadened. Extending beyond the cyberlibertarian scope, a more pragmatic social mix is described by Maddox et al. (2017) as incorporating those with financial backgrounds and those interested in emerging financial technologies and investment opportunities. A further cohort includes entrepreneurs interested in accessing new markets and business start-up opportunities opened through cryptocurrencies in digital spaces. Here we can see the beginning of a loop that starts with expansion of dreams towards an alternative techno-economic future (Swartz 2017) and folds back through a contraction into the centralised and existing systems of the fiat economy.

This dynamic of expansion and contraction of cryptocurrencies and their associated technologies is aptly positioned by Swartz and by Maurer et al. as traceable back to its origins within the cypherpunk and crypto-anarchist subcultures. Swartz (2018, 626) argues that for cypherpunks, privacy was a 'natural right' that could be achieved through cryptographic information systems outside of the influence of government and corporate entities. Their aims in writing code was simultaneously individualistic and populist; they sought to produce a communicative reality of free expression that gave rise to a new society predicated on privacy. For cypherpunks, the pseudo-anonymity of cryptocurrencies supported personal privacy by allowing the individual to selectively reveal personal financial and transactional information. This code-law is captured by Swartz in the notion of infrastructural mutualism. She articulates infrastructural mutualism as the ability to mutually build and support a collaborative platform upon which to transact free from the view and inference of corporate intermediaries (Swartz 2017). The prominence of this agenda within cryptocurrencies speaks back to their emergence during a proliferation of surveillant business models referred to earlier. Swartz (2017) also observes that infrastructural mutualism is tied to peer production, such as free software, peer-to-peer production, and commonsing practices. As such, infrastructural mutualists orient towards the blockchain as a decentralised, autonomous infrastructure with shared utility produced and maintained by all participants; links here to Deleuzian readings of the relationship between labour, technology and production are ripe but outside the scope of this contribution. Perhaps these relations are why we see the continued longevity of the blockchain within contemporary discussions (cf. Allen et al. 2018; Zhao et al. 2016) beyond their applications as a transparent ledger for assigning and transferring ownership of cryptocurrencies.

Bitcoin constricts – a carceral aloofness

Here we consider in more detail the polysemy within Bitcoin rhetoric and ideology as market forces impart familiar structures around the 'structureless' distribution of the blockchain. The community value that enabled and was exploited by Bitcoin proponents can be seen as competing narratives to the Bitcoin story. As Bitcoin became popular enough to make the evening broadcast news around December 2017, these narratives are sometimes paradoxically weaved together in the same breadth. 'Establishing an extra stream of income will allow you to start investing earlier'. This advice from Erik Finman, a Bitcoin multi-millionaire turned financial advisor, spread on Twitter during early 2018, when Finman was aged 19. In an interview in *Forbes* published a few hours later, Finman referred to his association with his brother, suggesting that 'we saw this as an incredible way to transcend the financial system including Wall Street. We discovered the incredible implications politically that this technology hasn't even begun to crack . . . yet!' (Munford 2018). The 'yet' that Finman refers to is a point of significant political, financial, and technical speculation.

Against speculation, however, is the evolving arc of Bitcoin practice, which shows a bend back to constraining forms of control. These seem to, for the majority of users, offer very different conceptions of the Bitcoin economy to Finman's account. Economies are aggregate things, and while Finman's suggestions or experiences are perfectly valid, they do not encompass the median or average Bitcoin experience of others. In aggregate, 2017 saw Bitcoin at the heady heights of trading, with prices reaching $19,694.68 USD per coin at 11 a.m. on the 17 of December. Since then, Bitcoin's price has declined steadily, trading variously between $3,800 USD and $8,000 USD in late 2018, which, considering history, means little. Yet these incredible swings of Bitcoin's monetary value offer insight into the practices that are steering this distributed communication medium away from radicality and towards the gravity of commercial interests.

These commercial interests manifest in ways that seem antithetical to the selfless ideology that blockchain is supposed to represent. For instance, in 2018, Statisgroup, a consultancy, suggested that 81% of initial coin offerings were total scams, with only 1.9% having successfully deployed a distributed ledger with a road map for their product and having publicly shown the code of their ledger. Meanwhile, the justice department has reportedly opened a criminal probe to market manipulation for Bitcoin and other digital currencies (Robinson and Schoenberg 2018); there is ample evidence to suggest that actors in a zero-regulation market behaved as a cynic (or regulator) might expect.

Other specific structural problems of Bitcoin mining show that their practical implications have been fully co-opted by monopolistic market structures – quite an irony, considering the libertarian overcurrents of blockchain rhetoric. Mike Hearn, a well-known Bitcoin developer, suggested as far back as early 2016 that the Bitcoin experiment was over, and that the platform was not working anymore. Hearn (2018) offers evidence of mining being a monopolistic enterprise centred in China, where over half of the hash power resides. He suggests that this monopolistic trend creates perverse incentives to meddle in the popularity of Bitcoin as a way to ensure control of its means of (coin) production. Hearn goes on to detail the technical and ideological problems of various forks of Bitcoin, where the one indisputable distributed ledger is thrown into dispute. Challengers to hegemonic notions of Bitcoin are DDOSed (DDOS stands for 'distributed denial of service') into submission at what seems to be the will of personal politics, which then contribute to the consternation of the network.

Recent scholarly work shows evidence of Bitcoin's personal enterprise. According to Hileman and Rauchs's (2017) work out of the Cambridge Centre for Alternative Finance, a majority of the Bitcoin hashing emanates from clustered processors occupying space together in mining facilities, while many of the firms involved are working through vertical and horizontal integration of Bitcoin practice to solidify their place in the market. These typical capitalistic monopoly-seeking behaviours are prima facie unsurprising but also present an antithetical narrative to the Bitcoin ethos and cryptocurrencies' libertarian ideals. Considered from a positivistic perspective, we can see the rush on Bitcoin is empirically unsustainable. The energy requirements taken by Bitcoin activities are growing at such a rate that they signal their own unsustainable bubble (de Vries 2018), where accelerating energy consumption needs are related to but distinct from Bitcoin's price. Mining bitcoins is now an enterprise that requires megawatts. This megawatt mining bends Bitcoin's arc back to a *literal* centralisation of *literal* power creation and distribution, with seemingly little irony to Winner's (1980) differentiation between the politics of centralised nuclear power and distributed solar power capacities. The technologies enabling blockchain's continuation require high degrees of hierarchical structure.

Finally, there is the ideological issue of (non)trust that is built into blockchain at both practical and ontological levels. First, consider Satoshi Nakamoto's (2008) premise:

> The root problem with conventional currency is all the trust that's required to make it work. The central bank must be trusted not to debase the currency. . . . Banks must be trusted to hold our money and transfer it electronically. . . . We have to trust them with our privacy, trust them not to let identity thieves drain our accounts . . . [while] e-currency based on cryptographic proof . . . can be secure and transactions effortless.

The implied ideal of 'e-currency' does not match the reality of mismanagement and 'breaches of trust' of Bitcoin. Consider clearing houses such as Mt. Gox, the re-centralisation of mining and ownership of bitcoins in the market, poor transfer rates, and wild swings of price based off unregulated market movers as examples. It seems that there are pertinent trust issues in Bitcoin's own ecology of practice. In the trustless (or more specifically trust-the-code) world of implementing blockchain, ideal human functioning imbues and requires ever expanding material ability to defend against software-enabled miscreants. This represents 'the next level' of neoliberal self-help rather than 'the next level' of Internet distributed communication – for students continuing to differentiate the two.

Conclusion

By way of conclusion we offer some parting thoughts on the futures of Ethereum smart contracts and cryptocurrencies in general. To begin, consider how Ethereum 'smart contracts' relate to 'taking the Internet to the next level' of digital surveillance afforded through blockchain-based tracking and individualised data tracing. This solution offers surveillant technologies the likes of which could not be imagined though centralised brokers such as Facebook, the National Security Agency, or other actors. In essence, the publicity/existence of the blockchain draws on narratives of self-acted total information awareness and transparency. With this clarity, the active contract is inescapable to its subjects. While Facebook and other forms of Web 2.0-based surveillant technologies exist as central repositories, blockchain-based equivalents would provide ledgers of built personal data that are inescapable for their subjects, while ever growing and intersecting data traces decrease the likelihood of pseudo-anonymity. If Web 2.0 turned to corporate control, Web 3.0 could be corporeal.

Proponents suggest that this, among other, unique aspects of blockchain technology, offers a model of oversight that upends risk and opportunity in current social, economic, and legal regimes. This utopic vision, we argue, is mostly unproven or readily disproven by evidence of the re-centralisation of control via blockchain. The washing in (and out) of the blockchain tide exposes mixed results as to where our feet are placed in the sand of our communication-life floor. The adoption of cryptocurrencies and associated technologies has been hampered reputationally by a history potholed with disputes, divergence, hacks, and scams within the community. Consequently, the emphasis within public discourse and within the community over the past five years has shifted from Bitcoin to blockchain. This shift in focus reflects the movement of efforts from a vision of social change and the rise of peer-to-peer payments to the possible applications of an 'immutable' ledger based upon novel technologies accounting for trust (Nelms et al. 2018). Meanwhile, the rise of investment speculation into cryptocurrencies has shifted attention away from social adoption and the possibility of financial inclusion to value volatility, centralisation, and questions of legitimacy. Yet the signal continues. The last five years have also seen cryptocurrencies move to a wider range of applications. The technical wicked problems involved include scalability, speed of transactions, frictionless transfer across national borders, and the cap on the number of coins that can be generated as a way to create value through supply scarcity. These technological challenges drive innovators and a start-up ecosystem of fintech companies linked to crypto-cyberlibertarian ideals with high levels of variability.

We have demonstrated that radical turns in technological innovation confront sociotechnical practices of adoption and, as their ideological tide washes away, they turn back towards integrated structures of political economy over time. Perhaps one way of seeing beyond the arc of an established media frame of expansion and contraction is to view its aftermath. Within this chapter we have considered that the normative curve of social adoption of new media such as blockchain parallels the structural tensions towards expansion and contraction. We have argued that in the aftermath of contraction, the culture of socio-technological appropriation transforms the latent potentials of existing technologies. We have also argued that the emergence of 'human programming' is an encoded vulnerability within Web 3.0 media. Digital tokens don't die, they just evolve to be increasingly transactionally irrelevant yet socially expository.

Bibliography

Agamben, G., 2009. *'What is an apparatus?' and other essays*. Stanford University Press.

Allen DWE, Berg C, Lane AM and Potts J. 2018. 'Cryptodemocracy and its institutional possibilities'. *The Review of Austrian Economics* (pp. 1–12). doi:10.1007/s11138-018-0423-6

Arnold M. 2003. 'On the phenomenology of technology: The "Janus-faces" of mobile phones'. *Information and Organization* 13(4): 231–256.

Augot D, Chabanne H, Clémot O and George W. 2017. 'Transforming face-to-face identity proofing into anonymous digital identity using the bitcoin blockchain'. arXiv:1710.02951 [cs.CR].

Baran P. 1964. *Memorandum: On Distributed Communications: I. Introduction to Distributed Communications Networks*. Santa Monica: Rand Corporation.

Barratt MJ, Lenton S, Maddox A and Allen M. 2016. '"What if you live on top of a bakery and you like cakes?" – Drug use and harm trajectories before, during and after the emergence of Silk Road'. *International Journal of Drug Policy* 35(2016): 50–57.

Beer D. 2009. 'Power through the algorithm? Participatory web cultures and the technological unconscious'. *New Media & Society* 11(6): 985–1002.

Brito, J. (2018). What does the EU's General Data Protection Regulation mean for open blockchain networks? Retrieved from https://coincenter.org/link/what-does-the-eu-s-general-data-protection-regulation-mean-for-open-blockchain-networks.

Brunton, F. 2015. 'Heat exchanges'. In *The MoneyLab Reader: An Intervention in Digital Economy*. Institute of Network Cultures.

Brunton F and Nissenbaum H. 2015. *Obfuscation: A User's Guide for Privacy and Protest*. Cambridge, MA: MIT Press.

Dahlberg L. 2010. 'Cyber-Libertarianism 2.0: A discourse theory/critical political economy examination'. *Cultural Politics* 6(3): 331–356.

Davidson S, De Filippi P and Potts J. 2018. 'Blockchains and the economic institutions of capitalism'. *Journal of Institutional Economics* 14(4): 639–658. doi:10.1017/S1744137417000200

de Jong E, Tkacz N and Velasco P. 2015. '"Live as friends and count as enemies": On digital cash and the media of payment'. In *The MoneyLab Reader: An Intervention in Digital Economy*. Institute of Network Cultures.

de Vries A. 2018. 'Bitcoin's growing energy problem'. *Joule* 2(5): 801–805. doi:10.1016/j.joule.2018.04.016

Ermann L, Frahm KM and Shepelyansky DL. 2018. 'Google matrix of bitcoin network'. *The European Physical Journal B* 91(6): 127.

Foucault M. 1980. 'The confession of flesh (L. M. Colin Gordon, John Mepham, Kate Soper, Trans.)'. In C Gordon (Ed.), *Power/Knowledge: Selected Interviews and Other Writings, 1972–1977* (pp. xi, 270). Brighton: Harvester.

Fuchs C, Hofkirchner W, Schafranek M, Raffl C, Sandoval M and Bichler R. 2010. 'Theoretical foundations of the web: Cognition, communication, and co-operation. Towards an understanding of Web 1.0, 2.0, 3.0'. *Future Internet* 2(1): 41–59.

Galloway AR. 2004. *Protocol: How Control Exists After Decentralization*. Cambridge, MA; London: MIT Press.

Gillespie T. 2018. *Custodians of the Internet: Platforms, Content Moderation, and the Hidden Decisions that Shape Social Media*. New Haven: Yale University Press.

Golumbia D. 2016. *The Politics of Bitcoin*. Minneapolis: University of Minnesota Press.

Greenfield A. 2017. *Radical Technologies: The Design of Everyday Life*. Brooklyn: Verso Books.

Hearn M. 2018. 'The resolution of the bitcoin experiment'. *Mike's Blog*. Retrieved from https://blog.plan99.net/the-resolution-of-the-bitcoin-experiment-dabb30201f7

Hileman, G. and Rauchs, M., 2017. *Global blockchain benchmarking study*. Cambridge Centre for Alternative Finance, University of Cambridge, 122.

Heemsbergen L. 2018. 'Killing secrets from Panama to paradise: Understanding the ICIJ through bifurcating communicative and political affordances'. *New Media and Society* https://doi.org/10.1177/1461444818804847

Hu, T.-H. 2015. *A Prehistory of the Cloud*. Cambridge: MIT Press.

Joselit D. 2002. 'Tale of the tape. Radical software.' *Artforum* 40(9).

Kondor D, Pósfai M, Csabai I and Vattay G. 2014. 'Do the rich get richer? An empirical analysis of the Bitcoin transaction network.' *PLoS ONE* 9(2): 1–10.

Lessig L. 1999. *Code: And Other Laws of Cyberspace*. New York: Basic Books.

Luxemberg R. 1917. *The Accumulation of Capital*. Retrieved from www.marxists.org/archive/luxemburg/1913/accumulation-capital/ch26.htm

Maddox A, Singh S, Adamson G and Horst H. 2017. 'The digital frontier of research ethics: A digital and face-to-face ethnographic study of cryptocurrency use and financial inclusion'. *Proceedings of CHI '17, CHI Conference on Human Factors in Computing Systems*,

Denver, CO, USA, May 06–11, 2017. https://ethicalencountershci.files.wordpress.com/2017/03/paper-9-maddox-et-al.pdf

Maddox A, Singh S, Horst H and Adamson G. 2016. 'An ethnography of bitcoin: Towards a future research agenda'. *Australian Journal of Telecommunications and the Digital Economy* 4(1).

Marx K. 1857/1973. *Grundrisse: Foundations of the Critique of Political Economy*. Trans Martin Nicolaus. Retrieved from www.marxists.org/archive/marx/works/1857/grundrisse/

Maurer B, Nelms TC and Swartz L. 2013. '"When perhaps the real problem is money itself!": The practical materiality of bitcoin'. *Social Semiotics* 23(2): 261–277.

Munford M. 2018. 'Cryptocurrencies and the Blockchain: Q&A With Erik Finman, Teenage Whiz Kid'. *Forbes*. Retrieved from www.forbes.com/sites/montymunford/2018/01/22/cryptocurrencies-and-the-blockchain-qa-with-erik-firman-teenage-whizz-kid/#297369be2270

Nakamoto S. 2008. *Bitcoin: A peer-to-peer electronic cash system*. Available at: https://bitcoin.org/bitcoin.pdf

Nelms TC, Maurer B, Swartz L and Mainwaring S. 2018. 'Social Payments: Innovation, Trust, bitcoin, and the Sharing Economy'. *Theory, Culture & Society* 35(3): 13–33.

O'Reilly T. 2005. *What Is Web 2.0: Design Patterns and Business Models for the Next Generation of Software*. Retrieved from http://oreilly.com/web2/archive/what-is-web-20.html

Parikka J. 2012. 'New materialism as media theory: Medianatures and dirty matter'. *Communication and Critical/Cultural Studies* 9(1): 95–100.

Potts J, Rennie E and Goldenfein J. 2017. 'Blockchains and the crypto city'. *it – Information Technology* 59(6): 285–293.

Rauchs M and Hileman G. 2017. *Global Cryptocurrency Benchmarking Study* (No. 201704-gcbs). Cambridge: Cambridge Centre for Alternative Finance, Cambridge Judge Business School, University of Cambridge.

Reid F and Harrigan M. 2013. 'An analysis of anonymity in the bitcoin system'. In *Security and Privacy in Social Networks* (pp. 197–223). New York: Springer.

Robinson M and Schoenberg T. 2018. 'U.S. launches criminal probe into bitcoin price manipulation'. *Bloomberg*. Retrieved from www.bloomberg.com/news/articles/2018-05-24/bitcoin-manipulation-is-said-to-be-focus-of-u-s-criminal-probe

Russell M. 2014. *Mining the Social Web*. Newton: O'Reilly Media Inc.

Sassen S. 2015. 'When money becomes an extraction tool rather than exchange medium: Foreword to the MoneyLab Reader'. *MoneyLab Reader* 1: 9–12.

Swartz L. 2017. 'Blockchain dreams: Imagining techno-economic alternatives after bitcoin'. In S Banet-Weiser and M Castells (Eds.), *Another Economy Is Possible: Culture and Economy in a Time of Crisis* (pp. 86–106). Malden: Polity.

Swartz L. 2018. 'What was Bitcoin, what will it be? The techno-economic imaginaries of a new money technology'. *Cultural Studies* 32(4): 623–650. doi:10.1080/09502386.2017.1416420

Tracey M. 1998. *The Decline and Fall of Public Service Broadcasting*. Oxford: Oxford University Press.

Winner L. 1980. Do artifacts have politics? *Daedalus* 109(1): 121–136.

Zambre D and Shah A. 2013. *Analysis of Bitcoin Network Dataset for Fraud*. Unpublished Report.

Zhao JL, Fan S and Yan J. 2016. 'Overview of business innovations and research opportunities in blockchain and introduction to the special issue'. *Financial Innovation* 2(1): 28.

Chapter 11

Blockchain and data market

The case of Wibson from a critical perspective

Guillermina Yansen

Introduction

Recently, Bitcoin, one of the most widespread blockchain based cryptocurrencies, has attracted the world's attention. Soon, literature noted that its true novelty was its underlying technology, blockchain. Blockchain is a way to create decentralized peer-validated time-stamped ledgers, a priori transparently and anonymously. In the case of Bitcoin it registers cash transactions, but it can be applied to a variety of goods (Preukschat, 2017). Thus, researchers began to focus on the decentralized nature of such technology, underlining its potential to "democratize" the circulation of goods and empower the "community" in different areas of social and economic life (Kosten, 2015; Atzori, 2015; Vigna and Casey, 2016). In fact, several times, democracy and decentralization are used as interchangeable terms to refer to the potential of blockchains to disrupt different types of centralized information intermediaries (Scott, 2014).

In this context, Wibson was launched.[1] Based on an Ethereum blockchain, Wibson is a proprietary and for-profit mobile app that intends to connect producers (and owners) of data (primarily individuals) with data buyers (mainly organizations and companies). If data producers currently freely give their data away through nonexclusive licenses to platforms such as Facebook or Google, which profit from them, Wibson proposes to data producers the opportunity of selling their data through the app.[2] Wibson tells us that "In the Wibson marketplace, citizens, for the first time, will be able to participate in a decentralized data marketplace that provides both financial incentives and control over their personal information, all without sacrificing privacy" (Wibson, 2017). As we will see in detail, Wibson is free for data sellers, charging a fee to buyers. It also offers validation mechanisms in which associated companies check the data (Aitken, 2018; Jiménez, 2018). Through blockchain, Wibson promises to truly disrupt the current logic of social media business, "democratizing" this market. To stakeholders interested in obtaining data, it promises that access to users' validated data is not going to be controlled and centralized by companies like Google or Facebook; avoiding intermediaries, entry barriers to business would be torn down or at least reduced. To users – data owners – Wibson guarantees that they are going to be able not only to control their data but to receive monetary benefits from it.

This sounds like good news. However, a critical approach must go further. In fact, several authors have called the attention to the evolution of blockchains, emphasizing various issues.

First, there is no such thing as "a blockchain technology" (Pilkington, 2016; Yli-Huumo et al., 2016; Preukschat, 2017) but instead several kinds of blockchain that combine with other technologies to function. In this sense, the first expression of blockchain, the public blockchain, like the one Bitcoin is based on, is not the most extended. Synthetically, a public blockchain is accessible to every Internet user (see details in the last section – Pilkington, 2016). But now all kinds of private and hybrid blockchains are emerging (Shrier et al., 2016). These share some characteristics and differ substantially in others, such as the concentration of some type of information on the user community (Preukschat, 2017). This has brought into question the effectively decentralized and thus "democratic" natural or intrinsic character of blockchains, particularly focusing on those related to the so-called entrepreneurs in the capitalist context (Herian, 2018). Hence, it is worth taking into account the particular features of each blockchain. Wibson is a proprietary app supported by a private blockchain and linked to an increasingly centralized Internet in its various layers (Zukerfeld, 2010). It is worth pointing, thus, to a fundamental actor: the company behind the app, Gran Data, a for-profit actor.

Furthermore, some scholars have questioned blockchain capacity to empower the community (Scott, 2014; Pel, 2015). They noticed that the community of users does not refer to the construction of communal ties but to "a refuge in a defensive individualism mediated via mathematical contractual law" (Scott, 2014: 20). In fact, Wibson was not born in a vacuum. The use of data by major for-profit actors had already been targeted by different associations and states, and that could be read as a background for the app's launch. In this sense, one can ask whether this cultural and institutional arena leads to a discussion of public utility of data traffic or, instead, contributes to cement other capitalist forms without questioning the relationship between the public and the private sphere. There are thus social or exterior features of blockchains to take into account, mainly regulation. "Empowering individuals", Wibson stands as a clear expression of an individualism that hides its commercial presence behind mathematical, "neutral" laws.

In this chapter we will advance in the study of Wibson, pointing out these and other possible criticisms. Diverse concepts are involved in this case study (democracy, decentralization, transparency, governance, commercialization, etc.), and we cannot analyze all of them. But what we can do is to put Wibson and similar blockchain-based apps in their right place: first, within capitalism and in a period of increasing commercialization of digital information (DI), and second, in between a process of substitution of one kind of centralization of data market (that which includes Internet giants such as Facebook and Google) to another kind of centralization (the one that includes Wibson).

Wibson is a paradigmatic case to observe the way in which the potentials of blockchain technology are being subsumed to the logic of the commodification of the Internet and, thus, leaving aside the discussions about the meaning of the public. It represents, put bluntly, another version of capitalistic dispute.

After this introduction, this manuscript is structured as follows. In the next two sections, we will place blockchain technology in the context of informational capitalism and particularly in the field of data commodification. The final section will describe the functioning of blockchain in general and of Wibson in particular. Regarding Wibson, we will focus on (1) the actors that participate in the process of data production and commercialization (individual actors, investors, the company that owns the app, etc.), trying to clarify the types of exchanges that take place between them, and (2) the discursive foundations on which the app is based. Finally, we present the conclusions.

This chapter is mainly theoretical. Methodologically, it is based on secondary sources (Wibson's official website, white paper and forum – called "Medium" – and other related journalistic materials) in order to characterize Wibson App and its discourse. Unfortunately, there is still no academic literature addressing Wibson or similar apps.

A theoretical starting point: informational capitalism, informational goods and intellectual property

In this work we start from the idea that the present times can be named as "informational capitalism" (Castells, 1997). Contrary to the notion of a "knowledge society", this concept aims to stress, on the one hand, the economic and social importance of knowledge, particularly that which is supported on digital information (DI). On the other, it stresses the capitalistic character of this stage. "Capitalism itself has undergone a process of profound restructuring" (Castells, 1997: 2). We mention briefly two of its structural features, those essential to this manuscript.

First, in informational capitalism, the "productivity and competitiveness" of agents "fundamentally depend upon their capacity to generate, process, and apply efficiently knowledge-based information" (Castells, 1997: 77), more precisely digital information (Zukerfeld, 2010). DI differs from other kinds of knowledge because of its "replicability": it can be copied with costs tending to zero. Thus, videos, texts, images, software, databases and, generally, all goods made of pure DI (here "informational goods" – IG), escape from the logic of commoditization of traditional or non-digital goods (Cafassi, 1998; Boutang, 2004; Rullani, 2004; Zukerfeld, 2010). Informational goods are, in this sense, non-rival and non-excludable, features that could lead to treat them as public goods, non-commodifiable goods by nature (Ostrom and Ostrom, 1977).

Second, related to the first, knowledge regulation (that is, intellectual property) has expanded and grown dramatically in recent years, acting as the characteristic knowledge "enclosure" of the present stage (Boutang, 1999; Zukerfeld, 2010).

The film, music and software industries (among others) have been applying different strategies to prevent the replicability of DI and informational goods (by drawing upon technological developments such as rights digital management or by staging "exemplary" trials to so-called pirates) while at the same time taking advantage of this replicability (using free licensed goods and even applying selective violation of certain intellectual property rights) (Zukerfeld, 2010). Today, the dispute for commoditization of DI has reached the growing field of user-generated data. Internet giants such as Google or Facebook take advantage and commercialize enormous amounts of data coming from nonprofit users. Blockchain, and specifically Wibson, join in this dispute.

In the next section we describe briefly the socioeconomic importance of data commoditization on the Internet. We do so centered on one current business model, the one with which Wibson aims to compete.

Data values: an extended business model

For profit usage, exploitation and commercialization of big amounts of data exceed that related to nonprofit users of the "social media". Even more, data has always been important to economic production (Rullani, 2004). From the beginning of the twentieth century, for example, Taylorism entered the factories, enabling capture of data from the working process. Also, consulting companies have done the same in different ways across the word, many before digital revolution. Nowadays, firms capture – generally through censorships – and analyze big amounts of data from their own production process (Srnicek, 2017). Meanwhile, state agencies have access to data from citizens and use it for different purposes. The Snowden case became famous after revealing a business political alliance from which data of phone calls and platform usage had been intercepted (Van Dijck, 2014). So-called data brokers such as Axciom collect, analyze and commercialize big amounts of data from available public records and consumer surveys, although there is not an effective way to prove all of their sources (Roderick, 2014). Each of these processes of acceding and exploiting data has its own characteristics, regulations and actors.

This chapter refers to not all but one particular kind of capitalist exploitation of data, and particularly to one extended kind of business model that makes profit from nonprofit users' data on the web in a specific way. Although it could combine different strategies, this model consists mainly of freely providing a service (an email, a social network, a streaming service, a search engine, etc.) in exchange for users' data. That is the case of Facebook, Twitter, LinkedIn, Skype, WhatsApp, YouTube, Gmail, Hotmail and so on. These are for-profit platforms or apps where advertisers can sell us things based on the information they collect on us, being big information intermediaries (Zukerfeld, 2010; Van Dijck, 2014; Scott, 2014). As Zukerfeld (2010) poses: instead of basing their business on the enforcement of intellectual property rights of their outputs, excluding those who don't pay for it (meaning the service or IG they offer), these platforms aim to be inclusive, inviting people to freely share their data (bringing the inputs)[3] so they profit on related services and goods.

During recent years, this model has been subject to all kinds of debates about privacy boundaries, abuses and lack of transparency by corporations. In fact, after years of debate, in 2018 the General Data Protection Regulation (GDPR) was enacted, a European Union law on data protection and privacy. In particular, Cambridge Analytica (CA) and Facebook have recently been in the eye of the storm, since it came to light that CA had collected and sold to politicians big amounts of user data from Facebook, affecting voter opinion in different countries. However, the relation between Facebook and CA is not much different from those that establish the abovementioned platforms with other companies. Platforms and apps daily share users' data with third parties for the purpose of customized marketing in exchange for free services. Whatever happens inside these companies (and in between them) happens behind the data owners' backs.

Privacy and transparency are truly important, surely, but they do not pose the only nor the main question that these current extended practices do: what about value? In this business model, users not only give up part of their privacy and control of data, but part of their economic value as producers of data[4] (Petersen, 2008; Zukerfeld, 2010; Fuchs, 2010; Scholz, 2014; Srnicek, 2017 and so on).

Data serves to improve productive processes, to develop new goods and services, to better know and predict people's behavior, to discover new market "needs", to position a good in the more profitable place and so on. Realistic or not, the metaphor of data as the twenty-first-century oil serves to show the current economic importance of the data market (Kenney, In Olma, 2014). Generally speaking, the data industry is estimated to be worth more than $100 billion and growing at almost 10% a year (The Economist, 2010). The biggest companies in the information sector are making great investments on data management and analytics. Axciom, a giant data broker from the United States, for example, "collects and analyzes over 50 trillion data transactions a year, storing detailed entries for more than 190 million consumers and 144 million households in the USA alone, . . . recording US$1.1b in revenues in 2011" (Roderick, 2014: 1–2). Specifically regarding the business model in which we're interested, that of user-generated data, Facebook "generated nearly $27 billion in revenue in 2016 via its advertising products, which is equivalent to around $20 per monthly active user per year" (Aitken, 2018). Barely a few years back, Google obtained gains for over $17 million USD just on advertising sells (Reischl, 2008). As some scholars have pointed out, nowadays data comes potentially from nearly a half of the world population, and access to the Internet is growing fast (Kenney, in Olma, 2014; Srnicek, 2017).

Thus, Wibson comes to operate within one of the most profitable branches of the information sector, potentially competing with giant companies like Facebook and Google. Wibson's CEO, Mat Travizano, has said that the app is not intending to compete with them. Instead, he aims to compete with data brokers (i.e., Axciom) which, in his own opinion, are different than Google or Facebook since they do not give anything to users in exchange for data (Jiménez, 2018). But independently of the Wibson CEO's opinions or intentions, to discover whether Wibson really potentially competes with these Internet giants, we can ask this question: why would users freely give away their data and lose control of it if they could obtain control and money through Wibson? And more important, why would a company turn to Facebook, facing high costs and getting unvalidated data, if it can have access to validated data and separately negotiate the prices with individuals through Wibson? Indeed, we will see soon how Wibson took note of both abovementioned current debates on the web (transparency and control of users' data on the one hand and economic value of users' data on the other) and uses that to promote itself, even specifically naming Google and Facebook and describing how they operate and where their profits come from, to illustrate the motives behind the launching of the app.

Blockchain and Wibson

Blockchains: from its origins to its recent applications

Recently, Bitcoin, one of the most widespread blockchain-based cryptocurrencies, has attracted the world's attention. Soon, literature noted that its truly novelty was its underlying technology, blockchain. Blockchain is a way to create decentralized peer-validated time-stamped ledgers. As Brett Scott states, "That is a fancy way of saying it is a method for bypassing the use of centralised officials in recording stuff" (Scott, 2014). More precisely, blockchain is a ledger that is distributed among different participants or nodes and is cryptographically protected and organized in mathematically related blocks of transactions in a way that cannot be altered (Preukschat, 2017). The more nodes it has, the stronger it becomes, to the extent that more participants are registering and controlling data circulation, reducing the possibility of double transactions. In the case of Bitcoin, it registers cash transactions, but it can be – and has been – applied to a wide variety of goods (diamonds, artistic works and now user data, etc.). Proof of existence, EverLedger, Ascribe, etc., are known examples (Scott, 2014; Preukschat, 2017; Herian, 2018). Thus, researchers began to focus on the decentralized "nature" of such technology, underlining its potential to "democratize" the circulation of goods and empower the "community" in different areas of social and economic life (Kosten, 2015; Atzori, 2015; Vigna and Casey, 2016).

However, starting from that limited definition, as Preukschat explains, there is no such thing as "a blockchain technology" (Pilkington, 2016; Yli-Huumo et al., 2016; Preukschat, 2017) but instead several kinds of blockchain that combine with other technologies to function. The decentralized,[5] open[6] and pseudo-anonymous[7] blockchain is the public[8] blockchain. In the end, it means that "there is free and unconditional participation of everyone in the process of determining what blocks are added to the chain, and what its current state is" (Buterin, 2015b in Pilkington, 2016: 230). But all kinds of private and hybrid blockchains are emerging (Shrier et al., 2016). These share some characteristics and differ substantially in others, such as the concentration of some type of information on the user community (Preukschat, 2017). This aspect has led some critics to question the effectively decentralized, and thus democratic, natural or intrinsic character of blockchains, particularly focusing on those related to the so-called entrepreneurs in the capitalist context (Herian, 2018). Furthermore, several authors have shown that even in Bitcoin, which runs on a public blockchain, the decentralization can turn into recentralization (Scott, 2014; Pel, 2015; Zukerfeld and Rabosto, in Schuster, 2017).

Thus, first, it is worth taking into account the particular features of each blockchain.

More specifically, a blockchain can be private (only participants – registered/invited users – can access the database or some kind of information from it) or closed (not everyone, but certain users can participate in registering information, including the possibility of setting different levels of access for different kinds of users) and, additionally, can establish different degrees of identification of users. It all depends on the design (Lessig, 2009).

So, learning from the first public blockchains, such as that which Bitcoin is based on, certain models change the possibilities of usage. They keep some degree of decentralization because the database is distributed between nodes and none of them can alter the blockchain, but there is some concentration of information (some hierarchies between nodes) and not everyone can access it, only registered users. This is the case of Wibson. Wibson is a proprietary and for-profit app based on a private Ethereum blockchain.[9] Wibson does not store data itself, but, as I will detail soon, concentrates other valuable information, also maintaining the power to change rules at any time. Indeed, as the CEO and cocreator of Wibson explains, through Wibson, he wants to "create a data broker fair and transparent" (Jiménez, 2018).

It is thus worth pointing out a fundamental actor here: the company behind the app, Gran Data, a for-profit actor. This actor is the one who establishes either the entire design or the rules for the design (or redesign if necessary) of this app and the characteristics of its underlying blockchain. A new, different intermediary is born.

Next, it should be noted that private or public blockchains share one feature: they are potentially capable of tracing DI or IG at any time and registering the transaction instantly on the blockchain. That is: one informational good cannot be in two places at the same time. In other words, blockchain constitutes an effective way of inhibiting replicability of ID and IG. This feature is not necessary related to the commercialization or non-commercialization of those IG, but could clearly help the former.

To be sure, according to CEO of Wibson: "We are transforming personal data into a valuable asset which consumers can easily control and trade, just like more traditional assets" (Wallen, 2018).

Through blockchain, in Wibson, what is private remains private, and all participants in the blockchain and Wibson are geared toward that purpose. Whether the data is appropriated by Facebook, Gran Data or by an individual does not call into question whether that data should be public and preserved from commercialization. This is exterior to blockchain and has to do with regulation (particularly with the smart contracts attached to IG). In this sense, one can ask whether the current cultural and institutional arena leads to a discussion of public utility, care and transparency of data traffic or instead contributes to installing other capitalist forms, keeping unaltered the balance between the public and the private.

Related to that, some scholars have questioned the supposedly intrinsic capacity of these technologies to empower the community (Pel, 2015; Scott, 2014). They noticed that the community of users does not refer to the construction of communal ties, "people getting together in mutualistic self-help groups", but to "individuals acting as autonomous agents". Thus, this supposed empowerment comes "from retreating from trust and taking refuge in a defensive individualism mediated via mathematical contractual law" (Scott, 2014: 20). "Empowering individuals" through a blockchain-based app (Wibson, 2017), Wibson seems to be a relevant case, if not the best expression, of this individualism. As we will see, its incentive system contributes to it.

In the next section we detail how Wibson works and how it describes (and justify) itself discursively (Figure 11.1).

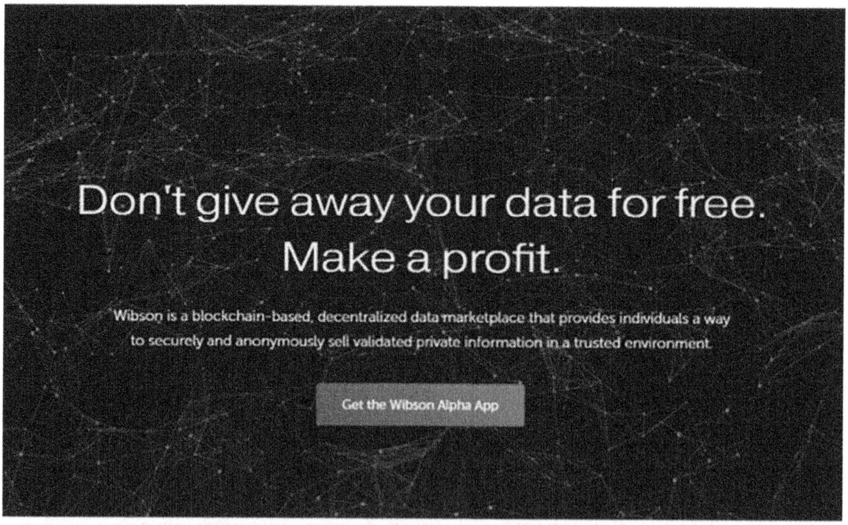

Figure 11.1 Wibson main page (Wibson.org)

Source: Author's own elaboration (screenshot) (2018)

The case of Wibson: functioning, actors, exchanges and discourses – a new emerging intermediary

What is Wibson according to Wibson?

Wibson identifies a "Challenge" in "today's economy": "data equals money. Unfortunately, it doesn't mean money for you", then points out guilty parties: "Giant tech companies cleverly use the Internet's underlying technical protocols to capture and control your personal information". Finally, Wibson proposes a "solution" to those "individuals" who are "the real owners of data": "The Wibson data marketplace provides infrastructure and financial incentives for individuals to securely sell private information that is validated for accuracy, all without sacrificing personal privacy" (Wibson, 2017). It is, according to Wibson and to sum up, "a decentralized data marketplace empowering individuals to monetize their own data, safely" (Wibson, 2017).

As we suggested earlier, here we can clearly see how Wibson takes note of current issues on data privacy, control and transparency, on the one hand, and on data economics or property, on the other, to justify and promote its business.

To be sure, it can be read in its "White Paper", in the section that describes the "motivation" for the app's launching, who these "giant tech companies" are. They "have cleverly used the underlying technical protocols to build layers of proprietary applications that capture and control massive amounts of personal data. . . . The top five companies (Google, Facebook, Apple, Microsoft and Amazon) boast a combined market value of almost $3.5 trillion" (Travizano et al., 2018: 2).

What is behind this "solution"?

Wibson is a proprietary and for-profit app launched in February 2017 by Gran Data company. Gran Data operates in the so-called field of big data (which includes capture and analysis of data) since 2007. It started offering services to corporations and, since 2017, it intends to include "individuals" through Wibson. Although its headquarters are located in Silicon Valley, most of the company operates in Argentina, where it employs about 60 workers. First through Binaria and now through Wibson, the goals of the company have been always the same: "understand market trends and predict users' behavior", selling related services (grandata.com, 2018). In an interview, asked about Wibson's profit model, the cofounder said: "What I actually want is to use Wibson as a way to obtain data for my other company, Gran Data" (Jiménez, 2018).

Based on an Ethereum blockchain, Wibson offers a digital data marketplace and legal advice on data transactions, mainly connecting data producers (individuals) with data buyers (organizations or corporations). Synthetically, once a user installs the app – this reduces the "community" to registered users – the app links itself to different data sources (social media profiles, device location and others – see Figure 11.2). From the app, the user can see data buyers' offers. Meanwhile, the "notaries" check the fidelity of the data. Users then sell

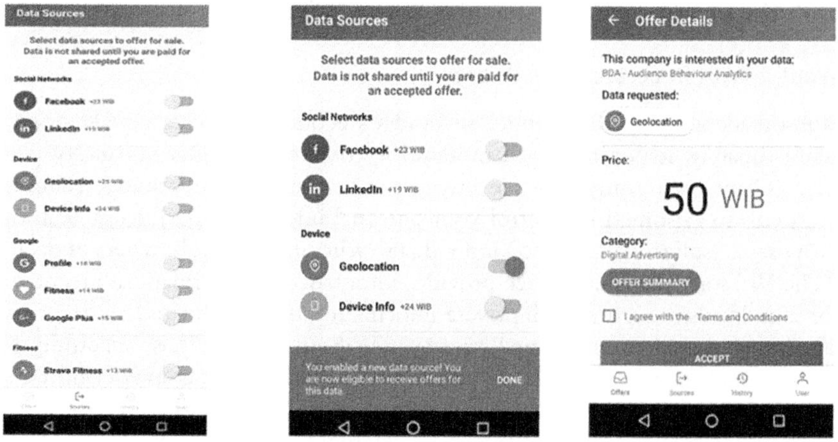

Figure 11.2 Wibson app, "Data Sources" and "Offer Details"; example of one source selected

Source: Author's own elaboration (screenshot of app) (2018)

data to a buyer, always monitoring where that data is, and receive a payment through Wibson. Thanks to blockchain, data can be always monitored by users, is encrypted and is not stored in any Wibson server, which only holds a record of the transaction, including the smart contract agreed upon between the seller and data buyer (Wallen, 2018).

Thus, Wibson's model includes the following actors and exchanges:

- Data sellers (registered users, mostly individuals): the app is free for them in monetary terms. When a transaction is completed, they win Wibson points (digital rewards that in the end represent money).[10]
- Data buyers (corporations or individuals). The app is free at the moment. Data buyers pay for and obtain data from users, not depending on Facebook or Google (but, by means of Wibson). If they want notaries to validate the data, they can add a payment that goes to Wibson. Thus, hat these actors are supposed to obtain access to validated data from users in a marketplace that a priori lacks the high entry barriers of the Internet giants. Here, money enters in the circuit. In this testing version of Wibson, data buyers don't differ from investors/partners, which, along with Wibson, will be the only buyers of data (Wibson, 2017 – Frequently asked questions).
- App investors/academic partners: from universities to big companies (including the telecommunication industry, banks and others), these actors can play two roles. Some of them are the aforementioned "notaries": they are in charge of verifying data (based on their own records), receiving a payment

from Wibson for the task. Others can use data to do research or for other purposes linked to their own business (Wibson, 2018b – medium). Any organization or corporation that concentrates information could potentially associate with Wibson and act as notary. They obtain data and also, of course, invest money on the app.

- The app (and the company behind it): Wibson can obtain some valuable things and make a profit in different ways. First, it receives investments from the "partners". Secondly, it receives money through the aforementioned payment from buyers who want verified data. Third, Wibson obtains information on user behavior (data buyers and sellers). Although, as we have seen, Wibson does not have access to the transacted data itself, like other apps and platforms, Wibson can have data of user behavior inside the app (logs, location, time of usage, amounts and kinds of interactions and transactions, interests) (Wallen, 2018). This could serve, of course, to make better versions of the app but also to sell related services, the so-called premium services, or even new apps.[11]

In this sense, terms and conditions of Wibson say:

> When using the Mobile Application, we will collect data that tells us about your app usage. We will use this usage data internally and only for research and development purposes. In addition, you will have the option to share with us different data contained in your mobile device or phone. . . . We collect this data to conduct internal testing of the Mobile Application and its use by you and other users for the purposes of research and state-of-the-art marketing. By delivering this data to us, you also authorize us to transfer it to Wibson Ltd., and our academic partners for related purposes.
> (Wibson, 2017 – Privacy Policy, Terms and conditions-)

How different are these terms from Facebook's? Should Wibson users rely solely on the code, or should they also trust Wibson? Of course, Wibson reserves the right to "make changes to the content and Services offered on the Mobile Application at any time" (Wibson, 2017 – Terms and Conditions-).

We have already seen infrastructure and exchanges between actors. To complete the understanding of Wibson functioning, let's see how the "incentives system" works. Like Bitcoin and other blockchains, Wibson has a "token model", called here "Wibson points". Its description is going to complete the previously suggested idea of an individual interest moving the "community" as a "common goal".

To date (in its "alpha" version) and as we have mentioned, Wibson is using Wibson points in order to incentivize "users" to interact in the app. But in the near future, the "token model" is going to consist of "Wibcoins", a Wibson cryptocurrency. So, to the extent that more users enter the app and the blockchain, Wibcoins will appreciate, and, simultaneously, Wibson will be stronger as an intermediary. In short, this system enables network participants to work together toward a common goal, the growth of the network and the appreciation of the token. Through this system, finally, interests of users (in individual terms) and app interests converge.

Conclusions

This chapter aimed to characterize an extended way of using blockchain technology in the field of circulation and commercialization of user-generated data through the case of Wibson.

To do this, we've placed this for-profit and blockchain-based app in context: first, in the general context of informational capitalism; second and more specifically, in the middle of a great expansion of the commercialization of user-generated data and the subsequent debates that took place as a response, in economic and social terms. These debates came to question the role that the Internet giants had been playing on that regard. The time to erase those intermediaries had come, and the decentralized nature of blockchain would come to help in that sense.

However, we've shown, first, that there is no such thing as "a blockchain" but different kinds of blockchains, and there are not, in this sense, "natural or intrinsic features" of blockchain technology. In particular, through a private blockchain, in Wibson, intermediaries do not disappear but change hands. Indeed, data brokers have changed: from Facebook or Google to Wibson, giving to "individuals" some monetary retribution and control of their data. In this sense, Wibson seems to be telling its users "Don't trust me, I don't store your data; trust in the blockchain community". But Wibson keeps the power to regulate the permissions and the rules of the app. As we've seen, the ideas of "giving control back to individuals" and "pay a fair share for their data" have turned into Wibson's discursive justification for its existence as a new intermediary in the growing digital data market. Users had already – before Wibson's own existence – been convinced of the evil of giants.

Second, but related to it: through Wibson, blockchain serves to develop another way of commercialization of informational goods (specifically data) on the Internet. Thus, Wibson helps to show that a certain degree of decentralization – controlled decentralization – of the data market doesn't represent a democratization of the data market; it works as a tool to raise a dispute against the Internet giants for one of the most important sources of profit these days: user data. This is an inter-capitalist dispute, in which community – turned into individuals for profit actors – is just a medium.

Leaning on certain attributes of the blockchain technology, apps like Wibson keep the disruptive potentials of the digital technologies in between the boundaries of capitalism. Thus, the question about nonprofit interests on data and public utility of data remains unanswered. If the commodification of the Internet has steadily advanced over the years in the realms of infrastructure, software and content, now it's time for data.

Notes

1 At the moment this paper was written, the mobile app was in an "alpha" testing phase.

2 It is worth noting that, while not identical to Wibson and without the same notoriety on the specialized press, other similar apps and platforms like Dock.io and Bitclave.com have emerged recently. Thus, this text focuses on a business field that, although emergent, exceeds the existence of an isolated case.

3 In regulatory terms, these platforms rely on gray areas or loopholes on the legislation, combining the appropriation of reusable contents (such as those licensed under CC or GPL) with the violation of unknown user's property rights (Zukerfeld, 2010). This is a different situation from that of the so called "data brokers".

4 We are not discussing the extent in which data itself (the so called "raw data"), without further treatment, produces economic value. Indeed, the usual distinction between data and information is difficult to sustain since algorithms that process data are part of the same platforms and apps in which data is produced. Neither is it suitable to call "workers", and specifically unpaid workers, to data producers. As I have shown, based on the literature review, I am simply assuming data is an indispensable input that costs very little to companies in comparison to the great profit that it enables.

5 There is no center, no "third parties", no "intermediaries"; each node is equal to the next one. In Bitcoin, blockchain aims to avoid banks. In Wibson, blockchain aims to avoid Facebook, Google and Wibson itself centralizing data in their own servers.

6 Anyone with minimal technical knowledge, a computer and software can became a user.

7 Blockchain users cannot be personally identified, but their addresses can be traced.

8 The blockchain is accessible to every Internet user, whether or not she is a user of the blockchain.

9 This is a testing private network built over the public blockchain Ethereum (Wibson, 2018a – Medium-).

10 Currently, Wibson points can be exchanged for Visa gift codes, Spotify subscriptions and Uber credits, depending on the country of residence (Wibson, 2017).

11 To be sure, "If you send or transmit any communications . . . to Company . . ., suggesting or recommending changes to the Mobile Application or Materials . . . all such Feedback is, and will be treated as, non-confidential and non-proprietary. . . . Company is free to use, without any attribution or compensation to you, any ideas, know-how, concepts, techniques, or other intellectual property and proprietary rights contained in the Feedback, whether or not patentable, for any purpose whatsoever, including but not limited to, developing, manufacturing, having manufactured, licensing, marketing and selling, directly or indirectly, products and services using such Feedback" (Wibson, 2017 – Terms and Conditions-).

References

Aitken, R. (2018). Can blockchain challenge 'FANG' tech giants for control over our data? *Forbes*. Available at www.forbes.com/sites/rogeraitken/2018/02/28/can-blockchain-challenge-fang-tech-giants-for-control-over-our-data/#1662d12f3367. Last access: 08/04/2018.

Atzori, M. (2015). Blockchain technology and decentralized governance: Is the state still necessary? *Papers SSRN*.

Boutang, Y. M. (2004). Riqueza, propiedad, libertad y renta en el capitalismo cognitivo. In *Capitalismo cognitivo, propiedad intelectual, y creación colectiva*. Madrid: Traficantes de sueños, pp. 107–120.

Cafassi, E., 1998. Internet: políticas y comunicación (Vol. 3). Editorial Biblos.

Castells, M. (1997). *Power of identity: The information age: Economy, society, and culture*. Oxford: Blackwell Publishers, Inc.

The Economist. (2010). Data, data everywhere: A special report on managing information. *The Economist*, 27 February. Available at www.emc.com/collateral/analyst-reports/ar-the-economist-data-data-everywhere.pdf. Last access: 17/09/2018.

Fuchs, C. (2010). Labor in informational capitalism and on the Internet. *The Information Society*, 26(3), 179–196.

Gran Data. (2018). Official website. Available at https://grandata.com/

Herian, R. (2018). Blockchain and the distributed reproduction of capitalist class power. In Gloerich, I., Lovink, G., and De Vries, P. (eds.) *MoneyLab reader 2: Overcoming the Hype*. Institute of Network Cultures, Amsterdam, pp. 43–51.

Jaimovich, D. (2018). Wibson, una app Argentina para ganar dinero con los datos personales. *Infobae.com*, 7 de mayo de 2018. Available at www.infobae.com/tecno/2018/05/07/wibson-una-app-argentina-para-que-puedas-ganar-dinero-con-tus-datos-personales/. Last access: 17/07/2018.

Jiménez, M. (2018). Wibson, la 'app' que permite a cualquier persona ganar dinero con sus datos personales. *El País*. Available at https://elpais.com/tecnologia/2018/02/27/actualidad/1519749269_061405.html. Last access: 03/04/2018.

Kosten, D. (2015, October 31). Bitcoin manifesto. Crypto-socialism – What's next? or what does it mean sharing economy and distributed trust? *Social Science Research Network*. Available at https://mpra.ub.uni-muenchen.de/73568/1/MPRA_paper_73568.pdf. Last access: 01/05/2019.

Lessig, L. (2004). *Free culture – The nature and future of creativity*. London: Penguin.

Lessig, L. (2009). *Code: And other laws of cyberspace*. Read How You Want.

Olma, S. (2014). *Never mind the sharing economy: Here's platform capitalism*, Blog, October 16. Available at http://networkcultures.org/mycreativity/2014/10/16/never-mind-the-sharing-economy-heres-platform-capitalism/. Last access: 5/7/2018.

Ostrom, V., and Ostrom, E. (1977). Public goods and public choices. In Savas, E. S. (ed.) *Alternatives for delivering public services: Toward improved performance*. Boulder, CO: Westview Press, pp. 7–49.

Pel, A. (2015). *Money for nothing and bits for free: The geographies of bitcoin*. Thesis. Department of Geography and Planning University of Toronto. Available at https://tspace.library.utoronto.ca/handle/1807/70121

Petersen, S. (2008). Loser generated content: From participation to exploitation. *First Monday*, 13(3).

Pilkington, M. (2016). Blockchain technology: Principles and applications. In Olleros, F. X., and Zhegu, M. (eds.) *Research handbook on digital transformations*. Edward Elgar Publishing, p. 225.

Preukschat, A. (2017). *Blockchain. La revolución industrial en Internet*. Barcelona: Gestión 2000.

Reischl, G. (2008). *El engaño Google: una potencia mundial incontrolada en Internet*. Barcelona: Medialive Content.

Roderick, L. (2014). Discipline and power in the digital age: The case of the US consumer data broker industry. *Critical Sociology*, 40(5), 729–746.

Rullani, E. (2004). El capitalismo cognitivo, ¿un déjà-vu? In *Capitalismo cognitivo, propiedad intelectual, y creación colectiva*. Madrid: Traficantes de sueños, pp. 99–106.

Scholz, T. (2014). Platform cooperativism vs. the sharing economy. *Big Data & Civic Engagement*, 47.

Schuster, M. (2017). Entre las criptomonedas y el criptocapitalismo. Entrevista a Andrés Rabosto y Mariano Zukerfeld. Revista electrónica. *Nueva Sociedad*. Available at http://nuso.org/articulo/entre-las-criptomonedas-y-el-criptocapitalismo/. Last access: 09/04/2018.

Scott, B. (2014). Visions of a techno-leviathan: The politics of the bitcoin blockchain, JUN 1 2014. *E-International Relations.* Available at www.e-ir.info/2014/06/01/visions-of-a-techno-leviathan-the-politics-of-the-bitcoin-blockchain/. Last access: 06/06/2015.

Shrier, D., Wu, W., and Pentland, A. (2016). Blockchain & infrastructure (identity, data security). *MIT Connection Science*, 1–18.

Srnicek, N. (2017). *Platform capitalism.* Cambridge: Polity Press.

Travizano, M., Minnoni, M., Ajzenman, G., Sarraute, C., and Della Penna, N. (2018). *Wibson: A decentralized marketplace empowering individuals to safely monetize their personal data* (White Paper). Available at https://wibson.org/wp-content/uploads/2018/10/Wibson-Technical-Paper-v1.1.pdf. Last access: 28/11/2018.

Van Dijck, J. (2014). Datafication, dataism and dataveillance: Big data between scientific paradigm and ideology. *Surveillance & Society*, 12(2), 197–208.

Vigna, P., and Casey, M. J. (2016). *The age of cryptocurrency: How bitcoin and the blockchain are challenging the global economic order.* Macmillan.

Wallen, J. (2018). Blockchain-run platform offers European consumers opportunity to profit from own personal data. *Forbes*, July 23. Available at www.forbes.com/sites/joewalleneurope/2018/07/23/blockchain-run-platform-offers-european-consumers-opportunity-to-profit-from-own-personal-data/#72e330ac290a. Last access: 14/09/2018.

Wibson. (2017). Official website. Available at https://wibson.org/

Wibson. (2018a). Wibson launches consumer-controlled personal data marketplace. *Wibson Medium.* Available at https://medium.com/wibson/wibson-launches-consumer-controlled-personal-data-marketplace-87b572a392bb. Last access: 20/09/2018.

Wibson. (2018b). Wibson launch event recap: A wonderful evening in Barcelona. *Wibson Medium.* Available at https://medium.com/wibson/wibson-launch-event-recap-a-wonderful-evening-in-barcelona-8f71de002411. Last access: 05/05/2018.

Yli-Huumo, J., Ko, D., Choi, S., Park, S., and Smolander, K. (2016). Where is current research on blockchain technology? – A systematic review. *PLoS ONE*, 11(10), e0163477.

Zukerfeld, M. (2010). *Capitalismo y conocimiento. Materialismo cognitivo, propiedad intelectual y capitalismo informacional* (Tesis de Doctorado, FLACSO Argentina). Available at https://capitalismoyconocimiento.wordpress.com. Last access: 12/04/2018.

Part III

Technological aspects and consequences of decentralized technologies

Chapter 12

Applying smart contracts in online dispute resolutions on a large scale and its regulatory implications

Janet Hui Xue and Ralph Holz

1. Introduction

This chapter analyzes the feasibility of using smart contract technology to handle online dispute resolution (ODR) on a large scale. Online dispute resolution (ODR) is "referred to as the use of technology to carry out the dispute resolution process."[1] ODR combines alternative dispute resolution (ADR) and information and communication technology;[2] it can be used for disputes arising from both online e-commerce transactions and offline transactions such as purchases. ODR becomes particularly relevant in the context of cross-border e-commerce. It can include the traditional legal process, although it does not usually rely on it: the traditional legal process often involves a court, judge, and possibly a jury to decide a dispute.[3] However, ODR has a scalability problem: it cannot easily satisfy the sheer number of possible requests from millions of consumers, given how strongly e-commerce is still growing and the high number of intermediaries that are needed to support the financial transactions that ultimately enable e-commerce. Such intermediaries include a range of financial institutions: banks, brokers/dealers, and also other institutions that interact with the end users of a financial transaction; the term also includes infrastructure such as payment, clearing, and settlement systems.[4] Several ODR systems exist at international and regional levels, including eBay's ODR system[5] or the domain name dispute resolution used by ICANN.[6] However, no *globally* viable ODR model has emerged yet.[7] Recently, so-called smart contracts on blockchains have been suggested as a possible solution for "self-enforcing Online Dispute Resolution".[8] The claimed advantage is that smart contracts may be able to deal with disputes much faster and on a very large scale.

However, smart contract technology is in its infancy, and such advanced use has not been sufficiently explored yet. It is not entirely clear yet what smart contract platforms will eventually exist and which features they will support. Expectations of the viability of smart contract technology may be overly optimistic; there is also a certain degree of confusion regarding possible features and limitations. Importantly, while many use cases have been proposed, very few have been analyzed from the perspective of legal compliance. As a result, small and medium enterprises (SMEs) that wish to enter the financial industry, e.g., third-party payment suppliers, face much uncertainty when they consider blockchains and smart contracts for e-commerce. Even traditional regulatory authorities such as central banks and governments face some challenges.

This chapter identifies and illuminates the feasible regulatory space to help understand how smart contracts for ODR platforms can possibly be regulated and embedded within current law systems. The chapter first defines smart contracts and explains their relationship to blockchain. It presents their capabilities and limitations and how they are different from conventional, more centralized approaches, thereby highlighting a unique contribution that is of great help for future ODR platforms: the enforced transparency of the dispute process. Based on this technical analysis, the chapter proposes an approach how smart contracts can be useful in ODR platforms as they are used today, such as the EU ODR platform,[9] by outlining the principles applying to arbitrators and definitions of access control, e.g., the need for access for state actors. The chapter presents possible approaches to apply smart contracts to standardize the procedures of lodging cases on a large scale and handling disputes in an efficient manner. The proposals are based on lessons learnt in the last few years in the development of smart contracts on the Ethereum blockchain, currently the only major blockchain that supports smart contracts.[10] The chapter concludes with an analysis of implications for future regulation and legal compliance.

For the purpose of this chapter, we will not need to distinguish between public blockchains, which allow anyone to participate, and private blockchains, which require some form of permission by an authoritative entity (or group of entities) to participate. The possibilities and limitations of smart contracts are largely the same for both; the difference is mostly that the permission-based system used in private blockchain makes it easier to assign specific roles to certain participants. Hence, we limit ourselves to the more general case of public blockchain in the following discussion.

2. Blockchain: distributed ledgers, consensus, and trust

Blockchain is a form of distributed ledger technology: blockchain participants maintain a shared, joint view of all transactions that have ever occurred. Classically, solving the question how two parties can trust in the validity of a transaction would require intermediaries such as banks. Public blockchain replaces trusted intermediaries with a collective of a large network of participants that run a so-called consensus protocol; anyone can participate. The consensus protocol gives strong assurance in the validity of a transaction that the network as a whole has accepted. A number of consensus protocols exist. In the case of the famous Nakamoto consensus, employed in Bitcoin and in a variant also in today's Ethereum,[11] one can show that as long as a majority of the participants execute the consensus protocol faithfully, the entire network eventually will achieve a consistent view of all balances between any two parties. Building consensus requires each participant to group transactions into so-called blocks. Blocks have predecessors and successors, and hence they form a chain. Creating a block requires investing computational effort to solve a cryptographic problem. The first participant who successfully creates a new block and links it into the blockchain is rewarded with a certain amount of currency (Bitcoin or Ether, respectively, for Bitcoin and Ethereum). This is generally called "mining".

The cryptographic problem is defined such that participants of equal computational power have an equal probability of creating a new block. This construction ensures that the probability of fraud becomes extremely small and negligible – attempts to interfere with the consensus require the fraudulent participant to have more computational resources than most other participants combined.[12] As long as the part of the network that has a "computational majority" behaves faithfully to the protocol, the network will preserve a trustworthy record of all transactions ever made. The consensus protocol is implemented in software that every participant can run.[13] In this chapter, we always use the term participant as an entity participating in the network and consensus protocol.

3. Smart contracts: nature, execution, and distinctive features

The notion of smart contracts is an addition to the blockchain paradigm. A smart contract is a computer program that is executed by participants in a blockchain.[14] This is the same principle that web services employ: one can send and receive data from a web service via an interface and use it for further processing and display. With smart contracts, the difference is that every participant can create a smart contract and define a set of invocable routines (called "methods") for other participants to use and interact with the smart contract. A toy example would be a smart contract that implements and exposes the functionality of a calculator in its methods. Other participants in the network, and in principle also other smart contracts, can invoke these methods to obtain results; e.g., they might send numbers to a method called "sum" and receive the total sum as a result.

A smart contract is stored inside a transaction sent to the blockchain; hence once the network has achieved consensus, the smart contract becomes an immutable entry in the blockchain. All participants are required to execute a smart contract that is "invoked", i.e., interacted with. Interactions with a smart contract are again transactions.[15] This means that any interaction with a smart contract is also stored in the blockchain and hence transparent to the entire network.[16] This is a necessary prerequisite for participants to maintain a consistent view of the ledger. Smart contracts are identified by (cryptographic) addresses, in the same way that senders and receivers in the network are identified by such addresses (and in general not by their real-world identity). Just like users, smart contracts may even have control over digital assets.

The hope that has often been expressed for smart contracts is that they can be used to define the terms, rules, and penalties of true, legal contracts *and* also automatically execute and enforce the associated obligations, with specific events triggering transactions. This is often referred to as "self-enforcement". They can also help to simplify transactions where more than one party has to sign off in order for it to become valid. However, it is important to understand that smart contracts are still just computer programs, i.e., a collection of algorithms. This allows them to be utilized as means for payment, clearing, and settlement processes, which define ways to transfer funds and clear and settle securities and commodities, as well as their derivatives.[17] All of these are easily described algorithmically. In principle, this means that the procedures of handling dispute cases can also be encoded in a smart contract. However, smart contracts cannot be used to, e.g., reason about the validity of a claim if this requires interpretation of law. Furthermore, smart contracts always need to be invoked by transactions, which in turn requires the existence of a blockchain participant who can create such a transaction. At the time of writing, no blockchain system allows external events to be defined that would automatically trigger the creation of invoking transactions – some participant must always be involved.

A distinctive feature of smart contracts is that invoking a method requires a form of payment for the execution of the method. In Ethereum, for example, the operations defined in a smart contract add up to a total amount of "gas" that is required – "gas" here being an internal unit that measures the cost of execution. The participant (or contract) invoking the method must offer to pay for the required gas. The invoking party offers a "gas price", i.e. a conversion rate from Ethereum's internal currency, Ether, to gas, and a total amount of Ether they are willing to pay for the invocation. A participant who chooses the transaction for inclusion in a block must execute the invoked method. The gas spent is awarded as Ether to the first participant who creates a block that includes the invoking transaction. Smart contracts can themselves send and receive currency as specified by their authors; the authors can also endow a smart contract with currency to use before deploying it onto the blockchain.

Importantly, smart contracts can "protect" their methods and endowments by specifying conditions for access. Smart contracts have owners who have special access privileges, e.g., to empty the current holding or to shut down the smart contract (which makes further invocations impossible). Ownership is implemented using the typical asymmetric cryptography of blockchain; the owner's private key is needed to interact with the protected methods of a smart contract. In this sense, smart contracts implement the same form of access control that is common to most of computer security. It naturally means that all the known problems of access control – participants losing keys, keys being stolen, etc. – also apply to smart contracts. In classic computer security, access control is generally accompanied by operational procedures, like requiring only thoroughly vetted personnel within an organization being allowed to make changes or the four-eye principle to initiate transactions. Smart contracts can reproduce all these features; but by default, there are no operational procedures predefined. Together, this opens a classic regulatory space: in theory, smart contracts could be mandated to feature default access for certain (state) actors. Furthermore, regulation may impose on all owners of smart contracts an obligation to keep their keys for access control in a safe place.

The regulatory space extends beyond the authors of smart contracts. All smart contracts are run on the software provided by the developers of the blockchain. Hence, it is not difficult to "blacklist" certain transactions in the software and "rewrite history": if the majority of participants accept such a decision by the developers, then the effect is that of the transaction never having happened. While this seems to be a solution to deal with fraudulent smart contracts, it is important to note that it is a bottleneck: It is impossible for developers to keep track of all fraud.

In summary, the distinguishing feature of smart contracts is *not* their expressivity: smart contracts cannot express any computation or workflow that classic software could not also express. The appeal of smart contracts lies in the way *a larger network executes them and provides a transparent record of every invocation*. This is a fundamental difference to software as it is run today in financial institutions, insurance companies, government agencies, etc. A record of all transactions is stored with *all* participants in the blockchain.

Another limitation is also crucial: smart contracts cannot reason about the "meaning" of terms and whether they are fulfilled or not. They cannot make decisions that we traditionally associate with judges interpreting written law or ombudspeople mediating. In the context of ODR, this means that humans will still usually be required to assess cases, just as is the case now – there is no inherent decentralization here that smart contracts could add. Smart contracts do not remove the *human* scalability problem of ODR. Their potential lies in a *unification of technical procedures*.

As with all programs, smart contracts can contain flaws and errors that even highly experienced programmers will not spot;[18] this is inherent to the nature of computers.[19] This has repeatedly been shown to be highly problematic, with the case of "The DAO" being the most spectacular one. The DAO, short for Decentralized Autonomous Organization, was the first smart contract that attempted to implement the workflows of an entire organization and make it execute "autonomously", i.e., without human managerial activity. In the case of The DAO, the rules in the smart contract would have allowed investors to vote on projects to fund; profits would have flowed back to the investors. Anyone could become an investor by acquiring "The DAO tokens", which represented investor rights and were implemented with smart contracts.[20]

Unfortunately, in the case of "The DAO", a relatively simple coding error resulted in a massive breach, with the equivalent of 3.6 million Ether stolen by an attacker (then worth around $60 million USD). The attack could not be contained due to the autonomy of the smart contract. In the end, the

Ethereum developers intervened and blacklisted all transactions relating to The DAO in the next release of their software, eradicating the attack from history. While this is the best-known case, many others flaws have been reported, with surveys available.[21] In a recent study,[22] Brent et al. built a tool to investigate all 141,000 smart contracts in the Ethereum blockchain. They could show that up to 60 percent of smart contracts contained errors of the kind that made The DAO exploitable.[23] The authors also found that a single-digit percentage of smart contracts fail to secure their Ether holdings against unauthorized access.

4. A model combining smart contract technology with humans-in-the-loop

In the following, we present a regulatory model that combines smart contracts and human intervention as an extension of the principles of current ODR systems.[24] The model helps improve the efficiency of handling cases that are of a common nature (i.e., they are very similar) while maintaining the flexibility needed for legal reasoning and interpretation. In this model, the transparency provided by the blockchain's logging of all transactions is an invaluable source of information for later auditing; it also allows the collection of data about cases, complaint types, and outcomes for further investigation when necessary. This information is automatically time-stamped and available to all participants. Although we do not define exactly how case information is stored (e.g., supporting documents), we note that the blockchain itself usually does not offer such a feature. Such data is usually stored externally, but it can be referenced in the blockchain in an integrity-preserving way: any later attempt to modify referred documents would be immediately detectable.

Our model is based on a proposed application for smart contracts: so-called DApps – distributed applications. DApps are meant to be applications whose functionality depends fundamentally on interactions with smart contracts on the blockchain. A DApp can be implemented as a stand-alone (desktop) application, as an application running on a server, or even as a hybrid form, e.g., as a website where part of the functionality is implemented on the server and another part as JavaScript, executed in the browser. The key feature is always the interaction with smart contracts, for which the deployed blockchain environment provides an execution environment, including messaging and integrity-preserving references to external storage. We note that, at present, there is a huge gap between vision and reality. Current proposals for DApps focus on implementing them as websites, for example, by having every activity recorded in smart contract transactions on the blockchain or providing user-friendly interfaces to interact with smart contracts. An example would be the experimental prediction market Augur or the micro-payment functionality implemented in the new Brave web browser. Crucially, the implementation as a DApp adds transparency and also allows the use of the blockchain currency for payments.

In our model, the ODR is implemented as such a DApp: an online application allows access via the browser, and the blockchain is responsible for transparency and payment. We show this in Figure 12.1. This establishes a foundation for further-reaching ODRs: other ODR systems can be linked to an existing one by invoking the methods that the smart contracts implement. The result is that different ODRs can implement the same processes, with the blockchain guaranteeing auditability for all.

Using transparent audit records which are broadcast throughout the entire network is also notable because it creates another form of checks and balances: it exercises pressure on the human arbitrator and thus contributes to disincentivizing unfair or biased judgement.[25] The steps leading up to a case (which is presented to the arbitrator) can be defined in code that is transparent to everyone. The arbitrator cannot easily abuse their power. Once a human arbitrator has made their decision, the remaining steps of ODR, e.g., payout of settlements or rejections, can then be facilitated in smart contracts as well. This establishes a completely transparent chain of events from initial claim to outcome. The standardization helps to streamline the process and make it faster. Smart contracts also allow the establishment of feedback channels. These range from simple positive/negative "voting" (thumbs up/down) to more complex designs, e.g., providing feedback while at the same time expressing support for

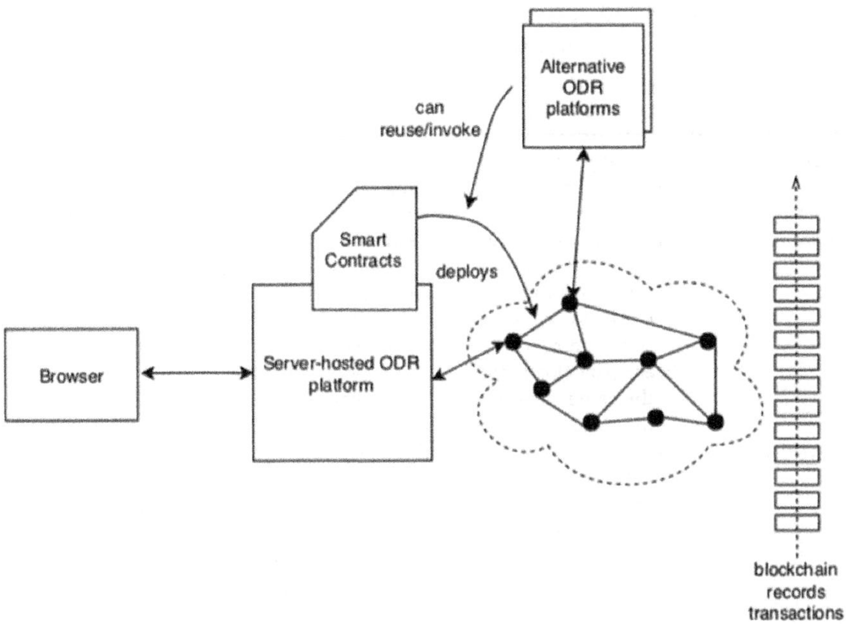

Figure 12.1 ODR platform implemented as a server-hosted application, which is accessible via the browser. Functionality is implemented in smart contracts deployed on a blockchain. The blockchain keeps track of all transactions.

another proposal. Votes are again transparent throughout the network. This lends itself naturally to feedback regarding agreement or disagreement with the decision of the arbitrator, either by affected parties or by external parties who are merely observing the ODR.

In addition to transparency, standardization may be the strongest contribution smart contracts make in our model: larger regulatory bodies can provide templates that (partially or completely) define an ODR process. The points where human arbitrators must interact would be well defined in the template. In this way, efficiency would be combined with sufficient room for further reasoning and interpretation requiring legal judgement. Companies can choose (or be mandated) to use the template. For example, the EU could standardize certain features of ODR platforms EU-wide; these templates could also be used outside the EU in efforts to harmonize the ODR implementation. Typical templates can be provided to lodge complaints, categorize dispute cases, and prioritize the processing of cases based on certain characteristics (e.g., urgency, monetary harm). The human decision remains a part of the overall process, but the human interaction would occur at precisely defined moments, with clearly specified inputs and outputs. Only more exotic cases might have to be done outside of this system (but still with a record of this fact kept). Payments could be transparently linked to decisions; even more complex financial structures can be implemented in transparent ways. An example could be debt issuances, where par value, tenor, and payment structure are parameters of a smart contract template. We summarize these aspects of our model in Table 12.1.

Table 12.1 Smart contracts in ODR

Aspect	*Relevant features of smart contracts*	*Immediate effects of using smart contracts*	*Outcome*
Transparency	Every participant has the same view of the definitions/methods of the smart contract. Every participant has the same view of the outcome.	Each participant can view dispute cases. Each participant can vote/provide feedback on decisions made by the arbitrator.	Better checks and balances exercise pressure on arbitrators.
Efficiency	Well-defined processes with clear hand-over points to human arbitrators.	Certain amount of templating allows for categorization of cases. Linked into feedback and payout mechanisms.	Shorter time to dispute resolution, immediate payout.
Standardization	Templated smart contracts to mandate procedures and principles of handling cases.	Reuse of well-defined procedures, reducing overhead. Possible to define variants based on templates.	Harmonization of implementation of ODR while leaving flexibility.

However, we emphasize that the use of smart contracts is not without risks, as discussed earlier in terms of access control and ownership of smart contracts.

5. Regulatory implications and potential from the use of smart contracts in ODR

The claimed potential of blockchain-based smart contracts is to make complex exchanges more transparent and reduce the means of undesired interference with transactions.[26]

However, traditional regulators like central banks and governments need to adapt to the possibilities and limitations of the new regulatory space. Concerning the regulation of smart contracts in ODR systems, this means striking a balance between the efficient processing of cases and creating an inclusive environment for increased participation, allowing those participants with fewer social resources to redress their interests in a more efficient way. Both increases, in efficiency and participation, may be gained by standardizing processes in code. Taking the EU ODR platform as described in our model as an example, EU-wide legal regulatory standards become easier to implement; at the same time, all participants can be given both the right and means to access and view the transaction record and, on a voluntary basis, provide feedback for the decision-making process. Importantly, a record of all feedback is kept, and attempts to abuse the mechanism can be tracked. In the following, we discuss the changed nature of co-regulation, with a particular focus on errors in smart contracts and regulatory implications.

5.1 Changed nature of co-regulation

This new model does not preempt regulatory manipulation as it exists in traditional models of regulation. Governments can still mandate certain functionality in smart contracts, and they can be authors of ODR smart contract templates. Co-regulation takes place but changes in nature: in this context, it means that many more actors have equal rights to view and provide feedback on the processes built into smart contracts. Co-regulation would imply a combined approach of regulating by code and regulating by law. However, in such a hybrid co-regulation approach, many principles need to be further clarified: how is access control defined, i.e., which parts of smart contracts can be activated, updated, or deactivated, by whom, and under which conditions?

This form of co-regulation opens participation in the regulatory process to any interested actor. Primary actors include the traditional actors as we know them from the regulation of financial systems, but also new intermediaries (brokers, dealers, and other entities interacting with end users) and finally individual consumers. Traditional regulators as we know them from the current financial system continue to exist but would adopt an additional role: the templated processing of ODR cases allows decisions to be analyzed on a much larger scale, while taking the amount and quality of feedback into account. Intermediaries are typically objects of ODR cases – payment suppliers would be a typical example. An ODR case should ideally contain a record of financial transactions relating to the disputed exchange. As is the case today, intermediaries in these transactions may often be located in different jurisdictions. This is a classic cross-border issue. The advantage of templated ODR smart contracts would be that intermediaries find it more acceptable to participate in the ODR process thanks to the code being unambiguous, hence reducing uncertainty and the potential for disputes about how to interpret the ODR process itself. Individual consumers are empowered in two ways. First, the existence of templated ODR contracts makes it less likely that they will be subjected to conditions predetermined by corporations alone without reasonable opportunity to negotiate terms. Second, consumers can provide much more immediate feedback and catch the attention of regulators, who can react faster to a growing number of similar disputes. This may help prevent unfortunate results as in previous settings, where single courts often did not enforce terms proffered by consumers in a contract.[27]

5.2 Errors in smart contracts

Even though code is unambiguous, smart contracts can still contain errors. Two kinds of errors can occur. The first kind of error we need to consider is when the developers of the smart contract misinterpret the (legal) meaning of ODR processes and implement them incorrectly. The second error occurs when the creators' interpretation is correct, but their use of the programming language results in an exploitable bug: seemingly correct code can be the target of an attack such that the attacker can "take over" the smart contract, i.e., cause it to run incorrectly and execute steps that are controlled by the attacker and not intended by the original developer. Errors of the second kind can often, but not always, be detected by automated tools – a variety exist, e.g., the one by Brent et al.,[28] Kalra et al.,[29] or Luu et al.,[30] to name a few. Theoretical limitations make it impossible to universally identify all possible errors. As of today, errors of the first form cannot be detected automatically at all as no machine can reason about the correctness of a mapping of a legal interpretation to code. This is still a task for humans.

5.2.1 Co-regulation: intervention in the case of errors

Incorrectly executing code should be halted and any wrongly executed steps undone. However, the blockchain execution model makes intervention of any kind relatively difficult. It would require (human) intervention by a recognized actor with an appropriate mandate. To fix an error of the first kind, the erroneous smart contract would have to be terminated and replaced or updated. This is a lengthier process and likely more costly than an advisory and clarification issued by a traditional regulator. However, it is relatively clear wherein the problem lies, the record of previous transactions can be rolled back in an orderly fashion, and an update mechanism in the smart contract may be able to solve the problem.

In the case of the second error, intervention may be significantly harder and financial loss harder to prevent. The problem is the presence of an active attacker who is taking active steps to corrupt the processes. A faulty smart contract can be terminated or changed to prevent further losses just like in the first kind of errors, but time is of the essence: as we have seen in the case of The DAO, heavy losses can be incurred within very little time. Undoing the damage also required intervention and crucial changes to the actual blockchain software. To do this in our ODR model, governments or multi-government bodies are likely the only actors in a position to mandate such changes and see them applied within a short time. Any delay would harm the trust of actors in the ODR process. An advantage of using blockchain-based smart contracts, however, would be that (criminal) investigation would be simplified because experts can view the audit trail and transaction history, which also provides the necessary information in short order to determine each party's liability and possible compensations to be made. To address this second risk of smart contracts, the code for ODR processes may well need to be written and maintained by engineers employed by a given organization (e.g., the EU, to stay in our example) – for many, this might incur substantial changes in their operational models.

5.2.2 Co-regulation: risk allocation and responsibilities in case of erroneous smart contracts

Intervention by governments is not the only (co-)regulatory implication that one needs to take into account. We argue that smart contracts do not obviate the need for a number of classic supporting mechanisms that are implemented outside the actual blockchain/smart-contract system.

Risk allocation: Since errors in smart contracts are unavoidable, organizations that rely on them need a clear understanding of their legal obligations and the obligations of their partners with respect to risk allocation and distribution. In particular, financial organizations must consider how risks should be allocated if their trade partners lose funds – an important consideration in the case of intermediaries.[31] Such arrangements need to be in place outside of the definitions of the smart contract, and before its deployment begins or the risk materializes.[32] Inconsistent understanding between different traders would otherwise collide with legal compliance in terms of liability and agreement about which party needs to become involved in which way.

Technical support for risk allocation: As risk allocation must be defined outside the smart contract, there remains a need for technical infrastructure and support to define, assess, and quantify risks and develop strategies to handle risks of different kinds. Smart contracts cannot eliminate this cost; the infrastructure support must provide the room for legal interpretation. The aftermath of the attack on The DAO may serve to illustrate the consequences of unclear risk allocation and procedures. Since The DAO was advertised precisely with the understanding that all rules were laid out in non-ambiguous terms in code, was the attacker not within their rights to exploit the bug and extract the funds? This question was considered seriously by the developers of Ethereum and led to a split of the community. The main developers decided to change the blockchain software such that all transactions relating to the attack would be ignored by participants – in essence "rewriting the immutable blockchain". However, a sizable faction disagreed and continued to work with the old software, hence creating a second, "forked" blockchain *with identical smart contracts running*. We also note that support infrastructure of the kind required has been envisioned but not yet implemented in existing ODR platforms, either. For example, it is absent in the current EU-wide portal for ODR, which was established in 2016, under Regulation (EU) No 524/2013 on online dispute resolution for consumer disputes,[33] which allows consumers and traders to submit complaints which can be directed and addressed through the platform.[34]

Some old regulatory challenges still remain: As we have shown, regulation implemented in smart contract code does not exclude traditional regulators and intermediaries from participation. However, once errors as described earlier occur in smart contracts, with potentially high financial losses, then judges and juries must still review and interpret the meaning of code and its legal basis.[35] The blockchain system may seem to make it harder for attackers to disguise their real identity because executing (attacking) a method in a smart contract may require a form of authentication. However, attackers may simply compromise the identity of another, legitimate participant by classic identity theft and use the assumed identity to stage their attack. The problems of attribution of attack and liability for protecting one's identity are the same as of today. This may be exacerbated by a high number of intermediaries, including those in other jurisdictions, who participate in the ODR system.

6. Summary

Smart contracts, run on blockchains, are often cited as a game-changing innovation that can make ODR systems more scalable. In this chapter, we have analyzed this view critically and mapped the regulatory space and implications of using smart contracts for ODR.

We gave an in-depth description of the technology behind smart contracts and highlighted their technical potential but also their limitations. In terms of expressivity, smart contracts do not replace the human arbitrator, as they cannot reason about the validity of a claim in the context of law. All steps of a smart contract, including the creation of the initial claim and the final decision by the arbitrator, are triggered by participants in the ODR system.

However, smart contracts do offer some true advantages. We provide a model that makes good use of these to improve the ODR process. First, the blockchain system provides complete transparency about the executed steps, creating an audit trail that is hard to forge and where details can easily be retrieved by participants. This leads to much higher accountability for the arbitrators in the decision-making process. For ODR, governments can implement regulation in the form of providing smart contract templates that define procedures that are legally required. Templates contain the standardized methods that can be executed by a multitude of ODR platforms, eliminating the need to implement them independently and hence reducing the degree of legal uncertainty in terms of compliance. Such smart contracts also provide a unified way to gather data about ODR outcomes and claims, thus allowing the effectiveness of the ODR process to be more easily analyzed and with a higher degree of confidence. Importantly, an efficient feedback mechanism can be implemented to collect opinions from participants whether or not the outcome met their expectations. This allows for a new form of co-regulation.

Ultimately, smart contracts are not a panacea. First, they introduce new problems, as they may contain errors of two kinds: wrong procedures due to legal misunderstandings and errors that make the code vulnerable to exploitation. We showed that intervention is not easy in either case, and damage can occur fast and be hard to undo. A classic set of mechanisms and support infrastructure still needs to be in place to deal with risk assessment and risk allocation in case of errors.

Notes

1 See Cortés, Pablo. *The Law of Consumer Redress in an Evolving Digital Market: Upgrading from Alternative to Online Dispute Resolution*. Cambridge: Cambridge University Press, 2017, p. 44.

2 Consumer ADR systems differ significantly from traditional out-of-court processes employed between commercial parties by relying on commercial arbitration and mediation processes. See Cortés Pablo, *The Law of Consumer Redress in an Evolving Digital Market: Upgrading from Alternative to Online Dispute Resolution*. Cambridge: Cambridge University Press, 2017, p. 3.

3 ODR has often been considered an online form of ADR. It aims to provide a tailored a solution to a conflict between several parties. According to the FTC, there are two types of dispute resolution: mediation and arbitration. The former one refers to a mediator acting as a neutral third party, facilitating dialogue to help the parties solve the problem. The latter solution depends on the parties reaching an agreement. Arbitration is associated with a stronger force than mediation but is less formal than court. The parties may appear at hearings, present evidence, or call and question each other's witnesses. An arbitrator or panel can make a decision after the cases have been presented; a decision may be legally binding. See the original explanation from FTC: Alternative Dispute Resolution, www.consumer.ftc.gov/articles/0162-alternative-dispute-resolution.

4 David Mills et al., *Distributed Ledger Technology in Payments, Clearing, and Settlement*, Finance and Economics Discussion Series Divisions of Research & Statistics and Monetary Affairs Federal Reserve Board, Washington, DC, p. 4, www.federalreserve.gov/econresdata/feds/2016/files/2016095pap.pdf.

5 eBay, *Dispute Resolution Overview*, https://pages.ebay.com/services/buyandsell/disputeres.html (accessed 7 November 2017).

6 ICANN, www.icann.org/resources/pages/dndr-2012-02-25-en (accessed 7 November 2017).

7 See Chapter I "Online Dispute Resolution and Prevention: A Historical Overview" in Ethan Katsh and Orna Rabinovich-Einy (eds.), *Digital Justice: Technology and the Internet of Disputes* (Oxford: Oxford University Press, 2017); Louis Del Duca, Colin Rule, and Zbynek Loebl Facilitating Expansion of Cross-Border ECommerce – Developing a Global Online Dispute Resolution System (Lessons Derived from Existing ODR Systems – Work of the United Nations Commission on International Trade Law), *Penn State Journal of Law & International Affairs*, https://elibrary.law.psu.edu/cgi/viewcontent.cgi?article=1004&context=jlia.

8 Pietro Ortolani, "Self-Enforcing Online Dispute Resolution: Lessons From Bitcoin" 36 (2016) *Oxford Journal of Legal Studies*, 595, 595–596, 598–602.

9 European Commission, *Online Dispute Resolution: Resolve Your Online Consumer Problem Fairly and Efficiently Without Going to Court*, https://ec.europa.eu/consumers/odr/main/?event=main.home2.show (accessed 27 May 2018).

10 *Solidity: High-Level Language for Implementing Smart Contracts*, http://solidity.readthedocs.io/ (accessed 27 May 2018).

11 Ethereum intends to eventually switch over to a different form of consensus; at the time of writing, this has not been sufficiently specified to include it in discussions.

12 The initial belief was that an absolute majority is required. Due to participants being able to collude, it is currently believed that the required computational power is on the order of 25 percent of the network's total computational power.

13 It is conceivable that some entities choose not to be part of the execution of the consensus protocol; in this case they become relying parties. They are not participants by our definition.

14 The concept of smart contracts was first introduced in the mid-'90s by Nick Szabo. Nevertheless, their implementation remained theoretical until blockchain development. For an overview see Nick Szabo, "Formalizing and Securing Relationships on Public Networks" (1997) 2 (9) *First Monday*, http://journals.uic.edu/ojs/index.php/fm/article/view/548/469 (accessed 31 May 2016).

15 Smart contracts can also have so-called internal transactions: these are executions of code that are completely determined by the invocation of a smart contract. As all participants must execute the invocation, these internal transactions are not stored in the blockchain, but they can always be inferred later by executing the smart contract invocation.

16 The execution of smart contracts normally happens in a so-called virtual machine (VM). VMs emulate a computer system. They are very commonly in use, even in browsers, to provide a standardized execution environment for programs. Users are rarely even aware of their presence.

17 David Mills et al., *Distributed Ledger Technology in Payments, Clearing, and Settlement*, Finance and Economics Discussion Series Divisions of Research & Statistics and Monetary Affairs Federal Reserve Board, Washington, DC, www.federalreserve.gov/econresdata/feds/2016/files/2016095pap.pdf (accessed 7 July 2018).

18 Destefanis, Giuseppe, Michele Marchesi, Marco Ortu, Roberto Tonelli, Andrea Bracciali, and Robert Hierons. "Smart contracts vulnerabilities: a call for blockchain software engineering?" In *2018 International Workshop on Blockchain Oriented Software Engineering* (IWBOSE), pp. 19–25. *IEEE*, 2018.

19 We note a famous mathematical result: the computational logic that underlies all computers implies that there will always be programs that may contain errors that cannot be detected by another program.

20 Token is a term that is currently mostly used in the context of Ethereum. A token is implemented in (one or more) smart contracts: sending a certain amount of currency (Ether) to the respective smart contract results in the sender being awarded a certain

number of tokens. These tokens can either represent units of a new currency, or they can entitle the owner to execute certain functionality in smart contracts that accept these tokens. As such, tokens are a layer on top of Ethereum: they allow the development of applications that are based on tokens specific to the application's needs. Indeed, tokens are such a popular use case that the so-called ERC20 standard provides rules how they should be implemented.

21 Atzei, Nicola, Massimo Bartoletti, and *Tiziana Cimoli. "A Survey of Attacks on Ethereum Smart Contracts (sok)." In International Conference on Principles of Security and Trust*, pp. 164–186. Springer, Berlin, Heidelberg, 2017.

22 Lexi Brent, Anton Jurisevic, Michael Kong, Eric Liu, Francois Gauthier, Vincent Gramoli, and Ralph Holz, *Bernhard Scholz: Vandal: A Scalable Security Analysis Framework for Smart Contracts*, https://arxiv.org/abs/1809.03981.

23 Note that this does not necessarily mean that all these contracts are similarly exploitable in practice: the errors could also be in "harmless" methods.

24 For existing different ODR platforms, see Louis Del Duca, Colin Rule, and Zbynek Loebl, "Facilitating Expansion of Cross-Border E-Commerce – Developing a Global Online Dispute Resolution System (Lessons Derived from Existing ODR Systems – Work of the United Nations Commission on International Trade Law)" 1 (2012) *Penn. St. J.L. & Int'l Aff.* 59, http://elibrary.law.psu.edu/jlia/vol1/iss1/4.

25 Related standards to improve operator transparency are known to exercise pressure towards correct behaviour; for an analysis of a successful standard see: Johanna Amann, Oliver Gasser, Quirin Scheitle, Lexi Brent, Georg Carle, Ralph Holz: Mission accomplished? HTTPS security after DigiNotar. *Proc. ACM/USENIX 17th Annual Internet Measurement Conference (IMC)*. London, UK, November 2017.

26 See Paul H. Farmer, Jr., "Speculative Tech: The Bitcoin Legal Quagmire and the Need for Legal Innovation" 9 (2014) *J. Bus. & Tech. L.* 85, 89.

27 See, e.g., James Gibson, "Vertical Boilerplate" 70 (2013) *Wash. & Lee L. Rev.* 161, 167–69; Cheryl B. Preston and Eli W. McCann, "Unwrapping Shrinkwraps, Clickwraps, and Browsewraps: How the Law Went Wrong from Horse Traders to the Law of the Horse" 26 (2011) *Byu J. Pub. L.* 1, 23.

28 Ibid., 21.

29 Kalra, Sukrit, Seep Goel, Mohan Dhawan, and Subodh Sharma. "Zeus: Analyzing safety of smart contracts." In *25th Annual Network and Distributed System Security Symposium*, NDSS, pp. 18–21. 2018.

30 Luu, Loi, Duc-Hiep Chu, Hrishi Olickel, Prateek Saxena, and Aquinas Hobor. "Making smart contracts smarter." In *Proceedings of the 2016 ACM SIGSAC conference on computer and communications security*, pp. 254–269. ACM, 2016.

31 Stuart D. Levi et al., *An Introduction to Smart Contracts and Their Potential and Inherent Limitations*, https://corpgov.law.harvard.edu/2018/05/26/an-introduction-to-smart-contracts-and-their-potential-and-inherent-limitations/#16, (accessed 26 May 2018).

32 Risk allocation cannot be implemented in another smart contract: errors could also exist in that contract's definition.

33 European Commission, *Report from the Commission to the European Parliament and the Council on the Functioning of the European Online Dispute Resolution Platform Established Under Regulation (EU) No 524/2013 on Online Dispute Resolution for Consumer Disputes*, 13 December 2017, https://ec.europa.eu/info/sites/info/files/first_report_on_the_functioning_of_the_odr_platform.pdf; See Regulation, https://eur-lex.europa.eu/LexUriServ/LexUriServ.do?uri=OJ:L:2013:165:0001:0012:EN:PDF.

34 The platform, which was launched in January 2016, is available at https://webgate.ec.europa.eu/odr/ (accessed 13 Apr 2016).

35 If smart contracts proliferate, judges and juries will have to review them to determine their legal basis and evidentiary status.

Chapter 13

SmartAnvil

Open-source tool suite for smart contract analysis

Stéphane Ducasse, Henrique Rocha, Santiago Bragagnolo, Marcus Denker, and Clément Francomme

Relevance: the need to support tool building

Solidity's smart contracts are new computational units with special properties [Eth18c]: they act as classes with aspectual concerns; they respond to message calls as a remote object; their memory structure is more complex than that of mere objects; they are obscure in the sense that, once they are deployed, it is difficult to access their internal state; and they reside in an append-only chain.

There is a large spectrum of possible analyses that smart contracts could benefit from [DMO+18]. Some have already been proposed in the literature and others, not yet. Here is a non-exhaustive list: attack analysis [LCO+16, ABC17], general metric [TDMO18] and dedicated smart contract metrics analysis, gas consumption optimization [CLLZ17], gas cost prediction, dashboard [Few06], or contract visualization [ABC+13], to name a few.

There is a need to support the building of new generation tools to help developers [DMO+18]. Such support should tackle several important aspects, taking into account the specificities of smart contracts: (1) the general structure and semantics of contracts, (2) the object nature of published contracts, and (3) the overall chain composed of block and transactions. Several analysis tools exist such as Oyente [LCO+16], BlockSci [KGC+17], and others [BLPB17, BDLF+16, Eth18b] but to the best of our knowledge, they focus on a single aspect of smart contracts, either static analysis or collecting mere data.

In this chapter, we present SmartAnvil, an open platform to build software analysis tools around various aspects of smart contracts. We illustrate the general components and we focus on three important aspects: support for static analysis of Solidity smart contracts, deployed smart contract binary analysis, and blockchain navigation and query. SmartAnvil is open source and supports a bridge to the Moose data and software analysis platform.

The contributions of this article are the descriptions of several components that compose the SmartAnvil open-source platform. The outline of the article is the following: First, we describe the general architecture and components of the platform. The next section describes the low-level components for static analysis, and then the low-level components to interact and analyze deployed contracts. Next we describe blockchain navigation and query support. The next to last section discusses the future extensions on the platform and also presents the related work on blockchain analysis platforms. Finally, we make our final remarks and conclusions.

SmartAnvil: open platform architecture

The SmartAnvil open platform is structured around several components to cover the different aspects of smart contract analysis. Figure 13.1 shows the key elements that we describe in the following. While SmartAnvil can work in isolation, SmartAnvil interacts with the Moose data and software analysis platform [NA05].

Solidity structural components

Parser/AST (SmaccSol). The first basic but important component for static analysis is a parser/AST. The component SmaccSol offers a full parser and AST model for Solidity. It is based on the Smacc Compiler-Compiler framework [LBGD18, BGLD17]. This parser corrected early grammar errors of the Solidity language [RDDL17].

Graph (SmartGraph). Based on SmaccSol, the SmartGraph component builds a semantic tree, where it enforces the rules that cannot be defined in syntax level. It also defines scopes, allowing one to easily lookup reified components, such as methods, types, parameters, arguments, contracts, etc. It supports powerful analyses and graph-like navigations by using simple queries over the tree. This component allows one to easily do static annotations or to build call-graphs.

Software Metrics (SmartMetrics). This component mixes the information provided by the previous components and the information provided by the Fog components supporting deployed contract analyses to offer a large set of metrics characterizing both the solidity code and the deployed contracts.

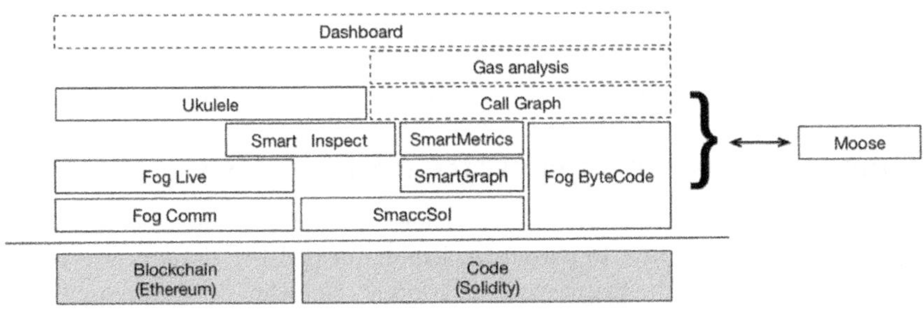

Figure 13.1 SmartAnvil components

Deployed contract components

The other set of components provides libraries to reverse engineer deployed contracts.

Drivers and Access to Contracts (FogComm). This component supports the access to the GETH- RPC API, implementing the primitives and related type marshaling for accessing deployed contracts, transactions, blocks, and more [BRDD18b].

Blockchain Element Reification (FogLive). This component extends FogComm by adding first citizen representations for blocks, transactions, and external/internal accounts. It also provides contract mirrors and contract proxies – built by techniques of reverse engineering and SmaccSol's AST analysis – for allowing a powerful connection to deployed contracts. It also provides the idea of Sessions, allowing cached and uncached interaction with the blockchain.

SmartInspect. This component leverages the implementation of contracts and mirrors in FogLive for gathering information. It exposes a contract's data in different formats to let the programmer access fine-grained information about the values of variables for a given deployed contract. It lets the developers inspect all the aspects of a deployed contract [BRDD18b].

Bytecode Reverse Engineering (Fog EVM ByteCode). This component extracts and interprets the stored hexadecimal code in deployed contracts, building a representation of the instructions and the relative memory layout. It also allows one to stream instructions and cut the contents into smaller pieces such as, lookup, methods, branching points, etc. It complements the SmartGraph and SmaccSol AST. This low-level information is interesting for fine-grained low-level analyses, for example, gas consumption analysis.

Transaction navigation

Query and Navigation (Ukulele). This component offers a query language to navigate and access transactions and deployed contracts. To achieve this, it implements different indexing strategies based on map reduce technologies, and it leverages the mirrors developed in FogLive. It has a small IDE to manipulate identified entities [BRDD18a].

Foundation for smart contract static analysis

Solidity [Eth18c] is a programming language used to specify smart contracts on the blockchain platforms, in particular, Ethereum [Eth14]. Solidity was originally designed to be the primary smart contract language for Ethereum. Even though other contract languages have been created for Ethereum (e.g., Serpent,

LLL), Solidity is still one of the major ones. Moreover, Solidity can also be used in other blockchain platforms such as Tendermint, Hyperledger Burrow, and Counterparty. Probably because of its popularity, a great amount of smart contract research deals with Solidity. Therefore, any proposed tool handling smart contracts should support Solidity to be well received.

Usually, static analysis is employed to examine programming language artifacts. Since Solidity is a programming language and smart contracts are its artifacts, we use static analysis techniques to implement tools for contract understanding and analyses [CCI90]. At their basis, most static analysis foundation techniques rely on ASTs (Abstract Syntax Tree). For instance, it is much easier to create code inspection tools on top of an AST than to rely on the purely textual contents of a contract. Therefore, to build static analyses for Solidity contracts, we need a way to create ASTs. Consequently, we require a parser to read Solidity source code and output a relevant AST representation of it.

In addition, we need a separate infrastructure from the Solidity compiler for the following reasons:

1. Since the Parser and AST represent a foundational part of a strong analysis tool, we need to fully control the parser and its production to avoid unwanted side effects in analyses using the produced ASTs.
2. Since the shape of the produced ASTs can severely impact the complexity of the analysis built on top, we need to control our ASTs.

Working with JSON AST produced by the Solidity compiler did not match the aforementioned requirements. In addition, we wanted to integrate with Moose (a data and software analysis platform) because it provides a rich and versatile set of tools [NA05] with a large ecosystem [Ber16, LKG07]. Therefore, developing a Solidity parser improves the support for better code analysis in Solidity [RDDL17]. To accomplish this, we used SmaCC (Smalltalk Compiler-Compiler) [BLGD17], relying on an adapted grammar specification of the Solidity language.

Challenges

The main challenge of designing a parser for Solidity is the inconsistencies among the documentation [Eth18c]. For example, in one part of the documentation it is stated that string literals are enclosed by either single or double quotes (section "Solidity in Depth" – "Types" – "String Literal"). However, in another part (section "Miscellaneous" – "Language Grammar") only double quotes are supported to define string literals. On the other hand, the official parser recognizes both single and double quoted string literals. This is just one example of several inconsistencies we found [RDDL17]. We decided to follow the official parser, i.e., if something is parseable in the official parser, then our parser should understand it as well. Even so, the inconsistencies in the documentation made the parser creation much more difficult because we lacked a reliable specification to follow.

Another challenge to create a parser is how often the Solidity language changes. The language specification is not stable, and syntactic rules are added or changed to support new versions of Solidity. For example, in version 0.4.21 (and below), there was no syntactic rule to handle a constructor; they were just a function definition with the same name as the contract. But that changed in version 0.4.22 (and above), where the constructor has a distinct syntax different from function (by using the constructor keyword). Therefore, any parser for Solidity needs to adapt to changes in the syntax, as the language is still under development.

We took into account these challenges when designing and developing our Solidity parser for Pharo.

Approach: SmaCC-Solidity

Creating a parser can be a difficult and time-consuming endeavor. Parser generators provide an easier way to tackle this problem [IM15]. Basically, we write the syntax specification using a formal grammar, and the generator automatically builds the parser. For example, there are many parser generation tools available now such as YACC [Mer93], ANTLR [Mil05], and SmaCC [BLGD17].

Generally, we can classify a parser as either top down or bottom up. A top-down parser starts its productions from the root element of the grammar, working its way down to the bottom leaves. A bottom-up parser works vice versa, starting from the leaves and working up to the root. Moreover, either type of parser usually works on a subclass of grammars. The most common subclasses are LL(k) for top down and LR(k) for bottom up parsers [ALSU06].

When we consider the Pharo Smalltalk environment, there are two prominent parser generation tools: PetitParser [BCDL13] and SmaCC [BLGD17]. Therefore, we had these two options to create our parser. We could also write the parser ourselves without relying on generators. We chose to develop our parser using SmaCC for the following reasons: (1) SmaCC requires a textual context-free grammar as input that is similar to the grammar provided for Solidity; (2) SmaCC generated parser can adapt more easily to future changes in the Solidity grammar; and (3) SmaCC produces an LR parser, which has interesting advantages over other types of parsers [ALSU06]. Moreover, both PetitParser and a manually written parser would be more difficult to adapt and maintain than SmaCC. Therefore, we claim that SmaCC is the better option to create our parser.

The SmaCC-Solidity parser is publicly available in GitHub (github.com/smartanvil/SmaCC-Solidity).

Illustrative example

Usually, someone uses a parser when he/she needs to perform static analysis on the source code. Let's suppose a developer wants to create a token contract. Roughly speaking, a token is a custom form of cryptocurrency managed by a contract. A token could represent loyalty points, bonds, game items, etc. In this scenario, the developer wants to first understand a well-used to-ken before coding his own. In this example, the developer gets the GolemNetworkToken (address: 0xa74476443119A942dE498590Fe1f2454d7D4aC0d) contract code and decides to build a visual representation of it. By using our parser and some classes from the Roassal package [Ber16], a few lines of code (Listing 13.1) is all it needs to build a simple visualization.

Listing 13.1 Visualization using SmaCC-Solidity

```
 1 ast := SolidityParser parse: sourcecode.
 2 b := RTMondrian new.
 3 b nodes: (ast sourceunits) forEach: [:contract |
 4     (contract className = 'SolContractDefinitionNode')
 5     ifTrue: [b shape box color: Color black.
 6       b nodes: (contract statements select:
 7         [:stt | stt className = 'SolStateVariableDefinition']).
 8       b shape box color: Color gray; size: [:f | f source
            lines size * 3].
 9       b nodes: (contract statements select:
10         [:stt | stt className = 'SolFunctionDefinitionNode']).
11       b layout flow]].
12 b.
```

In Listing 13.1, first we get the AST from parsing source code (line 1). Then we create a new Roassal visualization [ABC+13] where each contract is a big gray box (lines 2–4). Inside each contract box, we get the state variable definitions (i.e., contract attributes) and create black boxes representing it (lines 5–7). Moreover, for each function, we also create a gray box inside the contract, and the size of the function is related to its lines of code (lines 8–10). Finally, we define a standard layout for the visualization (line 11) and "return" the visualization object for show (line 12). The resulting visualization shows each contract on a big box, with smaller boxes inside representing attributes (in black) and functions (Figure 13.2).

Evaluation

For comparison, we verified if our parser could recognize the same Solidity contracts as the official parser. It is reasonable to assume that the official parser is the correct implementation. Therefore, any contract parsed by the official

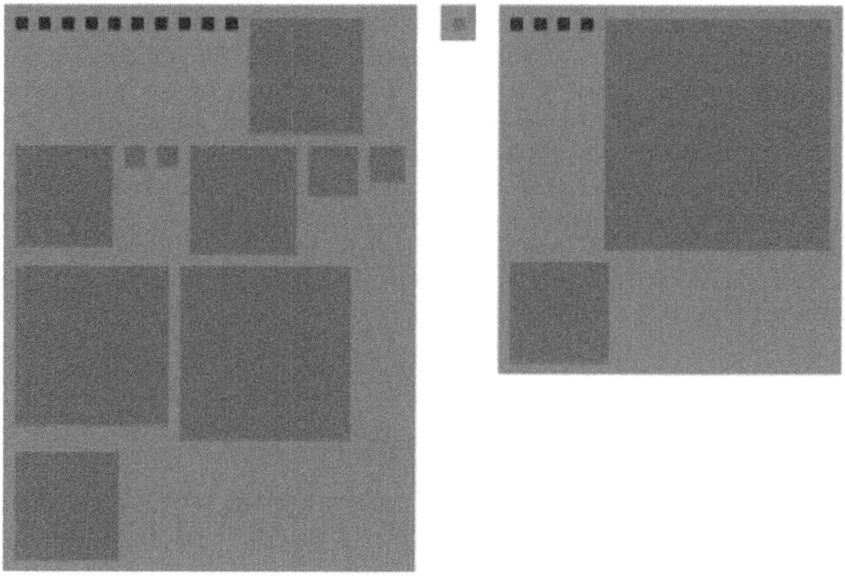

Figure 13.2 Contract functions using SmaCC-Solidity

should also be supported by our implementation. We used Etherscan to access Solidity contracts that were publicly available with their source code. All such contracts were correctly recognized by the official parser. Therefore, our evaluation was to verify if our implementation could parse them as well.

At the time of the experiment (August 2017), Etherscan had approximately 2,700 verified contracts in its database (in August 2018, the number of contracts was more than 40,000). From those 2,700, we selected only unique contracts from Solidity version 0.4.x, for a total of 1,175 contracts. Our implementation successfully parsed all 1,175 contracts. Consequently, we can claim our parser recognizes the same language artifacts as the official one.

Related work

We selected related work from two main topics: parsing conflicts and parser generators.

Isradisaikul and Myers [IM15] describe the difficulty in solving grammar conflicts with LALR parser generators. They propose an algorithm that generates better counterexamples for LALR parsers. A counterexample shows a parsing scenario that causes an ambiguity conflict in the LR method. Such scenarios help developers diagnose the conflict's source and identify problems in the grammar specification. The authors implemented their algorithm in

Java as an extension to the CUP parser generator, and they also evaluated their approach in 20 grammars against a state-of-the-art ambiguity detector. Their algorithm usually finds more counterexamples in less time than the compared techniques.

Passos et al. [PBB07] proposes a methodology to resolve conflicts in the LALR parsing method. The authors describe the challenges for handling conflicts without changing the defined language. They used YACC to generate a parser for the Notus language to illustrate the difficulty of resolving conflicts for LALR(1). The authors created a tool, called SAIDE, based on their methodology, which is an improvement over the regular methods available to handle conflicts in LALR parsers.

We are going to give a brief analysis of some well-known parser generation tools. SmaCC [BLGD17] is the parser generation tool we chose for this research. SmaCC can generate either LR(1) or LALR(1) bottom-up parsers. YACC [Mer93] is also a bottom-up LALR(1) parser generator. The original YACC was developed in C for Unix systems, but now we have implementations of it in several other languages. ANTLR [Mil05] differs from the previous tools because it is a top-down parser generator. ANTLR creates predictive LL(k) parsers, which are less sensitive to grammar irregularities than LR(1) and LL(1) parsers. There are implementations of ANTLR for languages such as Java, C++, C#, JavaScript, Python, and others. Unfortunately, as far as we know, there is no implementation of ANTLR for Pharo. Finally, PetitParser [BCDL13] is a scannerless parser generator that relies on parsing expression grammars. PetitParser is integrated with Moose, which facilitates its use on Pharo. The main problem with PetitParser is it does not read a grammar specification, and we must write the grammatic expressions using the PetitParser language.

Deployed smart contract analysis: inspection

Opaqueness is the major issue to analyze contract data [BRDD18b]. Smart contracts are opaque in the sense that, once they are deployed in the blockchain, it is very difficult to verify their internal state at run-time (i.e., the state stored in the contract defined by its internal attributes). By contrast, nowadays any programming language offers simpler ways to inspect object data. Developers use such inspection to access run-time data during development or maintenance activities. Similarly, developers could benefit from smart contract run-time inspection to verify the currently stored data. Moreover, from a business perspective, companies could use contract inspection to help clients verify and understand the information that is actually stored in the contract.

The difficulty of inspecting contract data is not a widely known problem [BRDD18b]. Currently, we have few tools to inspect contract information. Alternatively, developers resort to other practices to acquire a contract's internal state, such as creating getter functions to access data. For this reason, it is important to be able to develop tools that can be used for inspecting internal attributes. Moreover, the general concern is that a developer should be able to see the values stored in his own contracts.

Therefore, in this context, inspecting contract attributes is not only important but necessary for developers working with smart contracts.

Challenges

There are many challenges to pierce through the opaqueness problem and reveal contract information.

- **Binary and incomplete specification.** From the technical aspects, we only have the Ethereum API to access a binary representation of the contract. The first challenge we faced is an *incomplete* specification of the contract encoding performed by the Solidity compiler [Eth18c].
- **Inconsistent specification of hash computation.** Another challenge related to the specification is the hash computation for dynamic types. Static types use text as input for the hash calculation. However, dynamic types follow a different standard that it is not clearly specified in the documentation. For dynamic types, it is necessary to use binary data packed specifically for each type. For example, to access an array, it is necessary to pack the index number and the array position (offset) into a binary representation to obtain the correct hash. Other dynamic types would require a different input to get its hash.
- **Packed and ordered data.** We also highlight the challenges of decoding types, as the compiler packs as much data as possible into contiguous memory. Therefore, we need to know the specific types in the correct order to acquire the contract data, and that is not an easy task when we have an incomplete specification.

We acknowledge as a problem the challenges and difficulties of analyzing our own contracts deployed in the Ethereum blockchain database. To solve this problem, we propose an inspector that allows the user to perceive a clean representation of the instance's data attributes. Such an inspector is built using several components of the platform: FogComm, FogLive.

Approach: SmartInspect

SmartInspect [BRDD18a] is an internal state inspector for Solidity contracts based on a pluggable mirror-based reflection system. The goal of this tool is to allow the inspection of known contract instances based on their source code. The binary structure of the deployed contract is decompiled using a memory layout reification built from its source code. Therefore, only people with access to the source code and its deployed binary representation will be able to inspect its internal attributes. Moreover, a SmartInspect approach can introspect the current state of a smart contract instance without the need to redeploy it or develop additional code for decoding. SmartInspect is implemented in Pharo and it is publicly available in GitHub as part of the SmartAnvil tool suite (github.com/RMODINRIA- Blockchain/SmartShackle).

The general idea of the Smart Inspector is to decompile the storage layout encoded by the Ethereum API. By using the contract source code as reference, it is possible to know where the attribute values are stored in the encoded binary structure (Figure 13.3). It was a challenge to decompile the memory layout because the Solidity documentation [Eth18c] is incomplete regarding how some types are encoded. Therefore, we had to reverse engineer some of the encoding performed by the compiler ourselves.

After we decoded the memory layout, we still needed to apply our solution to any contract for a general reusable solution. We employ a mirror-based architecture [BU04] that mimics the structure of any contract for us to access the memory layout that we can decode. A mirror works like an independent meta-programming layer that splits the concern of reflection capabilities into a mirror object. First, we require the contract source code as input to start building the mirror. Then we parse the source code (using our Solidity parser described earlier) to create an AST (abstract syntax tree). By interpreting the

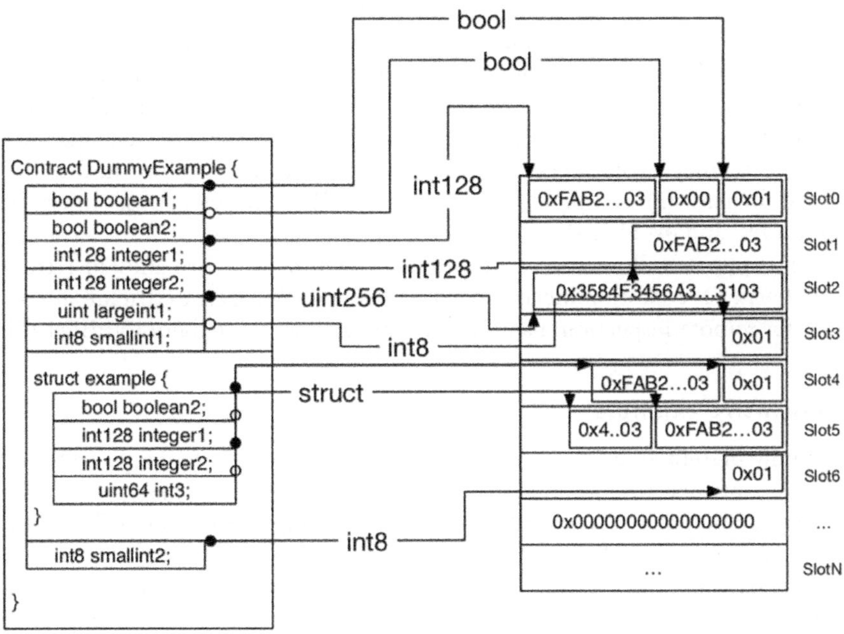

Figure 13.3 Memory layout representation

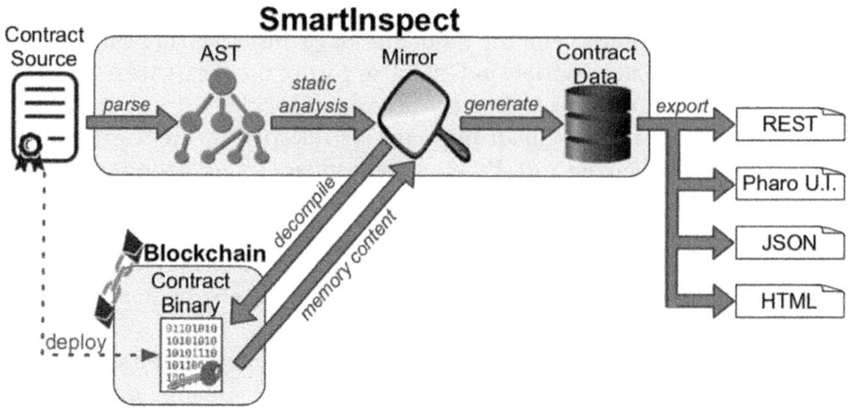

Figure 13.4 SmartInspect building process

AST, we are able to discover every type declared in the contract in the correct order. We require this information to decode the memory layout and access the contract data. Aiming at a general solution, we model configurable mirror objects that allow us to interact with deployed contract instances of the same configuration (usually meaning the same contract deployed in the blockchain).

Figure 13.4 shows a diagram of the whole process to inspect a contract; the pluggable reflective architecture generates a mirror for a given contract's source code by using its AST. Then we use this mirror to extract information from a remote contract instance deployed in the blockchain (which is encoded as a binary memory layout). The contract data we gathered is exposed in four different formats: (1) data proxy object (REST), (2) Pharo widget user interface, (3) JSON, and (4) HTML.

This approach allows us to access remote structureless information in a structured way. Our solution meets most of the desirable properties that are important for remote inspection, namely interactiveness and distribution [PBD+15].

Illustrative example

We now present an example of a smart contract written in Solidity and SmartInspect introspecting its contents. Let's suppose a scenario where a supervisor manages a poll that users are allowed to vote one single time. The poll is coded into a smart contract because it is used for management decisions that rely on the veracity and immutability of the information. Only the contract's supervisor is allowed to modify the list of voters. The following listing (Listing 13.2) highlights the most important code parts for this contract:

Listing 13.2 Solidity poll contract example

```
1 pragma solidity ^0.4.24;
2 /** @title Poll Contract Example
3   * @author RMoD-Blockchain Team
4   */
5 contract RmodPoll {
6   /* Type Definition */
7    enum Choice {POSITIVE, NEGATIVE, NEUTRAL}
8    struct PollEntry {address user; Choice choice; bool
       hasVoted;}
9
10  /* Attributes/Internal State */
11   PollEntry[] pollTable;
12   address private supervisor;
13
14   /* Constructor */
15   constructor() public {supervisor = msg.sender;}
16
17   /* Functions */
18   // Add the account as a voter in this poll
19   function addVoter(address account) public returns
       (uint) {. . .}
20   // Verifies if the account is already registered in
       this poll
21   function isRegistered(address account) public view
       returns(bool) {. . .}
22   // Returns the Voter's index in the pollTable
23   function voterIndex(address voterAccount) private view
       returns(int) {. . .}
24   // Function called by the voter to assert his vote
25   function vote(Choice myChoice) public {. . .}
26   // Verifies if everyone registered for this poll have
       voted
27   function everyoneHaveVoted() public view returns (bool)
       {. . .}
28   // Return the amount of votes for Positive, Negative,
       and Neutral
29   function countVotes() public view returns
       (uint,uint,uint) {. . .}
30 }
```

This contract defines two custom types: Choice (line 5) and PollEntry (line 6). A Choice models the answers to the poll (whether the vote was positive, negative, or neutral). A PollEntry is a record representing a vote, i.e., the voting user, the selected option, and if he/she has voted or not. Note that to refer to the voter we need an account address (using the primitive type address) that refers to an

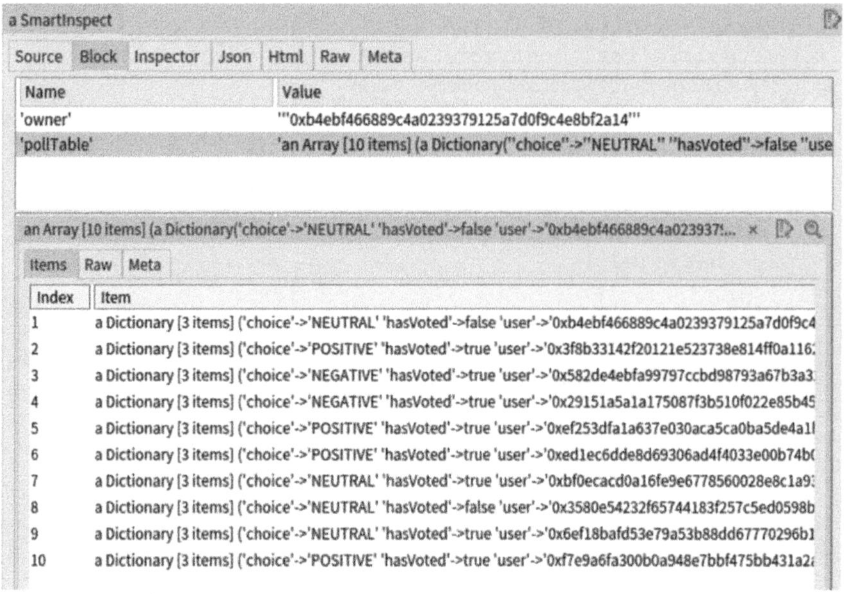

Figure 13.5 SmartInspect Pharo user interface screenshot

Ethereum account. The contract internally stores a poll table (an array of PollEntry, line 9) and an address to the poll's supervisor account (line 10). The poll table is an empty array where the supervisor will eventually store the poll information (i.e., the array will have an entry for each user that is allowed to vote). The supervisor's address is used for security checks, i.e., to ensure that only the supervisor can call some specific functions (e.g., addVoter function). It is not necessary to define and explain the remaining functions for this illustrative example.

Let's suppose that the poll needs to be closed soon and not everyone has voted. Therefore, the poll's supervisor will need to send reminders to the users who haven't voted yet. However, the contract's attributes were not defined as public. Moreover, we did not create any function to check for that information before deploying the contract. Since we cannot update the source code of a deployed contract instance, inspecting its internal state is the only way to know the accounts that have not voted. Because the supervisor has access to both the contract's source code and its deployed instance, he/she can execute SmartInspect to see the contract's data (Figure 13.5). Finally, the supervisor can see which users did not vote for this current poll instance.

Evaluation

We investigate whether SmartInspect implements the necessary and desirable features when compared to other inspectors. We identified six characteristics that are important for a blockchain remote inspector: privacy, extendibility, pluggability, consistency, reusability, and instrumentation. We detail the characteristics as follows:

- **Privacy:** Inspection should not breach or compromise data privacy by exposing data to unauthorized users. When considering smart contracts, a lack of privacy is dangerous, as it could be exploited by malicious users to acquire illicit advantages and resources.
- **Extendibility:** The inspector can be extended for other technologies. Ideally, a debugger or inspector should rely on a middleware that is extensible. For smart contracts, the inspector should be extensible over different smart contract languages and blockchain technologies.
- **Pluggability:** The inspector can be used on existing objects without the need to re-instantiate the objects or the system. For contracts, this means we can inspect existing deployed contracts without any dependency on the contract side or the need to redeploy the contract. An unpluggable approach has the disadvantage of requiring the redeployment of a contract, which has nontrivial transactional costs.
- **Consistency:** The representation used by the inspector must reveal the information in a consistent manner, i.e., the inspection must reflect the current state of the deployed contract.
- **Reusability:** The inspector can be reused for different contracts. Lack of reusability would require a developer to spend time redefining the inspection for each individual contract.
- **Instrumentation:** The inspector can alter the semantics of a process to assist in debugging. Basically, this is the mechanism to halt the process and inspect it at that point (e.g., breakpoints and watchpoints). This characteristic is not possible in blockchain platforms, as we cannot modify the deployed contract code to halt a function in the middle of its execution in the blockchain.

We analyzed SmartInspect and two other inspectors (Remix and Etherscan) according to the aforementioned characteristics for inspectors. We also compared two practices for accessing contract data: ad-hoc decoder and getter methods (Table 13.1).

Table 13.1 Related techniques comparison

Characteristic	*SmartInspect*	*Remix*	*Etherscan*	*Decoder*	*Getter*
Privacy	Yes	Yes	No	Yes	No
Extendibility	Yes	No	No	No	No
Pluggability	Yes	Yes	Yes	Yes	No
Consistency	Yes	Yes	Yes	Yes	Yes
Reusability	Yes	Yes	Yes	No	No
Instrumentation	No	No	No	No	No

As we can see from Table 13.1, SmartInspect's only characteristic flaw is related to *instrumentation* for remote debugging. However, this is a limitation imposed by the Ethereum blockchain technology rather than a design flaw in our approach.

Remix [Eth18b] is a suite of tools designed by the Ethereum Foundation for Solidity developers. Remix IDE is probably the most used tool in its suite. In the Remix tool suite, there is a full transaction debugger with inspection capabilities. Remix inspector only falls short in extendibility and instrumentation. It was designed specifically for Solidity and Ethereum, and as such, it is not extensible to other platforms. As we previously explained, instrumentation is not possible due to the characteristics of the Ethereum platform.

Etherscan is an analytics platform for Ethereum. It provides live information from Ethereum on blocks, transactions, contracts, etc. If a developer publishes his/her contract source code on Etherscan, then it will be possible to inspect the contract's data. However, by doing so, the developer will expose his contract source code and internal data to anyone, in a very easy way to access it. That is the reason why Etherscan inspection lacks privacy (unlike SmartInspect and Remix, which can expose the data to the developer only). Etherscan provides an API to access its services, but it is not extensible. Just like SmartInspect and Remix, Etherscan's inspector cannot support instrumentation.

An ad-hoc decoder uses the Ethereum API on the memory slots to manually fetch the data. This is a complex task, since it demands a deep understanding of the memory layout of each contract a developer plans to inspect. It also requires a developer to know the type of each attribute and code the ad-hoc decoder accordingly. Its advantages are that it allows access to data without loss of privacy and without the need to redeploy the contract. In fact, SmartInspect uses this concept of decoding memory layouts as a part of its inspection process.

Getter methods are a simple solution since they are cheap to implement and easy to test. The developer does not need to know the memory layout of a contract to create getter methods. However, if the developer forgets to make a getter for a given attribute, he/she will need to redeploy the contract and, most often, lose the data from the previous instance. Solidity does not support the return of many complex types (e.g., structs, mappings) on its functions. Therefore, a developer might need to adapt his/her data or function to provide access to a complex type. Moreover, the easy access to the data may cause a loss of privacy, since getter methods are a public part of the contract binary encoding.

Related work

Chis et al. [CNSG15] performed an exploratory study to better understand what developers expect from object inspectors, and based on that feedback, they propose a novel inspector model. The authors interviewed 16 developers for a qualitative study, and a quantitative study conducting an online survey where 62 people responded. Both studies were used to identify four requirements needed in an inspector. Then they propose the Moldable Inspector, which indicates a new model to address multiple types of inspection needs. We followed the lessons taken by the Moldable Inspector when creating SmartInspect. We deem noteworthy the multiple views aspect, as SmartInspect can present its inspected data in four different views (REST, Pharo U.I., JSON, and HTML).

Papoulias [PBD+15] gives a deep analysis of remote debugging. As discussed by the author, remote debugging is especially important for devices that cannot support local development tools. The author identifies four important characteristics for remote debugging: interactiveness, instrumentation, distribution, and security. Based on the identified properties, Papoulias proposed a remote debugging model called Mercury. Mercury employs a mirror-based approach and an adaptable middleware. We used Papoulias research as an inspiration to create SmartInspect, especially relying on a mirror for remote inspection.

Salvaneschi and Mezini [SM16] propose a methodology, called RP Debugging, to debug reactive programs more effectively. The authors discuss the idea that reactive programming is more customizable and easier to understand than its alternative, the observer design pattern. The authors also present the main problems and challenges to debug reactive programs and the main design decisions when creating their methodology. Although our inspector is from a different application domain, the RP Debugging design served as an inspiration to plan our own inspecting approach.

Srinivasan and Reps [SR14] developed a reverse engineering tool to recover class hierarchical information from a binary program file. Their tool also extracts composition relationships. They use dynamic analysis to obtain object traces, and then they identify the inheritance and composition information among classes on those traces. The authors' experiments show that their recovered information is accurate according to their metrics. The author's tool contrasts with SmartInspect, as we use static analysis and they use dynamic analysis.

Chain navigation and query language

Ethereum and other blockchains store a massive amount of heterogeneous data. In early 2017, Ethereum was estimated to have approximately 300GB of data [BLPB17]. Retrieving information from this massive amount of data is not an easy task. Moreover, the Ethereum platform only allows direct access to its *first-class* data elements, which includes blocks, transactions, accounts, and contracts [Eth14]. Therefore, if we search for a particular piece of information inside a data element, we would need a unique identifier (i.e., either the number or its hash) to access the block containing such information. Another alternative would be to directly access one block and sequentially access its parents to search for a data. Moreover, the information returned by the Ethereum platform when we access its blocks is encoded into a JSON-like structure that we need to interpret to acquire a specific item. Therefore, the Ethereum platform does not provide a semantic way to search for information nor an easy form to present such information.

In a classical database, when we need to search for a particular piece of information, we usually write a query to fetch, present, filter, and format such information. Database query languages like SQL provide a rich syntax to describe the data we want to acquire from the database. Since blockchain can be considered a database, it would be better if we could use a similar way to fetch information inside the blocks. In this context, users could benefit from a query language providing an easier way to fetch, format, and present the information extract from the blockchain platform.

Challenges

In this section, we describe in more detail the challenges when trying to acquire data from a blockchain. Although our research is focused on Ethereum, such problems are also present on other blockchain platforms as well.

- **Massive data.** Blockchain databases already possess a massive amount of data. In December 2017, Ethereum processed, on average, 876,000 transactions per day [BRDD18c]. Since the data in the blockchain cannot be deleted, the number of recorded transactions will only grow with time. Consequently, older information could get overwhelmed by new transactions and become "lost in time".
- **Heterogeneous data.** Blockchain not only stores a great amount of data but also manages a mixture of *first-class* elements such as transactions, blocks, accounts, and smart contracts. All of the *first-class* elements are different but interrelated by hashes. Even though Ethereum allows access to any of its *first-class* elements, the heterogeneity of the elements (each one with different meaning and high-level representation) complicates the acquisition of information.
- **Data opaqueness.** For flexibility reasons, Ethereum stores its information using a generic representation. Therefore, the stored data is opaque, since there is no metadata describing the information nor a simple way to know what was recorded. This opaqueness is useful and even necessary from the Ethereum standpoint because it allows the storage of arbitrary structures and behaviors. On the other hand, the opaqueness overcomplicates searching for information, since a user needs to access generic representations without any knowledge of its content.
- **Direct access.** In general, blockchain only allows direct access to its elements by using a unique identifier. This identifier is a hash number that is generated for every *first-class* element stored in the blockchain [Bit18]. The Ethereum platform, in particular, can also use a unique number (related to the order of the element) to access blocks and transactions [Eth18a]. The direct access complicates the user task in finding information because he will either need to: (1) store the identifiers for later usage or (2) perform a sequential access to gather the data.

To address these challenges, we proposed a query language that enables its users to acquire information more easily. We highlight the following benefits of using a query language to fetch information from blockchain: (1) describe structural and semantic filters to query for information; (2) reformat and transform the acquired data; (3) order the query results; and (4) limit the number of results returned.

Approach: Ukulele

In this section, we present the Ukulele version 0.9, a query language designed to acquire information from the blockchain. Ukulele is the improvement of our previous work, called Ethereum Query Language (EQL) [BRDD18c]. Ukulele is publicly available at GitHub as part of the SmartAnvil suite (https://github.com/smartanvil/UQLL). Ukulele syntax is based on the SQL language. The idea is to allow users to write queries as close to SQL as possible to facilitate the adoption of Ukulele, since SQL is a very popular language [SKS11, EN10].

Listing 13.3 shows the main elements of the Ukulele syntax. The syntax is described using EBNF (Extended Backus-Naur Form); we did not format the terminals *identifier* and *number* in double quotes to highlight that they are not literals. We omitted the Expression rule to not clutter the specification, but it follows a similar structure of SQL expressions.

Listing 13.3 Ukulele grammar in EBNF format

```
<SelectStatement> ::= <SelectClause> <FromClause>
    [<WhereClause>] [<OrderByClause>] [<LimitClause>]
<SelectClause> ::= "select" <Expression> {"," <Expression>}
<FromClause> ::= "from" <SourceBind> {"," <SourceBind>}
<WhereClause> ::= "where" <Expression>
<OrderByClause> ::= "order" "by" <Expression> ["asc" | "desc"]
<LimitClause> ::= "limit" number
<SourceBind> ::= identifier "as" identifier
<Expression> ::= . . .
```

As we can see from Listing 13.3, the syntax for Ukulele queries is very similar to the "Select" statement from the SQL language. The Ukulele "Select" statement consists of the following clauses: *select*, *from*, *where*, *order by*, and *limit*. Only the *select* and *from* clauses are required; the others are optional clauses. We also like to highlight that Ukulele, similar to SQL, is also case insensitive. Unlike SQL, the Ukulele "Select" statement does not have a *group by* clause. Although we have plans to support a *group by* clause in the future, the current version does not allow the usage of such a clause.

In the *from* clause of Ukulele, we need to use a collection. In Ukulele, a collection is a semantic representation of queried data. The Ukulele language has four predefined collections: *ethereum.blocks*, *ethereum.transactions*, *ethereum.*

accounts, and *ethereum.contracts*. Each one of those collections rep resents all first-class elements from a particular type (blocks, transactions, accounts, or contracts). We can use "eth" as an alias for "ethereum". It is possible to create custom collections from a subset of another one by creating "views" similar to SQL (Listing 13.4). Just like SQL, in which views can be used in place of a table in the *from* clause, so does Ukulele use views and collections.

Listing 13.4 Ukulele view grammar in EBNF format

```
<View> ::= "create" ("view" | "collection") identifier "as"
"("<SelectStatement> ")"
```

Ukulele already has a predefined structure of objects to act as a container for collection items. For example, when we retrieve information from a collection of blocks, the result will be presented as block objects. Therefore, each object type has attributes related to its storage structure (i.e., a block object will have different attributes than a transaction object). The attributes available for each object type are the following:

- **Block:** number, hash, parentHash, parent, nonce, timestamp, size, miner, difficulty, totalDifficulty, gasLimit, gasUsed, extraData, transactionsRoot, transactionsHashes, transactions, amountOfTransactions, uncleHashes, uncles.
- **Transaction:** hash, nonce, blockHash, blockNumber, block, transactionIndex, fromAddress, from, toAddress, to, value, gasPrice, gas, input, timestamp.
- **Account:** address, name, balance.
- **Contract:** descriptions, instances.
- **Contract.Instance:** address, name, balance, binaryHash, bytecode.

For a more detailed description of each attribute, see our first publication on EQL [BRDD18c]. One major improvement Ukulele has over EQL is handling contracts. For example, we can use contracts' internal attributes or functions in Ukulele queries. Moreover, we can handle the general structure of a contract (by using the contract object) or the deployed instances (the instances attribute of a contract object).

Internally, our implementation of Ukulele relies on indexes to increase its performance when querying data. Since each access to the blockchain to fetch data is a remote call, any form of optimization can improve the time required to acquire and present data. An index is a summarization of data stored into a structure that improves the performance of retrieval operations. The basic idea is to allow a more efficient search into the database. In our particular case, we index blockchain data (e.g., blocks, transactions) with its related hash to speed up fetching data.

For Ukulele, we implemented a binary search tree (BST) to serve as the index structure. The BST employs a two-dimensional array in which the first dimension of each entry is used for storing the property value and the second dimension is used for storing a set of hashes to the elements that correspond to this specific value. We chose this implementation because of its simplicity for selecting an interval of indexes in any comparison operation, such as “greater than”, “lesser than”. We acknowledge that BST has a high storage requirement. However, we wanted a simple and fast solution to our first implementation of Ukulele. Moreover, Ukulele builds these internal indexes automatically, without the need for user interaction. On the other hand, Ukulele also supports users creating their own custom indexes to speed up queries. The syntax to create custom indexes is similar to SQL (Listing 13.5).

Listing 13.5 Ukulele custom index grammar in EBNF format

```
<Index> ::= "create" ["unique"] "index" identifier "on"
    identifier "("identifier ")"
```

Illustrative example

For this example, we will show some of the new features of Ukulele (i.e., contract querying). Let’s suppose a smart contract that handles the selling of a product. The following listing (Listing 13.6) shows the essential code parts for the product contract.

Listing 13.6 Solidity product contract example

```
pragma solidity ^0.4.24;
/** @title Product Contract Example
* @author RMoD-Blockchain Team
*/
contract RmodProduct {
/* Type Definition */
enum State {ON_SALE, WAITING_SEND, RECEIVED, FINISH}

/* Attributes */
State private state = State.ON_SALE;
address private owner;
address private buyer;
uint private price;
string private itemName;

/* Constructor */
constructor(string _name, uint _price) public {
owner = msg.sender; itemName = _name; price = _price;
}
```

```

/* Functions */
// Returns the this product information (name,price)
function getInfo() public view returns(string,uint)
  {. . .}
// Buys this product
function buy() payable public {. . .}
// Inform the seller/owner the product was properly
  received
function received() public {. . .}
// Completes the sale, the owner terminate the con
  tract and get the money
function terminate() public {. . .}
}
```

As we can see, the contract (Listing 13.6) can be used to sell any product. In our example, the user only wants to query only about these product contracts. Therefore, he/she creates a view for this task (Listing 13.7). The "binaryHash" attribute of an instance is an MD5 hash of the contract's binary structured. Thus, by using this attribute someone can get all contracts with the same internal structure. In this case, the view query (Listing 13.7) is getting only RmodProduct contracts (Listing 13.6).

Listing 13.7 Ukulele create view example

```
CREATE VIEW RmodProductContracts (
SELECT instance
FROM eth.contract.instances AS instance
WHERE instance.binaryHash =
  '4d3c0777436de51258c7ba6c235a2e52'
) ;
```

Now, the user can employ the view to more easily query only product contracts. In this example (Listing 13.8), the user wants cheap products that are still up for sale.

Listing 13.8 Ukulele contract query example

```
SELECT instance.itemName, instance.price, instance.state
FROM RmodProductContracts AS instance
WHERE instance.price < 40 AND instance.state = 'ON_SALE';
```

Figure 13.6 shows the results from this query (Listing 13.8).

Ukulele can also execute contract functions. Besides using functions for querying values, this feature can be used to execute a function that changes the contract state in a batch. For example, let's suppose a user wants to collect the

Figure 13.6 Ukulele contract query example results

sales on his products. Without Ukulele, the user would have to execute the function "terminate" on each contract manually and one at a time. Using Ukulele, the same user can just write a simple query (Listing 13.9).

Listing 13.9 Ukulele block query example

```
SELECT instance.itemName, instance.terminate()
FROM RmodProductContracts AS instance
WHERE instance.owner = '0xca35b7d915458ef540ade6068dfe2f44e8fa733c'
AND instance.state = 'RECEIVED';
```

Evaluation

We compared Ukulele against Presto and Web3 on the supported features designed for acquiring data in the blockchain. The features we analyzed were the following:

- **Query language:** The implementation offers a query language to specify the data you want to fetch. Lack of a query language can make it more difficult to acquire complex information.
- **Group functions:** The implementation supports the use of aggregate (group by) functions. Lack of group functions limits transformation on the data and what it is possible to acquire.

- **Join data:** Checks whether it allows different data sources to be joined. Ideally, it should allow merging data from different platforms as well (e.g., blockchain and NoSQL).
- **Views:** Indicate if the implementation supports the definition of views or some similar feature. Views allow the user to save his queried data for later usage.
- **Tool support:** See if there is a tool support to specify, check, and show the acquired data as well as the commands used to fetch such data. Lack of tool support can hinder the adoption of the implementation.
- **Data source:** Checks if the implementation can fetch any type of first-class elements stored in the blockchain.

Web3 is the official Ethereum API coded in Javascript that implements an interface to the remote procedure call (RPC) protocol [Eth18a]. Web3 is not a query language; all data is gathered by using its API interface. Even though Web3 can access any data stored in Ethereum, it can only fetch by direct and sequential access. Therefore, the user must search the information manually among the collected data. Although not a very polished solution to gather data, Web3 and its underlying protocol is the basis to access Ethereum data. Both Ukulele and Presto use Web3 (or another related API) to access the blockchain platform and perform its search (Table 13.2).

Presto is a querying engine to run SQL on other platforms, including Ethereum blockchain. Moreover, Presto supports full SQL syntax for querying, such as joins, group functions, etc. However, it does not support another auxiliary syntax, such as views. There is no tool support to edit queries or view the results. Another flaw in Presto is that it can only acquire Ethereum data related to Blocks and Transactions. Therefore, Presto cannot show information on contracts or accounts.

Ukulele is a query language implemented to automate searching for information in Ethereum. As we previously mentioned, Ukulele is still under development, and the current version does not support group functions. Moreover, the current version of Ukulele is able to join multiple data sources from Ethereum, but it is not possible to merge such data with different platforms (such as NoSQL). There is no tool support for Ukulele, although one is currently under development. The

Table 13.2 Related techniques comparison

Feature	*Ukulele*	*Presto*	*Web3*
Query language	Yes	Yes	No
Group functions	No	Yes	No
Join data	Partial	Yes	No
Views	Yes	No	No
Tool support	No	No	No
Data source	All	Partial	All

major advantage Ukulele has over Presto is that Ukulele can fetch any data from Ethereum first-class elements (blocks, transactions, contracts, and accounts).

Related work

In this section, we discuss some related work on blockchain research focused on search and navigation. Tools and implementations (e.g., Presto) that were not originated by research are not presented here.

Morishima and Matsutani [MM18] propose a new way to search for blockchain information by using GPUs. They argue that blockchain full nodes could turn into a bottleneck for the platform if the search performance is not improved. The authors evaluate the performance of their approach against the existing practice and other methods and conclude that their proposal throughput is 3.4 times higher than the second highest approach. Although the work of Morishima and Matsutani is about searching blockchain data, it has a different purpose than Ukulele. Ukulele was designed to help users search for complex data. On the other hand, Morishima and Matsutani designed their approach to improve the performance of searching for data in blockchain nodes. The similarity is that both research deals with the internal structure of the blockchain and searching for data in that platform.

Ruta et al. [RSI+17] discuss a new semantic-enhanced layer for blockchain platforms focusing on the supply chain application domain. They propose a framework for online object discovery to implement their layer on a Hyperledger blockchain. Their approach adopts a semantic matching between queries and objects, which allows users to find supply chain information more easily. Unlike Ukulele, there is no query language. However, it does use semantic information to fetch blockchain information. Ukulele provides a rich syntax for querying information, but it does not use semantic-enhanced objects and information to improve the search.

Discussion and related work

In this section, we discuss our future research and tools, and then we present related work on blockchain analysis platforms and tool suites.

Future research and tool development

As a platform, SmartAnvil should support a large range of analysis. We are focusing on the foundations of the tools. We see the following topics as the next components around SmartAnvil.

Metrics. It is not possible to control what you do not measure, and this statement is the basic wisdom on why we need to use metrics [Hev97]. Metrics are useful to assess the internal quality of a software as well as the productivity of the development team. Since the '90s, there has been a plethora of proposed software metrics [LH93, CK94, LK94, HM95, BMB96, Hev97, TNM08]. The reason for so many different metrics is because specific domains or characteristics require measurements tailored for their particular needs. Usually, applying a metric designed for one domain to another leads to a mismatch or incompatibility. For instance, the domain mismatch led to the "adaptation" of procedural programming metrics for the object-oriented paradigm.

Due to the extremely fast growing pace of smart contract usage, in this new software paradigm, measuring code quality is becoming as essential as it is in out-of-chain software development. However, traditional software metrics do not capture the specific aspects of smart contracts. Therefore, we need metrics designed for smart contracts.

Gas estimation. In the Ethereum platform, any transaction that changes the internal state of a contract is charged a special resource called Gas [Eth18c]. The name was inspired by the view that this resource is the fuel for running contracts [Eth16]. Therefore, Gas units correspond to the execution of computation instructions. The idea is to avoid infinite loops (and the halting problem), encourage efficient code, and make users pay for the computation resource they used.

Even though the unused gas is refunded back to the user, optimizing this resource is the key to having a transaction approved quickly. Since the miner is awarded the used gas cost, he/she will prefer to mine transactions that optimize his/her gains. In this context, a better estimation of the gas by the user may encourage miners to process such a user's transaction.

Estimating how many gas units a contract function is going to require is not a simple task. The Remix IDE gives an estimate if the function does not contain loops or external calls. Consequently, Remix is not reliable to estimate gas on any function. Therefore, we require better estimation tools to assess the amount of gas consumption.

Security recommendations. The number of smart contracts is growing at a fast rate, and developers are not yet accustomed to code in this new environment. Bad programming practices in a smart contract can turn into terrible security flaws [DMO+18]. For example, the infamous "DAO attack" was caused by insecure coding practices on the contract that allowed an attacker to drain approximately 50 million dollars' worth of cryptocurrency [LCO+16, TVI+18]. As an analogy, we can think of web applications that had SQL-injections flaws, which would be simple to avoid if developers designed and adopted a more secure coding practice.

Most security flaws in smart contracts can be traced to poor coding that could be avoided if the developer had more expertise with the environment and the programming language. A simple and elegant way to give such expertise to developers is to create a recommendation system that warns developers of problematic code and suggests a better way to accomplish the same program. In this context, we claim it is important to give security recommendations for contract developers.

Dashboard. To make all the information gathered by future tools useful in practice, care has to be taken to create presentations that target developers and even other stakeholders like management and customers. We plan to explore how Dashboards can support both viewing data and defining conditions that should automatically notify developers in case of problems [Few06].

Related work

In this section, we discuss related work on blockchain analysis platforms and tools.

Porru et al. [PPMT17] acknowledge the need to develop specialized tools and techniques for blockchain oriented software (BOS). The authors define the term BOS as a software that interacts with blockchain. The authors describe issues and challenges faced when working with blockchain from a software engineering point of view. They also analyze 1,184 GitHub projects using blockchain, and they propose new ideas and practices to improve the state of the art on BOS. The authors present very interesting research possibilities that inspired several components on the SmartAnvil platform.

Bartoletti et al. [BLPB17] propose a framework for blockchain analytics coded as a Scala library. Their framework works on both Ethereum and the Bitcoin platform, and it employs a general-purpose abstraction layer to promote reuse. One great feature of the authors' framework is the ability to integrate data from other sources besides blockchain, such as a NoSQL database. The authors contrast their framework features against five other tools, but they do not conduct a performance comparison. This work is interesting because the authors combine blockchain data with a secondary database. Unlike SmartAnvil, their framework does not support querying or analysis of contracts, only blocks and transactions. Moreover, the query language is a specific syntax based on a Scala API, and it is not as popular as SQL-based queries. Finally, their framework focuses only on gathering data and does not support other tools such as inspection or static analysis.

Kalodner et al. [KGC+17] implement an open-source blockchain analysis platform called BlockSci. They designed their platform with a specific concern for performance by using an in-memory database and actual pointers instead of hash linkage. For instance, the authors claim it is 15 to 600 times faster than other tools. They support the following blockchains: Bitcoin, LiteCoin, Namecoin, and Zcash. The authors focus their analysis on financial transactions. Therefore, their analysis is not well polished for blocks, and it specifically does not support smart contracts. This contrasts with the SmartAnvil platform, which was designed to help smart contract developers as well as providing tools for other first-class elements (such as transactions and blocks).

Etherscan (*https://etherscan.io*) is also an analytics platform connected to the Ethereum platform and providing on-the-fly blockchain information on accounts, contracts, transactions, blocks, etc. Similar to SmartAnvil, Etherscan also has an inspector and other tools to interact with Ethereum. Etherscan does not have a query language, but it supports simple searches on blockchain elements. Although Etherscan is free to use, it is not open source. Therefore, it is not possible to extend any Etherscan features or components, unlike SmartAnvil, which is open source to encourage developers to contribute to improving our tools.

Remix [Eth18b] is an open-source suite of tools developed by the Ethereum Foundation. Although Remix is mostly recognized for its IDE component, it does provide many other tools such as inspection, transaction debugger, gas estimation, etc. Since it is developed by the Ethereum Foundation, Remix is always integrated with the latest Ethereum APIs. Remix is coded in JavaScript, and it is under the MIT open-source license. SmartAnvil shares some similar tools with Remix (e.g., inspector, parser). However, both suites have distinguished tools that are absent in the other. For instance, SmartAnvil has a query language, a smart graph, and integration with Moose. On the other hand, Remix has a transactional debugger and a full IDE.

There are tools designed to improve the security of smart contracts. Oyente [LCO+16] is a tool that flags potential security flaws on smart contracts. Oyente uses static analysis on the contract binary code to make security recommendations. SmartCheck [TVI+18] is another tool using static analysis that identifies unsecured patterns on contract source code and warns the user about better practices. Bhargavan et al. [BDLF+16] proposed an unnamed framework to convert smart contract to their own functional language, F*, which was design to better verify the correctness and security of smart contracts. Although SmartAnvil does not support security verification or recommendation of smart contracts, this is important for smart contract developers, and we plan to add a tool for such tasks in the future.

Conclusion

In this chapter, we presented a set of analysis tools showcasing our SmartAnvil platform to cover different aspects of smart contracts analysis. For each tool, we showed the importance of each and the main challenges when developing them.

First, we presented the basic tool to support static code representation of Solidity smart contracts, our parser, SmaCC-Solidity. Having full control over our parser and its representation allows us to avoid any problems with future changes in the Solidity language (which is not stable). The parser is used on other SmartAnvil tools such as SmartInspect and SmartMetrics. Developers can use this parser to increase the integration between Solidity and Pharo by implementing more tool support, or build their own static analysis tools on the resulting AST.

Second, we showed SmartInspect, our internal state inspector for Solidity smart contracts. As we explained, contracts are opaque, because once they are deployed, it is very difficult to see their run-time state, defined by their internal attributes. SmartInspect can pierce through the opaqueness and show to developers the live state of their own contracts while assuring a level of privacy that few other tools support. The inspector can see the contents of any contract instance of the given source code without needing to redeploy or develop any ad-hoc code to fetch the information. Contract inspection can help developers to better understand their contracts and even find bugs more easily.

Third, we presented Ukulele, a query language that allows users to retrieve information from the blockchain by writing SQL-like queries. This tool automates the task of sequentially searching into generic opaque structures and provides an easier way to specify the information we want to acquire in a higher abstraction level. Ukulele distinguishes itself by being able to search through all first-class elements such as blocks, transactions, accounts, and contracts. Other tools usually cannot search contract instances, leaving potential useful information behind. On the other hand, Ukulele is even able to call contract functions inside its queries.

For future work, we plan to extend the platform with more tools, such as: (1) improved metrics suite (our current SmartMetrics tools still needs improvement); (2) gas estimation of contract functions; (3) recommendation system to suggest secure programming practices; (4) a dashboard to facilitate the usage and interaction with blockchain and smart contracts.

Bibliography

[ABC+13] Vanessa Peña Araya, Alexandre Bergel, Damien Cassou, Stéphane Ducasse, and Jannik Laval. Agile Visualization With Roassal. In *Deep Into Pharo*, pages 209–239. Square Bracket Associates, September 2013.

[ABC17] Nicola Atzei, Massimo Bartoletti, and Tiziana Cimoli. A Survey of Attacks on Ethereum Smart Contracts. In *Proceedings of International Conference on Principles of Security and Trust*, volume 10204, pages 164–186. Springer, 2017.

[ALSU06] Alfred V. Aho, Monica S. Lam, Ravi Sethi, and Jeffrey D. Ullman. *Compilers: Principles, Techniques, and Tools*, 2nd edition. Addison-Wesley Longman Publishing Co., Inc., Boston, MA, 2006.

[BCDL13] Alexandre Bergel, Damien Cassou, Stéphane Ducasse, and Jannik Laval. Petitparser: Building Modular Parsers. In *Deep Into Pharo*, chapter 18, pages 377–411. Square Brackets Associates, 2013.

[BDLF+16] Karthikeyan Bhargavan, Antoine Delignat-Lavaud, Cédric Fournet, Anitha Gollamudi, Georges Gonthier, Nadim Kobeissi, Natalia Kulatova, Aseem Rastogi, Thomas Sibut- Pinote, Nikhil Swamy, and Santiago Zanella-BéguelIn. Formal Verification of Smart Contracts: Short Paper. In *2016 ACM Workshop on Programming Languages and Analysis for Security*, PLAS '16, pages 91–96. ACM Press, New York, NY, 2016.

[Ber16] Alexandre Bergel. *Agile Visualization*. LULU Press, 2016.

[Bit18] BitCoin.org. Bitcoin Developer Reference. *Bitcoin Core APIs*, 2018. Bitcoin Project 2009–2018.

[BLGD17] John Brant, Jason Lecerf, Thierry Goubier, and Stéphane Ducasse. *Smacc, a Smalltalk Compiler-Compiler*, 2017. www.refactory.com/Software/SmaCC/.

[BLPB17] Massimo Bartoletti, Stefano Lande, Livio Pompianu, and Andrea Bracciali. A General Framework for Blockchain Analytics. In *1st Workshop on Scalable and Resilient Infrastructures for Distributed Ledgers*, SERIAL '17, pages 7:1–7:6. ACM Press, New York, NY, 2017.

[BMB96] Lionel C. Briand, Sandro Morasca, and Victor Basili. Property-based Software Engineering Measurement. *Transactions on Software Engineering*, 22(1): 68–86, 1996.

[BRDD18a] Santiago Bragagnolo, Henrique Rocha, Marcus Denker, and Stéphane Ducasse. Ethereum Query Language. In *1st International Workshop on Emerging Trends in Software Engineering for Blockchain (WETSEB)*, pages 1–8, May 2018.

[BRDD18b] Santiago Bragagnolo, Henrique Rocha, Marcus Denker, and Stéphane Ducasse. SmartInspect: Solidity Smart Contract Inspector. In *2018 International Workshop on Blockchain Oriented Software Engineering (IWBOSE)*, pages 9–18, March 2018. Electronic ISBN: 978-1-5386-5986-1.

[BRDD18c] Santiago Bragagnolo, Henrique Rocha, Marcus Denker, and Stéphane Ducasse. Ethereum Query Language. In *2018 IEEE/ACM 1st International Workshop on Emerging Trends in Software Engineering for Blockchain (WETSEB)*, pages 1–8, May 2018.

[BU04] Gilad Bracha and David Ungar. Mirrors: Design Principles for Meta-level Facilities of Object-oriented Programming Languages. In *Proceedings of the International Conference on Object-Oriented Programming, Systems, Languages, and Applications (OOP- SLA'04), ACM SIGPLAN Notices*, pages 331–344. ACM Press, New York, NY, 2004.

[CCI90] Elliot Chikofsky and James Cross II. Reverse Engineering and Design Recovery: A Taxonomy. *IEEE Software*, 7(1): 13–17, January 1990.

[CK94] Shyam R. Chidamber and Chris F. Kemerer. A Metrics Suite for Object Oriented Design. *IEEE Transactions on Software Engineering*, 20(6): 476–493, June 1994.

[CLLZ17] Ting Chen, Xiaoqi Li, Xiapu Luo, and Xiaosong Zhang. Under-optimized Smart Contracts Devour Your Money. In *Proceedings of SANER*, pages 442–446. IEEE, 2017.

[CNSG15] Andrei Chis, Oscar Nierstrasz, Aliaksei Syrel, and Tudor Gîrba. The Moldable Inspector. In *2015 ACM International Symposium on New Ideas, New Paradigms, and Reflections on Programming and Software (Onward!), Onward!* , pages 44–60. ACM Press, New York, NY, 2015.

[DMO+18] Giuseppe Destefanis, Michele Marchesi, Marco Ortu, Roberto Tonelli, Andrea Bracciali, and Robert M. Hierons. Smart Contracts Vulnerabilities: A Call for Blockchain Software Engineering? In *2018 International Workshop on Blockchain Oriented Software Engineering*, IWBOSE@SANER 2018, Campobasso, Italy, March 20, 2018, pages 19–25, 2018.

[EN10] Ramez Elmasri and Shamkant Navathe. *Fundamentals of Database Systems*, 6th edition. Addison-Wesley Publishing Company, USA, 2010.

[Eth14] Ethereum Foundation. Ethereum's White Paper, 2014.

[Eth16] Ethereum Community. Ethereum Homestead Documentation, 2016.

[Eth18a] Ethereum Foundation. Json RPC, 2018.

[Eth18b] Ethereum Foundation. Remix Documentation Release 1, 2018. https://remix.readthedocs.io/en/latest.

[Eth18c] Ethereum Foundation. Solidity Documentation Release 0.4.24, 2018.

[Few06] S. Few. *Information Dashboard Design*. OReilly, 2006.

[Hev97] A. R. Hevner. Phase Containment Metrics for Software Quality Improvement. *Information and Software Technology*, 39(13): 867–877, 1997.

[HM95] M. Hitz and B. Montazeri. Measure Coupling and Cohesion in Object-oriented Systems. *Proceedings of International Symposium on Applied Corporate Computing (ISAAC '95)*, October 1995.

[IM15] Chinawat Isradisaikul and Andrew C. Myers. Finding Counterexamples From Parsing Conflicts. In *36th ACM SIGPLAN Conference on Programming Language Design and Implementation*, PLDI '15, pages 555–564. ACM Press, New York, NY, 2015.

[KGC+17] H. Kalodner, S. Goldfeder, A. Chator, M. Möser, and A. Narayanan. BlockSci: Design and Applications of a Blockchain Analysis Platform. *ArXiv e-prints*, September 2017.

[LBGD18] Jason Lecerf, John Brant, Thierry Goubier, and Stéphane Ducasse. A Reflexive and Automated Approach to Syntactic Pattern Matching in Code Transformations. In *IEEE International Conference on Software Maintenance and Evolution (ICSME'18)*, Madrid, Spain, September 2018.

[LCO+16] Loi Luu, Duc-Hiep Chu, Hrishi Olickel, Prateek Saxena, and Aquinas Hobor. Making Smart Contracts Smarter. In *CCS'2016 (ACM Conference on Computer and Communi- cations Security)*, 2016.

[LH93] W. Li and S. Henry. Object Oriented Metrics that Predict Maintainability. *Journal of System Software*, 23(2): 111–122, 1993.

[LK94] Mark Lorenz and Jeff Kidd. *Object-Oriented Software Metrics: A Practical Guide*. Prentice-Hall, 1994.

[LKG07] Adrian Lienhard, Adrian Kuhn, and Orla Greevy. Rapid Prototyping of Visualizations Using Mondrian. In *Proceedings IEEE International Workshop on Visualizing Software for Understanding*, Vissoft'07, pages 67–70. IEEE Computer Society, Los Alamitos, CA, June 2007.

[Mer93] Gary Merrill. Parsing Non-lr(k) Grammars With Yacc. *Software Practice and Experience*, 2(8): 829–850, 1993.

[Mil05] Ashley Mills. Antlr Tutorial, 2005.

[MM18] S. Morishima and H. Matsutani. Accelerating Blockchain Search of Full Nodes Using Gpus. In *26th Euromicro International Conference on Parallel, Distributed and Network-based Processing (PDP)*, pages 244–248, March 2018.

[NA05] Oscar Nierstrasz and Franz Achermann. Separating Concerns With First-class Names- Paces. In Robert E. Filman, Tzilla Elrad, Siobhán Clarke, and Mehmet Aksit, editors, *Aspect-Oriented Software Development*, pages 243–259. Addison-Wesley, 2005.

[PBB07] Leonardo Teixeira Passos, Mariza A. S. Bigonha, and Roberto S. Bigonha. A Methodology for Removing Lalr(k) Conflicts. *Journal of Universal Computer Science*, 13(6): 737–752, June 2007.

[PBD+15] Nick Papoulias, N. Bouraqadi, Marcus Denker, Stéphane Ducasse, and Luc Fabresse. Mercury: Properties and Design of a Remote Debugging Solution Using Reflection. *Journal of Object Technology*, 2015.

[PPMT17] S. Porru, A. Pinna, M. Marchesi, and R. Tonelli. Blockchain-oriented Software Engineering: Challenges and New Directions. In *Proceedings of the 39th International Conference on Software Engineering Companion*, pages 169–171, 2017.

[RDDL17] Henrique Rocha, Stéphane Ducasse, Marcus Denker, and Jason Lecerf. Solidity Parsing Using Smacc: Challenges and Irregularities. In *Proceedings of the 12th Edition of the International Workshop on Smalltalk Technologies*, IWST '17, pages 2:1–2:9. ACM Press, New York, NY, 2017.

[RSI+17] Michele Ruta, Floriano Scioscia, Saverio Ieva, Giovanna Capurso, and Eugenio Di Sciascio. Supply Chain Object Discovery With Semantic-enhanced Blockchain. In *Proceedings of the 15th ACM Conference on Embedded Network Sensor Systems*, SenSys '17, pages 60:1–60:2. ACM Press, New York, NY, 2017.

[SKS11] Abraham Silberschatz, Henry Korth, and S. Sudarshan. *Database Systems Concepts*, 6th edition. McGraw-Hill, Inc., New York, NY, 2011.

[SM16] Guido Salvaneschi and Mira Mezini. Debugging Reactive Programming With Reactive Inspector. In *Proceedings of the 38th International Conference on Software Engineering Companion*, ICSE '16, pages 728–730. ACM Press, New York, NY, 2016.

[SR14] Venkatesh Srinivasan and Thomas Reps. *Recovery of Class Hierarchies and Composition Relationships From Machine Code*, pages 61–84. Springer Berlin Heidelberg, Berlin, Heidelberg, 2014.

[TDMO18] R. Tonelli, G. Destefanis, M. Marchesi, and M. Ortu. Smart Contracts Software Metrics: A First Study. *ArXiv e-prints*, February 2018.

[TNM08] Ewan Tempero, James Noble, and Hayden Melton. How Do Java Programs Use Inheritance? An Empirical Study of Inheritance in Java Software. In *ECOOP '08: Proceedings of the 22nd European conference on Object-Oriented Programming*, pages 667–691. Springer-Verlag, Berlin, Heidelberg, 2008.

[TVI+18] S. Tikhomirov, E. Voskresenskaya, I. Ivanitskiy, R. Takhaviev, E. Marchenko, and Y. Alexandrov. Smartcheck: Static Analysis of Ethereum Smart Contracts. In *2018 IEEE/ACM 1st International Workshop on Emerging Trends in Software Engineering for Blockchain (WETSEB)*, pages 9–16, May 2018.

Chapter 14

Managing CRM with Fabric Hyperledger blockchain technology

*Dario Pulighedd*u, *Roberto Tonelli, and Michele Marchesi*

Introduction

The possibilities offered by the new and appealing blockchain technologies involve not only financial applications but, thanks to the advent of the new blockchain generation that supports smart contracts and dApp development, can currently span across all the applications that up to now were reserved to software systems.

Up to a few years ago, the term blockchain was only associated with Bitcoin, the cryptocurrency decentralized system set up by the researcher Satoshi Nakamoto (Nakamoto, Bitcoin white paper), who provided the scheme and the software (https://github.com/bitcoin/bitcoin) for running exchanges of virtual money among owners of blockchain addresses on the Internet, exploiting the recent results obtained through digital cryptography, such as digital signatures and hashing.

Even if the initial purpose of the project was to invent and render available to the Internet users a trustless cash system without the control of a central authority, the final result was a new software technology enabling more generally the management and the exchange of information across the network and able to grant transparency, immutability, anonymity, integrity and other welcome features required and desired for information management.

Since then, blockchain technology evolved and improved rapidly, and now there are different blockchain brands and solutions for the most disparate purposes. The main improvement is certainly the possibility of running native computer programs in the blockchain environment, the so-called smart contracts, which are pieces of software code deployed on a blockchain and running thanks to a virtual machine that is Turing complete, uses an instructions set blockchain dependent and thus allows the performance of any kind of computation performed by usual computers. Typical well-known examples are the Ethereum and the Hyperledger blockchain systems (Ethereum white paper; Hyperledger white paper). The former runs on a permissionless public blockchain (even if a private blockchain can be set up), supports a cryptocurrency, the Ether, and a programming language to develop smart contracts, Solidity, and is the second most popular blockchain after Bitcoin. The latter runs on a permissioned and private blockchain explicitly conceived to support business organizations in managing their own business logic, providing the option to decide the desired blockchain setup, and runs "chaincode" (the equivalent of smart contracts) written in various programming languages, mostly in GO (https://golang.org/).

This new scenario opened up the possibility to develop decentralized software applications exploiting the intrinsic blockchain features of transparency, immutability, anonymity, and integrity of information already reported earlier. Nevertheless, the blockchain technology is not solely good news; mainly due to the fact that it is still in its youth, there are various drawbacks that are under investigation over different fields of research, like software engineering (Ortu, Destefanis, Swift and Marchesi, 2016; Ortu, Destefanis, Kassab and Marchesi, 2015; Ortu, Destefanis, Adams, Murgia, Marchesi and Tonelli, 2015; Ortu, Destefanis, Kassab, Counsell, Marchesi and Tonelli, 2015; Mantyla, Adams, Destefanis, Graziotin and Ortu, 2016; Ortu, Destefanis, Counsell, Swift, Tonelli and Marchesi, 2016), social networks and developers' attitudes (Ortu, Murgia, Destefanis, Tourani, Tonelli, Marchesi and Adams, 2016; Destefanis, Ortu, Counsell, Swift, Tonelli and Marchesi, 2017; Destefanis, Ortu, Counsell, Swift, Stephen, Michele and Tonelli, 2016; Destefanis, Tonelli, Concas and Marchesi, 2012), and micropatterns (Concas, Destefanis, Marchesi, Ortu and Tonelli, 2013).

In Tonelli, Pinna, Baralla and Ibba (2018), an approach to the implementation of microservices by means of an architecture based on smart contract deployed in the Ethereum blockchain is presented. The architecture has two levels. The first level provides the ABI (the Ethereum application binary interface) for software applications and the user interface in which ABIs are embedded. The second layer is composed by the set of smart contracts running in the blockchain. In the model, each microservice is implemented by means of an atomic smart contract. Communication between levels takes place with remote procedure calls, through the Web3 Ethereum library 3, which includes the execution of blockchain transactions.

In Lenarduzzi, Tonelli, Marchesi and Lunesu (2018), the management of Scrum/Kanban Agile software projects is designed by means of blockchain applications. The duties of the product owner for certifying the correctness of the outcomes are delegated to one or more smart contracts deployed on the Ethereum blockchain and written in Solidity. In the model, an agreement with the customer allows the smart contracts to automatically enable payments and to introduce penalties or grants on the basis of the outcome. Product owner duties and work can thus be relieved, allowing the allocation of resources to more profitable and productive tasks.

In Marchesi, Ortu, Tonelli, Destefanis, Bracciali and Hierons (2018), the digital wallets produced by Parity for holding and exchanging Ethers among blockchain addresses and accounts in the Ethereum blockchain are examined, investigating problems that can arise with particular smart contract features. The paper analyzes a case study where a bug discovered in a smart contract library, and perhaps "unsafe" programming, allowed an attack on Parity, a wallet application, causing the freezing of about 500,000 Ethers (about $150 million USD,)in November 2017.

In Bragagnolo, Rocha, Denker and Ducasse (2018), an application, SmartInspect, allows the inspection of known contracts based on its source code, focusing on the debugging properties of interactiveness and distribution. This reflective approach allows a user to see the contents of any contract instance of the given source code, without needing to redeploy or develop any ad-hoc code to decode the memory representation.

In Sousa, Bessani and Vukolic (2018), a Byzantine fault-tolerant (BFT) ordering service is implemented for Hyperledger on top of the BFT-SMART state machine replication/consensus library, with optimizations for wide-area deployment. The results show that the ordering service can process up to ten thousand transactions per second and write a transaction irrevocably in the blockchain in half a second, even with peers spread across different continents.

In Hulea, Rosu, Miron and Astilean (2018), is presented a solution for pharmaceutical cold chain management using distributed ledger technologies. An application framework based on the Hyperledger Sawtooth distributed ledger framework is proposed for shipment tracking that will deliver information to all stakeholders during the distribution phase of pharmaceutical products. The solution includes a custom transactions family and a sensors gateway for automatically collecting data from temperature tracking devices.

In Kinkelin, Hauner, Niedermayer and Carle (2018), is presented a Byzantine fault-tolerant configuration management system (CMS) that provides control over administrators, restrains their rights and enforces separation of concerns. The configuration management process required multiparty authorization for critical configurations to prevent individual malicious administrators from performing undesired actions and is supported on Hyperledger Fabric.

In this chapter we focus our attention on the applications of the blockchain technology to CRM (customer relationship management) systems that involve business and research together. We discuss a model for the realization of a management infrastructure that is secure by design and able to support, by proper configuration, requirements and procedures of a business organization. The model adopts a decentralization of the software product at the application level by means of blockchain technology. The back end is based on the open-source platform Hyperledger to support business-to-business and business-to-customer transactions, and a front end where the business information is natively protected by cryptographic techniques provided by the blockchain protocols in order to reduce the attack surface.

Customer relationship management systems

Customer relationship management is the answer to the need of business and enterprises to acquire and use a huge amount of data with an analytic approach in order to improve their performance (Barton, 2012). It has been shown that this approach can be extended to all markets and that the injection of a huge amount of data, with the information they carry and their analytic evaluation, contribute to improved productivity and profitability of about 5–6 percent on average. The data collection process needs three steps: combining external and internal information, detecting predictive models for performance, and creating and using informatics tool for processing information and for changing internal capabilities. One of the objectives is the segmentation of customers into levels so that the enterprise can better target offers according to the segment customers belong to. The purpose is the establishment of long-term relationships with customers, with mutual trust generating added value through adopting a one-to-one marketing strategy (Greenberg, 2009).

From the perspective of customers or central (state or international) guaranty units, the data acquired by enterprises and business societies can be a real social risk, in particular when data protection is not granted or correctly taken into account, especially nowadays, where data on customers are collected and maintained in decentralized structures accessible from the network, like cloud repositories of web servers. As a consequence, the more recent legal regulations impose the approach of "privacy by design" for CRM of any exposed business enterprise, as in the GDPR (General Data Protection Regulation). The enhanced attention on the privacy normative pushed vendors to create new products for granting security and privacy, but since the service and the applications were already designed and working, were introduced as intermediate layers between the application and the rest of the network as an add-on, such as firewalls, intrusion detection systems, intrusion prevention systems, web application firewalls, next generation firewalls and, ultimately, artificial intelligence.

It is, by contrast, desirable to have at one's disposal a CRM that is secure by design which breaks the architecture of traditional CRM and builds its infrastructure on an architecture that natively implements security, privacy, transparency and data integrity, as well as supports for customization of accesses and polices permissions to different hierarchical levels – in summary, a system that can manage data access, storage and exchange with the flexibility and efficacy of traditional CRM and at the same time manages security and integrity issues natively, as for blockchain technologies.

As a solution we present a model for CRM on Hyperledger Fabric, where customization of the architecture is native; access permission and control, as well as transaction control, are implemented by design; and security, privacy, immutability and integrity of data are natively granted by the blockchain technology. Our approach leverages the trust relying on the infrastructure publicly connected to the Internet and relies instead on cryptography based on Hyperledger Fabric in order to exploit its features of permissioned and private blockchain.

The Hyperledger project

Hyperledger (www.hyperledger.org) is an open-source project founded by the Linux Foundation in 2015 for supporting the collaborative development of distributed ledgers based on blockchain technology with the aim of improving collaboration between different sectors in distributed ledgers, giving particular attention to performances and reliability for supporting commercial transactions of technological and financial enterprises in the global distribution arena. The project includes and supports open and independent standards and protocols by means of a framework composed of specific modules, depending on the context. Among the modules there is blockchain for managing consensus and storage, services for identity management and access control, and smart contracts. Many big brands of the IT sector support the project, like Cisco, IBM, Intel, Hitachi, Fujitsu, SAP and others.

Hyperledger fabric

Among the many platforms, Fabric constitutes an open-source blockchain framework, originally developed by IBM under the name IBM Open Blockchain (OBC). The idea behind Fabric is to support a modular structure where the different blockchain nodes can be configured in order to play different roles and to support the execution of smart contract code, called chaincode in the Fabric jargon. The architecture allows users to configure which consensus algorithm runs the blockchain and the membership services, so that each participant can play different roles and holds different privileges.

A Fabric Hyperledger network includes:

- Nodes, which are peers that execute chaincode, have access to the ledger, approve transactions and interact with the applications;
- Ordering nodes, which check for network coherence and distribute approved transactions to the network nodes; and
- MSPs (membership service providers), which are implemented as certificate authorities and manage the certificates used in order to authenticate members identities and roles.

Fabric's purpose is the integration in projects using a distributed ledger technology (DLT) as a service. The languages supported for smart contracts chaincode are multiple and include Go, Java, Javascript, nodejs; namely, it does not provide proprietary or ad-hoc programming languages, and developers can use the programming language they prefer or are most accustomed to. As already mentioned, it offers the possibility to organize private and permissioned blockchain networks. The advantage for a business organization is that access is not anonymous and can be restricted. Furthermore, policies can be defined so that different users can hold different access privileges. The MSP provides the infrastructure for managing participants' identities, and given that each member has been previously authorized and its identity is well known, proof of work or similar protocols can be dismissed at will for guaranteeing network security and participants' honesty.

Hyperledger Fabric can be personalized for different needs and flavors and allows the possibility of creating channels devoted to a subset of participants for managing a sub-blockchain network with its own transactions hidden from the rest of the network and independent from the overall transaction flux, the ideal situation for concurrent business or for enterprises with different hierarchical levels. The concept of channel can also be extended to only two participants (https://ibm.ent.box.com/v/BlockFiles).

The Fabric distributed ledger has two components, the *world state* and the *transaction log*. Each node has its own copy of the ledger of each network it belongs to. The first component, the world state, accounts for the ledger state in a given moment, while the transaction log registers all transactions that conduced to the current state, namely, accounting for the chronology.

Chaincode

Smart contracts in Fabric are invoked by an application external to the blockchain when it has to interact with it. In most cases, chaincode interacts only with the world state but not with the transaction log. The chaincode can be implemented in different high-level programming languages, like Java, JavaScript and GO. They execute the code and make requests to the blockchain. By means of private channels, it is possible to create a transaction belonging only to a subset of the network. All data belonging to a channel are invisible to others. This feature enables a simple and at the same time secure management of privacy issues. An example of GO chaincode is shown here for executing queries on the ledger.

```
func (s *SmartContract) queryUser(APIstub shim.ChaincodeS-
    tubInterface, args []string) sc.Response {
  if len(args) != 1 {
    return shim.Error("Incorrect number of arguments. Expect
      ing UserID")
  }
  UserBytes, err := APIstub.GetState(args[0])
  if err != nil {
    return shim.Error(err.Error())
  }
  return shim.Success(UserBytes)
}
```

All transactions need to be attached to the ledger in the right order even if managed by chaincode belonging to different channels. This is managed with

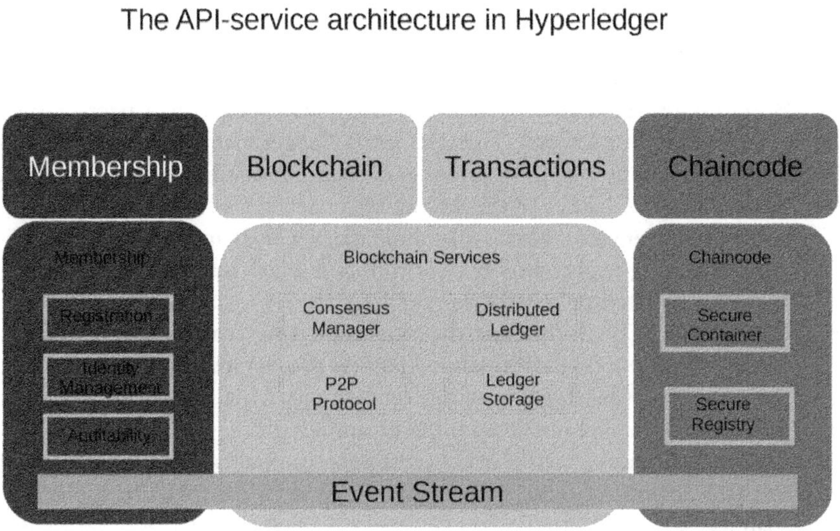

Figure 14.1 V2.0.0 architecture of Hyperledger (from Hyperledger white paper)

different possible choices of the consensus algorithm, like the SOLO and Kafka (https://github.com/hyperledger/fabric/tree/master/orderer/consensus/solo and https://github.com/hyperledger/fabric/tree/master/orderer/consensus/kafka) algorithms, or the Simplified Byzantine Fault Tolerance, in order to better take into account the relationships among network participants.

The Hyperledger Fabric White Paper specifies the main features of Fabric (see Figure 14.1 for the architecture). These are:

- **Scalability:** The possibility of adding dynamically new nodes into the network. The execution of chaincode is kept separate, and it is possible to add nodes for distributing the traffic flow.
- **Transactions:** Are deterministic, executed in a defined and constant time independent from the executing entity.
- **Identity:** Hyperledger Fabric provides a PKI (public key infrastructure) used for the controlling resources accesses. The PKI module can be integrated with preexisting solutions such as LDAP or AOUTH2.
- **Audit:** The possibility of performing auditing is included in Fabric, with managing events and a log allowing for a variety of checks based on the current network configuration.
- **Advanced queries:** Fabric allows users to query the current blockchain status, with queries defined and loaded into the blockchain during deploy of the business network. They can be invoked using APIs by users. Data

are distributed through transaction records made by key-value pairs corresponding to a commit in the blockchain.

- **Policy services:** Used for managing and controlling the policies, such as endorsement, consensus, and groups.
- **Blockchain services:** Manage the distributed ledger by a peer-to-peer communication protocol. The data in the ledger can be updated only by reaching consensus among nodes processing and validating transactions. Nodes compute hashes of the dataset after each block.
- **Consensus service:** This is a module that receives and executes transactions according to the chosen algorithm and interfaces with chaincode for checking transaction correctness.
- **Chaincode:** This is software that is executed for managing transactions. Chaincodes are executed in safe containers (boxes) inside validating nodes and are responsible for processing transactions requests and for verifying their validity in agreement with the business logic.
- **Channel:** Creates a virtual data partitioning to grant access to information and to transactions only in the part of the network participating in the channel.

The model

In order to ensure security by design for a CRM managing business and enterprises services, we designed and implemented an architecture where the interaction between the different parts of the network, the services and privacy and security issues and policies are implemented using Hyperledger Fabric.

In fact, every application or software system publicly connected to the Internet is exposed to hackers and attackers. CRMs hold personal and private data and information about thousands of people that are of immense value for business. The efforts and the resources spent on intrusions and on hacking such data in recent years not only constitute a hugely lucrative business but can (and have been) also used to undermine and influence people's beliefs and social aspects and relationships, such as in the cases where the data have been used for influencing elections in various countries. But keeping our attention on business and enterprises' CRM security, the project of a secure solution must adopt a "zero trust system" approach and must not rely on the public infrastructure connected to the Internet, such as hosting providers, connectivity solutions, servers, network devices and in general everything different from what runs inside endpoints, like PCs, and mobile and IoT devices. Zero-trust architecture also addresses threats that get inside the network – rather than focusing only on security issues on the perimeter like that performed by traditional security models – by leveraging micro-segmentation and granular perimeter enforcement based on user, data and location.

The principle of "defense in depth" must be adopted, where multiple protection layers are used to defend the system from external attacks. In particular, when analyzing web technologies, we have two systems interacting: the database (DB) and the web application. While the DB manages the storage and the interaction with data, the web applications manage the logic of the interactions among users and data. External users cannot interact directly with the DB and forward requests to the web-apps. Thus the latter are the first target, since they are exposed to informatics attacks being connected to the public network. If web-apps are not properly protected or security bugs are exploited, it is possible to steal data or to alter data integrity.

Inside relational DBs, it is possible to use security features for creating profiles with different privileges and permissions, but it is difficult and expensive to develop web-apps capable of using different profiles in the various different contexts. Traditional applications belong to the client-server architecture, which relies on and trusts the infrastructure hosting the application. These in general do not encrypt data, and a server attack can give complete access to the database. So, an "app server side" hacking could provide full access to a DB. Of course the DB can be encrypted, but usually encryption and decryption occur inside the database, and interaction with applications is not involved. It is thus desirable to have encryption directly with the client. Furthermore, if the web frameworks are replaced by a network of nodes in an untrusted environment where all transactions are executed if approved by authorized users and all operations are performed only with consensus of nodes, it would be more difficult for an external attacker to reach all the sensitive data.

This solution can be implemented through Hyperledger Fabric, where chaincode can manage interactions with databases and transactions are executed according to a selected consensus mechanism. In such architecture, web applications connected to the Internet are replaced by the Fabric blockchain. The graphical interface and the user interaction are delegated to an endpoint application where encryption is enabled on the client side end to end. The user interacts with Fabric back end through a channel after his requests are acknowledged by an ACL (access control list) and verified by chaincode, which is the only way to interact with the ledger.

Processing transactions

Transactions are processed according to a seven-step phase. In the first step, the application sends a request to an endorsing peer. Then the endorsement policies specify the number of nodes needed to sign a request. The nodes execute the chaincode to deploy the request and to simulate the read/write operations into the distributed ledger. In the third phase, the endorsing peers provide to the application the request of interaction with the blockchain, which is signed by the nodes. Then the application sends the transaction and the digital signature to the ordering service. The ordering service creates a block of transaction and delivers it to committing peers. These receive the transaction batch and, finally, for each transaction in the received block, verify the endorsement policy and check if there are potential conflicting transactions. If both checks are confirmed, the block is inserted into the distributed ledger and the blockchain status is updated.

Since only the digital signature and the read/write operations are broadcast inside the network, performance and scalability are optimized. The sharing of chaincode execution between different nodes with different tasks allows the service to be optimized even in the presence of overload and large transaction volumes. The separation of roles allows the dynamical increase of the network so that peers can be dynamically inserted.

The model architecture

The infrastructure of application and databases servers can be replaced by a business network built upon Hyperledger Fabric. The data are encrypted in the client and stored in a private blockchain. This is used as an intermediate layer, a middleware, which enables clients to communicate inside and outside the organization. The internal communications are implemented with specific ACL policies. Every interaction with the data stored into the distributed ledger occurs by means of chaincode invoked only by authorized users. Each operation on data, before it is accepted, is validated by the smart contracts deployed irreversibly on the blockchain. This ensures automation and security because interactions among the clients and database are executed on the basis of an access control list containing only valid operations, reducing the surface for external attacks.

Our first objective has been to realize a prototype working stand-alone where data flux occurs inside the software product but enabled to connect and integrate with preexisting external systems. Thus, we developed the client both in command line modality and in graphical user interface. A working example shows the synchronization of two folders by means of two noninteractive processes and the examination of data inside a graphic management system that interacts with the overall information system. The system can handle text whether or not it is encrypted and has been elaborated at "Eablock" and at "CLab" by one of the authors.

In the example reported in Table 14.1, the client iterates inside a folder containing ".log" files. The content and the names of every file are encrypted and inserted into the blockchain. Afterwards it is possible to examine the data inside a graphical platform (Figure 14.2).

The platform displays the list of the file content loaded into the blockchain that is recovered using user credentials, decrypting them inside the client and exposed to the user.

If an attacker were to enter into some of the nodes, the encrypted data could not be understood or interpreted. We enabled storing the encrypted contents as JSON files. Figure 14.3 shows part of a file content stored according to this standard.

Table 14.1 Screenshot of the messages provided by the client when iterates inside the data structure provided by the Fabric framework while encrypts and saves every element.

```
############ ########### ############
#                                   #
#              EABLOCK              #
#                                   #
#         YOUR SAFE BUSINESS        #
#                                   #
#             eablock.com           #
#          info@eablock.com         #
#                                   #
############ ########### ############
```

```
INFO: Downloading and Decryption of data ...
#
Result of Decryption (filename only)
   log.evtx
#
#
INFO: Downloading and Decryption of data ...
#
Result of Decryption (filename only)
   log.txt
#
#
INFO: Downloading and Decryption of data ...
#
Result of Decryption (filename only)
   log.xml
#
#
INFO: Downloading and Decryption of data ...
#
Result of Decryption (filename only)
   log_2.evtx
#
#
INFO: Downloading and Decryption of data ...
#
Result of Decryption (filename only)
   log_2.txt
#
#
INFO: Downloading and Decryption of data ...
#
Result of Decryption (filename only)
   log_2.xml
#
#
INFO: Downloading and Decryption of data ...
#
```

(Continued)

Table 14.1 (Continued)

Result of Decryption (filename only)
  log_3.evtx
#
#
INFO: Downloading and Decryption of data . . .
#
Result of Decryption (filename only)
  log_3.txt
#
#
INFO: Downloading and Decryption of data . . .
#
Result of Decryption (filename only)
  log_3.xml
#
#

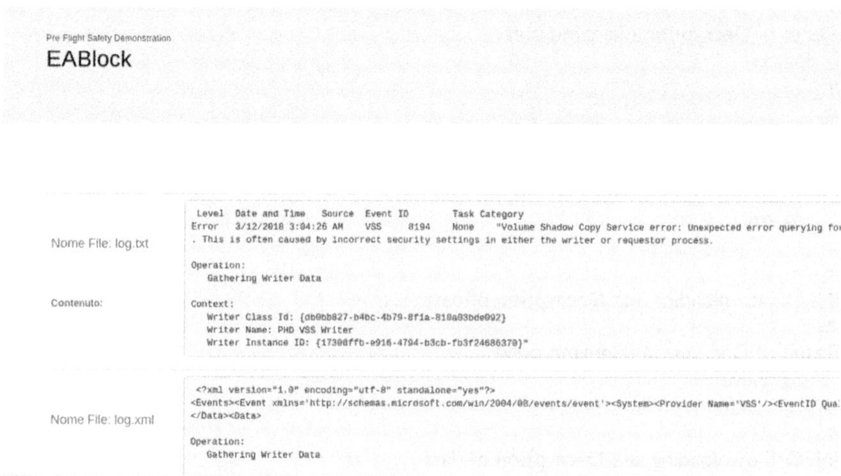

Figure 14.2 Screenshot of the Eablock client exposing the decrypted content from the Blockchain to the final user.

Since we also encrypt the file name, to steal a specific file becomes much more complicate for an attacker. Data can be recovered from the blockchain afterwards using the symmetric scheme.

Table 14.2 shows a screen where the client iterates inside the data structure provided by the Fabric framework and decrypts and saves every element.

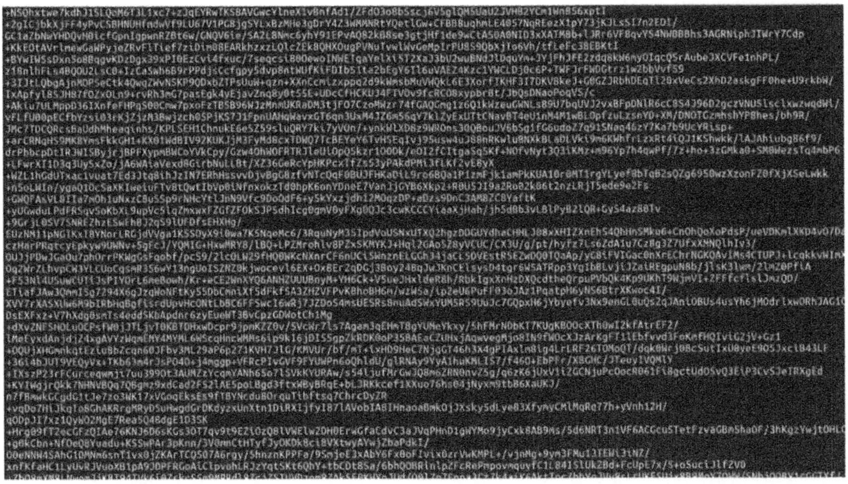

Figure 14.3 Screenshot of the messages provided by the client when iterates inside the data structure provided by the Fabric framework while encrypts and saves every element.

Table 14.2 Screenshot of the messages provided by the client when iterates inside the data structure provided by the Fabric framework while decrypts and saves every element.

```
############ ########## ############
#                                  #
#             EABLOCK              #
#                                  #
#        YOUR SAFE BUSINESS        #
#                                  #
#           eablock.com            #
#        info@eablock.com          #
#                                  #
############ ########## ############
```

```
INFO: Encryption and uploading to BlockCHain
#
    log.evtx
#
#
INFO: Encryption and uploading to BlockCHain
#
    log.txt
#
#
INFO: Encryption and uploading to BlockCHain
#
    log.xml
#
#
```

(*Continued*)

Table 14.2 (Continued)

```
INFO: Encryption and uploading to BlockCHain
#
   log_2.evtx
#
#
INFO: Encryption and uploading to BlockCHain
#
   log_2.txt
#
#
INFO: Encryption and uploading to BlockCHain
#
   log_2.xml
#
#
INFO: Encryption and uploading to BlockCHain
#
   log_3.evtx
#
#
INFO: Encryption and uploading to BlockCHain
#
   log_3.txt
#
#
INFO: Encryption and uploading to BlockCHain
#
   log_3.xml
#
#
```

Conclusions

In this chapter, we reported an analysis of the use of Hyperledger Fabric for managing CRM in a "secure by design" approach. Information security is the main target CRM must address in order to protect customer data from accesses by unauthorized parties. The use of blockchain technology natively supports encryption anonymization and decentralization, allowing the CRM to be built on a zero trust system support where there is no need of any trust in the infrastructure hosting software components. This allows data to be encrypted in the client application under the user control. The data are available and accessible only to authorized users and unintelligible to others. The native digital signatures allow precise identification of the sender, who cannot dissociate from any action. Data integrity is natively ensured on the blockchain by encryption and hashing functions that allow the prevention of any dishonest data alteration. The encrypted data are saved on a back end based on blockchain. We implement this scheme with a permissioned Blockchain that requires a precautionary verification of network participants. We use "Fabric" by Hyperledger, a project finalized with the creation of Blockchain for Enterprise. The permission structure of Hyperledger reduces the risk of security problems, allowing transactions only between authorized parts. With Fabric, chaincode can manage interactions with databases and transactions are executed according to a selected consensus mechanism. In such architecture, web applications connected to the Internet are replaced by the Fabric blockchain. The graphical interface and the user interaction are delegated to an endpoint application where encryption is enabled on the client side end to end. The user interacts with the Fabric back end through a channel after his requests are acknowledged by an ACL and verified by chaincode, which is the only way to interact with the ledger. The internal communications are implemented with specific ACL policies. Every interaction with the data stored into the distributed ledger occurs by means of chaincode invoked only by authorized users. Each operation on data, before being accepted, is validated by the smart contracts deployed irreversibly on the blockchain. This ensures automation and security because interactions among clients and the database are executed on the basis of an ACL (access control list) containing only valid operations, reducing the surface for external attacks. We realized a prototype working stand-alone in which data flux occurs inside the software product but is enabled to connect and integrate with preexisting external systems, and we developed the client both in command line modality and in graphical user interface. By means of this prototype, we show how the concept of CRM "secure by design" can be practically implemented relying on Fabric Hyperledger. Our research drives the existing research on CRM toward a blockchain approach that exploits the most relevant features of this new technology.

Acknowledgments

The authors are grateful to the ContaminationLab (C-Lab) of Cagliari University, which partially hosted the work and supported the Eablock project.

Bibliography

Barton, Dominic (2012). "Making Advanced Analytics Work", *Harvard Business Review.*

Bragagnolo, Santiago, Rocha, Henrique, Denker, Markus and Ducasse, Stephane (2018). "SmartInspect: Solidity smart contract inspector", *2018 International Workshop on Blockchain Oriented Software Engineering (IWBOSE)*, Campobasso, Italy, pp. 9–18. ISBN: 978-1-5386-5987-8.

Concas, Giulio, Destefanis, Giuseppe, Marchesi, Michele, Ortu, Marco and Tonelli, Roberto (2013). "Micro patterns in agile software", *International Conference on Agile Software Development*, pp. 210–222.

Destefanis, Giuseppe, Ortu, Marco, Counsell, Steve, Swift, Stephen, Marchesi, Michele and Tonelli, Roberto (2016). "Software development: Do good manners matter?", *PeerJ Computer Science*, vol. 2, p. 73.

Destefanis, Giuseppe, Ortu, Marco, Counsell, Steve, Swift, Stephen, Tonelli, Roberto and Marchesi, Michele (2017). "On the randomness and seasonality of affective metrics for software development", *Proceedings of the Symposium on Applied Computing*, pp. 1266–1271.

Destefanis, Giuseppe, Tonelli, Roberto, Concas, Giulio and Marchesi, Michele (2012). "An analysis of anti-micro-patterns effects on fault-proneness in large Java systems", *Proceedings of the 27th Annual ACM Symposium on Applied Computing*, pp. 1251–1253.

Ethereum white paper: https://github.com/ethereum/wiki/wiki/White-Paper

Greenberg, P. (2009). "CRM at the Speed of Light," in *Social CRM Strategies, Tools, and Techniques for Engaging Your Customers*. Fourth Edition. McGraw Hill, p. 30.

Hulea, M.E., Rosu, O., Miron, R. and Astilean A. (2018). "Pharmaceutical cold chain management: Platform based on a distributed ledger" (Conference Paper), *21st IEEE International Conference on Automation, Quality and Testing, Robotics, AQTR 2018*, 3 July 2018, pp. 1–6, Cluj-Napoca; Romania; 24 May 2018 through 26 May 2018; Category number CFP18AQT-PRT; Code 137740.

Hyperledger Fabric white paper: www.hyperledger.org/resources/publications#white-papers

Hyperledger white paper: www.hyperledger.org/resources/publications#white-papers

Kinkelin, H., Hauner, V.E., Niedermayer, H.E. and Carle, G. (2018). "Trustworthy configuration management for networked devices using distributed ledgers" (Conference Paper), *IEEE/IFIP Network Operations and Management Symposium: Cognitive Management in a Cyber World, NOMS 2018*, 6 July 2018, pp. 1–5, Taipei, Taiwan; 23 April 2018 through 27 April 2018; Category numberCFP18NOM-ART; Code 137784.

Lenarduzzi, Valentina, Tonelli, Roberto, Marchesi, Michele and Lunesu, Maria Ilaria (2018). "Blockchain applications for Agile methodologies", *19th International Conference on Agile Processes in Software Engineering and Extreme Programming. XP proceedings.*

Mantyla, Mika, Adams, Bram, Destefanis, Giuseppe, Graziotin, Daniel and Ortu, Marco (2016). "Mining valence, arousal, and dominance: possibilities for detecting burnout and productivity?", *Proceedings of the 13th International Conference on Mining Software Repositories*, pp. 247–258.

Marchesi, Michele, Ortu, Marco, Tonelli, Roberto, Destefanis, Giuseppe, Bracciali, Andrea and Hierons, Robert (2018). "Smart Contracts vulnerabilities: A call for Blockchain Software Engineering?", *International Workshop on Blockchain Oriented Software Engineering (IWBOSE)*, pp. 19–24. doi:10.1109/IWBOSE.2018.8327567.

Nakamoto, Satoshi, "Bitcoin: A Peer-to-Peer Electronic Cash System", Bitcoin white paper.

Ortu, Marco, Destefanis, Giuseppe, Adams, Bram, Murgia, Alessandro, Marchesi, Michele and Tonelli, Roberto (2015). "The JIRA repository dataset: Understanding social aspects of software development", *Proceedings of the 11th International Conference on Predictive Models and Data Analytics in Software Engineering*, p. 1.

Ortu, Marco, Destefanis, Giuseppe, Counsell, Steve, Swift, Stephen, Tonelli, Roberto and Marchesi, Michele (2016). "Arsonists or firefighters? Affectiveness in agile software development".

Ortu, Marco, Destefanis, Giuseppe, Kassab, Mohamad, Counsell, Steve, Marchesi, Michele and Tonelli, Roberto (2015). "Would you mind fixing this issue? An Empirical Analysis of Politeness and Attractiveness in Software Developed Using Agile Boards", *Agile Processes in Software Engineering, and Extreme Programming*, pp. 122–140.

Ortu, Marco, Destefanis, Giuseppe, Kassab, Mohamad, and Marchesi, Michele (2015). "Measuring and understanding the effectiveness of JIRA developers communities", *Proceedings of the Sixth International Workshop on Emerging Trends in Software Metrics*, pp. 3–10.

Ortu, Marco, Destefanis, Giuseppe, Swift, Stephen and Marchesi, Michele (2016). "Measuring high and low priority defects on traditional and mobile open source software", *Proceedings of the 7th International Workshop on Emerging Trends in Software Metrics*, pp. 1–7.

Ortu, Marco, Murgia, Alessandro, Destefanis, Giuseppe, Tourani, Parastou, Tonelli, Roberto, Marchesi, Michele and Adams, Bram (2016). "The emotional side of software developers in JIRA", *2016 IEEE/ACM 13th Working Conference on Mining Software Repositories (MSR)*, pp. 480–483.

Sousa, J., Bessani, A. and Vukolic, M. (2018). "A Byzantine Fault-Tolerant ordering service for the Hyperledger Fabric blockchain platform" (Conference Paper), *Proceedings – 48th Annual IEEE/IFIP International Conference on Dependable Systems and Networks, DSN 2018*, 19 July 2018, Article number 8416470, pp. 51–58, Luxembourg; 25 June 2018 through 28 June 2018; Category number E6445; Code 138141.

Tonelli, Roberto, Pinna, Andrea, Baralla, Gavina and Ibba, Simona (2018). "Ethereum Smart Contracts as Blockchain-oriented Microservices", *International Workshop on Microservices: Agile and DevOps Experience (MADE18).*

Chapter 15

Privacy with Ethereum smart contracts

Duarte Teles and Isabel Azevedo

Introduction

Data privacy has been an important issue over the last few decades. Several big corporations have been known for mishandling and misusing data collected from individuals. User privacy must be ensured in software applications, which was reinforced by the approval of the European Union's General Data Protection Regulation. Compliance with the GDPR is mandatory: penalties range from a minimum of 10 million Euros or 2 percent annual turnover (whichever is higher) to 20 million Euros or 4 percent annual turnover (whichever is higher) (European Union, 2016).

In 1996, computer scientist and cryptographer Nick Szabo first conceived the idea of smart contracts (Szabo, 1996). Generally, these are self-enforcing agreements (like real-world contracts), although expressed in computer code that, when executed, dictates the terms and conditions of the contract, without any of the parties involved trusting each other. Currently, they can be stored on a blockchain; thus, they inherit the characteristic properties of a blockchain: immutable, public and decentralized. Smart contracts, once created and deployed, cannot be further altered or tampered with. The overall process for creating them must involve careful design, testing and execution, or multiple unpatchable bugs and errors will potentially be explored by attackers at some point in the future. For example, the Decentralized Autonomous Organization (DAO) (Falkon, 2017) and Parity hacks (Parity Technologies, 2017; Petrov, 2017) resulted in millions of US dollars in stolen funds.

Two of the most well-known blockchains are Bitcoin (Bitcoin Project, 2018) and Ethereum (Ethereum Foundation, 2018). The former was created by an unknown person under the pseudonym of Satoshi Nakamoto, who pioneered the concept of digital currency enforced by cryptography with the aim of solving the double spending problem. The latter is currently the biggest blockchain to support smart contracts, which was specifically designed and created with an extended execution model for smart contracts (Ethereum Foundation, 2014). Ethereum also supports the development of decentralized applications (DApps), which embrace its smart contracts and properties.

Under the GDPR (European Union, 2016), individuals are entitled to two major rights: "right to erasure" and "right to rectification". In this case, since both blockchains are immutable, how can they comply with these two individual rights? Further, can DApps be developed in compliance with the GDPR, even while acknowledging this issue?

In this chapter, the authors first discuss the basic concepts of the GDPR. Then the multiple approaches for developing DApps while attending to the GDPR will be presented, although some may not be able to fully comply with the regulation. Furthermore, a series of universal steps also are provided for anyone interested in developing DApps to be able to fully comply with the regulation. Finally, a case study is considered: DFiles, an open-source DApp developed with decentralized technologies such as Ethereum, its smart contracts and the Interplanetary File System (IPFS) (Protocol Labs, 2018), while following the principles of blockchain software engineering (Destefanis et al., 2018). Here, we attempt to answer the following questions:

- Can DApps be fully compliant with the GDPR?
- Is it feasible to protect user data by encrypting it in Ethereum (Homestead)?

The short answer for the first question is that DApps can in fact be compliant with the GDPR, albeit with severe limitations. A possible approach to ensure their compliance is data encryption, which leads to the second question: it was found that protecting personal data by encrypting it is, as of late 2018, unfeasible, as explored later in this chapter. Ethereum and the IPFS must rapidly improve to allow other privacy scenarios or at least ensure encryption is in fact possible for medium to large file sizes.

The General Data Protection Regulation

Before the GDPR, big companies could collect, process and store their users' data with less restrictions. The European Union, however, drafted a new law to further ensure users have their important data private and protected from organizations' data mishandling and possible data breaches. In May 2016, this massive legislation was passed and was enforceable (European Data Protection Supervisor, 2018), although penalties were only applicable nearly two years later, on May 25, 2018. Understanding the regulation in its entirety can take a few months to one to two years. For the sake of space, only its most important aspects are covered.

The regulation introduces some new concepts:

- **Data subject (or individual):** "any person whose personal data is being collected, held or processed" (EU GDPR Compliant, 2018).
- **Personal data:** any information "relating to an identified or identifiable natural person ('data subject'); an identifiable natural person is one

who can be identified, directly or indirectly, in particular by reference to an identifier such as a name, an identification number, location data, an online identifier or to one or more factors specific to the physical, physiological, genetic, mental, economic, cultural or social identity of that natural person" (European Union, 2016).

- **Processing:** "any operation or set of operations which is performed on personal data or on sets of personal data, whether or not by automated means, such as collection, recording, organization, structuring, storage, adaptation or alteration, retrieval, consultation, use, disclosure by transmission, dissemination or otherwise making available, alignment or combination, restriction, erasure or destruction" (European Union, 2016).

Lawful basis and rights

When processing data from data subjects, there must be a lawful basis to do so. These are interconnected with the data subject's rights; some who do not apply under a particular lawful basis, while others may apply for almost all of them, as shown in Table 15.1.

There are several lawful bases to choose from – *consent*, *legal obligation*, *public task* and *legitimate interests* – with consent being the most widely used in traditional software applications. It refers to the permission to process the personal data of individuals for specific purposes. It must be requested with clear, concise and explicit language and without pre-ticked boxes or other default consent methods (European Union, 2016).

There are multiple individual rights that are new to the GDPR.

They are all equally important, as they may apply for some lawful bases for processing and not to others (Table 15.1). These include *rights to be informed*, *access*, *rectification*, *erasure* and *data portability*.

Ethereum and other blockchains generally comply with most of these rights. However, the main issue at stake here is the right to erasure, as it interferes with the immutability present in a blockchain. According to (ICO, 2018), this

Table 15.1 Differences between the rights to erasure and data portability

	Right to erasure	*Right to data portability*
Consent		
Legal obligation	X	X
Vital interests		X
Public task	X	X
Legitimate interests	X	

Note: Individual rights that do not apply to certain lawful bases are marked with an "X"

Source: ICO (2018)

right, although not always applicable, states that data subjects can request their personal data to be deleted without undue delay. The immutable nature of blockchains contradicts this right, as data cannot be deleted.

General data protection regulation compliance in Ethereum DApps

One of the biggest challenges for DApps development is the compliance with the General Data Protection Regulation, mainly because of some blockchain characteristics that do not allow for records to be deleted or altered, as already mentioned. However, most blockchains fully comply with the rights of access and data portability, as they have distributed ledger technology built in. This section presents three different approaches toward possible GDPR compliance using the Ethereum Blockchain and its smart contracts. These are:

1 **DApps with purely decentralized technologies:** In purely decentralized applications, achieving full GDPR compliance is, as of this writing, not possible, as most DApps use consent as their lawful basis for processing. The individual's right to erasure is the culprit here, as immutable data in the Ethereum blockchain cannot be deleted. However, there are two small special cases when purely decentralized apps might actually comply with the regulation. These are when the lawful basis for processing personal data is either in the public interest or a legal obligation. In these rare cases, the right to erasure does not apply, and thus, GDPR compliance can be achieved.

2 **DApps with a mixture of centralized and decentralized technologies:** DApps that use both centralized and decentralized technologies (such as the authors' case study) can be fully GDPR compliant. To achieve this, the solution is twofold: first, a thorough analysis must be performed to determine what parts of the whole system contain mutable data such as user information (email, home address or phone number). This will then be developed using centralized solutions with data and a matching hash stored in one or more databases. Second, Ethereum smart contracts can be developed as usual, with other data stored in them, in addition to the same hash of the centralized systems as a link between them. With this, in the event data is deleted in the centralized system, the hash linking both systems (centralized and decentralized with smart contracts) is broken. Therefore, this data cannot be tied directly to a specific individual, which is outside of the scope of the GDPR, as seen in Figure 15.1.

3 **Standard centralized applications with smart contracts:** Centralized software applications may not need to fully convert to decentralization. They sometimes may need to adopt only the distributed ledger technology in the Ethereum blockchain to record, for example, user

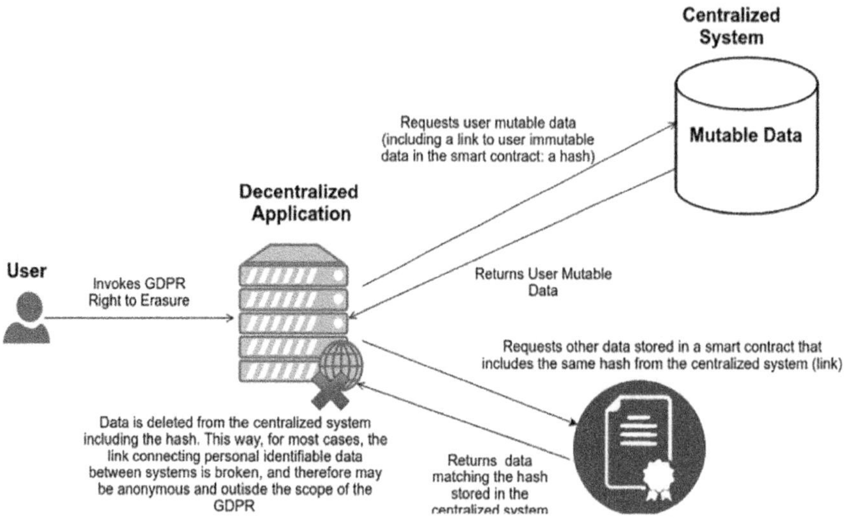

Figure 15.1 GDPR right to erasure; generic compliance for DApps

transactions. GDPR compliance, in this case, is straightforward: these software applications record the Ethereum address of their users in a centralized database. They then can link transactions to users. In the event users request their accounts to be deleted, the transactions are still openly available, albeit not tied to any specific individual and therefore outside of the scope of the GDPR.

GDPR compliance guideline for Ethereum DApps

As already discussed, GDPR compliance poses a significant challenge for decentralized applications. The fines for noncompliance are astronomically high, which ensures organizations are committed to obeying it. In this section, the authors provide a simple guideline to comply, in the best manner possible, with this regulation, despite key issues regarding the design of blockchains (including Ethereum) such as immutability:

1 Identify the lawful basis for processing personal data. Most of them give individuals the right to erasure, which by default is incompatible with the immutable nature of blockchains. However, as previously stated, this right does not apply if the lawful basis is only to comply with legal obligations or public tasks.

2 If consent is the lawful basis, analyze the parts of the software application that contain mutable data and ensure it is stored in centralized systems; store everything else in one or more smart contracts.
3 In one or more smart contracts, store a hash that links a centralized part with a decentralized component, such as Ethereum. In other words, most DApps today should have a centralized component, such as traditional databases, to store mutable data, combined with the power of decentralized technologies such as Ethereum and its smart contracts to store immutable data.
4 If the user invokes the right to be forgotten, delete his mutable data in the centralized system. This way, the link (hash) between the centralized and decentralized systems is broken and data in the latter might still be accessible, although it cannot be linked to a specific individual, which is outside of the scope of the GDPR, as shown in Figure 15.1.
5 In some cases, personal identifiable information is stored in one or more smart contracts. To comply with the GDPR, one possible approach is to encrypt this personal data. The authors' case study aims to understand whether this is feasible.

Case study: Dfiles

In the first half of this chapter, the GDPR was briefly discussed in addition to generic steps for any DApp to potentially comply with this regulation.

In this section, the authors present a case study – DFiles – with the aim of answering two important questions:

- Can DApps be fully compliant with the GDPR?
- Is it feasible to protect user data by encrypting it in Ethereum (Homestead)?

DFiles is an open-source decentralized application[1] developed with decentralized technologies such as the IPFS and Ethereum smart contracts, plus a centralized component for user authentication. Further, DFiles also aims to adhere to blockchain software engineering by going through each software development phase:

- Requirement gathering and analysis;
- Design;
- Implementation; and
- Testing.

Moreover, this section also thoroughly discusses the core engine behind DFiles, its Ethereum smart contract, from the code itself, to design patterns adopted, to security and testing.

The authors also briefly demonstrate the core functionality regarding DFiles, where a statistical analysis is performed comparing two versions of the same DApp: one where user-uploaded files are encrypted and another where they are not. The goal is to understand if encryption is feasible (and thus achieving user data protection and privacy) by comparing the total transaction cost and elapsed upload time for the same files in each version. This analysis is paramount to fully understand if the aforementioned (albeit generic) GDPR compliance plan for DApps is feasible, with special attention to the right to erasure.

Finally, the conclusions of this case study are presented.

Blockchain software engineering

In standard, centralized software applications, there are several phases to properly develop software applications: the software development life cycle. In decentralized applications, however, there must be special attention to develop secure smart contracts with a special emphasis on testing.

The first major phase is *requirement gathering and analysis*, where typically the *functional requirements* of a system are drafted. The most important ones in DFiles are:

1. The DApp must be able to communicate with the Ethereum Blockchain via the user's MetaMask (Consensys, 2018b) Google Chrome/Firefox extension;
2. Encrypt user files before their upload process to the IPFS;
3. Upload user files to the IPFS;
4. Register each user-uploaded IPFS file hash in an Ethereum transaction (smart contract);
5. List all the user-uploaded files to IPFS;
6. Download and decrypt all the user's uploaded files.

The second phase is *design*, where the overall system architecture is defined. The DFiles system architecture is shown in Figure 15.2.

The DFiles DApp has two main components:

- **Front end:** Responsible for displaying data to the user with Web3JS.
- **Back end:** Interacts with the front end to fetch business logic from multiple sources:
  - User authentication with a centralized system (NodeJS/Express) and a database. Here, a pair of private/public keys is generated to encrypt the user's files.
  - IPFS for decentralized file storage.
  - Ethereum smart contract that stores user upload file hashes.
- **Full stack:** The Truffle framework[2] was used as a bridge between the front end and back end with the Web3JS API.[3]

The DApp is connected to a local IPFS node, which simulates the connection to the IPFS network. Similarly, DFiles is also attached to a MetaMask private

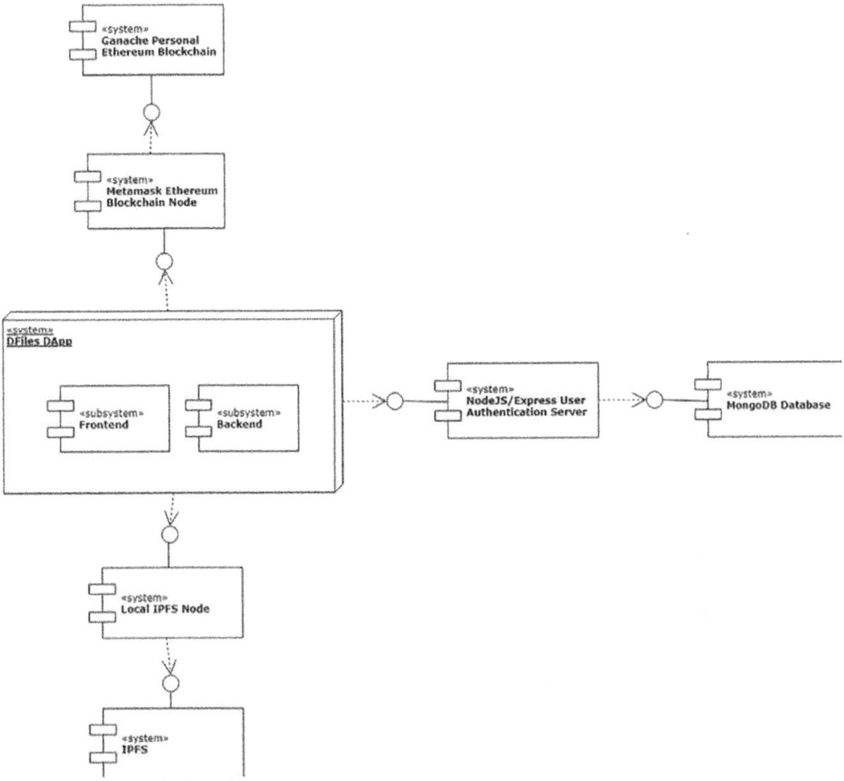

Figure 15.2 DFiles system architecture

Ethereum node that is connected to a private version of the Ethereum Blockchain (via MetaMask's Google Chrome/Firefox extension), where one can deploy smart contracts, develop applications and run tests: Ganache (Consensys, 2018a).

The last two phases are *implementation*, where the actual coding is taken place, and *testing*. All these phases will become clear when the DFiles core smart contract is detailed, with special focus on the latter. There is also *deployment*, which is discussed in section "Limitations and Future Work".

The core smart contract

Developing Ethereum smart contracts requires a substantial amount of design and testing to ensure they are bug free, as they cannot be changed once deployed. In DFiles, the core smart contract, **Files.sol**, was developed using the popular Ethereum programming language Solidity and Web3JS for interacting with it in the front end.

```
// A structure that contains information about the user's files
struct File {
string name; // the file's name
string extension; // the file's extension
uint32 size; // the file's size
string hash; //the IPFS file hash
string timestamp; // the transaction timestamp is stored in the JavaScript and is in the Unix Epoch time;
string ethereumAccount; // the user's Ethereum Address that uploaded the file
}
//The files belonging to each user (or address)
mapping(address => File[]) private userFiles;
```

Code Extract 15.1 Files.sol smart contract data structures

From the multiple readily available Solidity design patterns, only the Ownable one was chosen, due to the simplicity of the developed smart contract. Its implementation was provided by OpenZeppelin.[4] The code was inherited from the Files.sol smart contract. Then the overall data structures to use was decided on – for the user files, a mapping to link the user's Ethereum address to a File structure, **userFiles**. This structure stores data about a file – Code Extract 15.1.

A function was then developed to add files to the userFiles mapping, as displayed in Code Extract 15.2.

Finally, two read-only functions were created to return the index of a given file and to return the mapping's length. These allow one to save a substantial amount of gas by iterating the mapping via Web3JS in the front end.

The complete code of the Files.sol source code is available at Bitbucket.[5]

One of the final phases in BOSE is testing, especially when regarding smart contracts. The truffle framework provides a nice suite for unit testing.[6] The following tests were performed:

- Creating a new file object with the same properties as the smart contract's structure, inserting it in the test blockchain, fetching the inserted data and then comparing it to the original file object. If it is the same, then the test passes. Otherwise, it fails.
- Creating a new file object, inserting it the test blockchain and attempting to loop through an invalid file index (nonexistent file). If the loop fails, there are no files at that index, and therefore the test passes.

Short presentation

In this section, the core functionality of the DFiles DApp is presented. Furthermore, how files' encryption and the decryption of files work is also explained.

First and foremost, users register an account and sign in (this is handled via the NodeJS/Express centralized server). Then they are taken to the Upload Files page to select which file to upload, as shown in Figure 15.3.

```
/// @notice This function inserts information of a file to the
userFiles array: name, size, extension in addition to a timestamp and
the IPFS file hash
/// @param _name file name
/// @param _hash IPFS file hash
/// @param _extension file extension
/// @param _size file size
/// @param _timestamp a timestamp
/// @param _ethereumAccount the user Ethereum account calling this con-
tract
function addFile(string _name, string _hash, string _extension, uint32
_size, string _timestamp, string _ethereumAccount)
public {
require(_size>0 && _size<=4294967295, "Invalid file size");
File memory file = File(_name, _extension, _size, _hash,_timestamp,
_ethereumAccount);
userFiles[msg.sender].push(file);
}
```

Code Extract 15.2 Adding file information in the Files.sol smart contract

Figure 15.3 DFiles file upload example

Once the "Upload File" button is clicked, the file is encrypted with the crypto-js API,[7] and the user's private key is stored in the centralized server. The user must then accept a transaction that uses the smart contract and stores several details about the file in the local Ethereum Blockchain (Ganache), as indicated in Figure 15.4.

The gas fee and total transaction cost depend on the gas price (in GWEI) and the predefined gas limit (this is important for the evaluation section). The file is then sent to a local centralized IPFS node, which returns a hash containing the encrypted file. After this, the user is presented with a successful message for its URL, as seen in Figure 15.5.

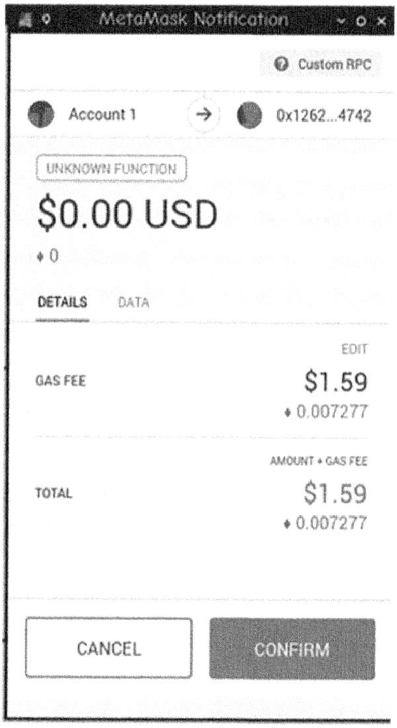

Figure 15.4 Ethereum MetaMask transaction prompt

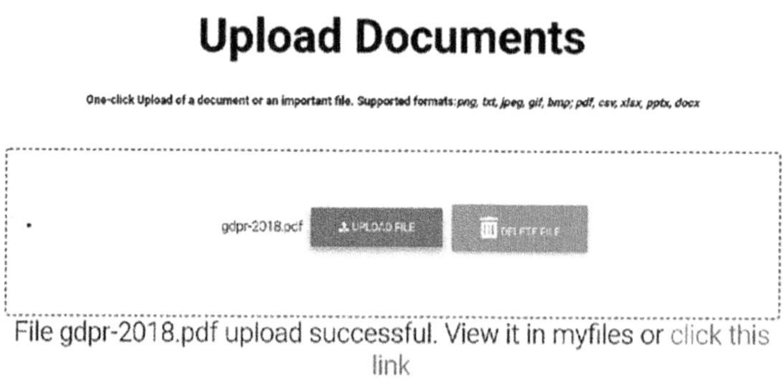

Figure 15.5 Document uploaded successfully message

Upon clicking the link, the user is presented with the file, but in encrypted form (Figure 15.6).

Finally, details of his files can be browsed, although these are not encrypted (Figure 15.7).

Once the user presses "Decrypt and download", the selected file is decrypted and downloaded. When the user invokes the GDPR right to erasure, all of his details, including the private key used to encrypt his files, are deleted. The files are still essentially in the IPFS node, although encrypted. Since they are inaccessible, they can be considered as the same as being deleted. This way, the

Figure 15.6 File encryption example

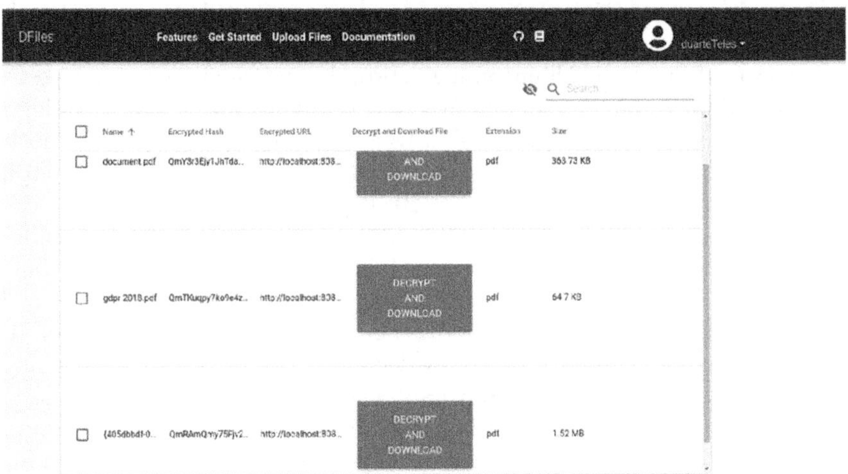

Figure 15.7 User uploaded files list

problem of immutability is solved. In the next section, a statistical analysis is performed to understand if this approach is feasible or not.

Evaluation

As previously discussed, the GDPR poses a significant challenge toward assuring DApps are compliant with it, mainly due to the right to be forgotten. In this section, a statistical analysis is performed to understand whether encrypting personal data (or files) is feasible or not before sending them to the IPFS node. This way, encrypted files persist for as long as the node serves them, but their content is still inaccessible to third parties, on par with file deletion.

In Ethereum, there is the concept of "gas":

> the execution fee that senders of transactions need to pay for every operation made on an Ethereum blockchain. The name gas is inspired by the view that this fee acts as cryptofuel, driving the motion of smart contracts. Gas is purchased for ether from the miners that execute the code.
>
> (Ethereum Foundation, 2016)

There are four important aspects related to gas:

- **Gas limit:** the maximum amount of gas to be paid in a transaction;
- **Gas used by transaction:** total gas that is consumed by the transaction;
- **Gas price:** price (in Ether) of one unit of gas specified in the transaction; and
- **Total transaction cost:** gas used * gas price.

Two versions of the DFiles DApp were developed: one without user authentication and file encryption, and another with both user authentication and file encryption/decryption. All upcoming statistical data is available at Bitbucket.[8]

First and foremost, 100 random files were selected with various extensions: .pdf, .docx, .xlsx and .pptx, although it was not possible to use them all due to hardware limitations. They were then divided into four different groups: small (1 KB–1 MB), medium (1 MB–20 MB), large (20 MB–200 MB) and extra large (200 MB–2 GB). In addition to this, for the same files and both versions of DFiles, the elapsed time from when the user clicks the "upload file" button, the file gets sent to the local IPFS node (encrypted or unencrypted) and the user clicks the button to accept the transaction is measured in addition to the total transaction cost in Ether (provided by MetaMask; it varies depending on the gas limit and gas price). Appendix A shows some of this collected data.

However, due to hardware limitations with file encryption, only files up to 14.2 MB were considered for the following statistical analysis. The total transaction cost and upload elapsed times were still recorded for comparison in the overall conclusion between files with and without encryption.

Small files

Table 15.2 shows a summary of the descriptive statistics for small unencrypted and encrypted files as well as the test results for their comparison. The complete data table is available in Appendix C.

- **Amount + gas fee (total):** The distributions are right-skewed for both unencrypted and encrypted files, i.e., most files exhibit small values (Fisher's skewness coefficient is positive in both file groups). The average amount is 0.0004024 ETH and 0.0003885 ETH for unencrypted and encrypted files respectively. The minimum value is 0.0003750 ETH and 0.0003640 ETH, respectively; the first quartile is 0.0003760 ETH and 0.0003640 ETH, respectively; the median is 0.0003770 ETH and 0.0003650 ETH, respectively; the third quartile is 0.0004380 ETH and 0.0004260 ETH, respectively; and the maximum is 0.0004720 ETH and 0.0004600 ETH, respectively. Therefore, it can be concluded that files with small values are predominant in both groups. Such concentration leads to very small variability, as shown by the coefficient of variation (8.4 percent and 8.5 percent, respectively).

In order to compare the distributions of both groups, the two samples were first tested for normality with the Shapiro-Wilk test (5 percent significance level). Normality is strongly rejected in both groups (p-value < 0.001). Therefore, a comparison of both samples was based on the Wilcoxon test (paired samples)

Table 15.2 Descriptive statistics and comparison test for small files

Small files		
Amount + gas fee (total) (ETH)		
	Unencrypted	*Encrypted*
Minimum	0.0003750	0.0003640
Maximum	0.0004720	0.0004600
Mean	0.0004024	0.0003885
Median	0.0003770	0.0003650
Wilcoxon test *p*-value	0.007	
Uploaded elapsed time (seconds)		
	Unencrypted	*Encrypted*
Minimum	2	3
Maximum	5	5
Mean	3.6	4.3
Median	4	4
Wilcoxon test *p*-value	0.001	
Size (MB)		
Minimum	0.01005	
Maximum	0.98400	
Mean	0.21550	
Median	0.06000	

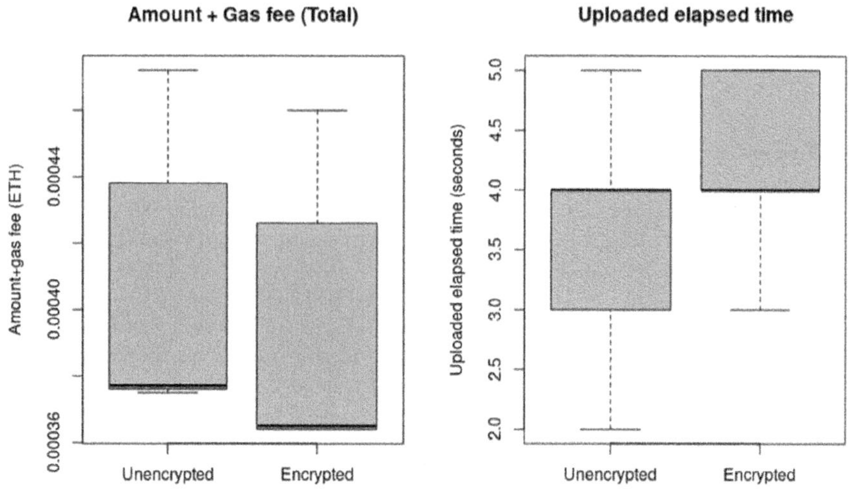

Figure 15.8 Boxplots for small files

whose *p*-value is 0.007. Therefore, the average amount + gas cost is larger for unencrypted files. Figure 15.8 clearly shows that conclusion.

- **Uploaded elapsed time:** The distributions are slightly left-skewed for both unencrypted and encrypted files, i.e., most files exhibit moderate and large times (Fisher's skewness coefficient is negative in both file groups). The average time is 3.6 seconds and 4.3 seconds for unencrypted and encrypted files respectively. The minimum value is 2 seconds and 3 seconds respectively, the first quartile is 3 seconds and 4 seconds respectively, the median is 4 seconds for both groups, the third quartile is 4 seconds and 5 seconds respectively and the maximum is 5 seconds for both groups. Therefore, it can be concluded that files with moderate and large times are predominant in both groups. Such concentration leads to a small variability as shown by the coefficient of variation (25.7 percent and 15.8 percent respectively).
- The results of the Shapiro-Wilk test show that normality is strongly rejected in both groups (p-value of 0.003 and 0.0001 respectively). The Wilcoxon test has a p-value of 0.001 and it can be concluded that time is larger for encrypted files. Figure 15.8 clearly shows that conclusion.

Medium files

Table 15.3 shows a summary of the descriptive statistics for medium unencrypted and encrypted files as well as the test results for their comparison. The complete data table is available in Appendix D.

Table 15.3 Descriptive statistics and comparison test for medium files

Medium files		
Amount + gas fee (total) (ETH)		
	Unencrypted	*Encrypted*
Minimum	0.0003750	0.0003630
Maximum	0.0004400	0.0004280
Mean	0.0004087	0.0003938
Median	0.0004225	0.0003805
Wilcoxon test *p*-value	0.0002	
Uploaded elapsed time (seconds)		
	Unencrypted	*Encrypted*
Minimum	5	6
Maximum	9	69
Mean	6.3	29.6
Median	6	19
Wilcoxon test *p*-value	0.0002	
Size (MB)		
Minimum	1.2	
Maximum	14.2	
Mean	6.5	
Median	5	
3rd quartile	12	

- **Amount + gas fee (total):** Most unencrypted and encrypted files are either large or small. The average amount is 0.0004087 ETH and 0.0003938 ETH for unencrypted and encrypted files, respectively. The minimum value is 0.0003750 ETH and 0.0003630 ETH, respectively; the first quartile is 0.0003753 ETH and 0.0003640 ETH, respectively; the median is 0.0004225 ETH and 0.0003805 ETH, respectively; the third quartile is 0.0004380 ETH and 0.0004268 ETH, respectively; and the maximum is 0.0004400 ETH and 0.0004280 ETH, respectively. Variability is very small as shown by the coefficient of variation (7.7 percent and 7.9 percent, respectively).
- The results of the Shapiro-Wilk test show that normality is strongly rejected in both groups (p-value < 0.001). The Wilcoxon test has a p-value of 0.0002 and it can be concluded that the average amount is larger for unencrypted files. Figure 15.9 shows that conclusion.
- **Uploaded elapsed time:** The distributions are right-skewed for both unencrypted and encrypted files, i.e., most files exhibit small and moderate times (Fisher's skewness coefficient is positive in both file groups). The average time is 6.3 seconds and 29.6 seconds for unencrypted

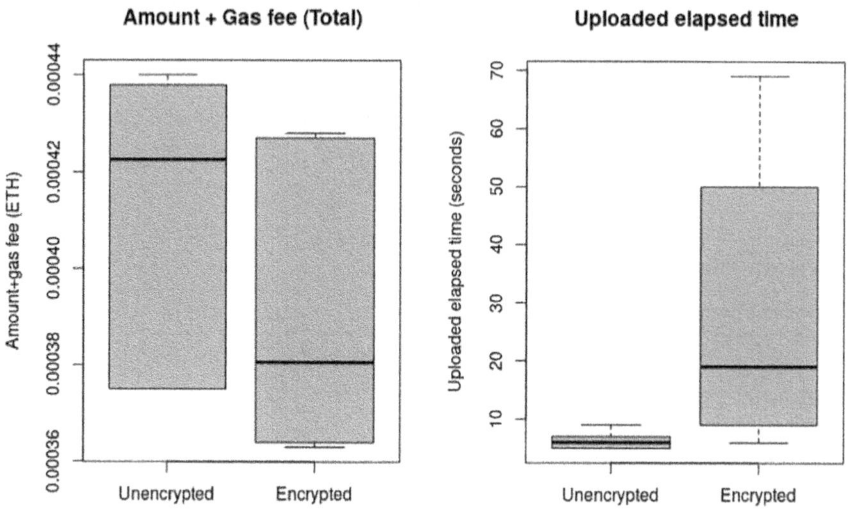

Figure 15.9 Boxplots for medium files

and encrypted files, respectively. The minimum value is 5 seconds and 6 seconds, respectively; the first quartile is 6 seconds and 10 seconds, respectively; the median is 6 seconds and 19 seconds, respectively; the third quartile is 7 seconds and 50 seconds, respectively; and the maximum is 9 seconds and 69 seconds, respectively. Therefore, it can be concluded that files with small and moderate times are predominant in both groups. However, variability is small for unencrypted files and is large for encrypted files, as shown by the coefficient of variation (18.8 percent and 82.2 percent, respectively).

- The results of the Shapiro-Wilk test show that normality is strongly rejected in both groups (p-value of 0.019 and 0.002, respectively). The Wilcoxon test has a p-value of 0.0002 and we conclude that the average time is larger for encrypted files. Figure 15.9 clearly shows that conclusion.
- **Size:** The distribution is right-skewed, i.e., most files exhibit small and moderate sizes (Fisher's skewness coefficient is positive). The average size is 6.5 MB. The minimum size is 1.2 MB, the first quartile is 3 MB, the median is 5 MB, the third quartile is 12 MB and the maximum is 14.2 MB. Therefore, it can be concluded that files with small and moderate sizes are predominant, but some files have a much larger size which leads to high variability, as shown by the coefficient of variation (72.3 percent).

Evaluation conclusion

The statistical analysis performed on small to medium files up to 14.2 MB shows the average total transaction cost is slightly larger in unencrypted files.

However, as expected, the average upload time was bigger for encrypted files. As for medium ones, the average total transaction cost is again slightly larger for unencrypted files, and the average upload time is larger in encrypted files.

In addition to this, if one compares the last recorded values for encrypted and unencrypted values from all categories (small, medium, large and extra large) in Appendices A and B, it clearly demonstrates that the last two file encryption times for files up to 800 MB are less than the upload elapsed time for encrypted files up to 14.2 MB.

The conclusion is that encrypting files to comply with the right to erasure is a valuable option for small to medium files up to 14.2 MB. From there, without considering hardware encryption limitations, upload times tend to grow exponentially. For this reason, encrypting medium to extra-large files is not feasible as of late 2018.

However, note that encrypting all files in DFiles could have not been necessary, as some would only contain data that cannot be tied to a specific individual – therefore not being considered personal data. The user could have selected an option whether or not to encrypt his files, whether or not they contain personal data. The problem with this is that users are not always truthful, and in this way they might upload sensitive files – files containing personal data about someone – which would be available out in the open and inside the scope of the GDPR. They could also resort to extortion – as data in DFiles is immutable – by uploading on purpose personal data about someone and then demanding money in exchange for their silence in telling the authorities responsible for applying fines for GDPR noncompliance. Therefore, file encryption, although time consuming and limited in the IPFS and Ethereum, is necessary to prevent these cases and to avoid communicating possible data breaches to the appropriate GDPR authorities.

Blockchain technology in general, as already discussed, has a very distinct and important characteristic: immutability. This ensures it is attractive to several major companies to combat fraud and have an unmodifiable record of transactions.

Therefore, Ethereum and the IPFS must advance to allow better privacy techniques unless the European Union drafts and passes laws that exempt DApps from parts of the GDPR that are highly difficult to comply with, such as the right to erasure.

Limitations and future work

Ethereum is clearly an exciting and evolving technology. However, there are several limitations that had a major impact on the authors' work. For instance, the severe gas cost of having smart contracts with loops discouraged its adoption in the DFiles core smart contract. Moreover, the lack of support for JSON objects is also a major aspect to take into consideration, as smart contracts in Solidity could potentially be more efficient if, instead of using a structure, a standard JSON object was used. On top of this, IPFS clearly has a long way to go for DApps to become mainstream. For starters, it has a growing problem of storing very large files, as demonstrated by DFiles. If encryption is required, then the maximum file size possible is much lower. It was proved that, due to hardware limitations and the current state of both Ethereum and IPFS, encryption was only possible for small to medium files. Ethereum, IPFS and data protection techniques will evolve significantly in the future, which will theoretically allow for either better encryption techniques or other privacy ones, thus shining a bright light for future DApps that require data privacy and protection.

As previously discussed, DFiles aims to demonstrate whether by encrypting personal data, GDPR compliance can be achieved. However, there are other problems associated with this approach, such as weak encryption algorithms that previously have proven to be highly secure. Examples of these include the MD5 and SHA1 ones (The Open Web Application Security Project (OWASP), 2018). For this reason, there is a slight possibility that the algorithms used in the most popular blockchains become obsolete for short periods of time – where data can be easily decrypted – before being replace by another, more secure one.

In addition to this, quantum computing could very soon become a reality, and for a substantial period of time, all data encrypted in most blockchains such as Ethereum as well as all the encrypted files stored in the IPFS via the DFiles DApp could be easily decrypted. This is, in the authors' opinion, the biggest threat to blockchain technology in the not-so-distant future.

As for future work in DFiles, instead of using a local IPFS node, the Infura[9] node could be used. This brings several advantages, as hardware limitations are minimized, but it brings a new set of problems, such as that files stored in the Infura IPFS node have no incentive to be kept for long.

Another aspect to improve is to deploy the DFiles smart contract to a test network such as Rinkeby and update the DFiles DApp to use this deployed smart contract instead of the local Ganache private Ethereum Blockchain. An early deployment has been done, but further testing is required. The smart contract is available in the Rinkeby test network.[10]

In short, in this section, the limitations of both IPFS and Ethereum were discussed, including DFiles' future work. However, there are some general conclusions that can be taken:

- IPFS file encryption is in its infancy; therefore, there are significant hardware and technology limitations preventing its mass adoption.
- Ethereum is a public ledger, and therefore it provides little to no privacy. The only possible approach is to encrypt data using other decentralized technologies such as the IPFS. Ethereum also has a substantial level of limitations – such as no JSON support and the discouragement of some computing loop instructions (for, while, for instance) due to high total transaction costs – that impact its worldwide adoption.

- Encrypting personal data for GDPR compliance purposes is severely limited and possibly discouraged. Both the IPFS and Ethereum should be considered special cases of the GDPR to avoid issues with data encryption.

Conclusion

In this chapter, first the most important GDPR concepts, in addition to the several lawful bases for processing personal data and the several individual rights, were presented. Its right to erasure interferes with blockchain immutability. On top of this, three scenarios were discussed concerning whether this right can or cannot be complied with, followed by a GDPR compliance guideline for Ethereum DApps.

To test this guideline, a case study was developed: DFiles. It is an Ethereum DApp built with a mixture of centralized and decentralized technologies such as Ethereum and IPFS. Its main objectives are to understand whether Ethereum (Homestead) DApps can comply with this regulation and if protecting personal data by encrypting it is feasible or not.

DFiles also adheres to the principles of blockchain software engineering by following the software development life cycle, albeit adapted for DApps. Its core smart contract is also explained, from the design patterns implemented to the main data structures and functions, in addition to a short presentation of its core features. In short, DFiles allows a user to upload and view his submitted files.

A statistical analysis to assert the feasibility of encryption in compliance with the right to erasure was then performed, albeit only for some files because of hardware limitations. Two variants of the DApp were created: one with file encryption and one without. Uploaded files were divided into four categories: small (1 KB–1 MB), medium (1 MB–20 MB), large (20 MB–200 MB) and extra large (200 MB–2 GB).

The total transaction cost in Ether plus the total elapsed time between the user clicking the upload button and it being uploaded were then measured in both versions. Its conclusions are then presented. In short, complying with the GDPR and its right to erasure is only feasible for encrypted files up to 14.2 MB.

Finally, the limitations of the case study and its future work were explained.

Notes

1 Accessed from https://bitbucket.org/duarte_1110199/dfiles-ethereum-dapp/src/master/.
2 Accessed from https://truffleframework.com/.
3 Accessed from https://github.com/ethereum/wiki/wiki/JavaScript-API.
4 Accessed from https://github.com/OpenZeppelin/openzeppelin-solidity
5 https://bitbucket.org/duarte_1110199/dfiles-ethereum-dapp/src/master/contracts/Files.sol.
6 Accessed from https://truffleframework.com/docs/truffle/testing/writing-tests-in-javascript.

7 Accessed from https://github.com/brix/crypto-js.
8 Accessed from https://bitbucket.org/duarte_1110199/dfiles-r-statistical-data/src/master/.
9 Accessed from https://infura.io/.
10 Accessed from https://rinkeby.etherscan.io/address/0x09C5b627354eF29c3B6507aAB a7386Ce240Fff9C.

References

Bitcoin Project. (2018). *Bitcoin – Open source p2p money*. Retrieved from https://bitcoin.org/en/

Consensys. (2018a). *Ganache*. Retrieved from https://truffleframework.com/docs/ganache/overview

Consensys. (2018b). *Metamask*. Retrieved from http://metamask.io/

Destefanis, G., Marchesi, M., Ortu, M., Tonelli, R., Bracciali, A., and Hierons, R. 2018. *Smart contracts vulnerabilities: A call for blockchain software engineering? Blockchain oriented software engineering (IWBOSE)*, International Workshop. Campobasso: IEEE.

Ethereum Foundation. (2014). *Solidity, the contract-oriented programming language*. Retrieved from https://github.com/ethereum/solidity

Ethereum Foundation. (2016). *Account types, gas, and transactions*. Retrieved from www.ethdocs.org/en/latest/contracts-and-transactions/account-types-gas-and-transactions.html

Ethereum Foundation. (2018). *Ethereum blockchain app platform*. Retrieved from www.ethereum.org/

EU GDPR Compliant. (2018). *What is a data subject*? Retrieved from https://eugdprcompliant.com/what-is-data-subject/

European Data Protection Supervisor. (2018). *The history of the general data protection regulation*. Retrieved from https://edps.europa.eu/data-protection/data-protection/legislation/history-general-data-protection-regulation_en

European Union. (2016). Regulation (EU) 2016/679 of the European Parliament and of the council of 27 April 2016 on the protection of natural persons with regard to the processing of personal data and on the free movement of such data. *Official Journal of the European Union*, 1–88.

Falkon, S. (2017, December 24). *The story of the DAO – Its history and consequences*. Retrieved from https://medium.com/swlh/the-story-of-the-dao-its-history-and-consequences-71e6a8a551ee

ICO. (2018, August 2). *Guide to the general data protection regulation (GDPR)*. Retrieved from https://ico.org.uk/media/for-organisations/guide-to-the-general-data-protection-regulation-gdpr-1-0.pdf

Parity Technologies. (2017, July 20). *The multi-sig hack: A postmortem*. Retrieved from https://paritytech.io/the-multi-sig-hack-a-postmortem/

Petrov, S. (2017, November 7). *Another parity wallet hack explained*. Retrieved from https://medium.com/@Pr0Ger/another-parity-wallet-hack-explained-847ca46a2e1c

Protocol Labs. (2018). *IPFS is the distributed web*. Retrieved from https://ipfs.io/

Szabo, N. (1996). *Smart contracts: Building blocks for digital markets*. Retrieved from www.fon.hum.uva.nl/rob/Courses/InformationInSpeech/CDROM/Literature/LOTwinterschool2006/szabo.best.vwh.net/smart_contracts_2.html

Appendix A

DFiles encrypted uploaded files statistical data

Table 15.4 Small files (1 KB–1 MB)

Gas fee (ETH)	*Gas fee (USD)*	*Amount + gas fee (total) (ETH)*	*Amount + gas fee (total) (USD)*	*Size (MB)*	*Uploaded elapsed time (seconds)*
0.000426	0.09	0.000426	0.09	0.013	5
0.000426	0.09	0.000426	0.09	0.0136	3
0.000428	0.09	0.000428	0.09	0.0137	3
0.000364	0.08	0.000364	0.08	0.0155	4
0.000428	0.09	0.000428	0.09	0.0162	4
0.000364	0.08	0.000364	0.08	0.0192	4
0.000364	0.08	0.000364	0.08	0.01005	4
0.000364	0.08	0.000364	0.08	0.02601	5
0.000427	0.09	0.000427	0.09	0.027	4
0.000365	0.08	0.000365	0.08	0.03004	4
0.000427	0.09	0.000427	0.09	0.04001	4
0.000365	0.08	0.000365	0.08	0.0591	4
0.000365	0.08	0.000365	0.08	0.06	3
0.000365	0.08	0.000365	0.08	0.067	4
0.00046	0.1	0.00046	0.1	0.0827	4
0.000426	0.09	0.000426	0.09	0.0842	5
0.000365	0.08	0.000365	0.08	0.1265	4
0.000364	0.08	0.000364	0.08	0.1848	4
0.000366	0.08	0.000366	0.08	0.193	5
0.000365	0.08	0.000365	0.08	0.2491	5
0.000366	0.08	0.000366	0.08	0.6608	5
0.000429	0.09	0.000429	0.09	0.7325	5
0.000365	0.08	0.000365	0.08	0.7349	5
0.000364	0.08	0.000364	0.08	0.9445	5
0.000364	0.08	0.000364	0.08	0.984	5

Table 15.5 Medium files (1 MB–20 MB)

Gas fee (ETH)	*Gas fee (USD)*	*Amount + gas fee (total) (ETH)*	*Amount + gas fee (total) (USD)*	*Size (MB)*	*Uploaded elapsed time (seconds)*
0.000365	0.08	0.000365	0.08	1.2	6
0.000427	0.09	0.000427	0.09	1.3	7
0.000426	0.09	0.000426	0.09	1.5	7
0.000365	0.08	0.000365	0.08	1.7	8
0.000426	0.09	0.000426	0.09	2.2	9
0.000428	0.09	0.000428	0.09	2.3	11
0.000364	0.08	0.000364	0.08	3.9	16
0.000364	0.08	0.000364	0.08	4.5	17
0.000426	0.09	0.000426	0.09	4.8	21
0.000363	0.08	0.000363	0.08	4.8	14
0.000427	0.09	0.000427	0.09	6.7	22
0.000427	0.09	0.000427	0.09	8	26
0.000365	0.08	0.000365	0.08	10.3	50
0.000428	0.09	0.000428	0.09	11.7	49
0.000364	0.08	0.000364	0.08	12	69
0.000364	0.08	0.000364	0.08	12.2	65
0.000364	0.08	0.000364	0.08	13.9	69
0.000396	0.08	0.000396	0.08	14.2	66

Appendix B

DFiles unencrypted uploaded files statistical data

Table 15.6 Small files (1 KB–1 MB)

Gas fee (ETH)	*Gas fee (USD)*	*Amount + gas fee (total) (ETH)*	*Amount + gas fee (total) (USD)*	*Size (MB)*	*Uploaded elapsed time (seconds)*
0.00044	0.1	0.00044	0.1	0.013	3
0.000438	0.1	0.000438	0.1	0.0136	3
0.00044	0.1	0.00044	0.1	0.0137	2
0.000375	0.08	0.000375	0.08	0.0155	2
0.000439	0.1	0.000439	0.1	0.0162	2
0.000375	0.08	0.000375	0.08	0.0192	3
0.000375	0.08	0.000375	0.08	0.01005	2
0.000375	0.08	0.000375	0.08	0.02601	4
0.000438	0.1	0.000438	0.1	0.027	3
0.000377	0.08	0.000377	0.08	0.03004	4
0.000438	0.1	0.000438	0.1	0.04001	3
0.000376	0.08	0.000376	0.08	0.0591	4
0.000376	0.08	0.000376	0.08	0.06	3
0.000472	0.11	0.000472	0.11	0.067	4
0.000438	0.1	0.000438	0.1	0.0827	4
0.000376	0.08	0.000376	0.08	0.0842	4
0.000375	0.08	0.000375	0.08	0.1265	5
0.000377	0.08	0.000377	0.08	0.1848	4
0.000376	0.08	0.000376	0.08	0.193	4
0.000377	0.08	0.000377	0.08	0.2491	4
0.000441	0.1	0.000441	0.1	0.6608	4
0.000376	0.08	0.000376	0.08	0.7325	4
0.000375	0.08	0.000375	0.08	0.7349	4
0.000376	0.08	0.000376	0.08	0.9445	5
0.000439	0.1	0.000439	0.1	0.984	5

Table 15.7 Medium files (1 MB–20MB)

Gas fee (ETH)	*Gas fee (USD)*	*Amount + gas fee (total) (ETH)*	*Amount + gas fee (total) (USD)*	*Size (MB)*	*Uploaded elapsed time (seconds)*
0.000376	0.08	0.000376	0.08	1.2	5
0.000438	0.1	0.000438	0.1	1.3	5
0.000438	0.1	0.000438	0.1	1.5	5
0.000376	0.08	0.000376	0.08	1.7	5
0.000438	0.1	0.000438	0.1	2.2	5
0.000438	0.1	0.000438	0.1	2.3	6
0.00044	0.1	0.00044	0.1	3.9	6
0.000375	0.08	0.000375	0.08	4.5	6
0.000438	0.1	0.000438	0.1	4.8	6
0.000375	0.08	0.000375	0.08	4.8	6
0.000438	0.1	0.000438	0.1	6.7	6
0.000439	0.1	0.000439	0.1	8	9
0.000376	0.08	0.000376	0.08	10.3	7
0.000439	0.1	0.000439	0.1	11.7	7
0.000375	0.08	0.000375	0.08	12	6
0.000375	0.08	0.000375	0.08	12.2	8
0.000375	0.08	0.000375	0.08	13.9	8
0.000407	0.09	0.000407	0.09	14.2	7
0.000439	0.1	0.000439	0.1	15.2	8
0.000375	0.08	0.000375	0.08	16.1	6
0.000441	0.1	0.000441	0.1	16.4	8
0.000376	0.08	0.000376	0.08	18	9
0.00044	0.1	0.00044	0.1	18.8	8
0.000375	0.08	0.000375	0.08	18.9	6
0.000439	0.1	0.000439	0.1	18.9	10

Table 15.8 Large files (20MB–200MB)

Gas fee (ETH)	*Gas fee (USD)*	*Amount + gas fee (total) (ETH)*	*Amount + gas fee (total) (USD)*	*Size (MB)*	*Uploaded elapsed time (seconds)*
0.000439	0.1	0.000439	0.1	20.8	12
0.000438	0.1	0.000438	0.1	21.1	9
0.000375	0.08	0.000375	0.08	23.2	9
0.000407	0.09	0.000407	0.09	24.6	7
0.00044	0.1	0.00044	0.00044	26.5	7
0.00044	0.1	0.00044	0.1	26.8	13
0.000438	0.1	0.000438	0.1	29.6	11
0.000376	0.09	0.000376	0.09	33.8	10
0.000375	0.08	0.000375	0.08	37.6	11
0.000377	0.09	0.000377	0.09	37.8	9
0.000375	0.08	0.000375	0.08	44	13
0.000375	0.08	0.000375	0.08	50.2	13

0.000472	0.11	0.000472	0.11	52.9	17
0.000472	0.11	0.000472	0.11	55.8	19
0.000472	0.11	0.000472	0.11	66.8	18
0.000375	0.08	0.000375	0.08	67.5	17
0.000375	0.08	0.000375	0.08	74.9	13
0.000439	0.1	0.000439	0.1	75.4	20
0.000473	0.11	0.000473	0.11	87.7	12
0.000439	0.1	0.000439	0.1	101.9	14
0.000375	0.08	0.000375	0.08	129.9	5
0.000375	0.08	0.000375	0.08	167.9	5
0.000375	0.08	0.000375	0.08	178.8	5
0.000375	0.08	0.000375	0.08	179.2	8
0.000375	0.08	0.000375	0.08	185.7	9

Table 15.9 Extra-large files (200 MB–2 GB)

Gas fee (ETH)	*Gas fee (USD)*	*Amount + gas fee (total) (ETH)*	*Amount + gas fee (total) (USD)*	*Size (MB)*	*Uploaded elapsed time (seconds)*
0.000375	0.08	0.000375	0.08	231.1	9
0.000375	0.08	0.000375	0.08	321.6	6
0.000375	0.08	0.000375	0.08	339	10
0.000375	0.08	0.000375	0.08	395.7	11
0.000375	0.08	0.000375	0.08	448.3	11
0.000375	0.08	0.000375	0.08	475	13
0.000375	0.08	0.000375	0.08	504.8	15
0.000375	0.08	0.000375	0.08	528	24
0.00042	0.09	0.00042	0.09	548.9	25
0.00042	0.09	0.00042	0.09	657.2	28
0.00042	0.09	0.00042	0.09	732	54
0.00042	0.09	0.00042	0.09	898.4	107

Appendix C

Descriptive analysis and comparison small files

Table 15.10 Amount + gas fee (total) (ETH)

Descriptive measures	*Unencrypted*	*Encrypted*
Minimum	0.000375	0.000364
Maximum	0.000472	0.00046
Mean	0.0004024	0.0003885
1st quartile	0.000376	0.000364
Median	0.000377	0.000365
3rd quartile	0.000438	0.000426
Standard deviation	0.0000339	0.000033
Coefficient of variation	8.40%	8.50%
Skewness	0.51	0.68
Shapiro-Wilk test		
Test statistic	0.7	0.68
p-value	< 0.001	< 0.001
Wilcoxon test		
Test statistic	262	
p-value	0.007	

Table 15.11 Uploaded elapsed time (seconds)

Descriptive measures	*Unencrypted*	*Encrypted*
Minimum	2	3
Maximum	5	5
Mean	3.6	4.3
1st quartile	3	4
Median	4	4
3rd quartile	4	5
Standard deviation	0.92	0.68
Coefficient of variation	25.70%	15.80%
Skewness	−0.33	−0.36
Shapiro-Wilk test		
Test statistic	0.86	0.78
p-value	0.003	0.0001
Wilcoxon test		
Test statistic	6.5	
p-value	0.001	

Table 15.12 Size (MB)

Descriptive measures	
Minimum	0.01005
Maximum	0.984
Mean	0.2155
1st quartile	0.0192
Median	0.06
3rd quartile	0.193
Standard deviation	0.31577
Coefficient of variation	146.50%
Skewness	1.4

Appendix D

Descriptive analysis and comparison medium files

Table 15.13 Amount + gas fee (total) (ETH)

Descriptive measures	Unencrypted	Encrypted
Minimum	0.000375	0.000363
Maximum	0.00044	0.000428
Mean	0.0004087	0.0003938
1st quartile	0.0003753	0.000364
Median	0.0004225	0.0003805
3rd quartile	0.000438	0.0004268
Standard deviation	0.0000315	0.0000313
Coefficient of variation	7.70%	7.90%
Skewness	−0.1	0.1
Shapiro-Wilk test		
Test statistic	0.69	0.69
p-value	< 0.001	< 0.001
Wilcoxon test		
Test statistic	171	
p-value	0.0002	

Table 15.14 Uploaded elapsed time (seconds)

Descriptive measures	Unencrypted	Encrypted
Minimum	5	6
Maximum	9	69
Mean	6.3	29.6
1st quartile	6	10
Median	6	19
3rd quartile	7	50
Standard deviation	1.2	24.3
Coefficient of variation	18.80%	82.20%
Skewness	0.71	0.63
Shapiro-Wilk test		
Test statistic	0.87	0.81
p-value	0.019	0.002
Wilcoxon test		
Test statistic	0	
p-value	0.0002	

Table 15.15 Size (MB)

Descriptive measures	
Minimum	0.01005
Maximum	0.984
Mean	0.2155
1st quartile	0.0192
Median	0.06
3rd quartile	0.193
Standard deviation	0.31577
Coefficient of variation	146.50%
Skewness	1.4

Chapter 16

A hierarchical structure model of success factors for (blockchain-based) crowdfunding

Felix Hartmann, Xiaofeng Wang, and Maria Ilaria Lunesu

Introduction

Crowdfunding is an important fundraising mechanism for new ventures and innovative projects. It is the practice of raising funds from a large number of people, typically using online platforms such as Kickstarter or Republic. Blockchain-based crowdfunding, represented by the surge of initial coin offerings (ICOs) and security token offerings (STOs), becomes a new and alternative form of crowdfunding and today can be considered one of the few functioning applications based on the blockchain technology.

Blockchain-based crowdfunding is an emerging economic phenomenon and a state-of-the-art strategy to finance ventures. Compared to traditional funding models like initial public offerings (IPOs), venture capitals (VCs) and first generation crowdfunding, blockchain-based crowdfunding is still highly unregulated. Projects launching blockchain-based crowdfunding offer to the public a fraction of ownership (stake) in a new digital platform or network and/or its product or services in the form of tokens/coins on a blockchain. The stake (tokens/coins) could represent a utility, security, asset, commodity, currency or collectible. Another main distinction from other forms of early stage venture investments is the fast liquidity that cryptoassets can gain on online secondary markets (centralized/decentralized exchanges).

The number of blockchain-based crowdfunding campaigns has increased drastically in the last few years. At the beginning of 2018, more established companies were also starting to explore the new funding opportunity. However, there is a lack of understanding of how to design a successful blockchain-based crowdfunding campaign and how to validate potential projects as an investor, partially due to the nascent nature of the phenomenon. A good understanding of the success factors of such campaigns would enable new ventures or entrepreneurs to design their blockchain-based fundraising initiatives properly, which in turn will help potential investors to seek main signals and drivers of outstanding projects. Based on this observation, we asked the following research question in our study:

RQ: What are the success factors for blockchain-based crowdfunding campaigns, and how are they related to each other?

In this study, we focused on the success factors that are internal to a venture or a project, which are under the control of those who launch campaigns. External factors that are out of the control of individual campaigns, such as the reference token price during the campaign period, are out of the scope of our study.

To answer the research question, we have applied a mixed-method approach. The literature review of the publications on the success factors of crowdfunding campaigns, especially that of ICO success factors, allowed us to identify an initial set of the determinants of blockchain-based crowdfunding success. Based on the list, we have analyzed a selected set of ICO evaluative websites to understand what factors were considered in practice but not reported in literature. After obtaining the extended list of success factors, we analyzed the relationships among them and built a model of the factors using interpretive structural modeling (ISM). The contribution of our work is a more extensive and structured understanding of what can lead to the success of (blockchain-based) crowdfunding campaigns.

The remaining part of the chapter is organized as follows: The next section describes the success factors that have been identified in the relevant literature. The research process is reported in the "Research Approach" section. The "Findings" section details the results of the study, which is further discussed in the "Discussion" section. The chapter ends with the "Conclusion" section in which the contribution of the study is highlighted and the future work outlined.

Literature review

During the last decade, many authors focused on crowdfunding success factors. Success factors are intrinsic to each crowdfunding project, and those fulfilled can lead to a successful campaign. There exist several, often controversial, studies on success factors in crowdfunding. Crowdfunding can be categorized in two main models: nonfinancial crowdfunding (reward and donation) and financial crowdfunding (equity, royalty and debt). Investors in financial crowdfunding platforms are different than the ones contributing to nonfinancial crowdfunding (Belleflamme et al., 2014). Financial crowdfunding backers do typically expected gains due to an increase in the value of their investments, as opposed to the potential reward, recognition or tax deduction in the case of nonfinancial crowdfunding.

Blockchain-based crowdfunding can also be categorized in these two main models. A company can offer utility tokens, payment tokens (cryptocurrencies) or security tokens (Hacker and Thomale, 2017). The utility token sale can be seen as a presale of a future product or service. Reward crowdfunding is a traditional crowdfunding model where an investor contributes comparatively small amounts of money to projects in return for some kind of reward. With this assumption, we can argue that a utility token sale shares similarities with nonfinancial crowdfunding such as reward-based crowdfunding. On the other hand, a security token sale is subjected to security regulations in many jurisdictions. One form of a security token offering (STO) is an equity token offering (ETO). In an ETO, a project sells part of its equity to a crowd of investors. With this assumption, it is arguable that STOs are similar to financial crowdfunding campaigns such as equity crowdfunding.

First, studies indicate a relationship between traditional crowdfunding success factors and token sale success factors (Fisch, 2018; Adhami et al., 2018; Lee et al., 2018). Therefore, we reviewed the literature on reward-based crowdfunding success factors to detect factors important to the nonfinancial crowdfunding model and equity crowdfunding literature to detect factors important to the financial crowdfunding model.

Nevertheless, blockchain crowdfunding campaigns have some intrinsic characteristics that are different from those of a traditional crowdfunding campaign or even an initial public offering (IPO). The information about the project is generally summarized in a white paper. The contained information is not bound by strict regulations such as the one contained in a prospectus in the case of an IPO. In the case of an ICO, the underlying technology is the blockchain. Smart contracts are tiny programs that can be uploaded to Github for third-party verification. The token sales are generally financed with decentralized cryptocurrencies such as Ether or Bitcoin, not with centralized fiat currencies, as is the case in traditional financing methods. For the above-argued reasons, we also reviewed recent literature to identify the success factors that apply to blockchain-based crowdfunding campaigns.

We report the identified factors using two main categories: project related and campaign related. Table 16.1 provides an overview of these factors, further grouped into subcategories.

Project-related success factors

Company characteristics

Industry: A study by Mamonov et al. (2017) on US-based equity crowdfunding sites states that crowdfunding projects in the real estate sector are by far more successful than those in other industries. This finding indicates that projects acting in certain industries will be more successful than those in other sectors. In the reward crowdfunding space, a study by Davies and Giovannetti (2018) finds evidence of great differences in the impact of project categories on the success of Kickstarter campaigns, with some categories positively affecting the probability of a project's success. By contrast, in the blockchain crowdfunding literature, we find a statement that ICO valuations are not different across industries (Fisch et al., 2018).

Table 16.1 A list of crowdfunding success factors from literature

Category	*Success factors reported in literature*		
	Success factor	*Effect*	*Study*
Project-related factors			
Company characteristics	Industry	+/−	(Davies and Giovannetti, 2018)(Fisch et al., 2018)(Mamonov et al., 2017)
	Location	+/−	(Rakesh et al., 2015) (Adhami et al., 2018) (Mamonov et al., 2017) (Ralcheva and Roosenboom, 2016) (Agrawal et al., 2015)(Adhami et al., 2018)(Fenu et al., 2018)
	IPO exit strategy	+/−	(Ahlers et al., 2015) (Vismara, 2016)
Strong partners	Reputable investors	+	(Mamonov and Malaga, 2018)(Kim and Viswanathan, 2013) (Ralcheva and Roosenboom, 2016)(Li et al., 2016)
Strong early adopters	Corporate customers as early adopters	+	(Mamonov and Malaga, 2018)
Project innovativeness	Intellectual capital	+/−	(Ralcheva and Roosenboom, 2016) (Ahlers et al., 2015) (Mamonov and Malaga, 2018)
Product stage	Product development stage	+	(Mamonov and Malaga, 2018)(Ralcheva and Roosenboom, 2016) (Loehrer et al., 2018)
Team composition	Team size (number of board members, number or advisors)	+/−	(Mamonov and Malaga, 2018) (Ralcheva and Roosenboom, 2016) (Frydrych et al., 2014) (Fisch, 2018) (Amsden and Schweizer, 2018) (Cerchiello and Toma, 2018)(Ahlers et al., 2015) (Fenu et al., 2018) (Stam and Schutjens, 2005)
	Female founder	+/−	(Frydrych et al., 2014) (Colombo et al., 2014) (Vismara et al., 2016) (Mohammadi and Shafi, 2018)
Team experience	Previous founder experience	+/−	(Gutsche and Sylla, 2017) (Kim et al., 2017)(Mamonov and Malaga et al., 2018) (Davies and Giovannetti, 2018) (Rakesh et al., 2015) (Colombo et al., 2014)
	Well-connected CEO	+	(Amsden and Schweizer, 2018)
	Team educational background	+	(Ahlers et al., 2015)
Founder dedication	Loyal CEO	+	(Momtaz, 2018)
	Financial commitment	+	(Loehrer et al., 2018) (Gutsche and Sylla, 2017) (Davies and Giovannetti, 2018)
Social media traction	Social network presence	+/−	(Mollick, 2014) (Vismara, 2016) (Cerchiello and Toma, 2018)(Amsden and Schweizer, 2018)(Davies and Giovannetti, 2018)(Zheng et al., 2014)

(*Continued*)

Table 16.1 (Continued)

Category	*Success factors reported in literature*		
	Success factor	*Effect*	*Study*
	Network interactions, updates and comments	+	(Hornuf and Schwienbacher, 2018) (Lukkarinen et al., 2016) (Lu et al., 2014) (Rakesh et al., 2015) (Gutsche and Sylla, 2017) (Kim et al., 2017) (Etter et al., 2013)
	Presence on Github	+	(Fisch, 2018) (Amsden and Schweizer, 2018)
Campaign-related factors			
Campaign design	Identity disclosure	+	(Kim et al., 2017) (Polzin et al., 2018)
	Quality signals (videos, pitches, etc.)	+/−	(Mollick, 2014) (Bi et al., 2017) (Chan and Parhankangas, 2017) (Courtney et al., 2017) (Frydrych et al., 2014) (Xu et al., 2016) (Kim et al., 2017) (Colombo et al., 2014) (Kuppuswamy and Bayus, 2015) (Mamonov and Malaga, 2018)
	Share of retained equity/tokens	+	(Ahlers et al., 2015) (Vismara et al., 2016) (Ralcheva and Roosenboom, 2016) (Lee et al., 2018) (Amsden and Schweizer, 2018)
	Lower funding target	+/−	(Amsden and Schweizer, 2018)(Lee et al., 2018) (Kim et al., 2017) (Colombo et al., 2014), (Mollick, 2014) (Kuppuswamy and Bayus, 2005) (Davies and Giovannetti, 2018) (Cordova et al., 2015) (Frydrych et al., 2014) (Mollick, 2014) (Vulkan et al., 2016) (Zheng et al., 2014) (Ahlers et al., 2015) (Vismara et al., 2016) (Mamonov and Malaga, 2018) (Ralcheva and Roosenboom, 2016) (Lukkarinen et al., 2016)
	Shorter campaign duration	+/−	(Mollick, 2014) (Kuppuswamy and Bayus, 2015) (Davies and Giovannetti, 2018) (Colombo et al., 2014) (Kim et al., 2017) (Zheng et al., 2014) (Cordova et al., 2015) (Frydrych et al., 2014) (Lukkarinen et al., 2016)
	Lower ticket size	+	(Lukkarinen et al., 2016)
	Well differentiated reward levels	+	(Kuppuswamy and Bayus, 2015) (Colombo et al., 2014) (Frydrych et al., 2014) (Kim et al., 2017) (Gutsche and Sylla, 2017)

	Campaign addresses more than one country market	+	(Gutsche and Sylla, 2017)
	Tokens allow contributors to access a specific service (or to share profits)	+	(Adhami et al., 2018)
	Using Ethereum	+	(Fisch, 2018) (Amsden and Schweizer, 2018) (Fenu et al., 2018)
	Number of tokens issued	+	(Fisch, 2018)
	KYC/pre-registration	-	(Lee et al., 2018)
	Presale	+/−	(Amsden and Schweizer, 2018) (Lee et al., 2018) (Adhami et al., 2018)
	ICO bonus/discounts	+/−	(Amsden and Schweizer, 2018) (Lee et al., 2018) (Adhami et al., 2018)
	Accepting multiple currencies (digital and fiat)	+	(Lee et al., 2018)(Amsden and Schweizer, 2018)
Campaign traction	Investors with large investments	+	(Ralcheva and Roosenboom, 2016) (Vulkan et al., 2016) (Hornuf and Schwienbacher, 2018)
	Early investments	+	(Lukkarinen et al., 2016) (Colombo et al., 2014) (Davies and Giovannetti, 2018) (Vulkan et al., 2016)(Agrawal et al., 2015) (Kuppuswamy and Bayus, 2015) (Etter et al., 2013) (Lee et al., 2018)
	Number of early backers	+	(Colombo et al., 2014) (Davies and Giovannetti, 2018) (Beier and Wagner, 2016)
	Average analyst rating	+	(Lee et al., 2018) (Fenu et al., 2018)
White paper quality	White paper availability	+/−	(Cerchiello and Toma, 2018) (Adhami et al., 2018)
	White paper content	+/−	(Cerchiello and Toma, 2018)(Fisch, 2018) (Amsden and Schweizer, 2018)
	Multi-language white paper	+	(Lee et al., 2018)
Campaign transparency	Information transparency about the startup	+/−	(Ahlers et al., 2015) (Lukkarinen et al., 2016) (Polzin et al., 2018)(Mamonov et al., 2017) (Gutsche and Sylla, 2017) (Kim et al., 2017)(Vismara, 2016)
	Code source is available	+	(Adhami et al., 2018) (Fisch, 2018)

Location: A study by Ralcheva and Roosenboom (2016) outlines that projects with headquarters in big cities are generally more successful in equity crowdfunding in the UK. A study by Agrawal et al. (2015) suggests that the proximity of an artist and its funders does not impact crowdfunding success. It seems that on Kickstarter, US-based projects have greater chances to succeed (Colombo et al., 2014). It is nevertheless difficult to state if location has a significant impact on crowdfunding success because there are only a limited number of projects in certain areas (Davies and Giovannetti, 2018). The importance of location seems not to be uniform for all the categories of projects on Kickstarter. Projects on games, comics and technology are relatively less dependent on their geolocation to attract funding (Rakesh et al., 2015). In the blockchain crowdfunding space, due to regulatory restrictions and uncertainties, choosing the right jurisdiction to set up the company offering the tokens plays a crucial role. A paper by Adhami et al. (2018) comes to the conclusion that the choice of a jurisdiction of reference for the token sale by project promoters is appreciated and adds to the probability of the campaign's success. Projects coming from certain regions seem to be more prone to be successful than others (Fenu et al., 2018). In contrast, a study by Fisch (2018) states that location of the venture does not impact on ICO valuation.

IPO exit strategy: Vismara et al. (2016) find that an IPO exit strategy does not affect the outcome of an equity crowdfunding campaign. Projects that declared an exit strategy within the next five years attracted fewer investors, but the amount raised did not differ. In contrast to this finding, Ahlers et al. (2015) find a positive effect of an IPO exit proposal on fundraising success.

Strong partners

Reputable investors: Mamonov and Malaga (2018) conducted an analysis of 133 projects across 16 Title III equity crowdfunding sites launched between May 2016 and February 2017. They find that there is a correlation between professional business angel and venture capital involvement and equity crowdfunding success. The positive effect on crowdfunding success could be derived by the leveraging effect of those reputable investors with respect to information asymmetry. Another study by Ralcheva and Roosenboom (2016) analyzes the performance of UK-based equity crowdfunding campaigns. The study concludes that business angel investments and winning grants increase the probability of campaign success. Meantime, Kim and Viswanathan (2013) find that investors with app development experience and investors with app investment experience have disproportionate influence on later investors in the crowd and help to reduce information asymmetry among the investor base. The lead investor´s credibility and his/her advocacy behaviors, as measured in identity certification, investment experience, percentage of their investment and comments for projects, are important factors affecting crowdfunding performance (Li et al., 2016).

Strong early adopters

Corporate customers as early adopters: A study by Mamonov and Malaga (2018) across 16 equity crowdfunding sites in the US found evidence of a positive correlation between the existence of corporate customers and equity crowdfunding success.

Project innovativeness

Intellectual capital: Previous studies acknowledge that one of the most important reasons for startups to patent is to secure funds (Graham et al., 2008). Surprisingly, the studies of Ahlers et al. (2015) and Mamonov and Malaga (2018) find no correlation between intellectual capital (as measured by patents) and funding success in equity crowdfunding. In contrast, another study by Ralcheva and Roosenboom (2016) contends there is a positive relation between intellectual capital protection and equity crowdfunding success in the UK.

Product stage

Product development stage: Mamonov and Malaga (2018) investigate the effects of the state of product development related to equity crowdfunding success. They find that companies in the beta or prototype phase are less likely to raise significant funding during their campaigns than projects that have completed product development. The study on equity crowdfunding in the UK by Ralcheva and Roosenboom (2016) finds an increase of campaign performance if a project already made a first sale. Another study states that the willingness to invest in an equity crowdfunding campaign is clearly affected by business development or achieved milestones, respectively (Loehrer et al., 2018). These results are somewhat in contrast to the blockchain crowdfunding performance in 2017. Many of the projects that conducted an ICO in that year had not nearly completed product development but were nevertheless quite successful (CB Insights, 2018).

Team composition

Team size: Mamonov and Malaga (2018) find that equity crowdfunding campaigns run by solo entrepreneurs were less successful than ones conducted by entrepreneurial teams. Ahlers et al. (2015) contend that a having a higher number of board members is linked to equity crowdfunding success. In a study on entrepreneurial legitimacy in reward-based crowdfunding, Frydrych et al. (2014) reveal that projects with pairs and teams demonstrate much higher success rates than projects with individuals. These findings imply that crowdfunding investors believe that bigger teams are able to handle unexpected difficulties in a much better way. A study by Stam and Schutjens

(2005) finds that team startups are relatively more successful than solo entrepreneur startups. Interestingly, this effect was only valid for the first three years of a venture. Larger teams might create more discussions and paralyze the decision-making process. Having advisors and mentors on board seems to influence equity crowdfunding performance positively (Ralcheva and Roosenboom, 2016). Fisch (2018), analyzing the effect of team size on the success of ICOs, finds no evidence of a connection between the number of founders and ICO success. In contrast, Cerchiello and Toma (2018) state that having a bigger team and more advisors has a positive effect on ICO success. Similarly, Amsden and Schweizer (2018) find that more advisors and a bigger team size in general are connected with a higher probability of tokens being traded after the token sale and with a higher probability of raising more funds. The study by Fenu et al. (2018), on the other hand, finds no relation between team size and ICO success.

Female founders: There exist several studies that state that female founders are disadvantaged in traditional finance and are less likely to receive institutional capital, private equity and bank financing (Becker-Blease and Sohl, 2007; Bigelow et al., 2014; Eddleston et al., 2016). Interestingly, there exists some literature that states that women entrepreneurs are more successful in reward-based crowdfunding (Frydrych et al., 2014). Colombo et al. (2014) find that individual proponents who are male are less likely to receive support in terms of backers and capital than are females or companies. In the equity crowdfunding space, Vismara et al. (2016) find that female founders are able to attract the same number of investors but raise lower funding. Interestingly another study on gender differences in the contribution patterns of equity crowdfunding investors finds that female investors are more likely to invest in projects in which the proportion of male founders is higher (Mohammadi and Shafi, 2018).

Team experience

Previous founder experience: In a study on success factors of crowdfunding projects on the Kickstarter platform, Gutsche and Sylla (2017) point out that founders with previous crowdfunding experience are more successful than those without experience. The paper highlights the importance of seeking external advice if the entrepreneurs and their team lack this experience. Other studies also confirm the importance of previous crowdfunding experience (Davies and Giovannetti, 2018). Backers tend to develop trust towards creators whom they have backed in the past (Rakesh et al., 2015). Serial creators could be able to create a supportive funder base over time. Kim et al. (2017) find a positive effect of founders' previous fundraising experience on crowdfunding success. The authors point out that this experience could be seen as a positive signal of founders' capability and competency. On the other hand, Colombo et al. (2014) find that the number of previously created crowdfunding campaigns, as indicators for social capital, was not significant in predicting the success of reward-based crowdfunding campaigns. Another study, by Mamonov and Malaga (2018), finds no significant relation between prior industry experience or serial entrepreneurial experience and equity crowdfunding success.

Well-connected CEO: A study by Amsden and Schweizer (2018) finds that projects with well-connected CEOs (measured through LinkedIn 500+) are more likely to sell tokens that are tradable after the token sale and to raise more funds.

Team educational background: A study by Ahlers et al. (2015) titled "Signalling in Equity Crowdfunding" analyzed 104 offerings between 2006 and 2011 based on data from the Australian Small Scale Offerings Board (ASSOB). The result shows that the number of team members holding an MBA was positively correlated to campaign success. This result could be linked to the better network those founders have on average. The study suggest that highly qualified board members can enhance the likelihood of attracting investors as well as increase the speed of raising capital.

Founder dedication

Loyal CEO: Loyal CEOs have to offer fewer incentives to attract investors to their ICOs. Loyal CEOs are able to raise a higher funding amount in a shorter time period and lower the probability of failure significantly (Momtaz, 2018).

Financial commitment: Time and money entrepreneurs dedicate to their business is important in the investment decision making of business angels and venture capital (Cardon et al., 2018; Busenitz et al., 2005; Prasad et al., 2000). This is in alignment with the findings of Leland and Pyle (1977), which state that founders anticipating success are willing to commit more of the initial investment. This, however, depends on the financial situation of the founders. In a research note on entrepreneurs financial commitment and crowdfunding success, Loehrer et al. (2018) clearly indicate a positive relationship between financial commitment of entrepreneurs and equity crowdfunding success. Furthermore, the studies by Gutsche and Sylla (2017) and Davies and Giovannetti (2018) state that founders could be able to trigger additional funding if they participate actively as backers to other projects on crowdfunding platforms.

Social media traction

Social network presence: Mollick (2014) finds that a proponent's number of Facebook friends is positively associated with the amount of capital raised in a crowdfunding campaign, although not having a Facebook account is better than having few Facebook friends. A study by Colombo et al. (2014) highlights the importance of internal social capital for success, measured by the number of contributors that are attracted during the campaign. A study by

Ordanini et al. (2011) underlines that initial capital raising is mostly done by social contacts that have been deployed outside the campaign (external social capital) and highlights the importance of those investments for campaign success because of its positive effects to increase internal social capital. A study by Zheng et al. (2014) demonstrates significant effects of social networks on reward crowdfunding success using data collected in China and the US using Facebook and Weibo. A study by Vismara et al. (2016) analyzed 271 UK-based equity crowdfunding campaigns. The study states that entrepreneurs with more LinkedIn connections are able to conclude a more successful campaign. In the blockchain crowdfunding space, a study by Davies and Giovannetti (2018) found the number of Facebook connections have a significant but not particularly strong effect on the probability of ICO success. A study by Cerchiello and Toma (2018) states that the simple presence of a Telegram channel can increase the likelihood of ICO campaign success. A study by Amsden and Schweizer (2018) states that having a communication channel on Telegram increases the probability of collecting more funds and that the tokens get listed on an exchange after the initial coin offering. Also, having an active Twitter account seem to have a positive influence on ICO success (Cerchiello and Toma, 2018).

Network interactions updates and comments: A study by Lukkarinen et al. (2016) suggests that the presence and activity of social networks is relevant for equity crowdfunding success. A study on equity crowdfunding in Germany come to the conclusion that posting updates by the entrepreneur increases subsequent investments, especially the subsequent day (Hornuf and Schwienbacher, 2018). A study by Gutsche and Sylla (2017) concludes that an ongoing dialogue with the community increases the success rate of campaigns. The author advises projects to interact frequently with their crowd, using as many channels as possible. A study by Kim et al. (2017) outlines that the number of comments and updates influence reward crowdfunding campaign success. A study by Etter et al. (2013) outlines the importance of an increase in Twitter messages after the start of a Kickstarter campaign. Lu et al. (2014) outline the importance of social media promotion activities during a Kickstarter campaign and its positive impact on success. A study by Rakesh et al. (2015) finds that rapid early promotion correlates with more promotion overall and highlights its importance for reward crowdfunding success. Projects promoted by influential Twitter users have the potential to attract more backers, and the backing habits of investors in Kickstarter are influenced by their social circle (Rakesh et al., 2015).

Presence on Github: A study by Fisch (2018) states that the simple presence of a Github page does not affect ICO valuation. The number of stars that are connected to a Github account, on the other hand, seem to be a better quality signal and increase the probability of campaign success (Fisch, 2018). Another study by Amsden and Schweizer (2018) states that being present on

Github (e.g., posting code updates) increases the probability of the token getting listed after the ICO.

Campaign-related success factors

Campaign design

Identity disclosure: In their study on the roles of founder and project features in reward-based crowdfunding, Kim et al. (2017) state that an identity disclosure has a positive and statistically significant relation to campaign success ratio. A study conducted in the Netherlands by Polzin et al. (2018) state that the information about the persons behind the project are especially important in reward and donation crowdfunding.

Quality signals (videos, pitches, etc.): Several studies highlight the importance of quality signals and their impact on crowdfunding success (Mollick, 2014; Bi et al., 2017; Chan and Parhankangas, 2017; Courtney et al., 2017; Frydrych et al., 2014; Xu et al., 2016; Kim et al., 2017). The study by Colombo et al. (2014) finds no significant correlation to external links nor to the number of images and videos on reward crowdfunding success. The study states that these factors are fully mediated by early contributions. On the other hand, the study of Kuppuswamy and Bayus (2015) on reward crowdfunding states that a video can attract more backers. In terms of equity crowdfunding, Mamonov and Malaga (2018) find no direct evidence of video material and campaign success, but Mollick (2014) suggests that signals such as videos and frequent updates are associated with greater success. Spelling errors seem to reduce the chance of success. It seems that on established crowdfunding platforms like Kickstarter, video pitches become a standard, and most projects are offering them (Frydrych et al., 2014).

Share of retained equity/tokens: The study by Ahlers et al. (2015) finds that retaining equity can be an effective signal to increase the likelihood of funding success. In other studies on equity retention and social network theory in equity crowdfunding, Vismara et al. (2016) and Ralcheva and Roosenboom (2016) come to the same result. This effect could be linked to the cost of retained equity if the business collapses and the potential increase in value if the project is successful. Founders who are convinced that the business will be successful will be more likely to retain as much equity as possible. Interestingly, in the blockchain-based crowdfunding space, the studies by Lee et al. (2018) and Amsden and Schweizer (2018) find that the same pattern is also true for ICOs. Projects that retain more tokens seem to be more successful. Lee et al. (2018) argue that "retaining more tokens could be an important governance indicator, the percent of tokens to be sold to investors measures management's skin in the firm" and that the result could be linked to former studies on the positive effects of signalling equity retention. It seems that investors are attracted by projects with a higher retention rate. Retaining a higher fraction of tokens could be seen as a signal of the founder's confidence in the project. Selling only a fraction of the tokens gives projects the possibility to sell unsold tokens in future financing rounds; this is comparable to seasoned equity offerings (SEOs) that are used by publicly traded companies. Nevertheless, in the case of most token sales, the tokens are not connected to any shareholder rights such as governance. The managers normally remain in full control over the company. In fact, this could change with the new trend of security token offerings such as ETOs which are bound by more prompt investor protection.

Lower funding target: In the equity crowdfunding space, Lukkarinen et al. (2016) studied the effects of funding target amounts and their relation to campaign success. The authors find that a high minimum funding target has a strong negative correlation with the number of investors and amount raised. On the other hand, the study found that an overall higher funding target is positively related to funding success. This could be explained because investors in the equity crowdfunding space expect that projects need to spend more to reach a significant increase in valuation. In line with this result, a study on equity crowdfunding by Ralcheva and Roosenboom (2016) finds that successful campaigns have higher targets. In contrast, a study by Mamonov and Malaga (2018) finds a negative effect of the target amount and crowdfunding success in equity crowdfunding. Higher targets led to worst results. A study on equity crowdfunding conducted by Vulkan et al. (2016) finds that increasing the funding target by one standard deviation decreases the probability of success by between 11 and 18 percentage points. Vismara et al. (2016) and Ahlers et al. (2015) find that the target capital is related to a higher number of investors but does not affect the overall amount raised. In the reward crowdfunding space, a study by Zheng et al. (2014) states that the crowdfunding goal is negatively related to campaign performance in the US and China. Several studies on crowdfunding confirmed that bigger funding goals are negatively associated with the crowdfunding success ratio (Kim et al., 2017; Colombo et al., 2014; Mollick, 2014; Kuppuswamy and Bayus, 2015; Davies and Giovannetti, 2018; Cordova et al., 2015). On the other hand, several studies find that successful campaigns with lower funding targets tend to get overfunded on average (Frydrych et al., 2014; Mollick, 2014; Vulkan et al., 2016). In the blockchain crowdfunding domain, the campaign's upper funding target is called "hardcap"; the minimum funding target is called "softcap." Interestingly, the softcap of successful and unsuccessful ICO campaigns are nearly identical and therefore seem to have no influence on campaign success. Not having a softcap nevertheless seems to have a negative relation to the amount raised during the ICO (Amsden and Schweizer, 2018). On the other hand, the hardcap of successful token sales seem to be double the size of the ones of unsuccessful token sales (Lee et al., 2018). The presence of a hardcap increases both the probability of a token getting traded and the amount raised (Amsden and Schweizer, 2018).

Shorter campaign duration: Some studies analyzed the impact of campaign duration to campaign success. In the equity crowdfunding space, Lukkarinen et al. (2016) find that campaign duration is negatively correlated with the number of investors but not related to the amount raised. The study propose that shorter campaign durations could encourage investors to act fast and signals decisiveness and the ability to deliver. In the reward crowdfunding space, several studies find that longer campaign durations have a negative impact to campaign success (Mollick, 2014; Kuppuswamy and Bayus, 2015; Davies and Giovannetti, 2018). Longer campaign duration could signal a lack of confidence. Some studies find no relation between reward crowdfunding campaign duration and campaign success (Colombo et al., 2014; Kim et al., 2017). Another study by Zheng et al. (2014) finds significant effects of campaign duration in China but not the US. A study by Cordova et al. (2015) finds a positive effect of longer campaign duration on reward crowdfunding success. Another study on Kickstarter found that the combination of a high funding target and a long funding period is associated with less successful crowdfunding campaigns and that shorter campaign duration is generally correlated with higher success; nevertheless, they found a low correlation between campaign duration and the funding ratio (Frydrych et al., 2014). Cordova et al. (2015) find that project duration increases the chances of success and leads to an increase in the dollar amount contributed per day on a given project.

Lower ticket size: A study by Lukkarinen et al. (2016) finds that a lower ticket size is correlated with crowdfunding success. The ticket size is the minimum investment an investor has to commit to participate in a crowdfunding campaign. This effect could be linked to the small funding availability of unaccredited investors.

Well-differentiated reward levels: There exists some literature on the effect of differentiated reward levels. Well-differentiated reward should be helpful to attract funding from the whole crowdfunding community because of the differing abilities and willingness to fund (Gutsche and Sylla, 2017) and increase the investor base (Kuppuswamy and Bayus, 2015). Lower reward levels could therefore lead to campaign failures because of the limited investor base (Kim et al., 2017). A study by (Frydrych et al., 2014) points out that more creative-oriented projects (e.g., art, design, music, etc.) tend to have a higher number of reward levels. The study nevertheless found no significant effect of the average number of rewards offered by successful and unsuccessful campaigns. Rewards that give a sense of community belonging seem to have a positive effect on crowdfunding success (Colombo et al., 2014). It seems that reward crowdfunding investors appreciate being part of a community.

Campaign addresses markets in more than one country: A study by Gutsche and Sylla (2017) highlights that it is important for projects with a higher funding goal to target more than one county. This gives projects the access to investors needed for higher crowdfunding success rates. The regulatory landscape nevertheless limits projects to run certain campaigns in specific markets. This is the case of financial crowdfunding in Europe. There are no unified regulations in place, and crowdfunding platforms face several difficulties in offering their campaigns over national borders (European Commission, 2017).

Tokens allow contributors to access a specific service (or to share profits): A study by Adhami et al. (2018) outlines that the right of access to services and the right to receive a share of company profits appear positively related to blockchain-based crowdfunding success.

Using Ethereum: Ethereum is the most widely adopted platform to launch blockchain-based crowdfunding campaigns. It seems that using Ethereum to build the project can increase ICO valuation (Fisch, 2018). Using the Ethereum network increases the probability of a high participation in an ICO (Amsden and Schweizer, 2018) and ICO success (Fenu et al., 2018).

Number of tokens issued: A study by Fisch (2018) argues that the number of tokens issued by the project increases the valuation of the crowdfunding campaign. Investors seem to be more likely to invest in a campaign where they are able to get more tokens for a certain investment than in projects where they have to invest higher amounts per token. A higher number of tokens offered also shortens the overall campaign duration. In fact, this characteristic seems to be a psychological bias. Investors seem to believe that if they get a higher amount of tokens, the investment is more valuable than if they get a smaller amount. This could be because they wrongly see tokens as a sort of equity investment.

KYC/pre-registration: Interestingly, projects that conducted a know your customers (KYC) process are less likely to conclude token sales successfully, according to a study by Lee et al. (2018). In their study, they also found that, similarly, ICOs that required advance registration or restricted sales in certain countries are also less likely to proceed. This should be linked to the exclusion of investors from countries with tight ICO regulations such as China, South Korea and the US.

Presale: Token presales seem to be strongly significant to ICO success (Adhami et al., 2018). If that's the case, a pre-ICO could be an interesting method to test the market before launching the main sale or to finance the main sale expenses. Also, Lee et al. (2018) find a positive correlation between token presales and ICO success. A successful presale normally is covered by high net worth investors and can create momentum due to higher flexibility in expenditures. A study by Amsden and Schweizer (2018) finds that tokens offered by projects organizing a pre-ICO are less likely to get traded after the token sale. This could be because many projects collect enough money from institutional investors, and those investors are more risk adverse against unregulated secondary marketplaces. Those projects also raise fewer funds.

ICO bonus/discounts: A study by Lee et al. (2018) finds that high bonus offers, defined as 20 percent or more, are more prevalent in failed ICOs. Bonuses can attract investors at an early stage but could also be considered as a negative signal to later stage investors who might consider the project as a lemon or scam. Another study, by Adhami et al. (2018), finds that bonus schemes are only marginally significant for the probability of success of the campaign. A bonus structure can help to attract early investors but is not related to ICO success (Amsden and Schweizer, 2018).

Accepting multiple currencies (digital and fiat): ICOs that accepted multiple (digital) currencies were more likely to succeed compared to ICOs that took just one currency. Given that major digital currencies such as BTC and ETH are drastically volatile, expanding the options of currencies, thus increased liquidity, can facilitate transactions (Lee et al., 2018). Accepting fiat currencies is negatively correlated with ICO success (Amsden and Schweizer, 2018). This could be because crypto investors are less confident in projects that are linked to traditional financial markets.

Campaign traction

Investors with large investments: A study conducted by Ralcheva and Roosenboom (2016) concludes that successful equity crowdfunding campaigns in the UK are able to attract investors who pledge significantly higher amounts of funds. Another study on equity crowdfunding in the UK (conducted by Vulkan et al., 2016) finds that the median pledge per investor is one-third higher for successful campaigns compared to unsuccessful ones. Additionally, the study states that the highest single investment in successful campaigns accounts for 30 percent of the funding goal. This highlights the importance of single high-value investments to drive successful campaigns. A study on equity crowdfunding in Germany state that investments of at least 5,000 Euro during the last seven days increase the overall funding amount of the following day (Hornuf and Schwienbacher, 2018).

Early investments: In the equity crowdfunding space, Lukkarinen et al. (2016) find that the amount of the share of the minimum target raised during the hidden phase from private networks is strongly positively related with both the final number of investors and the amount raised during the campaign. This effect could be triggered because of the later stage investors' confidence that early backers have undertaken some due diligence. In the reward crowdfunding space, we found several studies that analyzed the impact of early investors on campaign success. The studies by Colombo et al. (2014) and Davies and Giovannetti (2018) in the reward crowdfunding space highlight the importance of early investments and their positive influence on the overall crowdfunding success. A study by Vulkan et al. (2016) on equity crowdfunding in the UK found that successful campaigns on average collect 50 percent of their overall target within a week after the campaign starts. A study by Agrawal et al. (2015) highlights the importance of early F&F investments to attract "external" crowdfunding investors in the royalty crowdfunding space. Projects that raise under 28.8 percent of the overall investment target within one-sixth of the campaign are at high risk of failure on Kickstarter (Colombo et al., 2014). A study by Kuppuswamy and Bayus (2015) states that large early investments decrease the number of backers in the second phase. The authors think that this effect is triggered by the perception of investors that the project will be backed by enough persons. Successful projects nevertheless tend to attract additional funding in the last stage of the campaign. The funding curve of successful projects is therefore U-shaped. A study by Etter et al. (2013) outlines the importance of investments within the first four hours of the campaign. Early contributors seem to be crucial also in the ICO space, probably due to information cascades (Lee et al., 2018).

Number of early backers: In the reward crowdfunding space, a study by Colombo et al. (2014) outlines the importance of the number of early backers as an important signal of successful crowdfunding campaigns. Another study on Swiss-based reward crowdfunding conducted by Beier and Wagner (2016) confirms the importance of early backers on the overall crowdfunding success. Finally, a study by Davies and Giovannetti (2018) highlights the importance of the number of early backers in the first sixth of the campaign and its positive effect on reward crowdfunding success.

Average analyst rating: In the case of blockchain-based crowdfunding, independent analysts are taking part in the evaluation of such offerings. A study by Lee et al. (2018) finds that a high average rating by these analysts is an important signal to investors and can lead to a more successful ICO campaign. In the world where there is an absence of traditional underwriters, independent analysts seem to contribute when dealing with information asymmetry. In line with the previous finding, Fenu et al. (2018) find that a higher rating on ICOBench has a positive influence on ICO success.

White paper quality

White paper availability: A working paper by Cerchiello and Toma (2018) states that the presence of a white paper has a positive effect on ICO success. In contrast, a study by Adhami et al. (2018) states that the probability of success of an ICO is not affected by the availability of a white paper at all. The availability of such a document could be unimportant because the white papers have generally not been audited and aren't bound by any legal protection.

White paper content: A study by (Fisch, 2018) states that longer white papers have a positive effect on ICO success. A poor white paper may harm an ICO, and if that's the case, ventures would be better off having no white paper at all (Fisch, 2018). With respect to the content, more negative and specific words appear with higher frequency in unsuccessful ICOs (Cerchiello and Toma, 2018). Offering a more detailed white paper increases the chances of collecting more funds and of having a tradable token after the ICO finishes (Amsden and Schweizer, 2018).

Multi-language white paper: Projects that offer multi-language white papers and websites are more likely to be completed successfully (Lee et al., 2018). This could be linked to the reduced language barriers that those projects face. It remains unclear if such an approach will lead to expansive regulatory countermeasures in some countries in which the tokens will be ranked as securities in the near future. Offering material in certain languages could increase the suspicion that projects are directly targeting certain countries.

Campaign transparency

Information transparency about the startup: There exist a couple of studies that highlight the importance of financial projections in equity crowdfunding (Ahlers et al., 2015; Lukkarinen et al., 2016; Polzin et al., 2018). Ahlers et al., 2015 find that projects that disclose no financial projections or forecasts collect smaller amounts during their campaigns and that the provision of more details about the risks is positively related to crowdfunding success. Lukkarinen et al. (2016) focus on the importance of the provision of sales growth, EBITDA margin and valuation multiples. The availability of financials seems to be positively, albeit not very strongly, associated with the number of investors but not significantly related to the amount raised. The study by Polzin et al., 2018 used data collected by a survey conducted in the Netherlands with 1,278 respondents. The study finds that the provision of financial information is important in financial crowdfunding (e.g., equity or debt) and less important in nonfinancial financing (e.g., donation and reward). A study by Gutsche and Sylla (2017) highlights the importance of having a strong value proposition and communicating it clearly. A study by Kim et al. (2017) states that the elaboration of project details is a statistically significant indicator of reward crowdfunding success ratio. A study by Mamonov et al. (2017) analyzed 17 US-based equity crowdfunding websites. The study concluded that process standardization and due diligence performed by crowdfunding platforms can effectively reduce information asymmetry and lead to better crowdfunding performance. Vismara et al. (2016) find a positive effect of longer pitch durations on equity crowdfunding success.

Code source is available: A study by Adhami et al. (2018) states that the success of an ICO is strongly and positively affected by the presence of a set of codes for the blockchain project. The code source could be seen as a transparent proof of concept. Nevertheless, probably only a few investors are able to read it.

To sum up, it can be seen clearly from the reviewed crowdfunding literature that various factors can influence the success of a blockchain-based crowdfunding campaign. However, our current understanding on these factors and their effects is not consistent and unanimous. Even less clear is how these factors are interrelated to affect jointly the eventual crowdfunding success.

Research approach

The research process was divided in two steps based on the posed research question: (1) extending the success factors and (2) establishing the relationships among the success factors.

Extending the success factors

A particularity of blockchain-based crowdfunding is that investors rely on evaluations provided by rating platforms to make investment decisions. Different platforms use different evaluation mechanisms to decide the rating scores. Through analyzing these mechanisms, we could extract the factors that the evaluation websites consider important to take into consideration when evaluating a crowdfunding project and predicting its success. By contrasting the factors we obtained from this analysis to what we have obtained from literature, we could identify new factors that are not covered by the literature, thus extending the list of success factors presented in Table 16.1.

In our previous work, we identified a list of ICO evaluation websites and assessed their quality using two criteria – information richness and transparency of evaluation mechanism (Hartmann et al., 2018). In this study, we used three of the most transparent rating platforms in terms of evaluation mechanism. At the time our previous work was published, Cryptomoon was among the three most transparent rating websites. By the time of this writing, the website seems to have lost its focus on ICO ratings. We used three of the most transparent platforms that are still operational. We extended the set of success factors through a careful analysis of the three ICO evaluation websites. For each evaluation website, we searched for the documented evaluation mechanism used by the website to rate ICOs. Then we conducted a qualitative analysis of the document using the reported success factors from the literature as the seed categories to identify new success factors. The result of this step is reported in the first part of the "Results" section.

Establish the relationships among the success factors

In this step, we employed interpretive structural modeling (ISM), which is a systematic structure modeling approach introduced by Malone (1975) to analyze and build the element hierarchy connection model in graphic form. It is interpretive, as the judgment of experts decides whether and how the variables are related. Relying on expert knowledge, it disintegrates an intricate system into several elements and builds a multilevel structural model. It is structural because, on the basis of relationship, an overall structure is extracted from the complex set of variables. It is a modeling technique because the specific relationships and overall structure are portrayed in a graphical model (Sage, 1977). The hierarchical model allows a focused view of the implicit nature of the underlying associations between the variables. ISM has been used in various fields of study, such as knowledge management, supply chain management, project management and complex engineering problems. Since the purpose of this study is to develop a structured model of success factors for blockchain-based crowdfunding, ISM is an appropriate approach to use.

The various steps involved in applying the ISM technique in this study are as below:

1 Develop a structural self-interaction matrix (SSIM) of the success factors, which indicates pairwise relationship between the factors, using the experts' knowledge as input. The relationship between the two factors can be:

V: Factor i **influences** factor j;
A: Factor i **is influenced by** facto j;
X: Factors i and j **influence each other**; and
O: NO relation between Factors i and j.

2 Develop a reachability matrix: A set of rules are applied on the SSIM to transform it to a primary reachability matrix, then a final reachability matrix is generated by checking transitivity – transitivity of the contextual relation is a basic assumption in ISM which states that if element A is related to B and B is related to C, then A is related to C.
3 Partitioning of the reachability matrix into different levels.
4 Based on the relationships given in the final reachability matrix, drawing a directed graph (digraph) and removing the transitive links; replacing element nodes with the statements.
5 Classification of success factors using MICMAC (*Matrice d'Impacts Croise's Multiplication Appliquée a UN Classement*) analysis to identify the variables that are influential, dependent and necessary for the development of system model. Its main aim is to analyse interactions, i.e., the driving and dependency power of the variables.

The more detailed explanation of these steps and the intermediate and final results following these steps are presented in the second part of the following section.

Results

The extended success factors of blockchain-based crowdfunding

Table 16.2 shows the success factors that the three ICO evaluation websites used in their evaluation mechanisms to rate the ICOs. The rows in gray indicate the success factors reported in the literature and used by one or more of the three websites. The rows without gray background indicate new factors identified through the analysis of the websites, which are not covered by the literature. Most of the new factors fit well into the subcategories reported in Table 16.1. However, one factor – product quality – couldn't fit to any existing subcategory. Therefore, it is listed in Table 16.2 as a subcategory.

A hierarchical structure model of the success factors

1 Development of the structural self-interaction matrix (SSIM) of the success factors

We used LinkedIn to contact active blockchain investors. We started with a screening of well-known blockchain companies and searched for the list of the investment funds that have backed those projects. Then we searched for the

Table 16.2 The crowdfunding success factors used by the three ICO evaluation websites

Category	*Success factor*	*Used by (evaluation website)*
Project-related factors		
Company characteristics	IPO exit strategy	ICObench
	Competitive advantage	Cryptorated.com
	Information on company stage (Crunchbase: founding date, location/s, previous fundraising rounds)	Cryptorated.com
	Existence of strong direct competitors (negative)	Cryptorated.com
	Weak current market leaders	Cryptorated.com
	High difficulty in penetrating the market	Cryptorated.com
	Size of target market in millions	Cryptorated.com
Strong partners	Corporate partners	Cryptorated.com
	Company working with respectable law/ accounting firm	Cryptorated.com
Strong early adopters	Corporate customers as early adopters	Cryptorated.com
Project innovativeness	Highly decentralized business and technology model	Cryptorated.com
	High disruption level	Cryptorated.com
	Projects unique selling proposition	Cryptorated.com
	Developments have value beyond the platform	Cryptorated.com
Product stage	Product development stage	Cryptorated.com
Product quality	How good the quality of the product is	Cryptorated.com
Team composition	Team size (number of board members, number of advisors)	Cryptorated.com, ICObench
	Team project fit	Cryptorated.com
	Company looking for key team members = negative	Cryptorated.com
Team experience	Team previous blockchain experience	Cryptorated.com
	Team previous related industry experience	Cryptorated.com
Founder dedication	Committed founding team (number of team members on LinkedIn committed in other projects simultaneously = negative)	Cryptorated.com
Social media traction	Social network presence	ICObench
	Network interactions updates and comments	Cryptorated.com
	Presence on Github	Transparency monitor
Campaign-related factors		
Campaign design	Identity disclosure	ICObench
	Quality signals (videos, pitches)	ICObench
	Lower funding target	ICObench
	KYC/pre-registration	ICObench
	ICO bonus/discounts	ICObench

	Tokens have tangible, inherent, utility-based, functional value	Cryptorated.com ICObench
	Token reserve planned	Cryptorated.com
	Milestone-dependent releases	Cryptorated.com
	Vetting applied	Cryptorated.com
	Carefully planned and fully transparent fund allocation	Cryptorated.com
	Realistic funding goal	Cryptorated.com
	Long-term milestones available	Cryptorated.com
	Use of SAFT	Cryptorated.com
	Information on token price in ETH provided	Cryptorated.com
Campaign traction	Average analyst rating	ICObench
White paper quality	White paper comprehensiveness	Cryptorated.com
	White paper readability	Cryptorated.com
	Informativeness of white paper	Cryptorated.com
Campaign transparency	Information transparency about the startup	Cryptorated.com
	Code source is available	Transparency monitor
	Realistic business plan	Cryptorated.com
	Company conducted smart contract auditing	Cryptorated.com
	More detailed and reasonable road map	Cryptorated.com
	Token ticker provided	ICObench
	ICO start and end day provided	ICObench
	Information on token distribution provided	ICObench
	Token holder rights protected in trustless way	Transparency monitor
	ICO controlled by smart contract	Transparency monitor
	Smart contract easy to read and properly commented	Transparency monitor
	Smart contract handles other currencies in a trustless way.	Transparency monitor
	Smart contract store balance of those currencies	Transparency monitor
	If other currencies are used, token price provided	Transparency monitor
	Smart contract handle ETH in a trustless way	Transparency monitor
	Smart contract provide all tracking data via events	Transparency monitor
	Instruction on how to reproduce bytecode provided	Transparency monitor
	Source code provided on Etherscan	Transparency monitor

LinkedIn pages of the funds and screened their employees reported on LinkedIn. Several of these experts were contacted via LinkedIn, and their input was requested using the Excel template, as shown in the Appendix. In the Excel template, we also provided the definitions of the categories and subcategories of the factors, to facilitate them deciding the relationships between them.

Out of the 70 experts contacted who are working for 30 investment funds, ten replied, and four submitted the filled Excel file. One expert is an investment manager at a Chinese venture capital company focusing on the blockchain industry and has invested in enterprises such as Huobi, Coldlar, Bocheninc, Jinse Finance, Lianshang Technology, etc. The second expert is a top manager of a big investment firm in Singapore. He is a direct investor in the blockchain and venture capital space, specializing in quantitative and numerical finance, mathematics, political economics, macroeconomics, game theory, statistics, blockchain and cryptoeconomics. The third one is a founder of a digital assets hedge fund based in Singapore, focused on blockchain-based projects, decentralized protocols and ICOs. The firm invested in projects such as Fantom, Zilliqua, Golem, Ethereum, Tezos and others. The fourth expert is an entrepreneur, a cofounder of several blockchain-related startups and an active investor in the blockchain and cryptocurrency space.

The responses from the four experts were checked for interrater agreement using Fleiss' kappa (which is suitable for nominal categorical data from more than two raters), and the result showed slight agreement among the experts (kappa = 0.134).

We then proceeded to produce a unique dataset as the input for building the SSIM. The data unifying process followed the rules listed here:

1 If all four experts, or three out of four experts, or two out of four experts, agree on the relationship between two success factors, that relationship is preserved in the unique dataset. Among the 91 relationships (the total number of input asked from each expert), 77 were determined in this step.
2 If four experts are divided into two pairs by two different responses, we calculate the frequencies of the preserved responses per expert in the first step. The relationship agreed upon by the pair whose combined frequencies are higher than those of the other pair is preserved; if the two pairs' combined frequencies are equal, for each pair, Fleiss' kappa is calculated among the pair's responses and the unique responses achieved so far. The relationship specified by the pair with higher Fleiss' kappa value is preserved. Among the 91 relationships, 10 were determined in this step.
3 If all four experts disagree among themselves on the relationship between two success factors, we calculate the frequencies of the preserved responses per expert in the first two steps. The relationship specified by the expert with the highest frequency is preserved. If two or more experts have the same highest frequency, for each of these experts, Cohen's kappa is calculated between his/her responses and the unique responses achieved so far. The relationship specified by the expert with higher or the highest Cohen's kappa value is preserved. Among the 91 relationships, four were determined in this step.

Based on the obtained unique dataset, we built the structural self-interactive matrix as shown in Table 16.3.

Table 16.3 Structural self-interactive matrix for blockchain-based crowdfunding success factors

Success factor number	*Success factor name*	*Success factor number*													
		1	*2*	*3*	*4*	*5*	*6*	*7*	*8*	*9*	*10*	*11*	*12*	*13*	*14*
1	Company characteristics		X	V	X	O	O	V	X	O	O	V	V	O	V
2	Strong partners			X	V	X	X	X	X	A	X	V	V	V	V
3	Strong early adopters				A	A	A	O	O	X	V	V	V	O	O
4	Project innovativeness					O	V	A	X	A	O	V	V	V	O
5	Product stage						X	O	X	A	O	V	V	O	O
6	Product quality							A	A	A	V	O	V	V	O
7	Team composition								X	A	V	V	V	V	V
8	Team experience									A	V	V	V	V	V
9	Founder dedication										V	O	V	V	V
10	Social media traction											X	V	A	A
11	Campaign design												V	V	O
12	Campaign traction													A	A
13	White paper quality														V
14	Campaign transparency														

Note: **V:** Factor (row) i **influences** factor (column) j; **A:** Factor (row) i **is influenced by** factor (column) j;

X: Factors (row) i and (column) j **influence each other**; **O: NO relation** between Factors (row) i and (column) j

2 Development of the reachability matrix from the SSIM

In this step, the SSIM is converted into a binary matrix, called a reachability matrix (RM), by substituting V, A, X and O by 1 and 0 following the rules specified here:

Rule I: If the pair (i, j) is V, then replace it by 1 and make the (j, i) entry 0 in the initial RM;
Rule II: If the pair (i, j) is A, then replace it by 0 and make the (j, i) entry 1 in the initial RM;
Rule III: If the pair (i, j) is X, then replace it by 1 and make the (j, i) entry 1 in the initial RM;
Rule IV: If the pair (i, j) is O, then replace it by 0 and make the (j, i) entry 0 in the initial RM;
Rule V: If $i = j$, then make the (i, j) entry 1 in the initial RM.

Note: i stands for the row number; j stands for the column number

Table 16.4 The initial reachability matrix

Success factor number	*Description*	*Success factor number*													
		1	*2*	*3*	*4*	*5*	*6*	*7*	*8*	*9*	*10*	*11*	*12*	*13*	*14*
1	Company characteristics	1	1	1	1	0	0	1	1	0	0	1	1	0	1
2	Strong partners	1	1	1	1	1	1	1	1	0	1	1	1	1	1
3	Strong early adopters	0	1	1	0	0	0	0	0	1	1	1	1	0	0
4	Project innovativeness	1	0	1	1	0	1	0	1	0	0	1	1	1	0
5	Product stage	0	1	1	0	1	1	0	1	0	0	1	1	0	0
6	Product quality	0	1	1	0	1	1	0	0	0	1	0	1	1	0
7	Team composition	0	1	0	1	0	1	1	1	0	1	1	1	1	1
8	Team experience	1	1	0	1	1	1	1	1	0	1	1	1	1	1
9	Founder dedication	0	1	1	1	1	1	1	1	1	1	0	1	1	1
10	Social media traction	0	1	0	0	0	0	0	0	0	1	1	1	0	0
11	Campaign design	0	0	0	0	0	0	0	0	0	1	1	1	1	0
12	Campaign traction	0	0	0	0	0	0	0	0	0	0	0	1	0	0
13	White paper quality	0	0	0	0	0	0	0	0	0	1	0	1	1	1
14	Campaign transparency	0	0	0	0	0	0	0	0	0	1	0	1	0	1

The resulting initial reachability matrix is shown in Table 16.4.

The final reachability matrix is produced after including the transitivities. The result is shown in Table 16.5 (highlighted cells are the relations derived using the transitivity rule). The driving power of each success factor is calculated as the sum of the column values and shown as the last column of Table 16.5, whereas the dependence power of each success factor is calculated as the sum of the row values and shown as the last row of Table 16.5.

3 Partitioning of the reachability matrix into different levels

In this step, the final reachability matrix will be used (Table 16.5), to develop adjacency reachability R(s*i*) sets and adjacency antecedent A(s*i*) sets. R(s*i*) consists of constituent *i* itself and other constituents, i.e., constituents in the row that it may affect, whereas the antecedent A(s*i*) consists of constituents *i* and the other constituents, i.e., constituents in the column that may affect it.

R(si) ∩ A(si) results in the common constituents in both R(si) and A(si). Then a comparison between R(si) and R(si) ∩ A(si) is made. The success factor, for which R(si) and R(si) ∩ A(si) are equal, is judged as the topmost factor in the hierarchy and is assigned Level I. Once top-level constituents are identified, they are separated from the remaining constituents. This iterative procedure is continued until the levels of all variables are obtained. In this study, the process is completed in five iterations, which are shown in Table 16.6.

Table 16.5 The final reachability matrix

Success factor number	*Description*	*Success factor number*														*Driving power*
		1	*2*	*3*	*4*	*5*	*6*	*7*	*8*	*9*	*10*	*11*	*12*	*13*	*14*	
1	Company characteristics	1	1	1	1	1	1	1	1	1	1	1	1	1	1	14
2	Strong partners	1	1	1	1	1	1	1	1	1	1	1	1	1	1	14
3	Strong early adopters	1	1	1	1	1	1	1	1	1	1	1	1	1	1	14
4	Project innovativeness	1	1	1	1	1	1	1	1	1	1	1	1	1	1	14
5	Product stage	1	1	1	1	1	1	1	1	1	1	1	1	1	1	14
6	Product quality	1	1	1	1	1	1	1	1	1	1	1	1	1	1	14
7	Team composition	1	1	1	1	1	1	1	1	0	1	1	1	1	1	13
8	Team experience	1	1	1	1	1	1	1	1	0	1	1	1	1	1	13
9	Founder dedication	1	1	1	1	1	1	1	1	1	1	1	1	1	1	14
10	Social media traction	1	1	1	1	1	1	1	1	0	1	1	1	1	1	13
11	Campaign design	0	1	0	0	0	0	0	0	0	1	1	1	1	1	6
12	Campaign traction	0	1	0	0	0	0	0	0	0	0	1	1	0	0	3
13	White paper quality	0	1	0	0	0	0	0	0	0	1	1	1	1	1	6
14	Campaign transparency	0	1	0	0	0	0	0	0	0	1	1	1	0	1	5
Dependence power		10	14	10	10	10	10	10	10	7	13	14	14	12	13	

Table 16.6 Iterations showing partitioned levels

Success factor number	Reachability set R(si)	Antecedent set A(si)	Intersection set R(si) ∩ A(si)	Level
Iteration 1				
1	1,2,3,4,5,6,7,8,9,10,11,12,13,14	1,2,3,4,5,6,7,8,9,10	1,2,3,4,5,6,7,8,9,10	
2	1,2,3,4,5,6,7,8,9,10,11,12,13,14	1,2,3,4,5,6,7,8,9,10,11,12,13,14	1,2,3,4,5,6,7,8,9,10,11,12,13,14	I
3	1,2,3,4,5,6,7,8,9,10,11,12,13,14	1,2,3,4,5,6,7,8,9,10	1,2,3,4,5,6,7,8,9,10	
4	1,2,3,4,5,6,7,8,9,10,11,12,13,14	1,2,3,4,5,6,7,8,9,10	1,2,3,4,5,6,7,8,9,10	
5	1,2,3,4,5,6,7,8,9,10,11,12,13,14	1,2,3,4,5,6,7,8,9,10	1,2,3,4,5,6,7,8,9,10	
6	1,2,3,4,5,6,7,8,9,10,11,12,13,14	1,2,3,4,5,6,7,8,9,10	1,2,3,4,5,6,7,8,9,10	
7	1,2,3,4,5,6,7,8,10,11,12,13,14	1,2,3,4,5,6,7,8,9,10	1,2,3,4,5,6,7,8,10	
8	1,2,3,4,5,6,7,8,10,11,12,13,14	1,2,3,4,5,6,7,8,9,10	1,2,3,4,5,6,7,8,10	
9	1,2,3,4,5,6,7,8,9,10,11,12,13,14	1,2,3,4,5,6,9	1,2,3,4,5,6,9	
10	1,2,3,4,5,6,7,8,10,11,12,13,14	1,2,3,4,5,6,7,8,9,10,11,13,14	1,2,3,4,5,6,7,8,10,11,13,14	
11	2,10,11,12,13,14	1,2,3,4,5,6,7,8,9,10,11,12,13,14	2,10,11,12,13,14	I
12	2,11,12	1,2,3,4,5,6,7,8,9,10,11,12,13,14	2,11,12	I
13	2,10,11,12,13,14	1,2,3,4,5,6,7,8,9,10,11,13	2,10,11,13	
14	2,10,11,12,14	1,2,3,4,5,6,7,8,9,10,11,13,14	2,10,11,14	
Iteration 2				
1	1,3,4,5,6,7,8,9,10,13,14	1,3,4,5,6,7,8,9,10	1,3,4,5,6,7,8,9,10	
3	1,3,4,5,6,7,8,9,10,13,14	1,3,4,5,6,7,8,9,10	1,3,4,5,6,7,8,9,10	
4	1,3,4,5,6,7,8,9,10,13,14	1,3,4,5,6,7,8,9,10	1,3,4,5,6,7,8,9,10	
5	1,3,4,5,6,7,8,9,10,13,14	1,3,4,5,6,7,8,9,10	1,3,4,5,6,7,8,9,10	
6	1,3,4,5,6,7,8,9,10,13,14	1,3,4,5,6,7,8,9,10	1,3,4,5,6,7,8,9,10	
7	1,3,4,5,6,7,8,10,13,14	1,3,4,5,6,7,8,9,10	1,3,4,5,6,7,8,10	
8	1,3,4,5,6,7,8,10,13,14	1,3,4,5,6,7,8,9,10	1,3,4,5,6,7,8,10	
9	1,3,4,5,6,7,8,9,10,13,14	1,3,4,5,6,9	1,3,4,5,6,9	
10	1,3,4,5,6,7,8,10,13,14	1,3,4,5,6,7,8,9,10,13,14	1,3,4,5,6,7,8,10,13,14	II
13	10,13,14	1,3,4,5,6,7,8,9,10,13	10,13	
14	10,14	1,3,4,5,6,7,8,9,10,13,14	10,14	II

Iteration 3				
1	1,3,4,5,6,7,8,9,13	1,3,4,5,6,7,8,9	1,3,4,5,6,7,8,9	
3	1,3,4,5,6,7,8,9,13	1,3,4,5,6,7,8,9	1,3,4,5,6,7,8,9	
4	1,3,4,5,6,7,8,9,13	1,3,4,5,6,7,8,9	1,3,4,5,6,7,8,9	
5	1,3,4,5,6,7,8,9,13	1,3,4,5,6,7,8,9	1,3,4,5,6,7,8,9	
6	1,3,4,5,6,7,8,9,13	1,3,4,5,6,7,8,9	1,3,4,5,6,7,8,9	
7	1,3,4,5,6,7,8,13	1,3,4,5,6,7,8,9	1,3,4,5,6,7,8	
8	1,3,4,5,6,7,8,13	1,3,4,5,6,7,8,9	1,3,4,5,6,7,8	
9	1,3,4,5,6,7,8,9,13	1,3,4,5,6,9	1,3,4,5,6,9	
13	13	1,3,4,5,6,7,8,9,13	13	III
Iteration 4				
1	1,3,4,5,6,7,8,9	1,3,4,5,6,7,8,9	1,3,4,5,6,7,8,9	IV
3	1,3,4,5,6,7,8,9	1,3,4,5,6,7,8,9	1,3,4,5,6,7,8,9	IV
4	1,3,4,5,6,7,8,9	1,3,4,5,6,7,8,9	1,3,4,5,6,7,8,9	IV
5	1,3,4,5,6,7,8,9	1,3,4,5,6,7,8,9	1,3,4,5,6,7,8,9	IV
6	1,3,4,5,6,7,8,9	1,3,4,5,6,7,8,9	1,3,4,5,6,7,8,9	IV
7	1,3,4,5,6,7,8	1,3,4,5,6,7,8,9	1,3,4,5,6,7,8	IV
8	1,3,4,5,6,7,8	1,3,4,5,6,7,8,9	1,3,4,5,6,7,8	IV
9	1,3,4,5,6,7,8,9	1,3,4,5,6,9	1,3,4,5,6,9	
Iteration 5				
9	9	9	9	V

4 The structural model of the success factors for blockchain-based crowdfunding

The structural model demonstrating the relationships among the success factors is created from the initial reachability matrix (Table 16.4) and the partitioned levels (Table 16.6). In the directed graph, the top-level factors (Level I as shown in the Iteration 1, Table 16.6) are placed at the top of the group, the second-level factors (Level II) below the top-level ones, and so on until the base-level enablers (Level V) are placed at the lowest location. If the relationship between factors *i* and *j* exists, a directed arrow pointing from the influencing factor to the influenced factor is drawn. If the influence is mutual, a bidirectional arrow is drawn. The solid arrow line is used to connect two factors at two different levels. The dotted arrow line is used to connect two factors within the same level. The resulting diagram is a directed graph, as shown in Figure 16.1 (with number) and Figure 16.2 (with name), which demonstrates the hierarchical relationships among the factors.

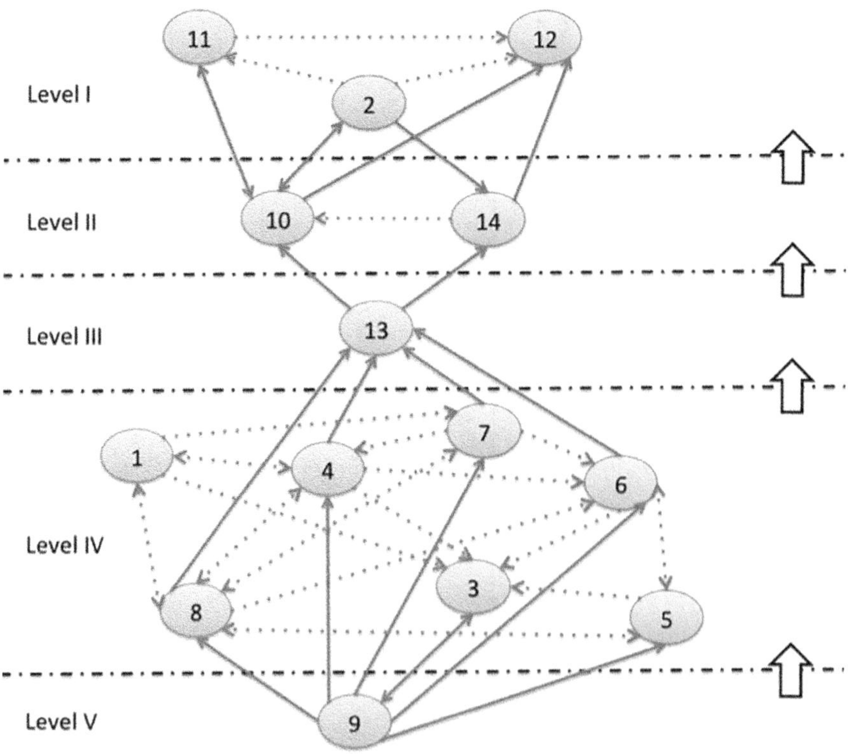

Figure 16.1 The directed graph of the factors

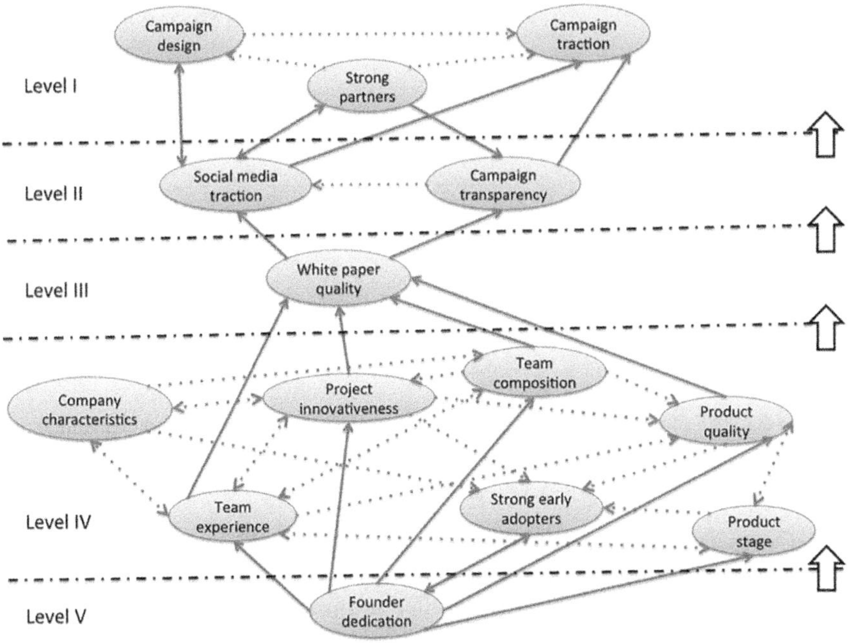

Figure 16.2 The model of blockchain-based crowdfunding success factors

5 MICMAC analysis of the success factor

In the last step of analysis, we classified the 14 success factors into four clusters as depicted by four quadrants in Figure 16.3, using the values displayed in Table 16.5 in terms of driving power and dependency power. It provides another perspective on these success factors.

Quadrant I – Autonomous variables: Factors in this quadrant have both weak driving as well as dependence power; they are less connected to the system. As shown in Figure 16.3, no success factors were classified in this quadrant.

Quadrant II – Dependent variables: Factors in this quadrant have weak driving but strong dependence power. As shown in Figure 16.3, all four campaign-related success factors are in this quadrant: campaign design, campaign traction, white paper quality and campaign transparency.

Quadrant III – Linkage variables: Factors in this quadrant have strong driving as well as strong dependence power, i.e., they are influenced by lower-level variables in the model and meanwhile significantly impact other variables. As shown in Figure 16.3, the majority of the factors (9 out of 14) are in this quadrant.

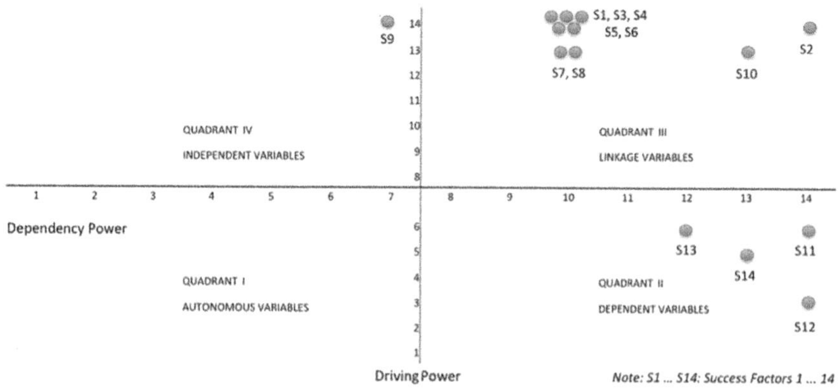

Figure 16.3 The MICMAC Analysis of Success Factors of blockchain-based crowdfunding

Quadrant IV – Independent variables: Factors in this quadrant have strong driving and weak dependence power. As shown in Figure 16.3, one factor, founder dedication, is classified in this quadrant.

Discussion

Our study revealed various determinants for the success of blockchain-based crowdfunding campaigns and depicted the intertwined relationships among different categories of success factors, both project related and campaign related.

A confrontation of Table 16.1 and Table 16.2 surfaces the fact that only a few success factors reported in literature are actually used in practice by ICO evaluation websites. In contrast, these websites are using many new success factors that are not reported in literature to evaluate ICOs. On the one hand, we could question the scientific and theoretical base of the evaluation mechanisms employed by these websites; on the other hand, it can be argued that, due to the fast development of the blockchain landscape, the gap between research and practice would always exist. Our study is one proof of it.

In the resulting model (Figure 16.2), we could see that the campaign-related factors, summarized into four categories, all sit at the top half of the model. They are relevant for the success of a crowdfunding campaign, but they are not as fundamental as project-related success factors, most of which are located in the bottom half of the model.

White paper quality, as a campaign-related success factor subcategory, is intrinsic to blockchain-based crowdfunding but has only been covered by a few recent papers due to limited literature on the topic. In comparison, from the analysis of the evaluation websites, we found more factors related to white paper quality: *white paper comprehensiveness*, *white paper readability*, and *informativeness of white paper*. The white paper quality category is a linkage variable lying in the middle of the model and therefore has both high dependency power and high driving power (as shown in Figure 16.3). The containing factors seem to be dependent on several underlying factor categories such as product quality, team experience, project innovativeness and team composition and influence several other factor categories including social media traction and campaign transparency.

Another two campaign-related factor categories, campaign traction and campaign design, are both heavily dependent on nearly all other categories and have little driving power. Several factors connected to the campaign traction category have been covered in the literature such as *investors with large investments*, *early investments*, *number of early backers* and *average analyst rating*. On the rating websites we found only *average analyst rating* is used in ICO evaluations, and no new factors were identified. In terms of campaign design, it is the most covered factor category in literature as well as on the evaluation websites. We found 15 factors covered in the literature; on the evaluation websites, we found five overlapping factors and nine new factors. Campaign design is a dependent variable with weak driving but strong dependence power (as shown in Figure 16.3). It is influenced by and influences social media traction.

The fourth campaign-related factor category is campaign transparency. The contrast of Table 16.1 and Table 16.2 reveals that campaign transparency as an important factor category is somehow overlooked by the literature, which only reported two factors that can be considered relevant, that is, *information transparency about the startup* and *code source is available*. In contrast, ICO Monitor, one of the three ICO evaluation websites, puts quite significant focus on campaign transparency, as demonstrated in Table 16.2, and uses many concrete factors to evaluate the transparency of an ICO. Among these factors, many are related to the use of smart contracts to control ICO in a transparent manner.

The project-related factors are subdivided into ten factor categories. They are located in all but one of the five hierarchy levels in the model. All Level V and Level IV categories are within this group. Most of them are in Level IV. The most fundamental factor, which is at the lowest level (Level V) of the model and the only element at that level, is founder dedication. We expected that the strong commitment of founders would impact the success of their crowd-fundraising initiatives, but the model highlighted how important and fundamental its impact could be. Surprisingly, the literature covers only two factors – *loyal CEO* and *financial commitment*. On the evaluation website, we found only one factor, *committed founding team*. Founder dedication has a strong driving and weak dependence power, and interestingly, it has a mutual influencing relationship with the strong early adopters category.

The second lowest level (Level IV) of the model is a dense layer. The linkages among the categories in this level are intensive, with quite a few of them bidirectional. It implies that company, team, project and product, the fundamental elements of a venture, always play the key role, even in a new and somehow unconventional fundraising mechanism. One category, company characteristics, has been covered in the literature, with *industry*, *location* and *IPO exit strategy* as three factors belonging to this category. Analysing the evaluation websites, we found IPO exit strategy as an overlapping factor and six new factors (see Table 16.2). Company characteristics is a key variable and would impact on team composition and strong early adopters. It is not surprising to see company characteristics influence other factors; however, it is somewhat surprising to see a mutual influence between it and team experience as well as project innovativeness, which means that the latter two could impact on company characteristics. It could be argued that truly innovative companies in the blockchain space need to choose a certain favourable jurisdiction to set up, and therefore the location of the company could be influenced by project innovativeness. In the meantime, more experienced teams could choose better company designs than less experienced teams.

Team categories, i.e., team experience and team composition, are located in the same level. Team experience acts as a linkage variable in our model, with strong driving and strong dependence power. On the evaluation websites, we find *team previous blockchain experience* and *team related industry experience* an important factor for ICO success. Similarly, team composition is also a linkage category, dependent on founder dedication and company characteristics and driving white paper quality, project innovativeness and product quality. Furthermore, it has a mutual influence with team experience. It is worth noting that one specific factor in the team composition category – *companies looking for key team members* – is considered negative and therefore has an adverse impact on the crowdfunding success. This indicates that blockchain-based crowdfunding backers also consider team related factors as an important investment evaluation variable.

Project innovativeness is also at Level IV. In the literature, we found only *intellectual capital (patents)* in the category of project innovativeness. On the evaluation websites, more factors were observed. As a linkage variable, product innovativeness is dependent on founder dedication and team composition, driving white paper quality, product quality and strong early adopters, and meanwhile having mutual influence with company characteristics and team experience.

In the same Level IV, there are product stage and product quality. In terms of product stage, we didn't find any new factors in the analysis of the evaluation websites. On the other side, product quality as a category only emerged in the analysis of the websites, not from the literature. What the specific factors are that can indicate product quality is yet to be understood. Both product stage and quality can influence strong early adopters.

It is somehow unexpected to see that strong early adopters appears in the same level with other more fundamental factor categories related to company, product and team. We found only one factor linked to this category in the literature – *corporate customers as early adopters*. In the analysis of the evaluation websites, we found this factor is used by one platform. Interestingly, it is the only category that has a mutual relationship with founder dedication, which seems somehow to increase the importance of this category.

The only two product related factor categories not located in the lower part of the model are social media traction (Level II) and strong partners (Level I). Not surprisingly, social media traction influences campaign traction. In contrast, it is somewhat surprising to see that strong partners is located in the top level of the model, as partnership is one of the fundamental aspects of a venture's business model. No sound explanation could be offered based on the literature and our own study, except that this might be due to the (mis)interpretations of the experts. Studying the literature, we found the *reputable investors (business angels, experts)* factor linked to this category. Analyzing the evaluation websites, we extended the category with two new factors – *corporate partners* and *working with respectable law/accounting firm*, which are significantly important partners, especially in the blockchain space.

Limitations of the study

There are several limitations in our study. First, there is a potential threat to the generalisability of the model we built. We were able to obtain responses only from a small number of experts. This limitation could affect the quality of the input data into the ISM process and eventually influence negatively the generalizability of the model. Second, it is possible that one or more experts made errors while filling in the Excel sheet due to time or comprehensiveness issues. The Excel sheet design could have been misleading. This is a potential threat to the internal validity of the study result. We tested the comprehensiveness of the sheet on several colleagues before sending it out to the experts. We also tried our best to ensure the reliability of the input for building the ISM by following a rigorously defined process to create a unique dataset.

Another issue is that the blockchain-based crowdfunding phenomenon is still in its infancy. It is still unclear which direction it will take in the future. The last years could probably be seen as a radical outlier in the future. In the coming years, it will be much more difficult and more expensive to raise capital due to regulation and higher competition. Some of the assumptions we identified in our study may be valid today but could lose their validity over the next years or even months.

Conclusion

In this chapter, we investigated the factors that could impact the success of blockchain-based crowdfunding campaigns, which nowadays have become an important means for new ventures and innovative projects to raise funds. By examining three major ICO evaluation websites, we extended the list of success factors reported by the literature, classifying them into project-related and campaign-related categories and subcategories. We then drew upon the knowledge of domain experts and built a hierarchical model of the success factors using the subcategories as the building blocks. The resulting model explicated the complex linkage among the success factors and highlighted the more fundamental driving factors behind the crowdfunding success.

Our findings could be used as a theoretical basis to further study the determinants and success indicators of blockchain-based crowdfunding initiatives. They could also provide entrepreneurs and investors in this domain with a holistic picture and understanding of the multiple forces at play in a crowdfunding campaign, especially in the blockchain arena.

Future work can validate the model built in our study by using a larger number of experts to improve the data quality of the input for the ISM process or using a different research design using more objective data. One future study we have planned is to conduct a quantitative analysis of correlation between success factors and the success of blockchain-based crowdfunding campaigns, using the hierarchical model built in this study (or part of it) as the research model.

References

Adhami, S., Giudici, G., and Martinazzi, S., 2018. Why do businesses go crypto? An empirical analysis of initial coin. *Journal of Economics and Business*.

Agrawal, A., Catalini, C., and Goldfarb, A., 2015. Crowdfunding: Geography, social networks, and the timing of investment decisions. *Special Issue: Innovation Economics II*, pp. 253–274.

Ahlers, G. K., Cumming, D., Günther, C., and Schweizer, D., 2015. Signaling in equity crowdfunding. *Entrepreneurship Theory and Practice*, pp. 955–980.

Amsden, R., and Schweizer, D., 2018. Are blockchain crowdsales the new "Gold Rush"? Success determinants of initial coin offerings. *SSRN*, p. 59.

Available at: www.sec.gov/oiea/investor-alerts-and-bulletins/ib_coinofferings [Accessed 18 July 2018].

Becker-Blease, J. R., and Sohl, J. E., 2007. Do women-owned businesses have equal access to angel capital? *Journal of Business Venturing*, pp. 503–521.

Beier, M., and Wagner, K., 2016. *User Behavior in Crowdfunding Platforms – Exploratory Evidence From Switzerland*. Hawaii: IEEE.

Belleflamme, P., Lambert, T., and Schwienbacher, A., 2014. Crowdfunding: Tapping the right crowd. *Journal of Business Venturing*, pp. 585–609.

Bi, S., Liu, Z., and Usman, K., 2017. The influence of online information on investing decisions of reward-based crowdfunding. *Journal of Business Research*, pp. 10–18.

Bigelow, L., Lundmark, L., Parks, J., and Wuebker, R., 2014. Skirting the issues: Experimental evidence of gender bias in IPO prospectus evaluations. *Journal Management*, pp. 1752–1753.

Busenitz, L. W., Fiet, J. O., and Moesel, D. D., 2005. Signaling in venture capitalist – New venture team funding decisions: Does it indicate long-term venture outcomes? *Entrepreneurship Theory and Practice*, pp. 1–12.

Cardon, M. S., Mitteness, C., and Sudek, R., 2018. Motivational cues and angel investing: Interactions among enthusiasm, preparedness, and commitment. *Entrepreneurship Theory and Practice*, pp. 1057–1085.

CB Insights, 2018. *Blockchain Investment Trends in Review*. s.l.: CB Insights.

Cerchiello, P., and Toma, A. M., 2018. ICOs success drivers: A textual and statistical analysis. *Dem Working Paper Series*, pp. 7–18.

Chan, C. S. R., and Parhankangas, A., 2017. Crowdfunding innovative ideas: How incremental and radical innovativeness influence funding outcomes. *Entrepreneurship Theory and Practice*, pp. 237–263.

Colombo, M., Franzoni, C., and Rossi-Lamastra, C., 2014. Internal social capital and the attraction of early contributions in crowdfunding. *Entrepreneurship Theory and Practice*, pp. 75–100.

Cordova, A., Dolci, J., and Gianfrate, G., 2015. The determinants of crowdfunding success: Evidence from technology projects. *Procedia: Social and Behavioral Sciences*, pp. 115–124.

Courtney, C., Dutta, S., and Li, Y., 2017. Resolving information asymmetry: Signaling, endorsement, and crowdfunding success. *Entrepreneurship Theory and Practice*, pp. 265–290.

CrowdfundingHub, 2016. *Current State of Crowdfunding in Europe*. Amsterdam: Crowd fundingHub.

Davies, W. E., and Giovannetti, E., 2018. Signalling experience & reciprocity to temper asymmetric information in crowdfunding evidence from 10,000 projects. *Technological Forecasting and Social Change*, pp. 118–131.

Eddleston, K. A., Ladge, J. J., Mitteness, C., and Balachandra, L., 2016. Do you see what I see? Signaling effects of gender and firm characteristics on financing entrepreneurial ventures. *Entrepreneurship: Theory and Practice*, pp. 489–514.

Etherscan, 2018. *Etherscan*. [Online] Available at: https://etherscan.io/tokens [Accessed 18 July 2018].

Etter, V., Grossglauser, M., and Thiran, P., 2013. Launch hard or go home! Predicting the success of Kickstarter campaigns. *In CHI*, pp. 591–600.

European Commission, 2017. *Identifying Market and Regulatory Obstacles to Cross Border Development of Crowdfunding in the EU*. s.l.: European Commission.

Fenu, G., Marchesi, L., Marchesi, M., and Tonelli, R., 2018. *The ICO Phenomenon and Its Relationships With Ethereum Smart Contract Environment*. Campobasso, 2018 International Workshop on Blockchain Oriented Software Engineering (IWBOSE).

Fisch, C., 2018. Initial Coin Offerings (ICOs) to finance new ventures: An exploratory study. *SSRN*.

Frydrych, D., Bock, A. J., Kinder, T., and Koeck, B., 2014. Exploring entrepreneurial legitimacy in reward-based crowdfunding. *Venture Capital*, pp. 247–269.

Graham, S. J., Merges, R. P., Samuelson, P., and Sichelman, T., 2008. High technology entrepreneurs and the patent system: Results of the 2008 Berkeley patent survey. *Berkeley Technology Review*.

Gutsche, J., and Sylla, S., 2017. Success factors of crowdfunding projects on the Kickstarter platform. In: *German-Turkish Perspectives on IT and Innovation Management*. s.l.: Springer, pp. 361–374.

Hacker, P., and Thomale, C., 2017. Crypto-securities regulation: ICOs, token sales and cryptocurrencies under EU financial law. *European Company and Financial Law Review*, Forthcoming.

Hartmann, F., Wang, X., and Lunesu, M. I., 2018. *Evaluation of Initial Cryptoasset Offerings: The State of the Practice*. Campobasso: IEEE.

Hornuf, L., and Schwienbacher, A., 2018. Market mechanisms and funding dynamics in equity. *Journal of Corporate Finance*, pp. 556–574.

icodata.io, 2018. *icodata.io*. [Online] Available at: www.icodata.io/stats/2017 [Accessed 21 May 2018].

Kim, K., and Viswanathan, S., 2013. The 'experts' in the crowd: The role of experienced investors in a crowdfunding market. *To Appear in MIS Quarterly*.

Kim, T., Por, M. H., and Yang, S. B., 2017. Winning the crowd in online fundraising platforms: The roles of founder. *Electronic Commerce Research and Applications*, pp. 86–94.

Kuppuswamy, V., and Bayus, B. L., 2015. Crowdfunding creative ideas: The dynamics of project backers in Kickstarter. *SSRN*.

Lee, J., Li, T., and Shin, D., 2018. The wisdom of crowds and information cascades in FinTech: Evidence from initial coin offerings. *SSRN*.

Leland, H. E., and Pyle, D. H., 1977. Informational asymmetries, financial structure, and financial intermediation. *The Journal of Finance*, pp. 371–387.

Loehrer, J., Schneck, S., and Werner, A., 2018. A research note on entrepreneurs' financial commitment and crowdfunding success. *Venture Capital*.

Lu, C. T., Xie, S., Kong, X., and Yu, P. S., 2014. Inferring the impacts of social media on crowdfunding. *WSDM'14*.

Lukkarinen, A., Teich, J. E., Wallenius, H., and Wallenius, J., 2016. Success drivers of online equity crowdfunding campaigns. *Decision Support Systems*, pp. 26–38.

Malone, D. W., 1975. An introduction to the application of interpretive structural modeling. *Proceedings of the IEEE*, 63(3), pp. 397–404.

Mamonov, S., and Malaga, R., 2018. Success factors in title III equity crowdfunding in the United States. *Electronic Commerce Research and Applications*, pp. 65–73.

Mamonov, S., Malaga, R., and Rosenblum, J., 2017. An exploratory analysis of title II equity crowdfunding success. *Venture Capital*, pp. 239–256.

Mohammadi, A., and Shafi, K., 2018. Gender differences in the contribution patterns of equity-crowdfunding investors. *Small Business Economics*, pp. 275–287.

Mollick, E., 2014. The dynamics of crowdfunding: An exploratory study. *Journal of Business Venturing*, pp. 1–16.

Momtaz, P. P., 2018. CEO loyalty and the pricing of initial coin offerings. *SSRN*.

National Park Service, 2015. *National Park Service*. [Online] Available at: www.nps.gov/stli/learn/historyculture/joseph-pulitzer.htm [Accessed 13 July 2018].

Ordanini, A., Miceli, L., Pizzetti, M., and Parasuraman, A. (2011). Crowd-funding: Transforming customers into investors through innovative service platforms. *Journal of Service Management*, 22(4), pp. 443–470.

Polzin, F., Toxopeus, H., and Stam, E., 2018. The wisdom of the crowd in funding: Information heterogeneity and social networks of crowdfunders. *Small Business Economics*, pp. 251–273.

Prasad, D., Bruton, G. D., and Vozikis, G., 2000. Signaling value to business angels: The proportion of the entrepreneur's net worth invested in a new venture as a decision signal. *Venture Capital*, pp. 167–182.

Rakesh, V., Chool, J., and Reddy, C. K., 2015. Project recommendation using heterogeneous traits in crowdfunding. *AAAI*.

Ralcheva, A., and Roosenboom, P., 2016. *On the Road to Success in Equity Crowdfunding*. [Online] Available at: https://ssrn.com/abstract=2727742 [Accessed 2018].

Sage, A. P., 1977. *Interpretive Structural Modeling: Methodology for Large-scale Systems* (pp. 91–164). New York, NY: McGraw-Hill.

Stam, E., and Schutjens, V., 2005. The fragile success of team start-up. *Papers on Entrepreneurship, Growth and Public Policy*.

Vismara, S. (2016). Equity retention and social network theory in equity crowdfunding. *Small Business Economics*, 46(4), pp. 579–590.

Vulkan, N., Åstebrob, T., and Sierrac, M. F., 2016. Equity crowdfunding: A new phenomena. *Journal of Business Venturing Insights*, pp. 37–49.

Zheng, H., Li, D., Wu, J., and Xu, Y., 2014. The role of multidimensional social capital in crowdfunding: A comparative study in China and US. *Information & Management*, p. 2014.

Appendix

The Excel sheet used to collect input from funds experts

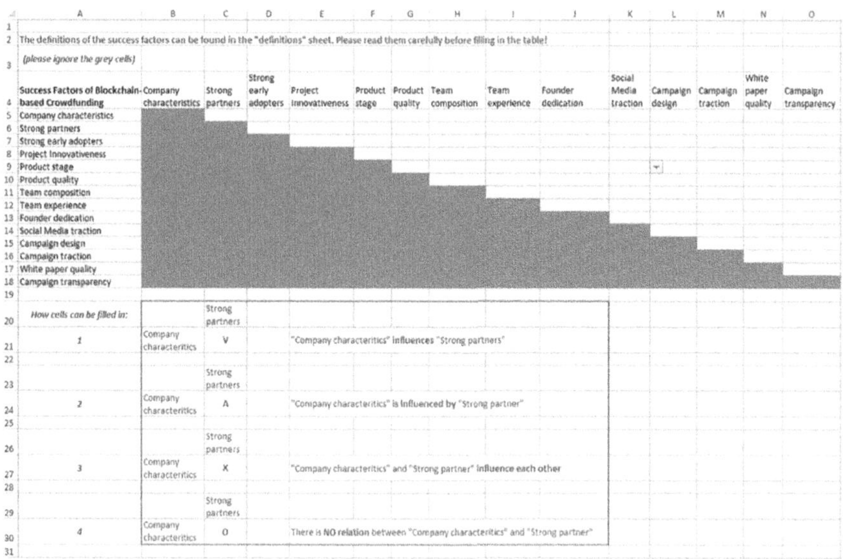

The definitions of the success factors can be found in the "definitions" sheet. Please read them carefully before filling in the table!

(please ignore the grey cells)

Success Factors of Blockchain-based Crowdfunding	Company characteristics	Strong partners	Strong early adopters	Project Innovativeness	Product stage	Product quality	Team composition	Team experience	Founder dedication	Social Media traction	Campaign design	Campaign traction	White paper quality	Campaign transparency
Company characteristics														
Strong partners														
Strong early adopters														
Project Innovativeness														
Product stage														
Product quality														
Team composition														
Team experience														
Founder dedication														
Social Media traction														
Campaign design														
Campaign traction														
White paper quality														
Campaign transparency														

How cells can be filled in:		Strong partners	
1	Company characteritics	V	"Company characteritics" **influences** "Strong partners"
		Strong partners	
2	Company characteritics	A	"Company characteritics" **is influenced by** "Strong partner"
		Strong partners	
3	Company characteritics	X	"Company characteritics" and "Strong partner" **influence each other**
		Strong partners	
4	Company characteritics	O	There is **NO relation** between "Company characteritics" and "Strong partner"

Index